EuroSLA Studies

Editor: Gabriele Pallotti

Associate editors: Amanda Edmonds, Université de Montpellier; Ineke Vedder, University of Amsterdam

In this series:

1. Pérez Vidal, Carmen, Sonia López-Serrano, Jennifer Ament & Dakota J. Thomas-Wilhelm (eds.). Learning context effects: Study abroad, formal instruction and international immersion classrooms

Learning context effects

Study abroad, formal instruction and international immersion classrooms

Edited by

Carmen Pérez Vidal

Sonia López-Serrano

Jennifer Ament

Dakota J. Thomas-Wilhelm

language
science
press

Carmen Pérez Vidal, Sonia López-Serrano, Jennifer Ament & Dakota J. Thomas-Wilhelm (eds.). 2018. *Learning context effects: Study abroad, formal instruction and international immersion classrooms* (EuroSLA Studies 1). Berlin: Language Science Press.

DOI:10.5281/zenodo.1300630
Source code available from www.github.com/langsci/180
Collaborative reading: paperhive.org/documents/remote?type=langsci&id=180

Cover and concept of design: Ulrike Harbort
Typesetting: Jennifer Ament, Sebastian Nordhoff
Proofreading: Arnaud Arslangul, Averil Coxhead, Aysel Saricaoglu, Caitlin Gaffney, David Coulson, Dietha Koster, Eliane Lorenz, Fatma Bouhlal, Gizem Mutlu Gülbak, Hamideh Marefat, Ineke Vedder, Luzia Sauer, Rowena Kasprowicz
Fonts: Linux Libertine, Libertinus Math, Arimo, DejaVu Sans Mono
Typesetting software: XƎLATEX

Language Science Press
Unter den Linden 6
10099 Berlin, Germany
langsci-press.org

Storage and cataloguing done by FU Berlin

Freie Universität Berlin

Contents

Contents

Acknowledgments

This edited volume is the outcome of intensive collaboration and cross-fertilization within the ALLENCAM research group. It owes its existence to a shared interest in examining language acquisition in different contexts. It is the culmination of several years of work carried out with constant mutual support, which is the best source of motivation and enjoyment when conducting research. Above all, we are grateful for the inspiring work carried out by all contributors, who have made the task of editing easy for us. We would particularly like to thank the Series Editor, Gabriele Pallotti, as the final quality of texts has substantially improved under his wise supervision and also Amanda Edmonds, whose advice has been invaluable. We are indebted for the financial support granted by the Spanish MICINN (through grant FFI2013-48640.C2-1-P) and the AGAUR (through grant SGR240).

Contributors

Jennifer Ament is currently a full-time researcher at Universitat Internacional de Catalunya in Barcelona. She holds a Master's degree specializing in Second Language Acquisition from Universitat Pompeu Fabra and is following the Doctoral programme in Linguistics at the same university. She is an experienced English language teacher and has worked at all levels of education in the North American, European, and Asian settings. Her main research interests are in the field of SLA, bilingual education, pragmatics, and language policy. She is currently analysing the effects of English-medium instruction (EMI) on the acquisition of pragmatic markers focusing on individual learner differences. She works as head of production for The Linguistics Journal and reviewer for the International Journal for Higher Education.

Pilar Avello has worked as a teaching and research assistant in the Department of Translation and Language Sciences at Universitat Pompeu Fabra. She completed her PhD within the Department's doctorate program in Applied Linguistics and has also taught language courses within the UPF graduate Translation and Applied Linguistics program. Her research adopts a multidisciplinary perspective which combines theoretical linguistics with a strong applied linguistics approach in relation to second language acquisition processes and outcomes. She has analysed how learning context effects influence the acquisition of English as a second language, with a focus on the development of phonological proficiency.

Júlia Barón is a full-time lecturer in the Institute for Multilingualism at the Universitat Internacional de Catalunya and a lecturer in the English and German Department at the Universitat de Barcelona. She holds a PhD in Applied linguistics and is a member of the GRAL research group (Grup de recerca en adquisició de llengües). She is also the coordinator of the GIDAdEnA group (Grup d'Innovació Docent en Adquisició i Ensenyament de l'Anglès). Her main research interests lie within the acquisition of English as a Foreign Language, more specifically of the acquisition of the target language pragmatics, as well as how different teaching methodologies affect the instruction of English as a foreign language.

Angélica Carlet is a professor of English Phonetics and Phonology and head of English at the Faculty of Education at Universitat Internacional de Catalunya, in Barcelona, Spain. She holds a PhD in English philology and a Master's Degree in second language acquisition from the Universitat Autònoma de Barcelona. The influence of one's native language phonology in the acquisition of a second language constitutes the main area of her research interest along with the effect of phonetic training for non-native speakers of English.

Carmen Del Río is currently a full-time TEFL teacher in Barcelona. She holds a PhD granted by the doctoral programme in Theoretical and Applied Linguistics Department of Translation and Language Sciences at Universitat Pompeu Fabra. Her research combines theoretical linguistics from within the field of phonetics, with a strong applied linguistics approach in relation to second language acquisition processes and outcomes in different learning contexts. She has focused on adolescent learners in mainstream education and study abroad. She is particularly interested in how pronunciation and phonetics penetrate the foreign language classroom in mainstream education and on teachers' approaches to pronunciation.

Maria Juan-Garau is currently Full Professor of Applied Linguistics at the Universitat de les Illes Balears. Her research interests centre on language acquisition in different learning contexts, whether naturalistic or formal, with special attention to study abroad and CLIL. Her work has appeared in various international journals and edited volumes. She has recently co-edited Content-Based Language Learning in Multilingual Educational Environments (Juan-Garau & Salazar-Noguera, 2015, Springer) and Acquisition of Romance Languages (Guijarro-Fuentes, Juan-Garau & Larrañaga, 2016, De Gruyter Mouton).

Leah Geoghegan is an EFL teacher at Caledonia English Centre. She holds an MA in Theoretical and Applied Linguistics from the Universitat Pompeu Fabra, specializing in language acquisition and learning, and is currently undertaking a second MA in Translation Studies at Portsmouth University. She was project manager and main writer for the website "Intclass" (www.intclass.org), a multimedia science tool for the promotion of three main foreign language contexts: study abroad, immersion and formal instruction. Her research interests include second language acquisition, English as a lingua franca and study abroad. She has contributed a chapter to the *Multilingual Matters* volume on Study Abroad, Second Language Acquisition and Interculturality.

Sonia López-Serrano is an English lecturer at the Department of Translation and Linguistic Sciences at Universitat Pompeu Fabra, where she is a member of the research group ALLENCAM (Language Acquisition from Multilingual Catalonia). She holds a Master's degree in Second Language Acquisition from the Universidad de Murcia, Spain, and is following the Doctoral programme in English Linguistics at the same university. Her research interests focus on instructed second language acquisition and L2 writing. In particular, she has conducted and published research on the language learning potential of writing tasks and the effects of different learning contexts on foreign language writing development.

Victoria Monje is a teacher of French as a foreign language and holds a Master's degree in Theoretical and Applied Linguistics from Universitat Pompeu Fabra. Her MA thesis (2016) was an innovative contribution to the larger Study Abroad and Language Acquisition (SALA) project, led by Professor Carmen Pérez-Vidal. Specifically, her research focuses on the acquisition of phonology of English as an L2.

Sofía Moratinos-Johnston is currently in the final stages of her doctoral studies in the Department of Spanish, Modern and Classical Languages of the Universitat de les Illes Balears, where she is also a lecturer. Her doctoral thesis focuses on language learning motivation in different learning contexts, which include formal classroom instruction, CLIL and study abroad. Apart from her research at the University of the Balearic Islands, she has also carried out research in the Centre for Applied Linguistics (University of Warwick) and the School of Education (University of Birmingham) as a visiting scholar.

Carmen Pérez-Vidal is currently an accredited professor of English at the Department of Translation and Linguistic Sciences at the Universitat Pompeu Fabra. Her research interests lie within the field of foreign language learning, bilingualism, and the effects of different learning contexts on language acquisition, namely study abroad, immersion and instructed second language acquisition. On this topic, she has conducted extensive research, as the leading researcher of the Study Abroad and Language Acquisition (SALA) project and has published internationally. She has edited the volume *Language Acquisition in Study Abroad and Formal Instruction Contexts* (Pérez Vidal, 2014), published by John Benjamins, and, more recently, contributed on the above topic to the Routledge Handbook of Instructed Second Language Acquisition, and to the Routledge Handbook on Study Abroad. In 2009, she was the launching co-coordinator of the AILA Research Network (ReN) on Study abroad.

Iryna Pogorelova is currently an academic coordinator and an instructor at the Master's Degree in Teacher Training in Foreign Language Instruction at Universitat Pompeu Fabra and Universitat de Lleida in Spain. She has recently completed her PhD at the Department of Humanities, Universitat Pompeu Fabra. Her dissertation investigated intercultural adaptation and the development of intercultural sensitivity of Catalan/Spanish undergraduate students during study abroad. She is also a member of the research group GREILI-UPF (Research Group on Intercultural Spaces, Languages and Identities). Her research interests include academic mobility and the development of intercultural competence and language acquisition in study abroad contexts.

Joana Salazar-Noguera is an associate professor at the Universitat de les Illes Balears, and since 2009 she coordinates the MA in Modern Languages and Literatures at the same university. She holds a PhD on English Philology. She has also taught at secondary education for eleven years and has published on the adequacy of EFL (English as a Foreign Language) methodologies in the Spanish educative context. Her most recent publications are the co-edited book Content-based learning in multilingual educational environments (Juan-Garau & Salazar-Noguera, 2015), and the article A Case Study of Early Career Secondary Teachers' Perceptions of their Preparedness for Teaching: Lessons from Australia and Spain (Salazar-Noguera & McCluskey, 2017).

Ariadna Sánchez-Hernández is a postdoctoral scholar of Applied Linguistics at Leuphana University of Lüneburg. She is a member of LAELA research group (Linguistics Applied to the Teaching of English Language) at Universitat Jaume I. She holds a Ph.D. in Applied Linguistics from Universitat Jaume I, a Master of Education in Curriculum and Instruction from Shawnee State University, and she has been a lecturer of Spanish at Ohio University. Her research interests include interlanguage pragmatics, second language acquisition, intercultural competence, acculturation, and the study abroad context.

Isabel Tejada-Sánchez is currently an Assistant Professor in the Department of Languages and Culture at the University of Los Andes in Bogotá, Colombia, where she has been a faculty member since 2014. Isabel completed her Ph.D. on Language Sciences and Linguistic Communication in a joint program at Universities Paris 8 and Pompeu Fabra. Her research interests lie in the areas of instructed second language acquisition, language teacher education, and language policy. She has taken part in several Applied Linguistics international conferences. In particular, she was member of the organizing committee of the 39th Language Testing Research Colloquium (LTRC). Dr. Tejada-Sánchez was also an ETS grantee between 2015 and 2017 within the English-language Researcher/Practitioner Grant Program.

Dakota J. Thomas-Wilhelm is currently a full-time English as a Second Language instructor in English as a Second Language Programs at the University of Iowa. He holds a Master's degree in Theoretical and Applied Linguistics specializing in Language Acquisition and Language Learning from Universitat Pompeu

Fabra and is following the Doctoral program in English Studies with a focus in Second Language Acquisition at Universitat Autònoma de Barcelona. His research interests lie within the field of SLA, English grammar instruction, and the design and implementation of linguistically-informed ESL materials and curriculum. In particular, his current focus concerns the designing of linguistically-informed materials to teach difficult grammar concepts using syntax and semantics.

Mireia Trenchs-Parera received her doctorate in Applied Linguistics from Teachers College-Columbia University, New York. She is an Associate Professor at the Department of Humanities, Universitat Pompeu Fabra, Barcelona, the lead researcher of group GREILI-UPF (*Grup de Recerca en Espais Interculturals, Llengües i Identitats*) and a senior member of the research group ALLENCAM. Her current research interests include studies on language attitudes, ideologies and practices and teaching and learning languages in multilingual and study abroad contexts. Her most recent research project deals with translingualism (The Translinguam Project). She has published her research in books from prestigious publishing houses (John Benjamins, Multilingual Matters, and Routledge, among others) and in recognized scientific journals (*Language and Linguistic Compass, International Journal of Bilingual Education and Bilingualism, Journal of Multilingual and Multicultural Development, Journal of Sociolinguistics, Canadian Modern Language Review,* and *English for Specific Purposes*).

Chapter 1

Context effects in second language acquisition: formal instruction, study abroad and immersion classrooms

Carmen Pérez-Vidal

Universitat Pompeu Fabra

Sonia López-Serrano

Universitat Pompeu Fabra; Universidad de Murcia

Jennifer Ament

Universitat Pompeu Fabra

Dakota J. Thomas-Wilhelm

University of Iowa; Universitat Autònoma de Barcelona

This volume within the EuroSLA Studies Series has been motivated by two fundamental reasons. Firstly, the assumption that applied linguistics research should first and foremost deal with topics of great social relevance, and, secondly, that it should also deal with topics of scientific relevance. Both ideas have led us to choose the theme 'contexts of language acquisition' as the topic around which the monograph would be constructed.

The aim of this introduction is to set the scene and present the three contexts on focus in the monograph and justify this choice of topic within second language acquisition (SLA) research, the perspective taken in this volume. Starting with the latter, in the past two decades the examination of the effects of different contexts of acquisition has attracted the attention of researchers, based on the idea that "the study of SLA within and across various contexts of learning forces a broadening of our perspective of the different variables that affect and

Carmen Pérez-Vidal, Sonia López-Serrano, Jennifer Ament & Dakota J. Thomas-Wilhelm. Context effects in second language acquisition: formal instruction, study abroad and immersion classrooms. In Carmen Pérez Vidal, Sonia López-Serrano, Jennifer Ament & Dakota J. Thomas-Wilhelm (eds.), Learning context effects: Study abroad, formal instruction and international immersion classrooms, 1–19. Berlin: Language Science Press. DOI:10.5281/zenodo.1300608

impede acquisition in general" (Collentine & Freed 2004: 157). The authors continue, "however, focusing on traditional metrics of acquisition such as grammatical development might not capture important gains by learners whose learning is not limited to the formal classroom (ibid: 158)". With reference to the social relevance of the topic, European multilingual policies in the past decades have been geared towards the objective of educating our young generations in order to meet the challenge of multilingualism (Coleman 2015; Pérez-Vidal 2015a), ultimately as an effect of "globalization and the push for internationalization [on campuses] across the globe"(Jackson 2013: 1). Indeed, the majority of European member states have embraced the recommendations made by the Council of Europe, encapsulated in the well-known 1+2 formula, according to which European citizens should have democratic access to proficiency in their own language(s) plus two other languages. In order to reach such a goal, a couple of decades ago the Council of Europe put forward a series of key recommendations to member states: i) an earlier start in foreign language learning; ii) mobility (the European Action Scheme for the Mobility of University Students, ERASMUS, exchange programme was launched in 1987, and since then more than three million students have benefitted from it); and iii) bilingual education, whereby content subjects should be taught through a foreign language (Commission of the European Communities. 1995). The latter recommendation has given rise to a number of immersion programmes at primary, secondary and tertiary levels of education, in parallel to the existing elite international schools (see the Eurobarometer figures and Wächter & Maiworm 2014, respectively). Such programmes are mostly taught through English, but also through French, German, Catalan, and other languages. Whether such learning contexts, which we have called 'international classrooms' and include classrooms at home and abroad (Pérez-Vidal et al. 2017), are de facto conducive to language acquisition is a matter which indeed needs to be investigated.

Against such a backdrop, this research monograph deals with the effects of different learning contexts mainly on adult, but also on adolescent learners' language acquisition. More specifically, it aims at comparing the effects of three learning contexts by examining how they change language learners' linguistic performance, and non-linguistic attributes, such as motivation, sense of identity and affective factors, as has been suggested not only by Collentine (2004) mentioned above, but also by a number of other authors (to name but a few, Pellegrino 2005; Dewaele 2007; Hernández 2010; Lasagabaster et al. 2014; Taguchi et al. 2016).

More specifically, the three contexts brought together in the monograph include i) a conventional instructed second language acquisition (ISLA) context, in which learners receive formal instruction (FI) in English as a Foreign Language (EFL); ii) a study abroad (SA) context, which learners experience during mobility programmes, with the target language no longer being a foreign but a second language, learnt in a naturalistic context; iii) the immersion classroom, also known as an integrated content and language (ICL) setting, in which learners are taught content subjects through the medium of the target language - more often than not English, hence the term English-Medium Instruction (EMI), and possibly English as a Lingua Franca (ELF) (Björkman 2013; House 2013). One last point needs to be made, concerning the issue of internationalisation, as is clearly stated in the title of the monograph:at any rate, the three contexts of acquisition on focus in this volume represent language/culture learning settings in which an *international stance* may be promoted in learners, as described below, in some cases also including the internationalization of the curriculum (Leask 2015).

In the SLA tradition in which the different chapters contained in the volume are framed, the comparison across contexts has been established under the assumption that contexts vary in the "type of input received by the learner (implicit vs. explicit), the type of interaction required of the learner (meaning-focus vs. form-focused)" (Leonard & Shea 2017: 185), and, most importantly, the type of exposure to the target language, with variations in the amount of "input, output and interaction opportunities available to them" (Pérez-Vidal 2014b: 23). As the focus is on three different learning contexts - SA, EMI, and FI - we suggest that they can be understood as situated on a continuum in which the most "interaction-based", with more favorable quantity and quality of input, would occur during a SA period. Second in order would be a semi-immersion context, as might take place EMI programmes, and the most "classroom-based" being FI in ISLA. Similarly, it is also along such a continuum, that these contexts make possible for learners to develop an attribute which Ushioda & Dörnyei (2012) refer to as an *international stance*. That is to say, learners have the opportunity to incorporate a new view of the world that integrates languages and cultures other than their own, often through the use of English as a lingua franca as a means of communication.

Turning to the cognitive mechanisms made possible in different linguistic environments or learning contexts, these have ultimately also been claimed to be different. DeKeyser (2007: 213) draws on skill acquisition theory, which distinguishes three stages - declarative knowledge, procedural knowledge and automatization - to suggest that, "a stay abroad should be most conducive to the third stage. It can – at least for some learners – provide the amount of practice necessary for the gradual reduction of reaction time, error rate, and interference with other tasks that characterize the automatization process". Similar cognitive perspectives might be applied to the classroom immersion context, on the assumption that it generates a 'naturalistic' academic context in which language is learnt through focusing on curricular content, one of the issues the monograph seeks to explore.

As for the existing set of findings concerning how learners develop their target language abilities in ISLA, research has reached considerable consensus around some of the main issues by now, although some remain controversial, some barely examined, and some entirely unexplored. Let us now turn to a brief presentation of current thinking.

Instructed SLA investigates L2 learning or acquisition that occurs as a result of teaching (Loewen 2013: 2716). This field of research theoretically and empirically aims to understand "how the systematic manipulation of the mechanisms for learning and/or the conditions under which they occur enable or facilitate development and acquisition of a [second] language" (Loewen 2015: 2). Formal instruction is a particular environment in instructed SLA that has been extensively researched for many decades.

In 1998, Michael Long reviewed eleven studies that examined the effect of FI on the rate and success of L2 acquisition. Of the studies that were reviewed, six of them showed that FI helped, three indicated that the instruction was of no help, and two produced ambiguous results. Long (1983) claimed that instruction is beneficial to children and adults, to intermediate and advanced students, as well as in acquisition-rich and acquisition-poor environments. His final conclusion was that FI was more effective than "exposure-based" in L2 acquisition. These findings led researchers to ask whether instruction (FI) or exposure (SA, EMI, etc.) produced more rapid or higher levels of learning.

Since Long's (1988) seminal review of the effects of FI, there have been a number of studies of the effect of FI. For example, Norris & Ortega (2001) conducted a meta-analysis of the effects of L2 instruction. Their study used a systematic procedure for research synthesis and meta-analysis to summarize findings from experimental and quasi-experimental studies between 1980 and 1998 that investigated the effectiveness of L2 instruction. Through their meta-analysis, they found that the literature suggests that instructional treatments are quite effective. They went on to investigate how effective instruction was when compared to simple exposure and found that there was still a large effect observed in favor of instructed learning.

Trenchs-Parera (2009) conducted a study on the effects of FI and SA as it related to the acquisition of oral fluency. Her results found that although both contexts have different effects on oral fluency and production, both of these contexts did have a positive effect. She went on to say that "the differences between these two contexts [FI and SA] may not fulfill the popular expectation that SA makes learners produce more native-like speech than does FI at all levels" (p. 382). While these results do indicate that FI can have a positive effect on L2 acquisition, they are unable to demonstrate that FI has learning effects that are conclusively more positive than those of more naturalistic environments.

We now turn to the examination of the effects of SA, often contrasted with ISLA, and occasionally also with at-home immersion. SA research has generated a wealth of studies, monographs, and handbooks on both sides of the Atlantic, starting in 1995 with Barbara Freed's (1995) seminal publication, followed by, to name but a few, Collentine & Freed (2004); Pellegrino (2005); DuFon & Churchill (2006), DeKeyser (2007); Collentine (2009); Kinginger (2009); Jackson (2013); Llanes & Muñoz (2013); Regan et al. (2009); Mitchell et al. (2015); Pérez-Vidal (2014a; 2017),and Sanz & Morales-Front (2018). Two periods can be distinguished in such research (Collentine 2009; Pérez-Vidal 2014). The first one was initiated by Freed's volume. In those years research mainly focused on the linguistic gains, or lack thereof, accrued with SA, with some attention paid to the impact of learner profiles and previous SA experiences (see for example, Brecht et al. 1995). Following that, new themes, besides linguistic impact, and new angles to approach them, have emerged throughout the second period. Following Collentine's (2009) tripartite distinction, such new themes include: (i) cognitive, psycholinguistic approaches looking into cognitive processing mechanisms displayed while abroad; (ii) sociolinguistic approaches analyzing input and interaction from a macro- and a micro-perspective; and, most centrally, (iii) sociocultural approaches derived from a paradigm shift from a language-centric (i.e. etic) approach to a learner-centric (i.e. emic) one (Devlin 2014). As established in Pérez-Vidal (2017: 341), indeed, within the latter paradigm, and in order to focus on the learner and his/her immediate circumstances, SA research has recently begun to investigate non-linguistic individual differences which affect learning in such a context, "that is: (a) intercultural sensitivity and identity changes; (b) affects, such as foreign language anxiety (FLA) or willingness to communicate (WTC) and enjoyment; (c) social networks, particularly through the use of new technologies and social platforms, and their effect on linguistic practice". Now, as DeKeyser (2014: 313) emphasizes, "a picture is beginning to emerge of what language development typically takes place [during SA] and what the main factors are that determine the large amount of variation found from one study to another".

Turning now to the positive effects of SA on learners' linguistic progress, in a nutshell, empirical studies paint a blurred picture. They seem to show that SA does not always result in greater success than FI in ISLA - some learners do manage to make significant linguistic progress while abroad, while others do not (DeKeyser 2007; Collentine 2009; Llanes 2011; Pérez-Vidal 2015b; Sanz 2014). In fact, what such results seem to prove, is the notorious variation in amount of progress made, which has often been attributed to the variation in learners' ability to avail themselves of the opportunities for practice that a SA context offers. These differences in turn are explained by learners' individual ability for self-regulation while abroad, as further discussed below Ushioda & Dörnyei (2012).

Looking at progress in more detail, empirical research has repeatedly shown that oral production seems to be the winner, with effects on fluency being significantly positive after SA, (Towell & Bazergui 1996; Freed et al. 2004; Llanes & Muñoz 2009; Valls-Ferrer & Carles 2014). One interesting related finding has been made concerning the nature of the programmes (Beattie 2014): robust immersion programmes organized at home and including a substantial number of hours of academic work on the part of the learners can be as beneficial as a similar length of time spent abroad (i.e.Freed et al. 2004). In contrast to the results for fluency in oral production, results for grammatical accuracy and complexity have been mixed, with DeKeyser (1991) not finding much improvement, whereas Howard (2005) or Juan-Garau et al. (2014), to name but a few, report that progress is made after a period spent abroad. The other main area of improvement is pragmatics, in particular when associated with the use of formulaic routines, and perception and production of speech acts (see for a summary Pérez-Vidal & Shively forthcoming), and particularly when paired with pragmatics instruction. This takes us back to the key question of how the nature of the exchange programme can affect linguistic outcomes. More specifically, issues such as type of accommodation, length of the stay, or initial level, have been found to significantly determine linguistic and cultural development while abroad. Concerning initial level, Collentine (2009) stated that there should be a threshold level which learners must reach to benefit fully from the SA learning context. Once that level has been reached, most studies report better results for their respective lower level groups, confirming that the kind of practice most common while abroad, that is interaction in daily communication, mostly benefits the less advanced learners, while academic work done outside the classroom may benefit the most advanced ones (Kinginger 2009). As for type of accommodation, home-stays with families have proved most beneficial An alternative option is with the so called *family learning housing*, where students reside with target language speakers of their own age, having signed a language pledge not to use any other language but the target language (Kinginger 2015). Length of stay also seems to be associated with advanced level learners, who may require longer periods to automatize the larger number of structures they have learnt at home than the lower level learners (DeKeyser 2014). However, interestingly, shorter periods abroad, of less than one month, may also significantly benefit EFL learners' fluency, accuracy and listening abilities (Llanes & Muñoz 2009). Three month periods may be more beneficial than six months (Lara et al. 2015). Listening has in fact clearly been shown to undergo significant progress while abroad (Beattie et al. 2014), as has reading (Dewey 2004). Writing and vocabulary have also been shown to significantly benefit from SA (Sasaki 2007; Sasaki 2011; Barquin 2012; Zaytseva et al. 2018).

Regarding learners' individual differences, age seems to play a role, as SA has been shown to be more beneficial for children than for adults in relative terms (Llanes & Muñoz 2013). Regarding aptitude, a certain level of working memory (Sunderman & Kroll 2009), phonological memory (O'Brien et al. (2007)) and processing speed (Taguchi 2008) seem to correlate with accurate L2 production, oral production and reception of pragmatic intentions, respectively. Finally, concerning the emotional variables underlying self-regulation during exchanges in the target language country, the expectation is that motivation will have a positive role and that anxiety, paired with the capacity for enjoyment, will as well. Dewaele et al. (2015) have found that SA benefits emotional stability, self-confidence and resourcefulness. While identity goes through a process of repositioning, this process is not exempt from difficulties, which often conditions degree of contact with target language speakers while abroad. More willingness to communicate and less foreign language anxiety seem to obtain during SA (Dewaele & Wei 2013; Dewaele et al. 2015).

Turning to the third type of context, although it is still in its infancy, immersion, the integration of content and language as an educational approach in primary, secondary (CLIL) and tertiary levels (ICL), has also given rise to a sizeable number of research studies (such as for example: Admiraal et al. 2006; Dalton-Puffer 2008; Airey 2012; Cenoz et al. 2014). The integration of content and language in higher education (ICLHE) came to be recognized in its own right in 2004, with the first conference examining this context, and has steadily grown to this day (Wilkinson 2004).

Findings from immersion and CLIL contexts, abundantly examined in the SLA literature, report that CLIL and immersion learners demonstrate language gains superior to learners who participate in FI alone, with equal or superior content learning outcomes (Wesche & Skehan 2002; Genesee 2004; Jiménez Catalán & Iragui 2006; Seikkula-Leino 2007). Specifically, gains are reported in receptive skills, vocabulary, morphology, and fluency, whereas fewer gains have been observed according to syntax, writing, pronunciation and pragmatics (Dalton-Puffer 2008), although results may be mixed (Pérez-Vidal & Roquet 2014). Research on non-linguistic outcomes has found that CLIL learners seem to be more motivated, or that CLIL can maintain students' interests and change attitudes towards multilingualism. Moreover, students generally perceive CLIL participation as a positive experience (Lasagabaster & Sierra 2009).

Turning now to adult education, the main focus of this monograph, a large body of research has been generated within the frame of ICLHE which is specifically interested in the widespread implementation of English-taught programs at mainly post graduate levels. This has come to be known as English medium instruction (EMI) which is characterized as a setting where English is used as a medium for instruction by, and for non-native English speakers in non-English speaking environments (Hellekjaer & Hellekjaer 2015). Researchers in this field have begun investigating the phenomenon from a wide variety of angles, for example by looking at the implementation and policy making end of the spectrum (Tudor 2007). What has been found is that the implementation of EMI must be carefully managed in order not to create tensions, considering the role of the first language, attitudes towards English, and the widespread effects of internationalization, not only affecting faculty and students, but also governing bodies and administration (Doiz et al. 2014). Others report on beliefs, attitudes and challenges from both the student/learner perspective and the faculty/institution's perspective. Findings show that stakeholders in EMI relate English instruction to internationalization very clearly, with some believing that one cannot exist without the other (Henry & Goddard 2015). This belief also proves to be a strong motivator for students to enroll in EMI courses (Margić & Žeželić 2015), although the experience does not always meet their expectations regarding language improvement and more support is often desired (Sert 2008). Finally, perhaps the least investigated aspect of EMI involves the assessment of outcomes measured in linguistic as well as non-linguistic terms.

On the one hand there are investigations looking at non-linguistic effects from EMI participation (Gao 2008; González Ardeo 2016). Research shows that a gradual implementation supporting both faculty and students is the most effective for maintaining and creating positive attitudes and motivation (Chen & Krak-low 2015). On the other hand, there are studies regarding the content learning implications of learning through a foreign language (Dafouz 2014). It has been argued that upon completion of a degree program there is no difference in con-tent knowledge (Dafouz & Camacho-Miñano 2016). A few studies investigating language outcomes from such a context (Lei & Hu 2014; Ament & Pérez-Vidal 2015; Ritcher 2017) show little evidence of language improvement from EMI par-ticipation. They also reveal that at this point there is simply not enough research to point to any clear conclusions. EMI is growing rapidly around the world and its close relationship with internationalization will ensure its continuance for time to come. What must be kept in mind is that, in order to properly implement, benefit from, and provide appropriate support to faculty and institutions offering EMI instruction, and maintain quality education, more research on this context must be carried out, specifically considering both linguistic and non-linguistic effects, which is precisely what this monograph aims to bring to light.

However, to our knowledge, no publication exists which places the three con-texts along the continuum already mentioned, as suggested in Pérez-Vidal (2011; 2014) with SA as 'the most naturalistic' context on one extreme, ISLA on the other, and ICL somewhere in between. The present monograph seeks to make a first attempt at filling such a gap, by including a number of studies analysing the effects of EMI, and another series of studies doing the same with SA, in contrast with ISLA. In such a comparison it is further assumed that EMI programmes are often experienced at the home institution either as an 'international experience at home' (internationalization at home), or as a preparation for the 'real' expe-rience of an SA period spent in the target language country, in which learners will most probably be expected to regularly attend academic courses. In such a circumstance, whatever the local language, quite probably some of the courses offered, if not all, will be EMI courses for international students, that is, they will be what we call 'international classrooms' (Coleman 2013; Leask 2015).

The monograph will thus be organized around the two contexts, EMI and SA, on the understanding that their effects will be contrasted with those obtained in ISLA, when appropriate. Both linguistic and non-linguistic phenomena will be investigated, employing quantitative but also qualitative methods, indepen-dently or combined. Regarding target countries in the immersion programmes examined, they include data from Spain and Colombia. Of the SA programmes scrutinized, data include exchanges having the following destinations: England, Ireland, France, Germany and Spain, in Europe, but also Canada, the USA, China, Brazil and Australia. The EMI chapters deal with tertiary level language learners, a section of the population which has received much less attention in research thus far, compared to secondary or primary learners, as mentioned above. Similarly, one SA chapter deals with adolescent learners, again a research population scarcely examined in such a context.

As for the internal organization of the volume, following the introduction by the editors, the first chapters will deal with EMI contexts of acquisition, and the remaining ones with SA contexts.

More specifically, we open up the monograph with four chapters devoted to the immersion context: three examine tertiary education data, and the last one primary and secondary. In Chapter 2, Dakota Thomas-Wilhelm and Carmen Pérez Vidal explore EMI in Catalonia, Spain, in contrast with ISLA, focusing on a syntactic phenomenon and its cognitive correlates, namely English countable and uncountable nouns. In Chapter 3, Jennifer Ament and Júlia Barón examine two EMI programmes with different intensity, also in Catalonia, looking into pragmatics, namely, the use of English discourse markers and their acquisition in the EMI context. Chapter 4, by Sofia Moratinos-Johnston, Maria Juan-Garau and Joana Salazar-Noguera, analyses a non-linguistic issue, that is, learners' linguistic self-confidence and perceived level of English according to the number of EMI subjects taken at university in the Balearic Islands, Spain. Chapter 5, by Isabel Tejada-Sánchez and Carmen Pérez-Vidal, closes the set of chapters devoted to immersion, by investigating the complexity, accuracy and fluency of written productions by young EFL immersion learners in Colombia.

Subsequently, the series of chapters on SA begins with Chapter 6, by Pilar Avello, which takes a fresh perspective and discusses the methodological intricacies associated with the measurement and analysis of pronunciation gains obtained during a sojourn abroad in an English-speaking country (England, Ireland, Canada, the USA, Australia). Chapter 7 by Victoria Monge and Angelica Carlet, contrasts ISLA and SA. These authors compare L2 phonological development, following a three-month period in any of the above-mentioned English-speaking countries, while controlling for proficiency level, in an attempt to follow up on Mora's (2008) seminal study with a reverse design. In Chapter 8 Carmen del Rio, Maria Juan-Garau and Carmen Pérez-Vidal contrast the impact of a three-month SA period and FI at home, in the case of adolescent EFL learners, an age band which has received comparatively less attention than others, focusing on the learners' foreign accent and comprehensibility, as judged by a group of non-native listeners, with the objective of assessing progress, following Trofimovich & Isaacs (2012). Motivation, identity and international posture is the focus of Chapter 9, in which Leah Geoghegan compares tertiary level students spending a SA in an English-speaking country with those in Germany or France, using qualitative research tools in order to gain a more detailed picture of the role of

ELF in SA. After that, Chapter 10 by Iryna Pogorelova and Mireia Trenchs explore intercultural adaptation during the experience of a SA period in different countries in Europe, but also in Canada, the USA, China, Brazil, and Australia. Finally, in Chapter 11 Ariadna Sánchez-Hernández deals with acculturation and pragmatic learning by international students in the USA, to close the series of chapters dealing with SA.

Acknowledgments

This work was supported by the Ministry of Economy and Competitiveness [FFI 2013-48640-C2-1-P]; by the AGENCIA UNIVERSITARIA DE RECERCA (AGAUR), in Catalonia, [2014 SGR 1568]; and by a EUROSLA workshop grant (2017). The monograph follows the EUROSLA workshop on the same theme celebrated at the Universitat Pompeu Fabra in Barcelona, Spain, 23-24 May, 2016.

References

Admiraal, Wilfred, Gerard Westhoff & Kees de Bot. 2006. Evaluation of bilingual secondary education in the Netherlands: Student's language proficiency in english. *Educational Research and Evaluation* 12(1). 75–93.

Airey, John. 2012. I don't teach language. The linguistic attitudes of physics lecturers in Sweden. *AILA Review* 25. 64–79.

Ament, Jennifer & Carmen Pérez-Vidal. 2015. Linguistic outcomes of English medium instruction programmes in higher education: A study on Economics undergraduates at a Catalan university. *Higher Learning Research Communications* 5(1). 47–68.

Barquin, Elisa. 2012. *Writing development in a study abroad context. Unpublished dissertation.* Barcelona: Universitat Pompeu Fabra.

Beattie, John. 2014. The 'ins and outs' of a study abroad programme: The SALA exchange programme. In Carmen Pérez-Vidal (ed.), *Language acquisition in study abroad and formal instruction contexts*, 59–87. Amsterdam: John Benjamins Publishing.

Beattie, John, Margalida Valls-Ferrer & Carmen Pérez-Vidal. 2014. Listening performance and onset level in formal instruction and study abroad. In Carmen Pérez-Vidal (ed.), *Language acquisition in a study abroad and formal instruction contexts*, 195–217. Amsterdam: John Benjamins Publishing.

Björkman, Beyza. 2013. *English as an academic lingua franca: An investigation of form and communicative effectiveness.* Boston/Berlin: Walter de Gruyter.

Brecht, Richard, Dan Davidson & Ralph Ginsberg. 1995. Predictors of foreign language gain during study abroad. In Barbara Freed (ed.), *Second language acquisition in a study abroad context*, 37–66. Amsterdam: Benjamins.

Cenoz, Jasone, Fred Genesee & Durk Gorter. 2014. Critical analysis of CLIL: Taking stock and looking forward. *Applied Linguistics* 35(3). 243–262.

Chen, Yih Lan Ellen & Deborah Kraklow. 2015. Taiwanese college students' motivation and engagement for English learning in the context of internationalization at home: A comparison of students in EMI and non-EMI programs. *Journal of Studies in International Education* 19(1). 46–64. doi:10.1177/1028315314533607.

Coleman, James A. 2015. Social circles during residence abroad: What students do, and who with. In Rosamond Mitchell, Nicole Tracy-Ventura & Kevin Mc-Manus (eds.), *Social interaction, identity and language learning during residence abroad* (EUROSLA monographs series 4), 33–51. Amsterdam: European Second Language Association.

Coleman, Jim. 2013. English-medium teaching in european higher education. *Language Teaching* 39(1). 1–14.

Collentine, Joseph G. 2004. The effects of learning contexts on morphosyntactic and lexical development. *Studies in Second Language Acquisition* 26(2). 227–248.

Collentine, Joseph G. 2009. Study abroad research: Findings, implications and future directions. In Michael H. Long & Catherine J. Doughty (eds.), *The handbook of language teaching*, 218–233. Malden, MA: Blackwell.

Collentine, Joseph G. & Barbara F. Freed. 2004. Learning context and its effects on second language acquisition: introduction. *Studies in second language acquisition* 26(02). 153–171.

Commission of the European Communities. 1995. *Teaching and learning: Towards a learning society. 449 white paper on education and learning*. Brussels: DGV.

Dafouz, Emma. 2014. Integrating content and language in European higher education: An overview of recurrent research concerns and pending issues. In Psaltou-Joycey Agathopoulou & Marina Mattheoudakis (eds.), *Cross-curricular approaches to language education*, 289–304. Cambridge: Cambridge Scholars.

Dafouz, Emma & Maria Camacho-Miñano. 2016. Exploring the impact of English-medium instruction on university student academic achievement: The case of accounting. *English for Specific Purposes* 44. 57–67.

Dalton-Puffer, Christiane. 2008. Communicative competence in ELt and CLIL classrooms: Same or different. Views. *Vienna English Working Papers* 17(3). 14–21.

DeKeyser, Robert. 1991. Foreign language development during a semester abroad. In Barbara Freed (ed.), *Foreign language acquisition: Research and the classroom*, 104–119. Lexington M.A.: D. C. Heath.

DeKeyser, Robert. 2007. Study abroad as foreign language practice. In Robert DeKeyser (ed.), *Practicing in a second language: Perspectives from applied linguistics and cognitive psychology*, 208–226. Cambridge: Cambridge University Press.

DeKeyser, Robert. 2014. Research on language development during study abroad: Methodological considerations and future perspectives. In Carmen Pérez-Vidal (ed.), *Language acquisition in study abroad and formal instruction contexts*, 313–327. Amsterdam/Philadelphia: John Benjamins.

Devlin, Anne Marie. 2014. *The impact of study abroad on the acquisition of sociopragmatic variation patterns: The case of non-native speaker English teachers. Intercultural studies and foreign language learning 13*. Oxford: Peter Lang.

Dewaele, Jean-Marc. 2007. The effect of multilingualism, sociobiographical and situational factors on communicative anxiety and foreign language anxiety of mature language learners. *The International Journal of Bilingualism* 11(4). 391–409.

Dewaele, Jean-Marc, Ruxandra S. Comanaru & Martin Faraco. 2015. The affective benefits of a pre-sessional course at the start of study abroad. In Rosamond Mitchell, Nicole Tracy-Ventura & Kevin McManus (eds.), *Social interaction, identity and language learning during residence abroad* (Eurosla Monograph Series 5), 33–50. European second language association.

Dewaele, Jean-Marc & Li Wei. 2013. *Is multilingualism linked to a higher tolerance of ambiguity?* Vol. 1. 231–240.

Dewey, Dan. 2004. A comparison of reading development by learners of Japanese in intensive domestic immersion and study abroad contexts. *Studies in Second Language Acquisition* 26(2). 303–327.

Doiz, Aintzane, David Lasagabaster & Juan Manuel Sierra. 2014. Language friction and multilingual policies in higher education: The stakeholders' view. *Journal of Multilingual and Multicultural Development* 35(4). 345–360. DOI:10.1080/01434632.2013.874433

DuFon, Margaret A. & Eton E. Churchill (eds.). 2006. *Language learners in study abroad contexts*. Clevedon, UK: Multilingual Matters.

Freed, Barbara F. (ed.). 1995. *Second language acquisition in a study abroad context*. Amsterdam: Benjamins.

Freed, Barbara F., Dan P. Dewey, Norman Segalowitz & Randall Halter. 2004. The language contact profile. *Studies in Second Language Acquisition* 26(2). 349–356.

Gao, Xuesong. 2008. Shifting motivational discourses among mainland Chinese students in an english medium tertiary institution in hong kong: A longitudinal inquiry. *Studies in Higher Education* 33(5). 599–614. . doi:10.1080/03075070802373107.

Genesee, Fred. 2004. What do we know about bilingual education for majority language students. In Fred Genesee andTessa Bathia & William Ritchie (eds.), *Handbook of bilingualism and multiculturalism*, 547–576. Malden: Blackwell Publishing.

González Ardeo, Mikel Joseba. 2016. Engineering student's instrumental motivation and positve attitude towards learning English in a trilingual tertiary setting. *Ibérica* 32. 179–200.

Hellekjaer, Glenn Ole & Anne-Inger Hellekjaer. 2015. From tool to target language: Arguing the need to enhance language learning in English-medium instruction courses and programs. In Slobodanka Dimova, Anna Kristina Hultgren & Christian Jensen (eds.), *English-Medium instruction in European higher education*, 317–324. Berlin: Walter de Gruyter.

Henry, Alastair & Angela Goddard. 2015. Bicultural or hybrid? The second language identities of students on an English-mediated university program in Sweden. *Journal of Language, Identity and Education* 14(4). 255–274. . doi:10.1080/15348458.2015.1070596.

Hernández, Todd A. 2010. Promoting speaking proficiency through motivation and interaction: The study abroad and classroom learning contexts. *Foreign Language Annals* 43(4). 650–670.

House, Juliana. 2013. Developing pragmatic competence in English as a lingua franca: Using discourse markers to express (inter)-subjectivity and connectivity. *Journal of Pragmatics* 59(A). 57–67.

Howard, Martin. 2005. Second language acquisition in a study abroad context: A comparative investigation of the effects of study abroad and foreign language instruction on the L2 learner's grammatical development. In Alex Housen & Michel Pierrard (eds.), *Investigations in instructed second language acquisition*, 495–530. Berlin: Mouton de Gruyter.

Jackson, Jane. 2013. Pragmatic development in study abroad contexts. In Carol A. Chapelle (ed.), *The encyclopedia of applied linguistics*, 1–12. Hoboken: Wiley-Blackwell.

Jiménez Catalán, Yolanda Ruiz de Zarobe, Rosa María & Jasone Cenoz Iragui. 2006. Vocabulary profiles of English foreign language learners in English as a subject and as a vehicular language. Views. *Vienna English Working Papers:* 15(3). 23–27.

Juan-Garau, Maria, Juana Salazar-Noguera & José Igor Prieto-Arranz. 2014. English L2 learners' lexico-grammatical and motivational development at home and abroad. In Carmen Pérez-Vidal (ed.), *Language acquisition in study abroad and formal instruction contexts*, 235–258. Amsterdam: John Benjamins.

Kinginger, Celeste. 2009. *Language learning and study abroad. A critical reading of research.* Houndmills: McMillian.

Kinginger, Celeste. 2015. Language socialization in the homestay: American high school students in China. In Rosamonda Mitchell, Nicole Tracy-Ventura & Kevin McManus (eds.), *Social interaction, identity and language learning during residence abroad* (Eurosla Monograph Series 5), 33–53.

Lara, Rebecca, Joan Carles Mora & Carmen Pérez-Vidal. 2015. How long is long enough? L2 English development through study abroad programmes varying in duration. *Innovation in Language Learning and Teaching* 9(1). 1–12. Special Issue, Festschrift Jim Coleman: Innovation in Language Learning and Teaching. DOI:0.1080/17501229.2014.995764.

Lasagabaster, David & Josep. Maria Sierra. 2009. Language attitudes in CLIL and traditional EFL classes. *International CLIL Research Journal* 1(2). 4–17.

Lasagabaster, David, Juán Manuel Sierra & Aintzane Doiz (eds.). 2014. *Motivation and foreign language learning: From theory to practice.* New York/Amsterdam: John Benjamins.

Leask, Betty. 2015. *Internationalizing the curriculum.* New York: Routledge.

Lei, Jun & Guangwei Hu. 2014. Is English-medium instruction effective in improving Chinese undergraduate students' English competence? *IRAL* 52(2). 99–126.

Leonard, Karen R. & E. Shea Christine. 2017. L2 speaking development during study abroad: Fluency, accuracy, complexity and underlying cognitive factors. *The Modern Language Journal* 101(1). 179–193.

Llanes, Àngels. 2011. The many facets of study abroad: An update of the research on L2 gains emerged during a SA experience. *International Journal of Multilingualism* 8(3). 189–215.

Llanes, Àngels & Carmen Muñoz. 2009. A short stay abroad: does it make a difference? *System* 37(3). 353–365.

Llanes, Àngels & Carmen Muñoz. 2013. Age effects in a study abroad context: Children and adults studying English abroad and at home. *Language Learning* 63(1). 63–90.

Loewen, Shawn. 2013. Instructed second language acquisition. In Carol A. Chapelle (ed.), *The encyclopedia of applied linguistics*, 2716–2718. Malden, MA: Blackwell Publishing.

Loewen, Shawn. 2015. *Instructed second language acquisition*. New York: Routledge.

Long, Michael. 1983. Does second language instruction make a difference? A review of research. *TESOL Quarterly* 17. 359–382.

Long, Michael. 1988. Instructed interlanguage development. In Leslie M. Beebe (ed.), *Issues in second language acquisition: Multiple perspectives*, 115–141. Cambridge, MA: Newbury House Publishers.

Margić, Branka. D. & Tea Žeželić. 2015. The implementation of English-medium instruction in croatian higher education: Attitudes, expectations and concerns. In Ramón Plo Alanstrué & Carmen Pérez-Llantada (eds.), *English as a scientific and research language*, 311–332. Berlin: De Gruyter.

Mitchell, Rosamond, Nicole Tracy-Ventura & Kevin McManus (eds.). 2015. *Social interaction, identity and language learning during residence abroad* (Eurosla Monographs Series 4). Amsterdam: The European Second Language Association.

Mora, Joan C. 2008. Learning context effects on the acquisition of a second language phonology. In Carmen Pérez-Vidal, Maria Juan-Garau & Aurora Bel (eds.), *A portrait of the young in the new multilingual Spain*, 241–263. Clevendon, UK: Multilingual Matters.

Norris, John M. & Lourdes Ortega. 2001. Does type of instruction make a difference? Substantive findings from a meta-analytic review. *Language Learning* 51. 157–213.

O'Brien, Irena, Norman Segalowitz, Barbara F. Freed & Joseph G. Collentine. 2007. Phonological memory predicts second language fluency gains. *Studies in Second Language Acquisition* 29(4). 557–581.

Pellegrino, Valerie A. 2005. *Study abroad and second language use: Constructing the self*. Cambridge: Cambridge University Press.

Pérez-Vidal, Carmen (ed.). 2014. *Language acquisition in study abroad and formal instruction contexts*. Amsterdam: Benjamins.

Pérez-Vidal, Carmen. 2011. Language acquisition in three different contexts of learning: Formal instruction, stay abroad and semi-immersion (CLIL). In Yolanda Ruiz de Zarobe, Juan Manuel Sierra & Francisco Gallardo del Puerto (eds.), *Content and foreign language integrated learning: Contributions to multilingualism in European contexts*, 103–128. Bern/Berlin: Peter Lang.

Pérez-Vidal, Carmen. 2014a. *Second language acquisition in study abroad and formal instruction contexts*. Amsterdam: John Benjamins.

Pérez-Vidal, Carmen. 2014b. Study abroad and formal instruction contrasted: The SALA project. In Carmen Pérez-Vidal (ed.), *Second language acquisition in study abroad and formal instruction contexts*, 17–57. Amsterdam: John Benjamins.

Pérez-Vidal, Carmen. 2015a. Languages for all in education: CLIl and ICLHE at the crossroads of multilingualism, mobility and internationalization. In Maria Juan-Garau & Joana Salazar-Noguera (eds.), *Content-based learning in multilingual educational environments*, 31–51. Berlin: Springer.

Pérez-Vidal, Carmen. 2015b. Practice makes best: Contrasting learning contexts, comparing learner progress. *International Journal of Multilingualism* 12(4). 453–470.

Pérez-Vidal, Carmen. 2017. Study abroad and ISLA. In Shawn Loewen & Masatoshi Sato (eds.), *The Routledge handbook of instructed second language acquisition*, 339–361. New York: Routledge.

Pérez-Vidal, Carmen, Neus Lorenzo & Mireia Trenchs. 2017. Una nova mirada a les llengües en l'educació: El plurilingüisme i l'internacionalització. In Josep M. Vilalta (ed.), *Reptes de l'educació a catalunya: Anuari 2015*, 139–195. Barcelona: Fundació Jaume Bofill i Edicions el Llum.

Pérez-Vidal, Carmen & Helena Roquet. 2014. CLIL in context: Profiling language abilities. In Maria Juan-Garau & Joana Salazar-Noguera (eds.), *Content-based language learning in multilingual educational environments*, 237–254. Berlin: Springer.

Pérez-Vidal, Carmen & Rachel Shively. Forthcoming. Pragmatic development in study abroad settings. In Nakoto Taguchi (ed.), *The Routledge handbook of study abroad research and practice*. New York: Routledge.

Regan, Vera, Martin Howard & Isabelle Lemée. 2009. *The acquisition of sociolinguistic competence in a study abroad context*. Clevedon: Multilingual Matters.

Ritcher, Karin. 2017. Researching tertiary EMi and pronunciation. A case from vienna. In Jennifer Valcke & Robert Wilkinson (eds.), *Integrating content and language in higher education; perspectives on professional practice*, 117–134. Frankfurt: Peter Lang.

Sanz, Cristina. 2014. Contribution of study abroad research to our understanding of SLA processes and outcomes: The SALA project, an appraisal. In Carmen Pérez-Vidal (ed.), *Language acquisition in study abroad and formal instruction contexts*, 1–17. Amsterdam/Philadelphia: John Benjamins.

Sanz, Cristina & Alfonso Morales-Front (eds.). 2018. *The Routledge handbook of study abroad research and practice*. New York: Routledge.

Sasaki, Mitsuko. 2007. Effects of study-abroad experiences on EFL writers: A multiple-data analysis. *The Modern Language Journal* 91. 602–620.

Sasaki, Miyuki. 2011. Effects of varying lengths of study-abroad experiences on Japanese EFL students' L2 writing ability and motivation: A longitudinal study. *TESOL Quarterly* 45(1). 81–105.

Seikkula-Leino, Jaana. 2007. CLIL learning: Achievement levels and affective factors. *Language and Education* 21(4). 328–341.

Sert, Nehir. 2008. The language of instruction dilemma in the Turkish context. *System* 36. 156–171.

Sunderman, Gretchen & Judith Kroll. 2009. When study abroad experience fails to deliver: The internal resources threshold effect. *Applied Psycholinguistics* 30. 1–21.

Taguchi, Naoko. 2008. Cognition, language contact, and the development of pragmatic comprehension in a study-abroad context. *Language Learning* 58(1). 33–71.

Taguchi, Naoko, Feng Xiao & Shuai Li. 2016. Effects of intercultural competence and social contact on speech act production in a Chinese study abroad context. *The Modern Language Journal* 100(4). 1–22.

Towell, Roger Hawkins, Richard & Nives Bazergui. 1996. The development of fluency in advanced learners of French. *Applied Linguistics* 17(1). 84–119.

Trenchs-Parera, Mireia. 2009. Effects of formal instruction and study abroad on the acquisition of native-like oral fluency. *Canadian Modern Language Review* 65(3). 365–393.

Trofimovich, Pavel & Talia Isaacs. 2012. Disentangling accent from comprehensibility. *Bilingualism: Language and Cognition* 15. 905–916.

Tudor, Ian. 2007. Higher education language policy in Europe: From principle to practice. In *Language teaching and learning in multicultural and plurilingual Europe*, 41–50. Vilnius: Vilniaus universiteto leidykla.

Ushioda, Ema & Zoltán Dörnyei. 2012. Motivation. In Susan M. Gass & Alison Mackey (eds.), *The Routledge handbook of second language acquisition*, 396–409. New York: Routledge.

Valls-Ferrer, Margalida & Mora Joan Carles. 2014. L2 fluency development in formal instruction and study abroad: The role of initial fluency level and language contact. In Carmen Pérez-Vidal (ed.), *Language acquisition in study abroad and formal instruction contexts*, 111–137. Amsterdam/Philadelphia: John c, content-based instruction, & task-based learning. In Robert Kaplan ed. Handbook of applied linguistics. Oxford: Oxford University Press. 207-228.

Wächter, Bernd & Friedhelm Maiworm (eds.). 2014. Bonn: Lemmens Medien GmbH.

Wesche, Michael & Peter Skehan. 2002. Communicative teaching, content-based instruction and task-based learning. In Robert Kaplan (ed.), *Handbook of applied linguistics*, 207–228. Oxford: Oxford University Press.

Wilkinson, Robert (ed.). 2004. *Integrating content and language: Meeting the challenge of a multilingual higher education.* Maastricht: Universitaire Pers Masstricht.

Zaytseva, Victoria, Imma Miralpeix & Carmen Pérez-Vidal. 2018. Vocabulary acquisition during study abroad: A comprehensive review of research. In Cristina Sanz & Alfonso Morales-Front (eds.), *2018. The Routledge handbook of study abroad research and practice*, 210–224. New York: Routledge.

Chapter 2

Exploring the acquisition of countable and uncountable nouns in English-medium instruction and formal instruction contexts

Dakota J. Thomas-Wilhelm

University of Iowa; Universitat Autònoma de Barcelona

Carmen Pérez-Vidal

Universitat Pompeu Fabra

The present study aims to explore the acquisition and mental representation of the countable and uncountable noun distinction in English as a foreign language (EFL) by two upper-intermediate Catalan/Spanish groups in two different learning contexts, formal instruction (FI) and English-Medium Instruction (EMI) (Coleman 2006; Izumi 2013), in contrast with baseline native speaker data, and with an interest in crosslinguistic influence. The FI group receives fewer hours of exposure to EFL, 3 per week, but in return, instruction on the phenomenon under study. In contrast, the EMI group is immersed in EFL, receiving 15-20 hours per week in the classroom, but receives no instruction on the phenomenon in question. Data were collected by means of two experimental tasks: one grammaticality judgment task and one picture-decision task. The results show that, although there is no significant difference between learning context overall, there are differences when the data are considered at the level of the noun-type. The lack of impact resulting from FI adds further evidence to the existing discussion related to explicit (FI) versus implicit (EMI) instructional contexts (Dafouz & Guerrini 2009; Pérez-Vidal 2009; 2011). In addition, these findings underscore the difficulty in the acquisition of countable and uncountable noun type distinctions at upper-intermediate levels.

Dakota J. Thomas-Wilhelm & Carmen Pérez-Vidal. Exploring the acquisition of countable and uncountable nouns in English medium instruction and formal instruction contexts. In Carmen Pérez-Vidal, Sonia López-Serrano, Jennifer Ament & Dakota J. Thomas-Wilhelm (eds.), *Learning context effects: Study abroad, formal instruction and international immersion classrooms*, 21–41. Berlin: Language Science Press. DOI:10.5281/zenodo.1300610

Dakota J. Thomas-Wilhelm & Carmen Pérez-Vidal

1 Introduction

At the intersection of semantics, syntax, and language acquisition is ongoing research about how semantics and syntax are related, and an extension of that is the question of how language learners acquire this relationship. Barner and Snedeker (2005: 42) pose a very important question: "how [does] the knowledge in one domain facilitate [the] acquisition of knowledge in the other?" The relationship between countable and uncountable nouns is an exemplar of this relationship between semantics and syntax. This study focuses on how English as a Foreign language (EFL) learners from two different language acquisition contexts, Formal Instruction (FI) and English-Medium Instruction (EMI), acquire countability distinctions in their target language using both behavioral and cognitive data, with a Grammaticality Judgment Test (GJT) and a Picture Decision Task (PDT), respectively (Chaudron 2003; Norris & Ortega 2003). The study presented in this chapter seeks to understand how EFL learners from each context comparatively recognize the countable/uncountable distinction and map it in their mental representations.

The study was conducted at a Catalan university in Spain where most of the subjects are taught in either Spanish or Catalan. However, following a relatively recent trend in Europe, English has increasingly become a third or additional language of instruction. Indeed, the so-called university EMI programs, modeled on similar programs existing at lower stages of education, have become current practice. Wächter & Maiworm (2014) conducted a survey during the 2006/07 academic year to determine the number of EMI programs in the European Higher Education Area. Through their survey, they were able to identify 2,389 programs that were taught though English. These findings are remarkable and even more so as the trend was confirmed by a subsequent survey showing that 6% of degrees in Europe take an EMI approach (Wächter & Maiworm 2014).

2 Literature review

Expressing quantity is something that is common in every language. Although it is more complex and developed in some languages than others, nouns, noun phrases, and quantifiers/quantification all have very specific positions and functions in language that allow us to refer to things in both the real and abstract worlds. As can be seen in Table 1, English has five main subclasses of nouns that can refer to objects and substances with physical existence (Leech & Svartvik 1975): (1) proper, (2) countable, (3) object-uncountable, (4) substance-uncountable, and (5) flexible. In the current study, we are only concerned with subclasses (2)-(5).

Table 1: Noun subclasses in English

	(1) Proper	(2) Countable	(3) Object-uncountable	(4) Substance-uncountable	(5) Flexible
I see...	John	*bottle	furniture	salt	cake
	*the John	the bottle	the furniture	the salt	the cake
	*a John	a bottle	*a furniture	*a salt	a cake
	*some John	*some bottle	some furniture	some salt	some cake
	*Johns	bottles	*furnitures	*salts	cakes

In English, countable nouns refer to countable items and carry the semantic feature of [+ COUNT] (and presumably [+ NEAT]). On the contrary, uncountable nouns refer to non-countable items with the semantic feature [– COUNT], and may be [+ NEAT] or [– NEAT]. According to Landman (2011), a noun is [+ *neat*] if the interpretation of its structures does not have overlapping minimal building blocks (e.g. *furniture* is comprised of *tables, chairs, sofas,* whereas a collection of just *tables* would not be considered *furniture*), and a noun is [– NEAT] if it is comprised of multiple and similar parts which overlap (e.g. *salt* is comprised of multiple, and similar, *grains of salt*). On the basis of such a distinction, uncountable nouns are further divided into object-uncountable and substance-uncountable. Object-uncountable nouns are the nouns which are composed of objects (e.g. *furniture, mail, luggage*) and carry the semantic features [– COUNT, + NEAT], making them "neat" uncountable nouns since their interpretation does not have overlapping minimal building parts. On the other hand, substance-uncountable nouns ("messy" uncountable nouns) are those which have the semantic features [– COUNT, – NEAT] and are composed of substances (e.g. *salt, toothpaste, milk*), whose minimal building parts overlap. Lastly, flexible nouns are those which can be used as either countable [+ COUNT]or uncountable nouns [– COUNT] (e.g. *chocolate/chocolates*). In this respect, it is important to note that in the present study, we follow Barner & Snedeker (2005) in positing that the interpretation of flexible nouns as one or the other is driven by the syntax in which they occur, i.e. in countable or uncountable syntactic constructions. This means that a flexible noun will be interpreted as either countable or uncountable given the context in which it appears. For example, if we compare the sentences *I like chocolate* and

She gave me two chocolates, the quantifier *two* in the latter sentence drives the interpretation of the flexible noun *chocolate* to being countable, while the use of the zero article, no quantifier, and singular form of the noun *chocolate* drives the interpretation to be substance-uncountable in *I like chocolate*, in the same way that *salt* is uncountable in the sentence *I need salt for my fries.*

Spanish, Catalan and English largely overlap in the way they treat countable and uncountable nouns. Indeed, in the three languages countable nouns (like *chair*) refer to countable items and mass-uncountable nouns (like *water*) denote non-countable items (Bruyne 1995; Wheeler et al. 1999; Butt & Benjamin 2004). The important difference is that some nouns that are treated as object-uncountable in English (thus appearing in the singular only in this language), in Spanish and Catalan have both a singular and plural form, expressing two different meanings. As can be seen in Tables 2 and 3, in Spanish or Catalan the singular form indicates an unspecified mass, while its plural refers to a plurality of objects; to express this meaning, English requires the addition of words that are countable elements. This is an important difference because one might expect that native speakers (NSs) of Spanish and Catalan might try to pluralize English uncountable nouns in trying to achieve the meaning that is similarly expressed in Spanish and Catalan.

Table 2: Pluralizing Spanish uncountable nouns

SINGULAR		PLURAL	
Spanish	English	Spanish	English
pan	*bread*	panes	*loaves of bread*
tostada	*toast*	tostadas	*pieces of toast*
equipaje	*luggage*	equipajes	*pieces of luggage*
basura	*garbage*	basuras	*bags of garbage*

In developmental research, many hypotheses have been discussed about how children are sensitive to syntactic information when acquiring nouns that refer to collections of things in English (Bloom & Keleman 1995). In the following paragraphs, we will describe the hypothesis put forth by Barner & Snedeker (2005) and argue for how it may also apply to foreign language acquisition.

Barner & Snedeker (2005) presented adults and 4-year old children with pictures and actual scenes, respectively, and asked the question *Who has more?* One of the stimuli contained one or two large objects, the other three or six smaller objects, whose combined mass was clearly smaller than that of the for-

Table 3: Pluralizing Catalan uncountable nouns

SINGULAR		PLURAL	
Catalan	English	Catalan	English
pa	*bread*	pans	*loaves of bread*
torrada	*toast*	torrades	*pieces of toast*
equipatge	*luggage*	equipatges	*pieces of luggage*
basura	*garbage*	basures	*bags of garbage*

mer object(s) (see Figure 3 for an example). All four classes of nouns addressed in the present study were tested, viz. countable, object-uncountable, substance-uncountable, and flexible.

Results show that, quite expectedly, both children and adults base their judgments on volume, or mass, for substance-uncountable nouns (e.g. a large chunk of *toothpaste* is perceived as being 'more' than three small ones), and on number for countable nouns (e.g. three or six small *shoes* are interpreted as 'more *shoes*' than one or two big ones). The crucial finding was that both children and adults use number rather than mass in their judgments of object-uncountable nouns. Thus, three small *chairs* and three small *tables* are seen as being 'more *furniture*' than a big table with a big chair. It thus seems that the inherent semantics of a word/concept like *furniture* (which denotes a set of individual objects) overrides the lexico-syntactic constraints posed by a given language like English, which treats it as an uncountable noun like *water*.

However, syntax does play a role in the case of flexible nouns, like *string*. Here, a plural syntactic context like *Who has more strings?* causes most participants to choose the picture with several small pieces of string, whereas a singular syntactic context like *Who has more string?* led to choosing the picture with one long piece of string.

Thus, 'individuation', i.e. the interpretation of a term as referring to an individual or a collection of individuals, can have at least three sources: inherent semantics, or world knowledge (the fact that furniture or silverware represent, in the real world, a collection of objects); lexical features (the fact that, at least in English, 'furniture' and 'silverware' are singular-only nouns); and syntactic context (e.g. the presence of quantifiers and plural morphology, in the case of flexible nouns).

3 Methodology

These are the research questions addressed in the current study:

RQ1. How do FI learners compare to EMI learners, and to NSs, in their ability to grammatically recognize different countable/uncountable noun distinctions?

RQ2. Are participants' judgments about quantity based on linguistic knowledge or non-linguistic world knowledge, and is there any difference in this regard among FI and EMI learners and native English speakers?

3.1 Participants

A total of 57 participants completed the two experiments included in this study in order to address our two research questions. Of the 57 participants, 33 were undergraduates completing language-specialty degrees (FI group) and 24 were undergraduates studying business-related degrees through English (EMI group). These two groups were chosen because the FI undergraduates received explicit instruction in the English language, while the EMI only received implicit instruction since the content of their courses was taught through the medium of English. All participants were Spanish/Catalan simultaneous bilinguals from a public university in Catalonia, Spain. All participants were controlled for their level of English, on the basis of the Cambridge Online Placement Test of English. The group represented a relatively homogeneous population having an intermediate level, that is a B.1.2 according to the Common European Framework of Reference. However, results from this test revealed that the FI group had a relatively lower level ($M = 17.55$, $SD = 3.80$) than the EMI group ($M = 18.38$, $SD = 0.57$). As can be seen by the standard deviations, the FI group had considerable variation in level. An independent samples t-test found that there was no significant difference in the English test scores for EMI and FI contexts ($t(34) = -1.235$, $p = .225$).

In terms of targetlanguage exposure, there are two main differences between the EMI and the FI group. Firstly, the students receiving EMI received more hours per week of English language exposure than the FI group. The EMI group was receiving all of their degree classes, at the time of the study, via EMI, which involved between 15-20 hours per week, according to the academic term. In contrast, the FI group only had a handful of classes that used English, for about three hours per week. Secondly, the FI class hours, as already mentioned, dealt with grammar and linguistics, and, most importantly, included instruction on the phenomenon in focus in this chapter, as part of their established syllabus. Such instruction was not extensive: it included one two-hour session and some homework practice amounting to another two hours, hence four hours in total. In contrast, the EMI instructional context had no explicit grammar instruction or attention to form and no specific training on countability. In other words, the language and grammar practice that students may obtain in this instructional environment is implicit, which, on its own, is not considered to lead to the same amount of progress as the combination of explicit and implicit teaching conditions (Ellis 2010). In sum, our groups show an interesting contrast: the EMI has more contact hours than the FI (15-20 hours vs. 3 hours per week); the FI has explicit instruction on countability, which EMI does not have.

A control group ($n = 26$) was also recruited and established for baseline data for the study. These NSs came from various English-speaking countries, speaking different world Englishes: American English ($n = 18$), Canadian English ($n = 4$), British English ($n = 3$), and Australian English ($n = 1$).

3.2 Data collection instruments and procedure

The data collection was carried out by means of two instruments: a Grammaticality Judgment Task (GJT), administered only in English (Experiment 1), and a Picture Decision Task (PDT) that was administered in English, Spanish, and Catalan (Experiment 2), respectively. Regarding RQ1, the GJT was chosen to provide insight into the participants' explicit knowledge of the grammaticality of countable, uncountable, and flexible nouns in different syntactic contexts. Regarding RQ2, a PDT was chosen following the work by Barner & Snedeker (2005).

GJTs have been used extensively in second language acquisition research and have been determined to be reliable and valid instruments for gathering insight into participants' explicit knowledge of the grammaticality of noun types in different syntactic contexts (e.g. Cowan & Hatasa 1994; Gass 1994; Cowart 1997; Ionin & Zyzik 2014, among others). In the present study, the GJT was administered in English only and consisted of 100 sentences which the participants had to individually rate based on whether each sentence sounded linguistically grammatical to them. For each item, participants had to choose one of the following options: *very natural – natural – not natural – not natural at all*.[1] Participants

---

[1] In order to avoid forcing the non-native speakers (NNSs) of English to choose between two extreme options (*very natural/not natural at all*), we decided to include the intermediate values *natural* and *not natural*, although the distinctions between *very natural/natural* and *not natural/not natural at all* were not taken into an account because of the decision to use a right-wrong approach for data analysis.

There are many furnitures to choose from.

- very natural

- natural

- not natural

- not natural at all

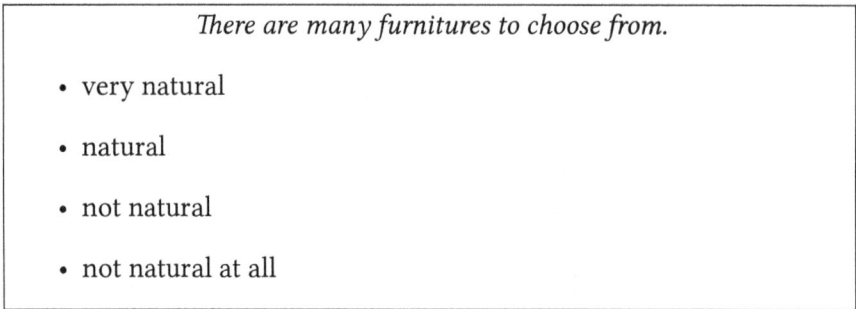

Figure 1: A sample item from the GJT

were required to give a judgment on each of the 100 items. A sample item from the GJT can be found in Figure 1.

As can be seen in Figure 2, GJT target sentences were created based on the five different noun types (countable, object-uncountable, substance-uncountable, [−COUNT] flexible, and [+ COUNT] flexible). After consulting specialists in both semantics and pragmatics of Spanish, Catalan, and English,[2] two *crosslinguistic statuses* were created. The nouns which acted and were used the same in all the languages were considered as the *match* condition, while those which differed between languages were considered the *mismatch* condition. The only category that consisted of mismatched tokens was object-uncountable. This created a total of five conditions. All items were presented in both grammatical and ungrammatical sentences. Overall, there were 50 experimental sentences and 50 fillers (25 grammatical and 25 ungrammatical).

Of the 50 experimental items, 27 were categorized as grammatical and 23 as ungrammatical. This imbalance was based on baseline data provided by the NSs, where 100% of the respondents accepted: *The boss asked me to get him a coffee*, as grammatically acceptable and 84.6% accepted *I'll take two sugars in my tea* as grammatically acceptable. For this reason, these two substance-uncountable nouns were considered as grammatically acceptable while the other substance-uncountable tokens that had the plural −*s* were coded as ungrammatical. In any case, these sentences were excluded from subsequent data analysis. All 100 items in the GJT and their answers were programmed into Qualtrics and randomized using the Qualtrics function for advanced randomization. One item was presented at a time. The task took the participants approximately 15 minutes to complete.

---

[2]Upon consulting with specialists in both semantics and pragmatics of Spanish, Catalan, and English, which allowed us to determine the crosslinguistic status, two conditions were created in order to devise the tokens for testing.

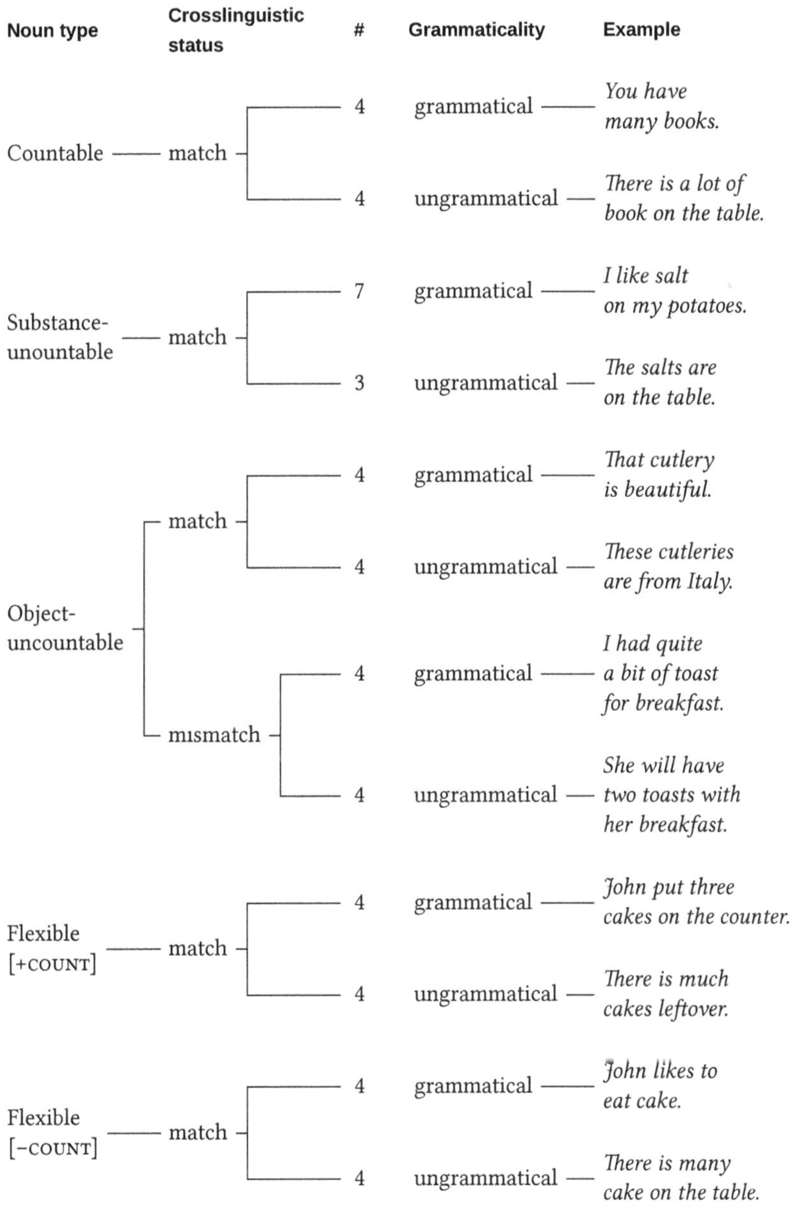

Noun type	Crosslinguistic status	#	Grammaticality	Example
Countable — match		4	grammatical —	*You have many books.*
		4	ungrammatical —	*There is a lot of book on the table.*
Substance-unountable — match		7	grammatical —	*I like salt on my potatoes.*
		3	ungrammatical —	*The salts are on the table.*
Object-uncountable	match	4	grammatical —	*That cutlery is beautiful.*
		4	ungrammatical —	*These cutleries are from Italy.*
	mismatch	4	grammatical —	*I had quite a bit of toast for breakfast.*
		4	ungrammatical —	*She will have two toasts with her breakfast.*
Flexible [+COUNT] — match		4	grammatical —	*John put three cakes on the counter.*
		4	ungrammatical —	*There is much cakes leftover.*
Flexible [−COUNT] — match		4	grammatical —	*John likes to eat cake.*
		4	ungrammatical —	*There is many cake on the table.*

Figure 2: Conditions for items in the GJT

For scoring in the case of the grammatical items, a right-wrong approach was taken. When coding the options that were available to participants during the AJT, a participant was awarded +2 points for answering *very natural*, +1 point for *natural*, -1 point for *not natural*, and -2 points for answering *not natural at all* for grammatical items and the inverse of the point system was used for scoring the ungrammatical items. If an answer was left blank, it was coded with an X to be excluded from data analysis. As already mentioned, the responses of *very natural* and *natural* were bundled together, as well as *not natural* and *not natural at all*, meaning that two scores of +2 carried that same weight as two scores of +1, which were later calculated into percentages of accuracy based on the grammaticality of the sentences. Mean percentages of accuracy were calculated with respect to the different conditions and classes. These were then made into percentages of accuracy for grammatical and ungrammatical items. The percentages of accuracy were used for the data analysis.

The second data collection instrument was the PDT, which was administered in English. This instrument provided information on quantificational judgments of countable/uncountable nouns by the participants. Modeled after the experiment by Barner & Snedeker (2005), this task sought to elicit quantity judgments (the choice of multiple items over a single item) of countable and uncountable nouns by non-native speakers (NNSs) of English belonging to the FI or EMI conditions, and compare those judgments to English NSs. Following the research conducted by Barner & Snedeker (2005), of particular interest was whether they would treat object-uncountable, such as *furniture* and *luggage*, and flexible nouns (e.g. *cake, string, chocolate*) presented in [+COUNT] syntax, as quantifying over individuals, or whether they would treat them as substance-uncountable nouns (e.g. *toothpaste, salt, pepper*) and quantify by mass. This was an important subquestion because of the differences between Catalan, Spanish, and English in regard to some of these nouns. The instrument consisted of 24 items in English. A sample PDT item can be found in Figure 3.

We administered a PDT in English to all groups, in which the following question was asked: *Where is there more...?* Upon seeing two pictures — one large item/group, or three small items/groups as shown in Figure 3 — this question forced participants to decide where there *was more* of that noun item. Although Barner & Snedeker (2005) posed the question *Who has more...?* in the framing of their experiment, the present study tested the question: *Where is there more...?*[3]

---

[3] It might be argued that this presentation may pose the participants with an ungrammatical sentence, for instance *Where is there more books?* We would like to emphasize here that we chose the use of the question *Where is*, and to not change *is* to *are* when presented with plural items, because in Spanish/Catalan, there is one word/verb form that accounts for both *there is* and *there are.*

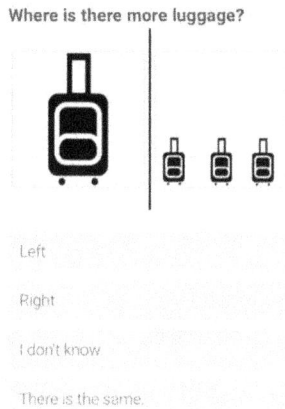

Where is there more luggage?

Left

Right

I don't know

There is the same.

Figure 3: A sample item from the PDT

We changed the question in order to provide the participants a linguistic form that had a similar structure throughout all three languages (e.g. English: *Where are there more books?* Spanish: *¿Dónde hay más libros?* Catalan: *On hi ha més llibres?*). This change in wording was made so that the data could be usable in another study that compared English, Spanish, and Catalan. Sample items and conditions for the PDT can be found in Table 4. The participants always chose from the answers: *left – right – I don't know – There is the same.* As shown in Figure 3, the three small objects always showed a combined volume and surface area smaller than the large object. This allowed responses based on number to be distinguished from those based on mass or volume.

Responses were rated by assigning a +1 if the picture with three small masses or items was chosen and a score of 0 if the picture of one large mass or item was chosen. A score of 0 was also assigned to *They have the same* responses and an X was assigned to *I don't know.* The X scores were later excluded from data analysis. The scores were calculated and analyzed as percentages of individuation (e.g. total number of 1s divided by the total number of that noun type presented). In the PDT, as with the GJT, target sentences were created based on the five different noun types (countable, object-uncountable, substance-uncountable, [–COUNT] flexible, and [+ COUNT] flexible).

Prior to participating in data collection, the participants completed two pre-participation questionnaires: a biodata and language use questionnaire and a quick English test. These questionnaires were web-based for all participants and

31

Table 4: Conditions for items in the PDT

Noun type	#	Crosslinguistic status	Example item
Countable	4	match	*Where is there more books?*
Substance-uncountable	4	match	*Where is there more salt?*
Object-uncountable	4	match	*Where is there more art?*
	4	mismatch	*Where is there more furniture?*
Flexible [+ COUNT]	4	match	*Where is there more cakes?*
Flexible [− COUNT]	4	match	*Where is there more cake?*

administered via Qualtrics.[4] The NSs were sent the information via an email containing links to the experimental tasks, as well as a sociolinguistic survey. They were asked to complete the surveys within three weeks, and those who completed all the tasks were included in the data analysis. NNS participants attended a data collection session in an on-campus computer lab during which they were administered the entire battery of instruments over the course of an hour and a half. The participants were offered a short break of 5-10 minutes between each of the data collection steps.

4 Results and discussion

4.1 Experiment 1

Experiment 1 allows us to address RQ1, that is, how the FI group would compare to the EMI and to NSs of English in their ability to grammatically recognize countable/uncountable noun distinctions, including object-uncountable noun, substance-uncountable nouns, and flexible noun types, and whether any influence from their two L1s would be revealed. In order to address this question, a series of one-way ANOVAs was run on the mean accuracy (scores out of 100) of the GJT with an alpha level set at 0.05. For the noun types tested, there was a statistically significant difference between groups as determined by one-way ANOVAs for countable nouns ($F(2,80) = 23.085$, $p < .001$), object-uncountable

---

[4]http://www.qualtrics.com, accessed 2015/01 – 2015/06

nouns ($F(2,80) = 96.938$, $p < .001$), flexible [+ COUNT] nouns ($F(2,80) = 22.894$, $p < .001$), and flexible [− COUNT] nouns ($F(2,80) = 18.619$, $p < .001$). There was no statistical difference between groups for substance-uncountable nouns ($F(2,80) = 1.806$, $p = .171$). Average accuracy rates are presented in Table 5.

Table 5: GJT sescriptive statistics

Group	Countable nouns	Object-uncountable nouns	Substance-uncountable nouns	Flexible [+ COUNT] nouns	Flexible [− COUNT] nouns
NSs	90.88	93.27	87.00	96.15	91.35
(*n* = 26)	(9.05)	(8.23)	(15.15)	(5.88)	(9.20)
FI context	83.71	46.97	80.30	75.76	71.59
(*n* = 33)	(19.13)	(11.49)	(17.50)	(17.10)	(15.40)
EMI context	64.84	79.17	78.13	73.44	76.69
(*n* = 24)	(8.99)	(18.26)	(19.59)	(13.45)	(11.36)

Looking at individual comparisons from a descriptive point of view, results of the GJT provided evidence that L2 English learners, from both the EMI and the FI, showed some difficulty in judging the grammaticality of constructions with countable and uncountable nouns in comparison to NSs of English. As visible in Table 5, the NSs performed with rates of accuracy nearly at ceiling across all the classes of nouns, with the exception of substance-uncountable nouns. All learner groups showed accuracy rates lower than those of the NS group in all categories. In Figure 4, it can be seen that the EMI participants performed, on average, lower than those in a FI context with the exception of object-uncountable nouns (e.g. *They have such beautiful furniture in their house* or *There are many furnitures to choose from*) and flexible nouns used in a [− COUNT] context (e.g. *John has some string in his bag*).

In order to test the significance of these differences among groups, post hoc tests using Tukey HSD were conducted. We will address each of the noun types individually.

As for countable nouns (e.g. judging the grammaticality of *There are six dogs playing in the park* versus *One third of the dog is in the garden*), a Tukey HSD post hoc test revealed that the FI learners (*M* = 83.71, *SD* = 19.13) were significantly different (*p* < .001) from the EMI learners (*M* = 64.84, *SD* = 8.99). The FI learners

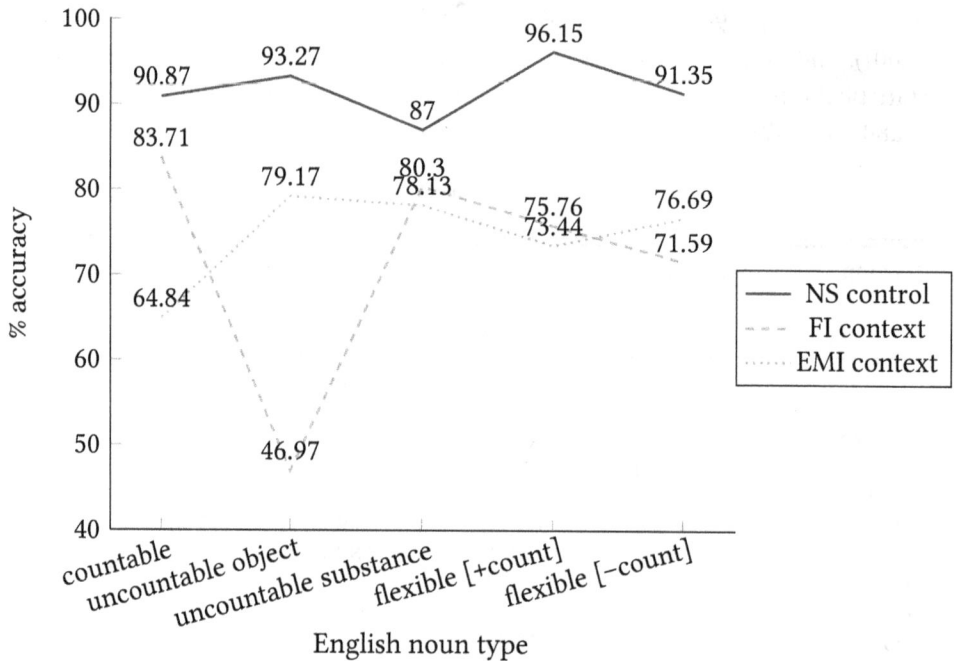

Figure 4: Profile plot of the participant groups' performance on GJT

were not significantly different from the NSs ($M = 90.87$, $SD = 9.05$, $p = .131$), while the EMI leaners were ($p < .001$).

For object-uncountable nouns (e.g. *They have such beautiful furniture in their house* vs. *There are many furnitures to choose from*), the FI learners' means of accuracy was below 50% ($M = 46.97$, $SD = 11.49$), which was much lower than the EMI learners ($M = 79.17$, $SD = 18.26$). A Tukey HSD post hoc analysis showed that this difference was significant with $p < .001$. When comparing the NNSs to NSs ($M = 93.27$, $SD = 8.83$), both learning contexts performed significantly lower ($p < .001$ for both groups).

In regard to substance-uncountable nouns, the NSs performed lower than 90% overall ($M = 87.00$, $SD = 15.15$), and both NNS groups' accuracy was quite close to this level. Thus, the difference with learner groups was not significant: $p = .314$ for the FI learners and $p = .178$ for the EMI learners. The FI learners were on average slightly more accurate ($M = 80.30$, $SD = 17.50$) than the EMI learner group ($M = 78.13$, $SD = 19.59$), although this difference was not significant ($p = .888$).

The data concerning flexible nouns do not show any relevant differences between the experimental groups. For flexible nouns presented with count syntax, henceforth flexible [+ COUNT], the NS group performed at high rates of accuracy (M = 96.15, SD = 5.88). The EMI learners performed with the lowest mean accuracy (M = 73.44, SD = 13.45), while the FI learners performed a little higher (M = 75.76, SD = 17.10). The difference between the two experimental groups was not significant (p = .796), although they both performed significantly lower than the NSs (p < .001 for both groups).

Flexible nouns presented in uncountable syntax, flexible [– COUNT], present a different picture, with the EMI learners achieving slightly higher rates of accuracy (M = 76.69, SD = 11.36) than the FI learners (M = 71.59, SD = 15.40), although this difference was not significant (p = .291). The NSs achieved significantly higher rates of accuracy (M = 91.35, SD = 9.20) than both of the experimental groups (p < .001 for both groups).

To summarize, the first research question explored the linguistic ability of both the FI and EMI experimental groups of NNSs in comparison to NSs in their ability to recognize grammatical and ungrammatical uses of countable/uncountable noun distinctions in English. The results of the GJT provided evidence that the NNSs, both FI and EMI, showed some difficulty, although not significant in all noun types. In comparison to NSs, differences were significant in the case of countable nouns for the EMI group, for both groups in the case of object-uncountables, and non-significant for substance-uncountable and for flexible nouns in countable contexts. They were again significant for both groups for flexible nouns in uncountable contexts.

When comparing learning contexts, the FI group performed significantly better than the EMI group with regard to countable nouns, while they performed only slightly higher with substance-uncountable nouns and flexible [+ COUNT]. The EMI group did perform slightly better than the FI group with regard to object-uncountable nouns and flexible [– COUNT] nouns. Thus, there was no clear trend favoring either FI or EMI. It must be remembered that the EMI group had around seven times more hours of exposure per week than the FI group (15/20 versus 3, respectively), potentially including many contexts for using these classes of nouns. On the other hand, the FI group had received explicit instruction, and more precisely 4 hours, on countability issues. Consequently, it can be stated that the contrast between both groups in terms of quantity and quality of exposure also results in mixed, or asymmetric, comparative results.

4.2 Experiment 2

Experiment 2 allows us to address RQ2: to what extent the judgments elicited with the PDT were based on linguistic or extra-linguistic knowledge and whether there are any differences among EMI and FI students and L1 English speakers.

We will now look at the results of the PDT in English and compare the EMI learners to the FI learners and the NSs. Results will be reported as percentages of individuation based on English noun type. It should be borne in mind that answers were scored by awarding +1 point if the participant chose the picture with three small masses or items and a score of 0 if the picture chosen represented a large mass or item. To calculate percentages of individuation, the positive numbers were added together and then divided by the total number of items in that category, which was always 4. In other words, if a participant chose the picture of three small items for *books, dogs,* and *doors,* but not for *windows,* then they would receive a score of 3. That score was then divided by 4 to get a percentage of individuation as 75%. One would predict lower percentages of individuation for uncountable-substance and flexible [– COUNT] items. For example, if a participant selected the picture of three small piles for *cake,* but the larger mass for *paper, stone,* and *chocolate,* then they would receive a score of 1 out of four. That would be converted into a percentage of individuation of 25%. In short, one would expect high percentages of individuation for countable, object-uncountable, and flexible [+ COUNT] nouns since those nouns are countable and, therefore, refer to objects that can be individuated and low percentages of individuation for substance-uncountable and flexible [– count] nouns since those nouns are uncountable and, therefore, refer to masses of substances.

In order to address this research question, a series of one-way ANOVAs was run on the mean percentages of individuation (scores out of 100) of the PDT, with an alpha value set at 0.05. For the noun types tested, there was no statistically significant difference between groups as determined by one-way ANOVA for countable nouns ($F(2,80)$ = .029, p = .972), object-uncountable nouns ($F(2,80)$ = 1.181, p = .312), or substance-uncountable nouns ($F(2,80)$ = .189, p = .828). As for flexible nouns, there was no statistical difference found for flexible [+ COUNT] nouns ($F(2,80)$ = .115, p = .892) nor flexible [– COUNT] nouns ($F(2,80)$ = .078, p = .925). Individuation rates are provided in Table 6.

Looking at individual comparisons from a descriptive point of view, results of the PDT provided evidence that L2 English learners, from both the EMI and the FI groups, showed very similar patterns of individuation (or qualificational judgments) to NSs of English. Table 6 shows the means of individuation for all the groups.

Table 6: PDT descriptive statistics

Group	Countable nouns	Object-uncountable nouns	Substance-uncountable nouns	Flexible [+ COUNT] nouns	Flexible [– COUNT] nouns
NSs (*n* = 26)	96.15 (15.32)	85.58 (20.22)	33.65 (42.98)	93.27 (20.69)	52.88 (42.03)
FI context (*n* = 33)	96.21 (11.04)	76.52 (25.72)	27.27 (36.10)	91.67 (18.40)	56.82 (38.16)
EMI context (*n* = 24)	96.88 (8.45)	81.25 (20.19)	30.21 (40.36)	93.75 (11.06)	54.17 (37.35)

Given the very similar results, post hoc tests using Tukey HSD showed no statistical differences among groups, with all *p* values higher than .715

These strong similarities among groups deserve some comments. The most striking, and perhaps unexpected, is that regarding object-uncountable nouns (e.g. *Where is there more furniture?*). English native speakers' individuation rate was the highest (*M* = 85.58), followed by EMI learners (*M* = 81.25) and FI learners (*M* = 76.52). This means that, even though in English some nouns are un-countable only (e.g. *luggage*, which may be grammaticalized as countable in Cata-lan/Spanish, i.e. *equipajes*), judgments seem to be based in all cases on semantics (the mental representation of individual objects) rather than on grammar (the mass- vs. count-noun distinction). This provides further evidence for Barner & Snedeker's (2005) claim that, for object-uncountable nouns, English speakers rely more on semantics than on their language's grammar.

Another rather unexpected finding was the proportion of participants who se-lected the individuating option for substance-uncountable nouns. Although all groups perceived these stimuli (such as *water*) to refer more to masses rather than to individuals, and thus tended to select the picture with the big object rather than the one with several small ones, about one third of the answers seemed to interpret some of the substance-uncountable nouns as being [+ INDIVIDUAL] (e.g. *milk* and *water*). This could be attributed to the fact that, in the PDT, the uncount-able substances which were liquid, appeared as "cups" of those substances and therefore might have been interpreted as [+ INDIVIDUAL].

A similar phenomenon was observed for flexible nouns. While all three groups consistently interpreted flexible nouns in terms of individuation in [+ COUNT] syntactic contexts (e.g. *Where is there more cakes?*), in [– COUNT] contexts (e.g. *Where is there more cake?*) about 50% of the responses individuated (e.g. chose the picture of three small *cakes*), while the other 50% did not individuate (e.g. chose the picture of one large *cake*). As with the substance-uncountable nouns, it is possible that the pictures that represented flexible nouns in the PDT did not provide appropriate interpretations of mass representations (e.g. a large cake instead of three small cakes). Thus, our experiment provides only partial evidence that syntax drives the individualized interpretation of flexible nouns presented in a [– COUNT] context, as was found by Barner & Snedeker (2005).

5 Conclusions

The present study evaluated the acquisition of English by Spanish/Catalan speakers from two different EFL learning contexts, conventional FI and EMI, to gauge their respective impact on learners' target language abilities vis-à-vis countability. To do so, we followed Barner & Snedeker (2005), who used a similar PDT to investigate English-speaking children's developmental patterns and adults' representations of countable-uncountable noun semantics, in addition to a GJT based on 100 items. No previous studies have investigated this phenomenon in NNSs, specifically from a bilingual background, in different learning contexts, FI and EMI, and with a crosslinguistic perspective.

Regarding RQ1, which looked into the EMI and FI participants' ability to recognize grammatical and ungrammatical uses of countable/uncountable noun distinctions in English, the results of the GJT provided evidence that the NNSs of English showed some difficulty, although not significant in all noun types, with regards to the judgments of countable and uncountable noun distinctions when used in grammatical and ungrammatical contexts in comparison to the NSs, irrespective of whether they were studying English in a FI or EMI context. Differences with NSs were significant in the case of countable nouns for the EMI group, in favor of the NSs, for both the FI and the EMI groups in the case of uncountable-objects, in favor of the NSs. Differences were non-significant for uncountable-substance and for flexible nouns in both countable and uncountable contexts. There were no clear and consistent differences between the EMI and the FI groups, which shows that both programs seem to have similar effects on this dimension of language performance, despite their obvious difference as regards amount of input (15-20 vs. 3 hours per week) and instructional approach (implicit vs. explicit).

Regarding RQ2, which enquired into the participants' judgments of individuation for different noun types, results have shown a large amount of similarity across groups when comparing the PDT data collected from NSs and NNSs of English. Most importantly, the fact that English L2 learners had similar response patterns as NSs regarding object-uncountable nouns, which receive different grammatical encodings in English versus Catalan/Spanish, supports Barner & Snedeker's (2005) theory that mental representations of object-uncountable nouns do represent individual objects, and provide additional evidence that mental representations do not seem to differ across speakers of different languages, regardless of how each language encodes them in the grammar (as countable or uncountable nouns). Our results also agree with Barner & Snedeker's (2005) conclusion that flexible nouns are interpreted based on the syntactic context in which they occur, although in our data the difference between [+ COUNT] and [– COUNT] contexts was not as clear-cut as in their original experiments.

This chapter and these conclusions do not come without consequences and limitations, though. We do believe that the presentation of the pictures makes the task to some extent unnatural, although this is true of many controlled experimental conditions. We also believe that expanding the research to all levels of learners would give some better insight into the acquisition process of countable and uncountable nouns.

Acknowledgments

We would like to thank Eloi Puig-Mayenco and Jennifer Ament for their help in participant recruitment and data collection, as well as their valuable comments throughout the writing process. In addition, we would also like to thank the anonymous reviewers and series editors for their insightful comments and suggestions throughout the review process.

References

Barner, David & Jesse Snedeker. 2005. Quantity judgments and individuation: Evidence that mass nouns count. *Cognition* 97. 41–66.

Bloom, Paul & Deborah Keleman. 1995. Syntactic cues in the acquisition of collective nouns. *Cognition* 56. 1–30.

Bruyne, Jacques de. 1995. *A comprehensive Spanish grammar*. Cambridge, MA: Blackwell.

Butt, John & Carmen Benjamin. 2004. *A new reference grammar of modern Spanish*. London: E. Arnold.

Chaudron, Craig. 2003. Data collection in SLA research. In Catherine J. Doughty & Michael H. Long (eds.), *The handbook of second language acquisition*, 762–828. Malden, MA: Blackwell.

Coleman, Jim. 2006. English-medium teaching in European higher education. *Language Teaching* 39(1). 1–14.

Cowan, Ron & Yukiko Abe Hatasa. 1994. Investigating the validity and reliability of native speaker and second language learner judgments about sentences. In Elain E. Tarone, Susan M. Gass & Andrew D. Cohen (eds.), *Research methodology in second language acquisition*, 287–302. Hillsdale: Lawrence Erlbaum.

Cowart, Wayne. 1997. *Experimental syntax: Applying objective methods to sentence judgments*. Thousand Oaks: SAGE Publications, Inc.

Dafouz, Emma & Michele C. Guerrini (eds.). 2009. *CLIL across educational levels: Experiences from primary, secondary and tertiary contexts*. Madrid: Santillana Educación.

Ellis, Rod. 2010. Second language acquisition, teacher education and language pedagogy. *Language Teaching* 43. 182–201.

Gass, Susan M. 1994. *Second language acquisition: An introductory course*. New York: Routledge.

Ionin, Tania & Eve Zyzik. 2014. Judgment and interpretation tasks in second language research. *Annual Review of Applied Linguistics* 34. 1–28.

Izumi, Shinichi. 2013. Focus on form (FonF). In Peter Robinson (ed.), *The Routledge encyclopedia of second language acquisition*, 244–249. New York: Routledge.

Landman, Fred. 2011. Count nouns – mass nouns, neat nouns – mess nouns. In Jurgis Skilters & Susan Rothstein (eds.), *The Baltic international yearbook of cognition, logic and communication 6*, 1–67. Riga: BICLYIC.

Leech, Geoffrey & Jan Svartvik. 1975. *A communicative grammar of English*. London: Longman.

Norris, John & Lourdes Ortega. 2003. Defining and measuring SLA. In Catherine J. Doughty & Michael H. Long (eds.), *The handbook of second language acquisition*, 716–761. Malden, MA: Blackwell.

Pérez-Vidal, Carmen. 2009. The integration of content and language in the classroom: A European approach to education (the second time around). In Emma Dafouz & Michele C. Guerrini (eds.), *CLIL across educational levels: Experiences from primary, secondary and tertiary contexts*, 25–40. Madrid: Santillana Educación.

Pérez-Vidal, Carmen. 2011. Language acquisition in three different contexts of learning: Formal instruction, stay abroad and semi-immersion (CLIL). In Yolanda Ruiz de Zarobe, Juan Manuel Sierra & Francisco Gallardo del Puerto (eds.), *Content and foreign language integrated learning: Contributions to multilingualism in European contexts*, 103–128. Bern/Berlin: Peter Lang.

Wächter, Bern & Friedhelm Maiworm (eds.). 2014. Bonn: Lemmens Medien GmbH.

Wheeler, Max, Alan Yates & Nicolau Dols. 1999. *Catalan: A comprehensive grammar*. New York: Routledge.

Chapter 3

The acquisition of discourse markers in the English-medium instruction context

Jennifer Ament

Universitat Pompeu Fabra

Júlia Barón Parés

Universitat Internacional de Catalunya; Universitat de Barcelona

This study focuses on the effects of the context of learning on language acquisition by comparing the production of discourse markers (DMs) in oral output of English-medium instruction (EMI) students (N = 7) with non-EMI students (N = 9). Data were elicited through an oral discourse completion task and a conversation task. Four types of DMs were identified: cognitive, interpersonal, structural and referential. Quantitative analysis reveals that EMI students tend to produce longer responses and more structural markers, as opposed to control students, who use more referential markers. A qualitative interpretation of the data suggests that the EMI participants mark their discourse for their own as well as for their interlocutor's benefit, specifically by using structural markers to ensure clear interpretation of utterances. The study further suggests that participation in an EMI program may lead to pragmatic benefits specifically in terms of the type and quality of DMs used, rather than of their frequency and overall variety. However, the study also indicates that this context alone may not be sufficient for the acquisition of all types of markers, and that there are many other factors at play in the acquisition of this pragmatic feature.

1 Introduction

This exploratory study examines the acquisition of discourse markers (DMs) in second language acquisition. The function of DMs as connectors in discourse makes them essential to smooth communication, as they facilitate the correct

Jennifer Ament & Júlia Barón Parés. The acquisition of discourse markers in the English-medium instruction context. In Carmen Pérez Vidal, Sonia López-Serrano, Jennifer Ament & Dakota J. Thomas-Wilhelm (eds.), *Learning context effects: Study abroad, formal instruction and international immersion classrooms*, 43–74. Berlin: Language Science Press. DOI:10.5281/zenodo.1300612

interpretation of an utterance and express the speakers' intentions (Ariel 1998). Despite the attested importance of these markers, DMs are seldom addressed in second language classroom instruction (Vellenga 2004). Thus, learners are left with the difficult task of, firstly, interpreting, and secondly, integrating them effectively into their own speech. As this volume highlights, the context of learning plays an important role in second language acquisition, for it has been found that different contexts of learning foster the development of different language skills. General conclusions from research are that, for optimal language learning to occur, participation in more than one context is desirable (Pérez-Vidal 2014b). More particularly, integrated content and language contexts, in which curricular subjects are taught through the medium of a second or foreign language, can lead to very positive outcomes in the domains of receptive skills, vocabulary, morphology, speaking, creativity, and motivation (Pérez-Cañado 2012). Regarding pragmatics, research shows that integrated context and language classes provide opportunities for incidental pragmatic learning (Taguchi 2015).

2 Literature review

The rationale and motivation for the present study are that, firstly, there are scarce data regarding the acquisition of DMs by second language (L2) learners, despite their importance for successful communication. Secondly, the ever growing importance of English-medium instruction (EMI) in Europe today has both social and political consequences. Thus, knowing more about language acquisition in this setting can help inform higher education institutions across Europe regarding what types of linguistic gains can be expected from participation in EMI programs and what kind of language support is needed for students receiving their education through EMI. The literature review consists of two parts: first, an overview of EMI will be provided to contextualize the present study. In the second part, DMs are identified and classified according to their functions, and studies examining their acquisition are discussed.

2.1 English-medium instruction

2.1.1 Policies

While many factors have contributed to the rise of EMI across Europe, the Bologna process was perhaps the most impactful (European Minister's of Education 1999). This large-scale policy change, which sought to encourage the mobility of students and faculty within Europe, had widespread effects on language policies across the European Union. In efforts to become more competitive and attractive to both faculty and students from other countries, universities began to offer degrees either partially or completely taught through languages other than the official language of the country, most notably English (Coleman 2006; Llurda et al. 2013; Pérez-Vidal 2015). In fact, the number of EMI courses tripled from 1998 to 2008 in Europe (Wächter & Maiworm 2008). The rapid implementation of EMI programs continues to rise to this day reaching nearly 6% of all programs offered in Europe (Smit & Dafouz 2012; Wächter & Maiworm 2014).

2.1.2 Contextualization

EMI can be defined as a context in which English is used as the language of instruction, in tertiary education, in non-English speaking countries (Hellekjaer & Hellekjaer 2015). However, different regions and even individual universities have integrated EMI into their specific context in unique ways, thus making EMI somewhat of an umbrella term, for which specific realizations may differ across institutions. For instance, some regions have found it necessary to protect local languages, as was the case in the autonomous regions of Catalonia and the Basque Country in Spain. When introducing EMI programs in these two regions, the decision was made to implement trilingual policies with a view to protect and promote learning of regional languages (See Pérez-Vidal 2008; and Doiz et al. 2014). Similarly, Nordic countries question if there is perhaps an over-reliance on English in academic contexts, and steps are being taken to protect national languages in research and education (Nordic Council of Ministers. 2006). Thus, as demonstrated, program structure or intensity of EMI differs according to each community's language needs. Some may have full EMI programs while others only a small percentage of EMI courses. Institutions differ as well according to what type of language support is offered to students, faculty and administration (regarding both English or national languages). Despite the differences in structure, when a course is offered through EMI, there are also some constants, such as a strong focus on content and little attention or support offered to aid language learning. Although EMI courses are now widespread, there is scarce research on how they are implemented in practice; only a handful of studies have been conducted, which reveal that lecturers do not focus on language, and that they may feel uncomfortable correcting errors as they are often non-native speakers of English themselves (Costa 2012). Lecturers are experts in their disciplinary fields and do not consider themselves language specialists; their aim, from their point of view, is therefore to educate students on their subject of expertise (Airey 2012; Unterberger 2012).

2.1.3 Research on EMI

Within the European Union, a body of research on EMI from a second language acquisition perspective has begun to emerge. Much of such research has taken a qualitative approach, investigating such topics as lecturers' and students' attitudes and beliefs towards EMI (Kling 2013; Kuteeva & Airey 2014). These studies seek to inform policymakers, program creators, language teachers, and professional development departments about how EMI is implemented in different institutions. Concerning content learning, research reveals that students find courses harder and the workload heavier when taught through English (Tazl 2011) and that EMI is not perceived as equal to first language instruction in terms of content delivery (Sert 2008). It has also been reported across a wide variety of contexts that students expect language gains when participating in EMI programs (Pecorari et al. 2011; Gundermann 2014; Lueg & Lueg 2015; Margić & Žeželić 2015). However, as mentioned above, there is hardly any language support provided to students during EMI degree programs, and language learning is not an explicit goal of such programs. Thus, investigating whether and how EMI leads to gains in linguistic competence is an area where more research is needed, and this chapter intends to offer a contribution in this direction.

2.2 Discourse markers

Discourse markers seem to play an important role both in first and second language acquisition, since they are constantly used by native speakers (NSs) and non-native speakers in interaction. As Yates (2011) points out, DMs help one interpret the speakers' attitudes towards the content of their messages and they tend to carry socio-pragmatic meaning. What some studies in SLA have found is that foreign and second language learners tend to use a narrower variety of DMs than NSs do, and that they seem to be less aware of the multifunctional uses of DMs (Vanda 2007; Yates 2011). However, even if DMs seem to be key elements in interaction, defining and categorizing them is a complex issue, as the literature in the field has shown (see Fischer 2006 for review). First of all, different terms such as pragmatic markers, discourse particles, discourse connectives, conversational markers, among others have been used to refer to these different linguistic items which have specific cohesive functions and important interpretive roles in conversation. Secondly, the multifunctional nature of some DMs has not been reflected in most of the categorizations presented so far, since most of these elements tend to have different functions depending on the context and situation where they are produced. Thirdly, one of the most problematic issues may be the grammaticalization of some DMs, for some tend to overlap syntactically with subordinating conjunctions or coordinators, while some others may simply connect different parts of discourse. All these issues have contributed to categorizations that fail to completely and accurately describe what discourse markers really show in terms of structure and function (Fischer 2014).

Even if no clear definitions can be found in the literature, many studies have identified some common characteristics among DMs. Most of them seem to show flexibility, that is, they are flexible in terms of their placement and use in discourse; additionally, they also encode speakers' intentions and interpersonal meanings (Carter & McCarthy 2006); they also carry little semantic meaning (Schiffrin 1987), but at the same time are essential to the natural flow of speech, as well as to correct interpretation (Neary-Sundquist 2013). Another aspect which has been reported in various studies is that hearers seem to rely on DMs to interpret and follow discourse (Blakemore 1992; Aijmer 1996), so, as (Leech & Svartvik 1975: 156) suggest, by using DMs "in speech or in writing, you help people understand your message by signaling how one idea leads on from another. The words and phrases which have this connecting function are like 'signposts' on a journey". Thus, these common characteristics are important elements for identifying discourse markers, which may have elusive referential meanings on the surface, but play important roles on different planes of communication (Schiffrin 1987).

In an attempt to describe how DMs are used by non-native speakers, in the present study it was decided to follow existing categorizations in order to assess their adequacy for analyzing learners' discourse. Therefore, following Maschler (1994) and Fung & Carter (2007), the present study analyzes DMs according to four functional categories: *cognitive, structural, referential,* and *interpersonal.* Each category serves several related functions. DMs in the *cognitive* category are thought to provide information on the cognitive state of the speaker and instruct the hearer as to how to construct their mental representation of the ongoing discourse. *Structural* DMs serve metalinguistic textual functions on how the flow of discourse is to be segmented. *Referential* DMs mark relationships between the utterances before and after the DM; these relationships may be marked by conjunctions, and may be completely grammatically integrated while at the same time functioning pragmatically (Fischer 2014), DMs in this category seem to be more syntactically and textually bound than the other DM categories. The final category, *interpersonal* DMs, are thought to be used to mark affective and social functions of spoken grammar, and indicate how the speaker feels towards the discourse statements (Andersen 2001). See Table 1 for a summary of the categories, functions and examples.

Table 1: Categorization of pragmatic markers according to functions

Functions	Example items
Cognitive	
Denote thinking process	*Well, I think*
Reformulation / self-Correction	*In other words, I mean*
Elaboration / Hesitation	*It's like / sort of, well*
Assessment of the listener's knowledge about utterances	*Right?*
Structural	
Opening and closing of topics	*Ok, right, well, now,*
Sequencing topic shifts	*Anyway(s), so, then, next*
Summarizing options	*And, so yeah*
Continuation of or return to topics	*Additionally, and so, and, plus*
Referential	
Cause / Contrast	*Because / But, although*
Consequence / Digression	*So / Anyway*
Interpersonal	
Mark shared knowledge	*You see, you know*
Indicate speaker attitudes	*Yes, of course, really, I agree*
Show emotional response / interest and back channel	*Great, sure, ok, yeah*

In the present study the use of DMs and their relationship to pragmatic competence is also explored, since, as (Müller 2005: 1) states "there is a general agreement that discourse markers contribute to the pragmatic meaning of utterances and thus play an important role in the pragmatic competence of the speaker". Furthermore, Sankoff et al. (1997) note that a learner's use of DMs may be a good indicator of the effect of L2 exposure on pragmatic competence. The present study thus intends to investigate how DMs may be acquired in EMI contexts.

2.3 The acquisition of pragmatic markers across contexts

2.3.1 Study abroad

A sojourn abroad has proven to be a positive learning environment for the development of pragmatic competence (Barron 2003; Schauer 2006). Cultural and linguistic immersion of this kind provides learners with increased opportunities to interact with NSs of the target language. Other benefits are that they are repeatedly exposed to daily routines, and have ample opportunities to practice a wide variety of communicative acts in many different social settings. These factors are believed to contribute to language learning. Research examining DMs show positive results: for example, Liu (2013; 2016) found that for Chinese students living in the United States both the increased exposure and increased socialization had significant positive effects on the frequency and variety of DMs produced. Similarly, Barron (2003) measured the use of pragmatic routines of 30 English-speaking learners of German through a written discourse completion task. She found that the exposure to input in the target language triggered important pragmatic development and more target like use of pragmatic routines. In a similar study on 128 international students who spent a study-abroad period in the United States, Sánchez-Hernández (2016) (see also Chapter 10 of this volume) found parallel results, showing that there was a relationship between the degree of acculturation and acquisition of DMs. These studies demonstrate how increased exposure, socialization and acculturation through a study-abroad period have measurable effects on pragmatic development.

2.3.2 Classroom settings: formal instruction and integrated content and language classes

While a classroom instructional setting does not offer the same variety of opportunities for learning or for practicing pragmatic skills as studying abroad can, it does show benefits of its own. Both instructed as well as incidental learning of pragmatics have been documented in previous studies (Nguyen et al. 2012; Bardovi-Harlig 2015). However, few studies report on the effects of explicit instruction on the acquisition of DMs; rather, most studies take language samples from classroom learners and report on their usage of DMs as learned incidentally. In the case of Bu (1996), oral data were gathered from interviews and recordings of English classroom discussions. She found that the Chinese learners in her study varied greatly regarding the types of DMs used when compared to NSs. She concluded that, while learners use many of the same DMs as English NSs, they do not employ them with the same functions as NSs do, and at times learners even give new and different functions to DMs that NSs never do (also found in Müller 2005). A study on Chinese learners of English by Liu (2013) also reported similar findings: Regarding the frequency of use of DMs in interviews, some markers were used significantly differently when compared to NSs. Those markers that learners used more frequently than the NSs were *just, sort of/kind of, but, well* and *then*, compared to *I think, yeah/yes* and *ah* which were used less frequently by the learners than by the NSs. The author argues that the difference between learners' and natives' use of DMs can be attributed to language transfer.

Among the studies investigating a larger range of DMs, Neary-Sundquist (2014) studied the relationship between proficiency level and pragmatic marker use. She reported that DM use rose with proficiency level, that lower proficiency learners used DMs much less frequently than NSs did, and that advanced learners reach NS levels for the frequency of use. With respect to the variety of markers used, she found that low-level learners overuse certain expressions while advanced learners make use of a larger variety of DMs. Another study comparing teenage learners in Hong Kong to a corpus of English NSs was conducted by Fung & Carter (2007). Through the analysis of interactions between students, they found that learners use referential markers at high frequencies, while other categories are used more sparingly, and that NSs use DMs for a much wider variety of functions. The authors argue that the use of DMs by the participants reflects the input they receive through their formal instruction in English courses. Regarding integrated content and language settings, Nikula (2008) studied adolescents' communication in content courses taught in English. She found this context to offer a wide variety of opportunities for pragmatic learning and practice. From classroom observation she reported students using DMs for a variety of pragmatic functions, such as mitigating or softening their communication acts. This gives evidence that content learning does allow learners to practice pragmatic routines, such as DMs. These studies show that although learners do not receive direct instruction on DM use, they can and do learn to use them implicitly, although more research is needed to know how the learning context specifically affects the acquisition of DMs.

3 The study

The goal of the present research is to investigate the effect of the EMI setting on the acquisition and use of DMs, in order to inspire future studies on similar larger populations and to provide empirical evidence as to what kinds of pragmatic outcomes can be expected from the EMI setting.

The research questions addressed in the present study are as follows:

1. Do EMI and non-EMI learners use DMs at similar frequencies and distributions, according to the four functional categories of DMs?

2. Are there differences between the frequency and distribution of DMs between EMI and non-EMI learners across tasks, viz. an oral discourse completion task and a conversation task?

4 Methodology

4.1 Participants

Sixteen second-year Economics undergraduate students from a university in Catalonia, Spain, were recruited to participate in this study. Results from a language background questionnaire revealed that all participants were Spanish/Catalan bilinguals and that these languages were also the languages of their previous education. All participants reported English as a third language. Participants reported having an English certificate at a B2 level according to the common European framework of references for languages.

Participants were divided into two groups: an immersion group (henceforth, IM group) (N = 7, age = 19) and a control group (henceforth CON) (N = 9, age = 19). The IM group was enrolled in an International Business degree, which is taught completely through English. Participants in the CON group were enrolled in either Economics or Business Administration at the same university but had only one of their courses taught through English in the second year of study. Each degree program consists of 425 contact hours per academic year. For the IM group, all 425 hours are delivered through the English language, while the CON group had an exposure of 35 contact hours. Data were collected during the participants' second year of study. Figure 1 illustrates the difference between groups in English contact hours per academic year.

4.2 Data collection instruments

Four instruments were used for data collection: two questionnaires (a language background questionnaire and a proficiency test) and two instruments for the elicitation of oral data (a conversation task, and an oral discourse completion task).

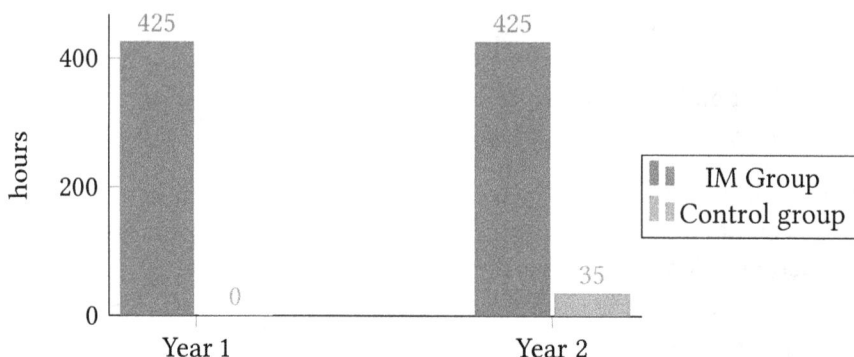

Figure 1: Exposure to EMI

4.2.1 Language background and proficiency level questionnaires

The language background questionnaire was designed to gather information on the participants' language background and learning history to ensure homogeneity of the groups. The online Cambridge placement test was used to ensure a homogeneous group according to general English proficiency; any participant who did not score over a B2 level was not included in the sample.

4.2.2 Conversation task

In order to gather spoken data through interaction, participants were asked to engage in conversation with another participant. Participants were asked three questions that required them to reflect on and discuss their motivations and attitudes towards English as a lingua franca, as well as towards their EMI courses (see appendix A).

4.2.3 Oral discourse completion task

A ten-item oral discourse completion task was used to elicit DMs (see appendix B). Discourse completion tasks as a research tool are supported by Usó-Juan & Martínez-Flor (2014); Parvaresh & Tavakoli (2009); Kasper & Rose (2002), and Hinkel (1997), and they are particularly valuable for eliciting DMs from L2 speakers (Roever 2009). However, they have been strongly debated in the literature, mainly because participants are often asked to write what they would say in a certain situation and this is considered an inaccurate representation of what they would actually say in real-time communication (Bardovi-Harlig 2015).

In order to address these concerns, an audio and visual discourse completion task was adopted. A video was created consisting of the researcher looking at the camera and recording the prompts for the ten discourse completion tasks, providing a pause of twenty-five seconds for the participants to respond before continuing to the next item. In this way, each item was orally contextualized and an interlocutor was provided to lower the cognitive load, thus enabling the participants to respond rapidly and as they would in an authentic interaction.

4.3 Procedure

Participants completed the web questionnaire and placement test via email before attending the testing session. Recording of data took place in sound-proof booths. Each booth had a large window and was equipped with a microphone, headset and computer. The participants could see and hear the researcher outside of the booth and were given a series of instructions to set up Audacity, the program used to record their response. The oral discourse completion task was administered first, by playing the video simultaneously on the participants' computer screens. Twenty-five seconds were given to respond to each prompt.

This was followed by the conversation task. For this task, participants were put into pairs in the booths, and recorded themselves. The researcher read each of the three questions out loud, the participants were told to include their opinions, personal experiences and anything else they felt they wanted to express in response to the statements. They had two minutes to discuss each question.

4.4 Data analysis

Audio files were transcribed into Codes for the Human Analysis of Transcripts (CHAT) using computerized language analysis (CLAN) software (MacWhinney 2000). The researcher identified and tagged each DM used in both the oral discourse completion task and the conversation task and assigned it a code according to its functional category (cognitive, structural, referential, or interpersonal). The transcriptions were then checked by another researcher. A single researcher coded the transcriptions twice to ensure consistency. A further 25% of the transcriptions were coded by a second researcher; and when there was a discrepancy, an agreement was reached through discussing the item and together deciding on how it should be coded. After coding, the frequency of use of each type of DM was calculated using CLAN. Tables 2 to 5 provide extracts from the data, giving three examples of each function.

Table 2: Exemplification from the data, according to function: Cognitive DMs

Examples from the data: Cognitive Function
i   *Yeah I've tried it and it doesn't fit me very well uhh I mean I would prefer another size or maybe another model that fits me better*
ii   *Please I'm not really well here ahh could you leave me alone for a minute please? It's like I'm a bit sick and I don't feel well I need some loneliness to recover myself please*
iii   *Umm well ahh I'm not sure it looks nice but I wouldn't wear it*

The markers were coded by taking into account the main function the DM was performing in the discourse, so that what may appear to be the same marker is, in fact, the marker performing different functions and therefore, would be coded accordingly. For example, the token of *well* marks a cognitive function in example (*iii*) in Table 2, and was so coded because we stipulated that in this context (i.e. utterance initial and occurring between two hesitation markers such as *umm*) that it signals a cognitive function (in this case, hesitation), and perhaps an effort to hold the floor while the speaker searches for a word or formulates their utterance in their mind. Looking at examples (*i*) and (*ii*) in Table 2, *I mean* functions to reformulate the message the speaker is conveying whereas *it's like* functions to signal an elaboration or exemplification of the previous utterance.

The structural markers were coded in the same manner, i.e. identifying the function of the marker in the discourse. For example, in example (*iv*) in Table 3 the structural marker *and then* functions to show temporal sequence (going to one city and afterwards to another) and also indicates an implied contrast between the two cities (the way English is spoken contrasts greatly between the two cities). In example (*v*), *and* functions to mark the summary of the speaker's opinion on the matter being discussed and *so* functions to mark the beginning of the speaker's turn as well as a slight shift in the topic, a shift from participant one's opinion to participant two's opinion. In example (*vi*), *so* serves to summarize the speakers' message.

The referential marker *because* in example (*vii*) in Table 4 functions to introduce a reason or cause for suggesting the weekend for the party. Example (*viii*) *but* marks a contrast between the two parts of the utterance, and example (*ix*) *so* marks the causal or consequential relationship between the first part of the utterance and the second.

Table 3: Exemplification from the data, according to function: Structural DMs

	Examples from the data: Structural Function
iv	*Yes and, umm, for example you can go to London and then you can go to U. S. and it's totally different so you can also*
v	*Participant 1: Umm ahh and the last ahh I would say that I see myself talking English in well, I hope to be in in United States or or somewhere*
vi	*Participant 2: hmm so I think that aah I I chose to to have lessons in English because I wanted to improve my my level I wanted to to keep practising it*
vii	*stop bothering me you know you're annoying me and my friends so I would really appreciate that you left right now*

Table 4: Exemplification from the data, according to function: Referential DMs

	Examples from the data: Referential Function
vii	*I would suggest you to do it on the weekend because we don't have so much homework from university*
viii	*I have tried on me but it doesn't fit*
ix	*It don't fit me because it's so small so I have to change*

Table 5: Exemplification from the data according to function: Interpersonal DMs

	Examples from the data: Interpersonal Function
x	*Well I kind of you know we don't have that much of a relationship with Laura and things have gone pretty badly lately.*
xi	*Yeah absolutely I love it but it's a little bit small for my size*
xii	*Oh yeah I love it but you know what it is too small*

The use of the interpersonal marker *you know* in example (*x*) in Table 5 functions to align the speaker with their interlocutor and mark the shared knowledge that the speaker and the interlocutor have about the speaker and Laura not having a good relationship. Examples (*xi*) *yeah absolutely* and (*xii*) *oh yeah* are used to express the speaker's attitudes and emotions towards what is being discussed. Below, data from each task is provided.

(1) Oral discourse completion task data:
1 **Well** I'm not sure about it **you know** Laura
2 it's a very chaotic girl **and** she's always
3 making noise maybe it's not such a good
4 idea inviting Laura if you feel to do it
5 ahh go ahead **but** in my opinion she
6 shouldn't be invited **you know**.

In (1), the speaker opens discourse and begins with the cognitive marker, *well,* denoting mental processing. The participant begins to share her opinion and uses the interpersonal marker *you know* to mark and confirm shared knowledge, with her interlocutor. She lets her interlocutor know that she is continuing to add information to the same topic using the structural marker *and.* Then in line 6, she uses the referential marker *but* to show contrast between what the speaker and hearer feel and restates her opinion, she finishes her turn by closing with the cognitive marker *you know* as an attempt to align with her interlocutor as well as to assess the interlocutor's reception of her message.

(2) Conversation data:
1 **OK**, I start umm I've been learning English
2 all my life **and I think** that I I would be
3 very competent and natural with English
4 speakers, native ones, **but I think** that
5 I've always can improve.

In this example the participant first uses the structural DM *OK* to mark the opening of discourse and begin her turn. Then another structural DM *and* is used in line 2, in order to indicate a continuation of the topic and to add information. It is followed by the interpersonal DM *I think* which gives an indication of the speaker's personal opinion towards the statement immediately following the marker. Then in line 4, a referential DM is used to contrast the information given after *but* with the statement that precedes it. This is then immediately followed by an interpersonal DM *I think* which expresses the speaker's attitudes and beliefs towards the following statement.

Below are examples of data from the IM group; P1, P2 etc. stand for Participant 1, 2 etc.

(3) P1: We are colleagues in the same class.
P2: Yes.
P1: **So** we probably agree.
P2: Yes the same.
P1: **And** how do you feel when you communicate with native English speakers?
P2: **Well** I don't feel comfortable.

In (3), participant 1 uses *so* to summarize opinions with her statement 'so, we probably agree'. Then she uses *and* as a structural marker to signal a shift in the topic, from what the speaker feels to what participant two feels towards what is being discussed.

(4) P3: Yes, it's difficult to reach the level of English that native speakers have, but I think that, umm it's very important in, in your life to, to do so. *So.*
P4: Yeah, **and well**, ahh, in, ahh, the future, I, I want to go to, for example, Londres (London), to find, to will find a homework, ahh because it's a nice city.

In (4), participant 3 uses *so* as a structural DM at the end of her utterance to sum up her opinion and mark the end of her turn, which participant 4 correctly interprets and uptakes with an appropriate response. She goes on to use *and* as a topic shift marker and *well* to mark the introduction of a new topic.

5 Results

This section first provides the results for research question 1 by presenting the findings from the discourse completion task and the conversation task together. Research question 2 is addressed in the second section by analyzing the two tasks separately. Before conducting inferential statistics, statistical assumptions were verified; for all but two of the variables, skewness and kurtosis values were out of normal distribution ranges. In addition, the sample size was small. It was thus decided to use non-parametric tests. Specifically, the Mann-Whitney test was carried out to detect any significant differences between the two groups of participants. Additionally, Cohen's *d* was calculated to determine effect sizes, using as a standardizer the pooled standard deviations of the two groups. The interpretation of the Cohen's *d* is as follows: *d* values between 0 and .5 are considered small effect sizes, values between .5 and .8 are considered medium effect sizes, and over .8 are reflections of large effect sizes.

5.1 Differences in frequency and variety of DM use according to the four categories across both tasks

To begin descriptive statistics were first calculated. Most notably the results reveal that, despite being given equal amounts of time to complete the tasks, participants in the IM group produced more words (M = 847.86, SD = 194), than the CON group (M = 555.89, SD = 166.59), which, according to the Mann-Whitney statistical test, proved to be significant, with a large effect size (U = 8, p = .013, d = 1.614). Furthermore, and probably as a consequence of this, the IM group produced more DMs (M = 104.43, SD = 24.61) compared to those in the CON group (M = 72.22, SD = 17.27) which also proved to be a significant difference, with a large effect size (U = 8, p = .013, d = 1.515). However, with respect to the ratio of DMs per 100 words, the CON group produced more than the IM group: IM (M = 12.4, SD = 1.47) versus CON (M = 13.24, SD = 1.42), although when tested for significance the result was not statistical (U = 25, p = .491). In order to assess the variety of DMs used, Guiraud's index was calculated, dividing the number of DM types by the square root of the number of DM tokens; the difference between groups was not statistically significant. Guiraud's index is a corrected version of the standard type/token ratio (TTR), which is less sensitive to variations in text length (Daller 2010). Table 6 reports descriptive and statistical results on the data from the two tasks together. Due to the significant difference in number of words spoken, it was decided to calculate all further tests based on the percentage of DMs produced with respect to the total number of words produced multiplied by one hundred.

In order to respond to research question 1 – *Do EMI and non-EMI learners use DMs at similar frequencies and distributions, according to the four functional categories of DMs?* – Further analyses with respect to the four functional categories were carried out. Table 7 shows the mean ratios of DMs produced per participant according to each category across both tasks as well as the mean percentage of occurrence of each category of DM with respect to the total DMs produced. Regarding this distribution, when both tasks were analyzed together, the IM group produced a higher proportion of cognitive (IM = 12.72%, CON = 11.85%), struc-

Table 6: Descriptive and statistical data for both tasks IM and CON groups

Group (N)	Words spoken	DMs spoken	DMs per 100 words	Mean DM' Guiraud Index
IM (7)	M = 847.86	M = 104.43	M = 12.4	M = 1.73
	SD = 194	SD = 24.61	SD = 1.47	SD = .13
CON (9)	M = 555.89	M = 72.22	M =13.24	M = 1.76
	SD = 166.59	SD = 17.27	SD = 1.42	SD = .19
Mann-Whitney test	U = 8	U = 8	U = 25	U = 18.5
	p = .013	p = .013	p = .491	p = .19
Cohen's d	d = 1.614	d = 1.515	d = - 0.58	d = -0.20

Table 7: DMs used according to DM category IM and CON group both tasks

DM Category	IM Group			CON Group		
	Mean	SD	% of all DMs	Mean	SD	% of all DMs
Cognitive	1.58	.46	12.72	1.56	.56	11.85
Structural	3.02	.96	24.49	2.40	.67	18.46
Referential	2.89	1.01	23.94	4.02	1.25	30.77
Interpersonal	4.74	1.13	37.62	5.01	1.57	36.92
DM frequency (tokens per 100w)	12.41	1.47	n/a	13.24	1.42	n/a
DM variety (types per 100w)	3.07	.74	n/a	3.97	.74	n/a

tural (IM = 24.49%, CON = 18.46%) and interpersonal markers (IM = 37.62%, CON = 36.92%), while the CON group tended to produce a higher rate of referential markers (IM = 23.94%, CON = 30.77%). The CON group also produced more DM tokens and types per 100 words, which is reflected in the slightly larger value of the Guiraud Index. This may indicate that the use of DMs was both more frequent and more varied than compared to the IM group.

A Mann-Whitney test was carried out in order to detect any significant differences between the groups regarding these values per 100 words. Results show there was a significant difference in the production of referential markers, with a large effect size ($U = 7$, $p = .010$, $d = 1.097$). Specifically, the CON group ($M = 4.33$, $SD = 1.25$) produced more referential DMs than the IM group ($M = 3.32$, $SD = 1.01$). Results for the remaining variables measured were not significant. The probability values for the differences and effect sizes are reported in Table 8.

Table 8: Comparison of IM and CON groups

Category of DM	Mann-Whitney Value	p-value	Cohen's d
Cognitive DMs	31	.958	.039
Structural DMs	20	.223	.749
Referential DMs	14	.064	-1.536
Interpersonal DMs	26	.560	.197
DM frequency (tokens per 100w)	25	.491	.581
DM variety (types per 100w)	13	.055	-1.211
Guiraud's Index	40	.40	-0.195

To summarize the results from research question 1, it was found that IM students spoke significantly more, and produced significantly more DMs in their texts, in absolute terms. However, looking at standardized values per 100 words, there were no significant differences detected between the groups. Regarding the distribution of the different categories of DMs, the CON group was found to produce a significantly higher ratio of referential DMs than the IM group.

5.2 Differences in frequency and variety of DM use in each task separately

Separate analyses were run for each task in order to address research question 2 - *Are there any differences between groups depending on the task, according to the four categories?*- Regarding the discourse completion task, descriptive statistics were calculated (see Table 9) and a Mann-Whitney test was then carried out to detect statistical significance (see Table 10). As in the previous section, all values discussed here are based on ratios per 100 words, given the significant differences in text length between the two groups.

The IM group ($M = 399.57$, $SD = 84.72$) produced significantly more words than the CON group, with a large effect size ($M = 287.33$, $SD = 100.34$) ($U = 12$, $p = .039$, $d = 1.209$). According to the distribution of DMs, results show tendencies for the IM group to produce a higher rate of structural (IM = 20.00%, CON = 15.73%) and interpersonal markers (IM = 41.40%, CON = 39.76%) than the CON group,

Table 9: Descriptive statistics for the oral discourse completion task

DM Category	Mean	SD	% of all DMs	Mean	SD	% of all DMs
Cognitive	1.06	.41	10.88	1.65	1.17	11.87
Structural	2.04	1.00	20	1.94	1.09	15.73
Referential	2.38	1.16	24.56	3.78	.91	28.78
Interpersonal	4.19	1.12	41.40	5.38	2.09	39.76
Mean words	399.57	84.72	n/a	287.33	100.34	n/a
DM frequency (tokens per 100w)	10.01	1.78	n/a	13.19	2.30	n/a
DM variety (types per 100w)	2.79	.49	n/a	3.49	1.48	n/a
Guiraud's Index	1.74	.20	n/a	1.54	.34	n/a

Table 10: Comparison of groups discourse completion task

Category of DM	Mann-Whitney value	p-value	Cohen's d
Cognitive	21	.266	-0.742
Structural	31	.958	.095
Referential	12	.039	1.34
Interpersonal	20	.223	.737
Mean Words	12	.039	1.209
DM frequency (tokens per 100w)	7	.010	1.546
DM Variety (types per 100w)	23	.401	-0.722
Guiraud's Index	19	.186	.752

while the CON group appears to produce higher rates of cognitive (IM = 10.88%, CON = 11.87%) and referential markers (IM = 24.56%, CON = 28.78%) than the IM group. The only significant difference between the groups was detected in the referential marker category, with a large effect size ($U = 12$, $p = .039$, $d = 1.34$).

However, despite speaking more, the results show the IM group ($M = 10.01$, $SD = 1.78$) produced significantly fewer DMs per 100 words than the CON group ($M = 13.19$, $SD = 2.30$), with a large effect size ($U = 7.00$, $p = .010$, $d = 1.546$). Furthermore, the CON group ($M = 3.49$, $SD = 1.48$) was found to produce a wider variety of DM types than the IM group ($M = 2.79$, $SD = .49$), although the result was not significant. Variety of types per 100 words is a measure that can be partially affected by text length (for example, longer texts will tend to have more repetitions of the same types). The Guiraud Index, which introduces a partial correction for these effects, is in fact slightly higher in the IM group (*M* = 1.74, *SD* = .20) than the CON group (*M* = 1.54, *SD* = .34), although this difference was not significant either.

In sum, significant differences were that the IM group spoke more than the CON group and that the CON group produced a higher frequency of DMs per 100 words, as well as a significantly higher proportion of referential DMs than the IM group.

Turning to the conversation task, descriptive statistics were calculated first (see Table 11), and secondly the data were analyzed statistically using the Mann-Whitney test (see Table 12). The descriptive statistics show that, during the conversation task, the IM group produced more words (*M* = 448.28, *SD* = 143.40), than the CON group (*M* = 268.56, *SD* = 84.14) a difference that proved to be statistically significant, with a large effect size (*U* = 9, *p* = .017, *d* = 1.529). The IM group also showed a higher frequency of DM production overall (*M* = 14.90, *SD* = 3.12) compared to the CQN group (*M* = 13.08, *SD* = 1.54), however, this difference failed to prove significant. The CON group produced a higher variety of DMs (*M* = 4.44, *SD* = 77) compared to the IM group (*M* = 3.35, *SD* = 1.42), and the difference was significant, with a large effect size (*U* = 10, *p* = .023, *d* = .954).

Table 11: Descriptive statistics for the conversation task

DM Category	IM Group Mean	SD	% of all DMs	CON Group Mean	SD	% of all DMs
Cognitive	1.95	.88	13.90	1.49	1.24	11.82
Structural	4.11	1.42	27.35	2.75	1.02	21.41
Referential	3.31	1.01	23.56	4.33	1.25	32.91
Interpersonal	5.52	2.53	35.20	4.51	1.58	33.87
Mean words	448.28	143.40	n/a	268.56	84.14	n/a
DM frequency (tokens per 100w)	14.90	3.12	n/a	13.08	1.54	n/a
DM Variety (types per 100w)	3.35	1.42	n/a	4.44	.77	n/a
Guiraud's Index	1.72	.30		1.98	.37	

Table 12: Comparison of Groups Conversation Task (ratios per 100 words)

Category of DM	Mann-Whitney value	p-value	Cohen's d
Cognitive	24	.427	.428
Structural	13	.050	1.100
Referential	14	.064	-0.898
Interpersonal	24	.427	.479
Mean Words	11	.034	1.529
DM frequency (tokens per 100w)	21	.226	.740
DM Variety (types per 100w)	10	.023	.954
Guiraud's Index	16	.10	.772

Concerning the categories of DMs, a statistically significant difference was detected in the use of structural DMs, with a large effect size ($U = 13$, $p = .050$ $d = 1.100$). Specifically, the IM group ($M = 4.11$, $SD = 1.42$) produced more structural DMs than the CON group ($M = 2.75$, $SD = 1.02$). Furthermore, the IM group tended to produce more cognitive and interpersonal DMs, and the CON group more referential DMs, although none of these differences were significant.

To summarize results from the conversation task, it was found that the IM group produced significantly more words and more structural DMs than the CON group and that the CON group produced a significantly higher variety of DMs than the IM group.

6 Discussion

This study did not find many statistically significant differences between the two groups, both because of the limited sample size and also because the two groups were rather similar with respect to several dimensions. However, the significant differences that were found offer some interesting points for discussion.

Regarding the first research question, findings show that students in an EMI program produced longer responses and dialogues. When calculating absolute scores, EMI students produced significantly longer stretches of speech and a significantly higher number of DMs. Both of these findings can be considered signs of increased oral fluency (Segalowitz & Freed 2004). However, when text length was controlled for via calculation of standardized values per 100 words, the differences were not sustained. While this points out that the two groups produce similar frequencies of DMs in proportion to the total length of text produced, it still evidences an increased oral fluency among the EMI students.

The second finding was that the non-EMI group had a very high frequency of use of referential markers. Previous research has suggested that this category might be easier or could be the first category of DMs to be acquired (Liu 2016). This is due to the main functions of referential DMs, namely to show cause and contrast, consequence and comparison. These markers are the type of DM most often addressed in the foreign language classroom due to their close relationship with syntax as well as their strong prevalence in written language (Fung & Carter 2007). This contrasts with the other categories which appear more frequently or even exclusively as oral markers and have fewer text-dependent functions (Andersen 2001). While the EMI students did integrate referential markers into their speech, they did not use them quite as frequently as the non-EMI group did; on the contrary, they had a slightly more even distribution of use of DMs over the four categories, which may be an indication of the EMI group employing a more appropriate distribution of DMs across functions. It might be the case that EMI students were able to select other more appropriate markers while the CON group seemed to rely more on referential markers. These findings echo those reported in Fung & Carter (2007), who found that L2 learners relied on referential DMs more than on the other DM categories.

Turning to the interpretation of the results in terms of the second research question, it was found that the non-EMI group produced a higher ratio of DMs to words during the discourse completion task. A possible explanation for this result may be that, due to the strict time limit during the discourse completion task, there may have been some cognitive competition as described by Skehan (1998), where some features are attended to at the expense of others. For example, in this case, providing a response within the time given may have been a difficult task for the non-EMI participants and, as a consequence, little attention might have been paid to how the message was delivered; in other words, they may have been more likely to repeat the same markers and utilize the same sentence structures to organize their discourse and convey their ideas to their interlocutors. This may be due to being unsure of how to continue a natural flow of conversation during the task. This interpretation would account for the difference in production of DMs between the groups. This effect of cognitive competition could be more prevalent in the non-EMI group, as they may speak English less often and might be less used to spontaneously using English, whereas the EMI students are accustomed to using English daily and thus might able to use DMs slightly more selectively.

Additionally, the EMI participants were found to produce significantly longer texts, which as mentioned above can be interpreted as a sign of fluency, since they were able to produce longer responses than the non-EMI group was in the same amount of time. We suggest this could be due to the constant and frequent exposure to EMI classes. However, in future research one might compare the results to NS data to confirm if the ratio of DMs produced by the groups is similar or different from NS usage.

Regarding the significant difference between the use of referential DMs as measured on the discourse completion task, this trend was also found when analyzing the two tasks together and has been discussed above. It seems that the referential category is more closely linked to grammar and what is taught in L2 classrooms. The functions of referential DMs appear to be the most transparent in their meaning and use, and thus, may be slightly easier to incorporate into the one's speech than the other DM categories (Liu 2016).

Turning to the conversation task, in addition to producing significantly longer responses, which has already been discussed, EMI students were found to use significantly more structural markers than the non-EMI group during the conversation task. This could be a reflection of a slightly higher or more sensitive pragmatic competence in their ability to signpost discourse while engaged in conversation, as was found in Wei (2011), whose advanced learners were reported to use more structural markers to highlight information. Furthermore, the use of structural markers could be a sign of increased linguistic complexity. This finding aligns with those from Neary-Sundquist (2014), who reported that higher proficiency learners used DMs to support and enable their fluency, and that as proficiency increases, learners can allocate more attention not only on delivering their message but on how they would like their message to be received. However, in the present study, our participants had the same proficiency and they only differed in terms of amount of exposure to the target language. This leads us to suggest that the number of hours of exposure available through immersion programs (as was the case for the IM group in this study), may provide learners with more opportunities for communication and thus make them more aware of how they express themselves while speaking English.

It was also found that the non-EMI group produced a wider variety of DMs overall compared to the EMI group during the conversation task. It seems that text length could be playing a strong role here. The EMI participants produced significantly longer responses on all tasks, and it is therefore much more likely that in a long text the same markers are used more than once. This interpretation is further supported by the non-significant findings of differences in variety found according to Guiraud's Index. When text length was controlled for, the significant difference between the groups was not sustained.

As mentioned in the literature review, the type of input in EMI is mainly via lectures (Hellekjaer & Hellekjaer 2015), a context where academic language with a formal tone is primarily used. Lecturers must cue their interlocutors as to when they are opening a topic, changing, returning to, or continuing a topic, as well as mark progression while explaining processes. These functions are carried out by structural markers (Andersen 2001), thus, making them one of the most salient categories of DMs that EMI students are exposed to. This may be why EMI students integrate more structural markers into their speech than the non-EMI students.

Despite the explanations provided as possible reasons for the differences according to task, the results do not seem to point towards a clear relationship between task and DM use, as was also found by Neary-Sundquist (2013). This clearly points to the need for more research in this area.

7 Conclusion

This preliminary study seems to provide evidence that the context of learning can make some difference in the learning of pragmatics. EMI students were found to produce significantly longer responses than the non-EMI group, including more words and more DMs in absolute terms, which is a sign of increased oral fluency. Furthermore, EMI students produced more structural DMs, which showed an effort on the behalf of these participants to produce more complex language and to signpost discourse clearly. The EMI students also had a more even distribution of use of DMs across categories. This could be a reflection of development in pragmatic competence: It seems as though the increased amount of time spent in EMI classrooms may lead learners to attend more to how they want their messages to be interpreted by their interlocutors. This pattern of use also reflects the type of input they receive, namely, academic lectures. Non-EMI students, on the other hand, produced more referential DMs, which seems to be the first category learned due to their transparent meanings, attention given to them in language classrooms as well as their prevalence in writing and formal speech (Fung & Carter 2007; Neary-Sundquist 2014; Liu 2016).

This study aimed to shed some light on the incidental acquisition of DM in the EMI classroom and we have identified some trends. However, the study was conducted on a small number of participants and the findings should be taken as preliminary. It is, therefore, important to carry out more studies in this context with more participants to confirm the trends found here.

Acknowledgments

The authors extend their gratitude to a number of researchers who offered their valuable insights comments and support during this project, Eloi Puig Mayenco, Andrew Lee, and Dr. Roy Lyster, as well as to the anonymous reviewers and editors of this monograph for their suggestions.

Funding

This study was supported by the Spanish Ministry of Science and Innovation (grant FFI2013-48640-C2-1-P).

Appendix A: Conversation task

1. Do you imagine yourself being a completely competent and natural speaker of English in the future? How do you feel when communicating with native speakers of English? What place do you see English having in your future?

2. Why do you believe courses are taught in English in your University? Why did you enroll in a degree program that is taught in English? How do you feel about being taught in English by non-native speakers of English?

3. Do you enjoy communicating in English with other Non-Native English speakers? Can you share any of your experiences using English as an international language?

Appendix B: Oral discourse completion task

1. **Contextualization:** Your best friend is inviting you to her birthday party. You will definitely be able to make it whenever she suggests because she is such a good friend. (Suggestion non-face-threatening)

2. **Researcher on video speaking directly to participant:** Hi, so I have just about everything for the party planned, which day do you think I should have it?

3. **Contextualization:** Your friend wants to invite Laura to the birthday party, a girl that your friend knows you don't get along with. Try to convince your friend to not invite Laura. (Suggestion face-threatening)

4. **Researcher on video speaking directly to participant**: Oh yes, and by the way, I ran into Laura the other day, we went out for coffee. I know you're not crazy about her, but I invited her to my birthday party. That will be ok, won't it?

5. **Contextualization**: Your friend is telling you all about her birthday plans; tell her what you think of them. (Opinion, non-face-threatening)

6. **Researcher on video speaking directly to participant**: As you know it's my birthday coming up next week, and I have a few ideas about what I'd like to do. I thought about inviting everyone for dinner at my house, maybe everyone could bring a dish, then, afterwards we could go out and celebrate in this bar I know where you can drink and dance.

7. **Contextualization**: You are shopping with a friend, they are trying on a hat that you think is very old-fashioned looking, and the colour (red) is terrible. You don't like it at all. (opinion face-threatening)

8. **Researcher on video speaking directly to participant**: Oh, I love just love hats, all kinds really. This red one is quite nice. What do you think, does it suit me?

9. **Contextualization**: Your friends gave you a sweater as a gift. You don't really like it and you want to return it. You need to ask your friend for the receipt so you can exchange it. (request, face threatening)

10. **Researcher on video speaking directly to participant**: So, have you had time to try on the sweater? Does it fit? We all hope you like it.

11. **Contextualization**: You are meeting your friend for a coffee and just missed the train; you'll now be a few minutes late. (apology non-face threatening)

12. **Researcher on video speaking directly to participant**: Hi, I am here waiting. Where are you?

13. **Contextualization**: Your friend's party started at 10. It is now 11 and you will not be able to go at all. You know she is going to be very disappointed. You call her and tell her. (apology, face threatening)

14. **Researcher on video speaking directly to participant**: Hi, where are you? Are you on your way?

15. **Contextualization:** Your friend has just picked you up in their car, and has all the windows down. You are cold and need to ask them to turn on the heat or roll up the windows.

16. **Researcher on video speaking directly to participant:** Nothing, researcher provides interlocutor only.

17. **Contextualization:** Your friend gets to the party and really looks great. You can tell that they cut their hair and have bought new clothes. You want to tell them how good they look. (Compliment, non-face threatening)

18. **Researcher on video speaking directly to participant:** Nothing, researcher provides interlocutor only.

19. **Contextualization:** You have been talking to this person at the party for a while and they are really starting to bother you. They keep making fun of your friends and you find it insulting, you find them offensive. You have tried to walk away, but they keep cornering you. You will have to tell them to leave you alone. (aggressive situation)

20. **Researcher on video speaking directly to participant:** Nothing, researcher provides interlocutor only.

References

Aijmer, Karin. 1996. Swedish modal particles in a contrastive perspective. *Language Sciences* 18(1). 393–427.

Airey, John. 2012. I don't teach language. The linguistic attitudes of physics lecturers in Sweden. *AILA Review* 25. 64–79.

Andersen, Gisle. 2001. *Pragmatic markers and sociolinguistic variation: A relevance-theoretic approach to the language of adolescents 84*. Amsterdam: Benjamins.

Ariel, Mira. 1998. Discourse markers and form-function correlations. In Andreas Jucker & Yael Ziv (eds.), *Discourse markers: Descriptions and theory*, 226–260. Amsterdam: Benjamins.

Bardovi-Harlig, Kathleen. 2015. Operationalizing conversation in studies of instructional effect in L2 pragmatics. *System* 48. 21–34.

Barron, Anne. 2003. *Acquisition in interlanguage pragmatics: Learning how to do things with words in a study abroad context*. Amsterdam: Benjamins.

Blakemore, Diane. 1992. *Understanding utterances: An introduction to pragmatics.* Oxford: Blackwell.

Bu, Jiemin. 1996. Swedish modal particles in a contrastive perspective. *Language Sciences* 18(1). 393–427.

Carter, Ronald & Michael McCarthy. 2006. *Cambridge grammar of English: A comprehensive guide; spoken and written English grammar and usage.* Cambridge: Cambridge University Press.

Coleman, Jim. 2006. English-medium teaching in European higher education. *Language Teaching* 39(1). 1–14.

Costa, Francesca. 2012. Focus on form in ICLHE lectures in italy: Evidence from English-medium science lectures by native speakers of italian. *AILA Review* 25. 30–47.

Daller, Michael. 2010. *Guiraud's index of lexical richness. In: British association of applied linguistics, September 2010.* Available from: http://eprints.uwe.ac.uk/11902.

Doiz, Aintzane, David Lasagabaster & Juan Manuel Sierra. 2014. Language friction and multilingual policies in higher education: The stakeholders' view. *Journal of Multilingual and Multicultural Development* 35(4). 345–360. DOI:10.1080/01434632.2013.874433

European Ministers of Education. 1999. *The declaration of bologna.*

Fischer, Kerstin (ed.). 2006. *Approaches to discourse particles.* Amsterdam: Elsevier.

Fischer, Kerstin. 2014. Discourse markers. In Klaus Schneider & Anne Barron (eds.), *Pragmatics of discourse*, 271–294. Berlin: De Gruyter Mouton.

Fung, Loretta & Ronald Carter. 2007. Discourse markers and spoken English: Native and learner use in pedagogic settings. *Applied linguistics* 28(3). 410–439.

Gundermann, Susanne. 2014. *Modelling the role of the native speaker in a Lingua Franca context.* EMI: Universität Freiburg dissertation.

Hellekjaer, Glenn Ole & Anne-Inger Hellekjaer. 2015. From tool to target language: Arguing the need to enhance language learning in English-medium instruction courses and programs. In Slobodanka Dimova, Anna Kristina Hultgren & Christian Jensen (eds.), *English-Medium instruction in European higher education*, 317–324. Berlin: Walter de Gruyter.

Hinkel, Eli. 1997. Appropriateness of advice: DCT and multiple choice data. *Applied linguistics* 18(1). 1–26.

Kasper, Gabriele & Kenneth R. Rose. 2002. *Pragmatic development in a second language.* Oxford, UK: Blackwell.

Kling, Joyce, Soren. 2013. *Teacher identity in English-Medium instruction: Teacher cognitions from a Danish tertiary education context.* University of Copenhagen dissertation.

Kuteeva, Maria & John Airey. 2014. Disciplinary differences in the use of English in higher education: Reflections on recent language policy developments. *Higher Education* 67(5). 533–549.

Leech, Geoffrey & Jan Svartvik. 1975. *A communicative grammar of English.* London: Longman.

Liu, Binmei. 2013. Effect of first language on the use of English discourse markers by 11 Chinese speakers of English. *Journal of Pragmatics* 45. 149–172.

Liu, Binmei. 2016. Effect of L2 exposure: From a perspective of discourse markers. *Applied Linguistics Review* 7(1). 73–98.

Llurda, Enric, Josep. M. Cots & Lurdes Armengol. 2013. Expanding language borders in a bilingual institution aiming at trilingualism. In Hartmut Haberland, Dorte Lønsmann & Bent Preisler (eds.), *Language alternation, language choice and language encounter in international tertiary education*, 203–222. Amsterdam: Springer Science & Business Media.

Lueg, Klarissa & Ranier Lueg. 2015. Why do students choose English as a medium of instruction? A Bourdieusian perspective on the study strategies of non-native English speakers. *Academy of Management Learning & Education* 14(1). 5–30.

MacWhinney, Brian. 2000. *The CHILDES project: Tools for analysing talk.* 3rd edn. Mahwah, NJ: Lawrence Erlbaum.

Margić, Branka. D. & Tea Žeželić. 2015. The implementation of English-medium instruction in croatian higher education: Attitudes, expectations and concerns. In Ramón Plo Alanstrué & Carmen Pérez-Llantada (eds.), *English as a scientific and research language*, 311–332. Berlin: De Gruyter.

Maschler, Yael. 1994. Metalanguaging and discourse markers in bilingual conversation. *Language in Society* 23(3). 325–366.

Müller, Simone. 2005. *Discourse markers in native and non-native English discourse.* Amsterdam: Benjamins.

Neary-Sundquist, Colleen. 2013. Task type effects on pragmatic marker use by learners at varying proficiency levels. *L2 Journal* 5(2). 1–21.

Neary-Sundquist, Colleen. 2014. The use of pragmatic markers across proficiency levels in second language speech. *Studies in Second Language Learning and Teaching* 4(4). 637–663.

Nguyen, Thi Thuy Minh, Thi Pham Hanh Pham & Minh Tam Pham. 2012. The relative effects of explicit and implicit form-focused instruction on the development of L2 pragmatic competence. *Journal of Pragmatics* 44. 416–434.

Nikula, Tarja. 2008. Learning pragmatics in content-based classrooms. In Eva Alcón Soler & Alicia Martínez Flor (eds.), *Investigating pragmatics in foreign language learning, teaching and testing*, 94–113. Clevedon, UK: Multilingual Matters.

Nordic Council of Ministers. 2006. *Deklaration om nordisk språkpolitik [declaration on a Nordic language policy]*. Copenhagen: Nordic Council of Ministers.

Parvaresh, Vahid & Mansoor Tavakoli. 2009. Discourse completion tasks as elicitation tools: How convergent are they. *The Social Sciences* 4(4). 366–373.

Pecorari, Diane, Philip Shaw, Aileen Irvine & Hans Malmström. 2011. English for academic purposes at swedish universities: Teachers' objectives and practices. *Iberica* 22. 55–78.

Pérez-Cañado, Maria Luisa. 2012. CLIL research in Europe: Past, present, and future. *International Journal of Bilingual Education and Bilingualism* 15(3). 315–341.

Pérez-Vidal, Carmen. 2008. Política lingüística universitària catalana dins l'EEES a la universitat pompeu fabra: El pla d'acció pel multilingüisme. In Joan Martí i Castell & Josep Maria Mestres i Serra (eds.), *El multilingüisme a les universitats en l'espai europeu d'educació superior (actes del seminari del CUIMPB-CEL 2007)*. 115–141. Barcelona: Institut d'Estudis Catalans.

Pérez-Vidal, Carmen. 2015. Languages for all in education: CLIL and ICLHE at the crossroads of multilingualism, mobility and internationalisation. In Maria Juan-Garau & Joana Salazar-Noguera (eds.), *Content-based language learning in multilingual educational environments*, 31–50. Berlin: Springer.

Pérez-Vidal, Carmen. 2014b. Study abroad and formal instruction contrasted: The SALA project. In Carmen Pérez-Vidal (ed.), *Second language acquisition in study abroad and formal instruction contexts*, 17–57. Amsterdam: John Benjamins.

Roever, Carsten. 2009. Teaching and testing pragmatics. In Michael Long & Catherine J. Doughty (eds.), *The handbook of language teaching*, 560–577. Oxford: John Wiley & sons.

Sánchez-Hernández, Adriana. 2016. *Pragmatic routines during study abroad programs; the impact of acculturation and intensity of interaction*. Paper presented at the International conference on intercultural pragmatics and communication, Split. 10–12 June 2016.

Sankoff, Gillian, Pierrette Thibault, Naomi Nagy, Hélène Blondeau, Marie-Odile Fonollosa & Lucie Gagnon. 1997. Variation in the use of discourse markers in a language contact situation. *Language Variation and Change* 9. 191–217.

Schauer, Gila. A. 2006. Pragmatic awareness in ESL and EFL contexts: Contrast and development. *Language Learning* 56(2). 269–318.

Schiffrin, Deborah. 1987. *Discourse markers*. Cambridge: Cambridge University Press.

Segalowitz, Norman & Barbara F. Freed. 2004. Context, contact and cognition in oral fluency acquisition: Learning Spanish in at home and study abroad contexts. *Studies in Second Language Acquisition* 26(2). 173–199.

Sert, Nehir. 2008. The language of instruction dilemma in the Turkish context. *System* 36. 156–171.

Skehan, Peter. 1998. *A cognitive approach to language learning*. Oxford: Oxford University Press.

Smit, Ute & Emma Dafouz. 2012. Integrating content and language in higher education: An introduction to English-medium policies, conceptual issues and research practices across Europe. *AILA Review* 25(1). 1–12.

Taguchi, Naoko. 2015. 'Contextually' speaking: A survey of pragmatic learning abroad, in class, and online. *System* 48. 3–20.

Tazl, Dietmar. 2011. English medium masters' programmes at an austrian university of applied sciences: Attitudes, experiences and challenges. *Journal of English for Academic purposes* 10(4). 252–270.

Unterberger, Barbara. J. 2012. English medium programmes at austrian business faculties. A status quo survey on national trends and a case study on programme design and delivery. *AILA Review* 25. 80–100.

Usó-Juan, Esther & Alicia Martínez-Flor. 2014. Reorienting the assessment of the conventional expressions of complaining and apologising: From single-response to interactive DCTs. *Iranian Journal of Language Testing* 4(1). 113–136.

Vanda, Koczogh Helga. 2007. Native speaker and non-native speaker discourse marker use. *Argumentum* 3. 46–53.

Vellenga, Heidi. 2004. Learning pragmatics from ESL & EFL textbooks: How likely? *Tesl-Ej* 8(2). 1–18.

Wächter, Bernd & Friedhelm Maiworm. 2008. *English-taught programmes in european higher education: ACA papers on international cooperation in education*. Bonn: Lemmens.

Wächter, Bern & Friedhelm Maiworm (eds.). 2014. Bonn: Lemmens Medien GmbH.

Wei, Ming. 2011. A comparative study of the oral proficiency of Chinese learners of English across task functions: A discourse marker perspective. *Foreign Language Annals* 44(4). 674–691.

Yates, Lynda. 2011. Interaction, language learning and social inclusion in early settlement. */International Journal of Bilingual Education and Bilingualism/* 14(4). 457–471.

Chapter 4

The effects of English-medium instruction in higher education on students' perceived level and self-confidence in ELF

Sofía Moratinos-Johnston
University of the Balearic Islands

Maria Juan-Garau
University of the Balearic Islands

Joana Salazar-Noguera
University of the Balearic Islands

Various studies (Seikkula-Leino 2007; Pihko 2007; Doiz et al. 2014) carried out in secondary education have demonstrated the motivating effects of content-and-language-integrated-learning (CLIL) programmes. However, they also indicate some problems with students' self-concept in foreign languages caused by the difficulties encountered by learners. Compared with the sizeable number of studies focusing on CLIL and affective factors in secondary schools, there is still a lack of similar research at university level, where the term 'Integrating Content and Language in Higher Education' (ICLHE) is preferred. At this level students may have problems fully understanding lectures because of vocabulary difficulties or the lecturers' pronunciation (Hellekjaer 2010). In this study, we compare students' linguistic self-confidence and perceived level of English according to the number of ICLHE subjects taken at university. Data was collected by means of a questionnaire administered to ICLHE students (n=155) and follow-up interviews (n=9). Results indicate a significant difference in participants' level of linguistic self-confidence between those students that have taken one or two ICLHE subjects and those that have taken more than four. Similar results emerge as regards the students' perceived

Sofía Moratinos-Johnston, Maria Juan-Garau & Joana Salazar-Noguera. The effects of English-medium instruction in higher education on students' perceived level and self-confidence in ELF. In Carmen Pérez Vidal, Sonia López-Serrano, Jennifer Ament & Dakota J. Thomas-Wilhelm (eds.), Learning context effects: Study abroad, formal instruction and international immersion classrooms, 75–99. Berlin: Language Science Press. DOI:10.5281/zenodo.1300614

level of English. These outcomes are corroborated by the interview data. They indicate that participants' initial lack of self-confidence diminishes as students become accustomed to using English in their content classes, find strategies to cope with the challenges and start to intervene more. They also note an improvement in their level of English, which is translated into greater levels of enjoyment. The present study thus seems to imply that the more ICLHE courses taken, the better in terms of boosting linguistic self-confidence and perceived level of English.

1 Introduction

The spread of courses 'Integrating Content and Language in Higher Education' (ICLHE) taught in English has been spurred by the fact that universities compete globally not only for international recognition, but also to attract foreign students and staff while promoting international research and networking (Coleman 2006; Graddol 2006; Lasagabaster 2015; Pérez-Vidal 2015). Other reasons include the promotion of multilingualism in education driven by the European Union and the Council of Europe which results in the introduction of courses that integrate language and content at all levels of education (Leuven Communiqué (2009). However, although ICLHE courses are becoming more and more common, differences can be noted in terms of their distribution across Europe. Whilst these courses are the norm in central and northern Europe, they are not so widely spread in southern Europe (Wächter & Maiworm 2014), possibly due to the lower proficiency levels found amongst university students and lecturers (Cots 2013; Arnó-Macià & Mancho-Barés 2015).

In Spain, *Content and Language Integrated Learning* (CLIL) was first implemented some two decades ago through a series of national and regional policies initiated in bilingual schools or the so-called "European sections" (Cañado 2010; Juan-Garau & Salazar-Noguera 2015). Similarly, the Spanish Ministry of Education recently introduced an initiative aimed at raising the international profile of Spanish universities, whereby one out of three degree programmes will be taught in English by 2020 (Spanish Ministry of Education 2015).

The advantages for students associated with the inclusion of ICLHE courses at university level are manifold, both academically and in terms of their future career development, be it locally or abroad. These advantages manifest themselves firstly as successful language acquisition, as shown by many studies (e.g. Coyle et al. 2010; Ruiz de Zarobe 2011; Pérez-Vidal 2013; Gené-Gil et al. 2015). However, there are also some authors (e.g. Seikkula-Leino 2007; Hunt 2011; Bruton 2013) that argue that there may be a loss of self-esteem linked to the fact that students are required to use a language they do not really know for academic communication, resulting in decreased language use and demotivation, which may hamper language acquisition. The fact that content is taught in a foreign language, and that this language may be above the current competence of the student, makes ICLHE a challenging endeavour requiring considerable effort and concentration on the students' part. In the same vein, Hood (2010) points out that, at the initial stages of instruction, enjoyment, motivation and self-esteem may suffer as students struggle to adapt to this new teaching approach. Hence, Cenoz et al. (2014) suggest the need for more research on some of these still unanswered questions. It is therefore worth investigating at what stage students start to feel more comfortable in their ICLHE classes. With this goal in mind, this study explores:

- students' linguistic self-confidence and perceived level of English according to the number of ICLHE subjects taken at university

- the reasons for any initial lack of confidence in their abilities

- the strategies that learners use to cope with the challenges.

2 Literature review

Linguistic self-confidence and self-perception of L2 achievement

Delving into the historical development of L2 motivational research (Dörnyei & Ushioda 2011), we find that during the *social psychological period* (1959-1990) Gardner & Lambert (1959) pointed out that there seemed to be two main factors affecting L2 achievement: language aptitude and a group of attitudinal and motivational variables that they referred to as the motivation factor. As a matter of fact, Gardner's (1985) most well-known contribution to the development of motivation research, the *socio-educational model,* aimed at explaining how these attitudinal and motivational components fostered second language acquisition (SLA). The relationship between motivation and *orientation* is a key feature in this model, which distinguishes between *integrative* and *instrumental orientations.*

A significant finding was the important role that the self-perception of L2 achievement played in successful SLA. These studies suggested that proficiency in English was associated with a concept that was labelled as 'Self-Confidence with English'. Students with high self-confidence:

> experienced little anxiety when speaking English in class or in real life situations, perceived themselves as being competent in their English abilities,

reported frequent use of English, had positive attitudes towards their English class, showed motivation and desire to learn English, had experiences with more than one language at home, and performed well on indices of achievement in English. (Sampasivam & Clément 2014: 24)

A strand within Gardner's *socio-educational model,* the *socio-contextual model,* proposed by Clément (1980), accounted for the above-mentioned findings and first developed the concept of '*linguistic self-confidence*', which was defined by social contact with the L2 group and modulated by its frequency and its quality. Thus, although the concept of linguistic self-confidence is largely defined socially, particularly within multilingual communities, it also has a cognitive component - 'the perceived L2 proficiency'. The more positive our self-perceived proficiency and the lower our anxiety levels, the higher our levels of linguistic self-confidence will be. Linguistic self-confidence also greatly influences the willingness to communicate (WTC) in the foreign language classroom (MacIntyre et al. 1998). For instance some studies in Asia indicate that, apart from cultural factors, individual factors such as self-confidence play an important role in classroom situations that demand interaction such as group tasks (Shao & Gao 2016; Eddy-U 2015; Yashima 2002). Again in a classroom environment, Dörnyei (2001) drew up a list of nine demotivating factors linked to a total of 75 occurrences, 11 of which were related to reduced self-confidence following a negative experience in class. There also seem to be differences in perceived self-confidence according to the level of proficiency. Lower proficiency learners feel demotivated earlier during their learning experience and blame internal factors such as unsatisfactory performance or reduced self-confidence, while higher proficiency learners tend to blame the teachers (Falout & Maruyama 2004).

While linguistic self-confidence is thought to have a positive effect on SLA and motivation (Dörnyei 2005), its opposite, 'anxiety', has a mostly negative effect. MacIntyre et al. (1994: 284) define it as 'the feelings of tension and apprehension specifically associated with second language contexts'. Horwitz et al. (1986) refer to the foreign language classroom environment as a context where learners are very likely to have difficulty understanding others and making themselves understood. Research shows that the effects of foreign language anxiety on the learner include forgetting previously learned material, decreased participation, negativity and avoidance behaviour (Gregersen & Horwitz 2002). Consequently, learners will only be confident in their linguistic abilities if they lack anxiety and have positive feelings about their proficiency in the L2. Sampasivam & Clément (2014) have put together a model describing the relationship between a number of factors that determine L2 confidence. At the centre of the model are richness and self-involvement. Richness refers to the various channels through which we receive the L2 input, which should be varied in form and allow for feedback to be effective. The fact that we are able to understand this rich input positively affects self-confidence, while self-involvement is related to the level of interaction that learners maintain in response to this input. Yashima (2002) claims that self-involvement is in turn shaped by the perceived importance of the contact experience and gives an example of this relationship which is related to the concept of *international posture*. People who value international communication are more likely to place more value on this type of contact experiences and be therefore more motivated to learn the L2, which in turn results in higher levels of L2 confidence (Yashima 2009).

The relationship between richness and L2 confidence is mediated by two variables: (1) frequency of contact; and (2) proficiency. An increased frequency of contact, even when low in richness, is expected to lead to an increase in L2 confidence. Similarly, proficiency is also associated with L2 confidence. Learners with adequate levels of proficiency are less likely to be overwhelmed by rich input, experiencing greater levels of satisfaction and confidence while beginners can suffer from anxiety if they are exposed to rich forms of contact Ozdener & Satar (2008).

The last variable described in Sampasivam & Clément's (2014) model is *quality*, which influences the relationship between self-involvement and L2 confidence. This variable refers to the pleasantness of the contact experience and how it positively or negatively affects self-confidence.

Since linguistic self-confidence and the self-perception of L2 achievement are thought to play an important role as regards motivation, WTC and subsequent SLA, these are variables worth considering when researching how the introduction of a teaching approach such as ICLHE affects the learners. More specifically, as this approach is supposed to foster interaction between teacher and learners and the learners themselves (Coyle 2007), WTC will become especially important in these classes. Moreover, ICLHE is also known to be cognitively demanding (Coyle et al. 2009) and therefore may affect each learner's self-esteem differently. In the next section, we will look at the nature of these challenges, their consequences and how the students tackle the difficulties they may encounter.

3 Content and language integration: the challenges, students' responses and the effects of increasing exposure to ICLHE

The sociocultural tenet that language use mediates language learning (Swain 2000) in an ICLHE context implies 'a level of talking, of interaction and dialogic activity which may be different to that of the traditional language or content classroom' (Coyle 2007: 554). Moreover, if the content is conceptually difficult, the added hurdle of the foreign language may make it even more difficult for students to assimilate both language and content simultaneously (Seikkula-Leino 2007). Some students may feel that they are expected to perform at a more advanced level than that which they consider realistically possible, resulting in a decreased lack of confidence, despite the improvement in their grades. There may be therefore a discrepancy between the progress revealed by formal assessment and the students' own perception of progress (Mearns 2012). If we now turn to the CLIL contexts, their demanding nature requires higher levels of concentration amongst students, who may perceive this as too much of an imposition (Hunt 2011) and feel more anxious, as Sylvén & Thompson (2015) and Santos Menezes & Garau (2013) confirmed. These studies were undertaken in secondary schools at initial stages of CLIL implementation, when students had not yet had much exposure to this new teaching approach. However, as exposure increases by the third grade of secondary education, differences between CLIL and non-CLIL students' anxiety levels seemed to decrease, as Doiz et al.'s (2014) study reveals.

As regards ICLHE research in Spain, Arnó-Macià & Mancho-Barés (2015) and Breeze (2014) discovered that ICLHE students were very aware of their low language proficiency level, including problems of comprehension and their inability to express complex content knowledge in a foreign language (Muñoz 2001; Feixas et al. 2009). Nevertheless, Aguilar & Rodríguez's (2012) study, targeting engineering students, reported satisfactory results in terms of vocabulary acquisition and listening skills, despite objections to the lecturer's level of English. It is precisely lecture comprehension, a skill that seems hard to master in ICLHE classes, which worries students. For example, Flowerdew & Miller (1992) discovered that some of the areas that students identified as difficult were handling the speed of lecture delivery, understanding new terminology and concepts and concentrating during extended periods of time. In Norway, Hellekjaer (2010) described difficulties understanding certain parts of the lecture because of unclear pronunciation, unknown vocabulary and difficulty taking notes. To all this Breeze (2014) added the high speed of delivery of lectures, which hinders comprehension. Finally, students also appreciated a clearer structure in lecture organization as Dafouz and Núñez (2010) pointed out. Although switching to a foreign language can have an initial negative effect that may adversely affect university students' grades, Klaassen (2001) found that differences in grades between students following ICLHE and traditional teaching methods were no longer noticeable after one year. The students had adapted to the language change thanks to a number of strategies that helped compensate for these negative effects. The strategies students used to overcome their language problems included: looking up difficult words and L1 use (see also Coonan 2007); researching the subject both before and after the lecture; relying on peers and teachers or tutors for help, and trying to improve their concentration skills (Flowerdew & Miller 1992). Airey & Linder (2007) found that some students would concentrate on taking notes instead of focusing on the contents. The solution in this case was to stop taking notes and read the textbook or class materials before the lecture instead.

To conclude, over the years there have been various studies analysing the impact of ICLHE courses, focusing on their effect on the students and the many challenges these have to face (e.g. Arnó-Macià & Mancho-Barés 2015; Aguilar & Muñoz 2014). We believe that more research is needed on the latter aspect, including analysing the point at which these challenges and their effects on students' linguistic self-confidence start to recede as a consequence of their increased exposure to ICLHE courses. These issues will be analysed in this study along with the strategies students use to overcome the difficulties they face, with a view to helping other students who are uncertain about their linguistic abilities.

4   The present study

The research questions that this study intends to answer are the following:

RQ1. At what stage do ICLHE students start to build up linguistic self-confidence and perceive an improvement in their level of English?

RQ2. Why do some ICLHE students display an initial lack of self-confidence and what strategies do these students use to overcome the difficulties they face?

5 Method

5.1 The study's design, setting and sampling decisions

Our study forms part of a larger project that examines motivation in different language learning contexts: Formal Instruction (FI), ICLHE and Study Abroad (SA) (Moratinos Johnston (forthcoming)). Within this project, we decided to focus specifically on students that had experienced ICLHE subjects, since the literature review had revealed the potential detrimental effects on their linguistic self-confidence caused by the challenges associated with simultaneous content and language learning.

Our study targets undergraduate students in the University of the Balearic Islands, a university which is also involved in a process of internationalization aiming to attract foreign students. In terms of the number of subjects taught in English, the degree that offers the most is obviously the English major degree. As for other degrees, the number varies according to the faculty and department policy. Some faculties, such as Tourism or Business and Economics, offer an optional pathway in English. For example, the Tourism Faculty requires students following the pathway to take 30 mandatory ECTS in English, study abroad for at least one semester and write a dissertation in English. The requirements in the Business and Economics Faculty are similar yet more demanding since students have to take at least 100 ECTS of the degree in English. Apart from all these ICLHE subjects offered on Tourism and Business and Economics degree courses, other degrees also offer a much smaller amount of ICLHE subjects, ranging from nine in the case of the Law degree to two in the case of Biochemistry. Considering that one of the aims of this study was to target students who had experienced ICLHE, the sampling technique chosen was *stratified random sampling* where 'the population is divided into groups or *strata* and a random sample of proportionate size is selected from each group' (Dörnyei 2007: 97). The stratification variables used were the different subject areas present in the university, which allowed us to include a higher proportion of students from the Tourism, Social Sciences and Law degrees, since these are the most popular degree courses.

A smaller sample was extracted, in order to carry out in-depth interviews. Participants were selected based on the results of a questionnaire (see for a detailed description 4.3 below). Since we were interested in obtaining a diverse sample, reflecting various levels of linguistic self-confidence, we looked at the participants' scores on this scale in the questionnaire, together with the number of ICLHE subjects they had taken. Nine students that showed a high variance on these measures and in L2 proficiency levels were thus selected.

5.2 Participants

In the present study, we analysed the data from a group of students (n=155) from the University of the Balearic Islands in Spain. The overall majority of these students know Catalan and Spanish, the two official languages in the region, Catalan being the local and Spanish the state language.

Table 1 presents an overview of the participants' main characteristics and the number of ICLHE subjects they took. These students were in their first (N=51), second (N=33), third (N=28) and fourth (N=43) year of their studies and the majority were between 18 and 22 years of age.

Table 1: Characteristics of the sample and number of ICLHE subjects taken

General information			
Sex	Female	94	60.6%
	Male	61	39.4%
Studies	Tourism	74	47.7%
	Modern languages	24	15.4%
	History	18	11.6%
	Primary Education	17	10.9%
	Business and Economics	12	7.8%
	Engineering and Science	10	6.6%
ICLHE	1 subject	54	34.8%
	2 subjects	23	14.8%
	3 subjects	24	15.5%
	4 subjects	4	2.6%
	> 4 subjects	50	32.3%

More than half of the students (66.9%) declared that they had an intermediate level of English (B1/B2), as shown in Figure 1. Amongst them, one third of the participants (35.1%) declared they had a B2, the minimum level of listening ability that Breeze (2014) recommends before one begins an ICLHE course, while (20.7%) stated that they had a C1 level or above, which probably means that these students could feel at ease and possibly learn more in their classes. The remaining students' (12.4%) perceived level ranged between a B1 to basic level (A1/A2) or non-existent.

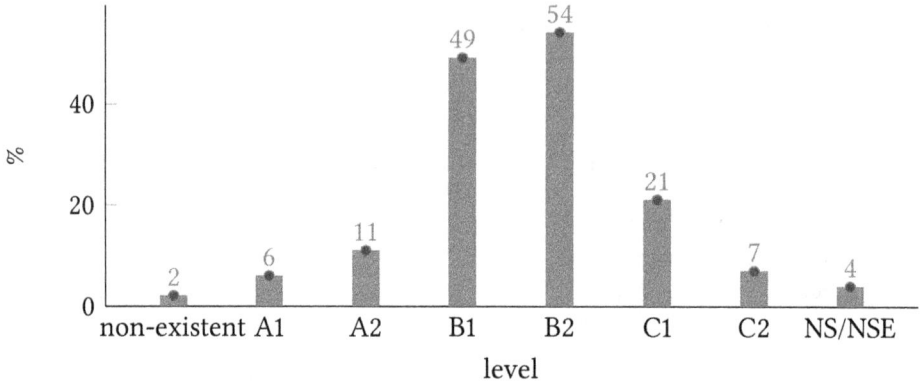

Figure 1: Perceived level of English of the participants. NS(E)= native speaker (equivalent).

Interviewees (n=9) were balanced for gender and came from a varied range of degree courses where ICLHE subjects were offered, as seen in Table 2 below.

Table 2: Characteristics of the interviewees

Initials	Gender	Degree	Year	No. ICLHE subjects	Perceived level of English
MG	male	Economics	2	2	C1
MV	male	Catalan	1	1	A2
MJG	female	Tourism	3	>4	B1
DM	male	Tourism	1	3	B1
MFS	female	English	4	>4	C1
LM	female	English	4	>4	C2
VC	female	History	1	1	A2
IM	male	History	1	1	A2
IR	male	History	1	1	B2

5.3 Instruments

A mixed-method approach was followed, as it offers the advantages of triangulation, complementarity and cross-validation of the findings (Ivankova & Greer 2015). Thus, two research instruments were used in our study, a questionnaire and interviews.

The questionnaire used in the survey was developed following Dörnyei's (2010) guidelines, and comprised two parts: the first consisted of 19 questions designed to establish the participants' linguistic profile (e.g. mother tongue and self-rated English proficiency level) and the types of language learning context experienced (FI, CLIL and SA), while the second part included 47 six-point Likert-type items (ranging from strongly disagree to strongly agree). These items were adapted from three previously published motivation questionnaires: Csizér & Kormos (2009) Motivation Questionnaire for College and University Students in Hungary, Taguchi et al.'s (2009) motivation questionnaires and Ryan's (2009) Motivation Factors Questionnaire. The items were translated and modified (where necessary) to suit the Spanish cultural context. The administration procedure involved first contacting UIB lecturers, whose ICLHE courses had been selected on a random basis. These lecturers then informed their students that a questionnaire would be administered to all those wishing to participate. On each occasion, the administrator (i.e. the first author of this paper) introduced the questionnaire which took on average 15 minutes to fill in. Response rates were high (over 98%).

In this study, we will focus on the findings revealed by the questionnaire as regards the two variables under scrutiny – the perceived level of English of the participants and their linguistic self-confidence as described below:

- Perceived level of English: participants rated themselves by choosing one of seven CEFR levels ranging from non-existent to native speaker/native speaker-like.

- Linguistic self-confidence (5 items adapted from Ryan's (2009) questionnaire): measuring the level of confidence that the participants had in their abilities as L2 learners and users. The items, three of which were negatively worded, were the following:

    1. I am sure I am able to learn a foreign language.
    2. I worry that other students will laugh at me when I speak English.
    3. Learning a foreign language is easy for me.
    4. I think I am the type who would feel anxious and ill at ease if I had to speak to someone in a foreign language.
    5. I always think that my classmates speak English better than I do.

The linguistic self-confidence scale was found to have a high internal consistency (Cronbach's alpha = .78).

Interviews were an additional instrument of this study. They were used to further interpret the findings revealed by the questionnaire data. Thus, the larger scale perspective was enriched by personal exchanges with the participants, following a model that Dörnyei (2007: 170) describes as 'questionnaire survey with follow-up interviews or retrospection'. This approach allows us to interpret unexpected results that may arise from the data by inviting the participants to explain them individually. In addition, the interviews became narrative accounts of the participants' language learning history. The learners' accounts described how they felt throughout different stages across microlevel timescales (Mercer & Williams 2014). Interviews also allowed the participants to point out and develop those factors that they themselves found the most relevant to their learning history.

The semi-structured interviews with set questions aimed at exploring:

- the participants' feelings at the time of their lessons,

- their language simultaneously,

- strategies used to overcome potential learning difficulties,

- their overall evaluation of the course (including the teacher, their peers, materials, impressions of their level of English and the fact that they were learning content and etc.).

These questions allowed us to investigate a wider topic area, resulting in nine in-depth narrative interviews in the participants' mother tongue, which lasted between 60 and 90 minutes. Participants' quotations are reported using an identification code, which includes the initials of their first and last name. After obtaining the participants' consent, all interviews were audio recorded and fully transcribed following Richards (2003) recommendations. Excerpts presented in this study were translated from Catalan or Spanish into English by the interviewer.

5.4 Data analysis

The questionnaire was piloted and went through reliability analysis by means of principal component analysis using SPSS 22. We then carried out normality tests, which showed the normality of the data, allowing us to use parametric tests.

The interviews were coded according to emerging themes, patterns or conceptual categories that helped structure the data in order to discover the wider picture developing from some of these recurring themes (Saldaña 2013). The conceptual categories in the theoretical framework on L2 confidence developed by Sampasivam & Clément (2014) were used as the basis for analysis. The goal was to identify the links between the recurrent themes and these conceptual constructs (Pavlenko 2007), yet also keeping an open mind for possible unexpected themes that might have appeared. The coding process was done using NVIVO 11.

6 Results and discussion

6.1 RQ1. Linguistic self-confidence and perceived level of English according to ICLHE subjects taken

In order to answer the first research question, we analysed whether there were any statistical differences between the participants as regards their levels of linguistic self-confidence and perceived level of English according to the number of ICLHE subjects taken using a one-way between groups ANOVA.

The results revealed that there was a statistical difference in terms of linguistic self-confidence $F (4, 154) = 3.98$, (p =.004) between the groups of participants divided according to the number of ICLHE subjects taken. The effect size, calculated using eta squared, was .09, which according to Cohen (1988) is considered a medium effect size. *Post hoc* comparisons with Tukey HSD indicated that the mean score for the students that had taken one (M=4.22) and two ICLHE subjects (M=3.92) were lower and significantly different from the group of students that had taken more than four subjects (M=4.76), who had higher levels of linguistic self-confidence on the six-point scale, as seen in Table 3. There were no statistically significant differences amongst the other groups. However, although the difference was only statistically significant after taking more than four ICLHE subjects, having done three subjects (M=4.61) already helped to improve the students' self-confidence. These findings are in line with Doiz et al. (2014) study that noticed a decrease in levels of anxiety in the third grade of secondary education as students progressed in their studies and became used to instruction in English. Furthermore, they confirm that the more frequent the contact with rich input, such as after taking multiple ICLHE classes, the higher the L2 confidence (Sampasivam & Clément 2014), although this pattern clearly emerges only with students taking more than four subjects in English.

As far as the perceived level of English is concerned, mean scores were calculated according to the students' self-ratings based on the Common European Framework Reference (CEFR) levels. This is a standardised linguistic competence

Table 3: Results for the linguistic self-confidence scale

No. of ICLHE subjects	N	Mean	SD
1 subject	53	4.22	.95
2 subjects	23	3.92	1.04
3 subjects	24	4.61	.88
4 subjects	4	4.06	1.70
>4 subjects	50	4.76	.94
Total	154	4.41	1

rating well-known to the majority of students, since it is used in most language schools, official exams and in the UIB to determine acceptable levels of competence to obtain a Bachelor's degree. The questionnaire gave students a choice on the following scale: 0=non-existent; 1=A1, Beginner; 2=A2 Elementary; 3=B1 Intermediate; 4=B2 Upper-Intermediate; 5=C1 Advanced; 6=C2 Proficiency; 7=native speaker/native speaker like (Ortega & Sheehan 2016).

Results revealed that again there was a statistical difference $F_{(4, 154)} = 14.95$ ($p \leq .001$) between the groups of participants regarding their perceived level of English. The effect size, calculated using eta square, was .4, which according to Cohen (1988) is considered a large effect size, indicating that the number of subjects taken plays an important role in determining the participants' perceived level of English. The *post hoc* comparisons using Tukey HSD showed that the mean score for the students that had taken one (M=3.17), two (M=2.96) and three ICLHE subjects (M=3.58) were lower and significantly different from the group of students that had taken more than four subjects (M=4.62) demonstrating that the latter group's perceived level of English tended towards a C1, as opposed to the B1 level of the 1-ICLHE subject group. The group that had taken 4 subjects did not differ statistically when compared with the others (Table 4); however, it was composed of four students only.

Overall, the results depicted in Table 4 show a general rise in the perceived level of English as the number of subjects increases. However, the 1-ICLHE and 2-ICLHE subject groups stated on average that their perceived level of English was an intermediate level (B1). This could indicate that although the students may experience linguistic gains, they still seem to consider their proficiency to be rather low, which could be related to the intrinsic challenges involved in the ICLHE approach. These results coincide with Arnó-Macià & Mancho-Barés (2015), Muñoz

Table 4: Results for the Perceived level of English scale

No. of ICLHE subjects	N	Mean	SD
1 subject	53	3.17	1.12
2 subjects	23	2.96	1.18
3 subjects	24	3.58	.97
4 subjects	4	3.25	1.50
>4 subjects	50	4.62	1.02
Total	154	3.68	1.27

Note: Students mean scores are calculated according to the following scale: 0=non-existent; 1=A1; 2=A2; 3=B1; 4=B2; 5=C1; 6 =C2; 7=native speaker/native speaker like

(2001), and Feixas et al. (2009) as regards the student's impression of their low proficiency level. Interestingly, for both linguistic self-confidence and perceived level of English, the 2-ICLHE subject group did not show an increased score, on the contrary, there was a very slight decrease, indicating that two ICLHE subjects did not seem to be enough for students to feel at ease in their classes. These and other issues are explored further in the analysis of the interviews described in the next section.

6.2 RQ2. Reasons for initial lack of self-confidence and strategies used to overcome it

6.2.1 Richness and proficiency

To answer our second research question, regarding the reasons for the participant's initial lack of self-confidence and the strategies used to overcome it, our interview data reveal that the link between richness and proficiency is an important part of our study, especially since we noticed that one of the most frequently used words amongst our participants was the word 'level'.

Rich forms of contact, as found in an ICLHE class, can provoke anxiety for those who consider they have low proficiency, and thus negatively affect levels of self-confidence. For instance, LM, an English degree student, who now defines her level of English as a C2 (>4 ICLHE subjects), describes how she confronted her first literature subject in English with a clear lack of self-confidence: 'at that moment I didn't have the level of English required to explain something that for me was very difficult or very complex such as a poem'. However, this feeling of anxiety seems to recede with time and practice. DM (Tourism, 3 ICLHE subjects) also found it hard to take notes in the ICLHE class initially: 'in the beginning I didn't know how to write the words, I still don't know how to, I write them as they sound, but I consider it a challenge, but you survive, you get used to it and you improve with the help of your peers and teachers'. MJG (Tourism, >4 ICLHE subjects), who defined her initial level as too low and who was anxious and struggled in her classes, describes her mixed feelings regarding her perceived language proficiency: 'every time I understand more, making less of an effort, of course, but I don't think that I have yet reached at all the level that I would like'. She further stated that her English level (B1) restricts the amount of questions that she asks the teacher, which means that she misses a lot of the finer points. MJG is an unusual case: unlike the majority of participants, she still does not perceive an important increase in her level of English after more than four ICLHE subjects. She believes that one of the ways ICLHE can be improved is by ensuring students have the right level of English from the outset to cope with the challenges this approach entails as well as including extra English language support. This would prevent students from being stressed, or making such an enormous effort, while allowing them to feel more confident to ask questions in class, etc. In summary, they would profit more fully from the whole experience. Some of the improvements mentioned, such as the need for higher initial English levels and language support, echo those expressed by previous studies researching student's experiences with ICLHE in Spanish universities (Aguilar & Rodríguez 2012; Arnó-Macià & Mancho-Barés 2015).

Sampasivam & Clément (2014) also point out that a context that is high in richness involves both being capable to comprehend and produce a response in the L2 and this will lead to higher levels of self-confidence. In other words, these rich contexts should include a certain degree of interaction, which is precisely what DM likes about his ICLHE classes: 'the teacher keeps on asking: what is your opinion? what did we refer to earlier...?' together with the fact that there is a lot of group work. At one point, he states: 'every Thursday we did project work in a group and in this group we share our English knowledge and this helps. It helps a lot'.

6.2.2 Self-involvement and quality

The forms of contact which require some interaction, as described in the previous section, will also lead to greater self-involvement, which is in turn affected by perceived importance. In other words, the greater the importance one attaches to L2 contact experiences, the greater the involvement and the more likely they are to lead to L2 confidence. According to Yashima (2002; 2009), learners with a strong international posture will also have higher levels of involvement and highly value L2 contact experiences. In contrast, our data revealed that MV (who took one ICLHE subject), a Catalan degree student, who is reluctant to accept English as the *lingua franca* and use it when he travels abroad, does not accept having to take an ICLHE subject either. His low English level (A2) does not help and he describes his experiences during his initial ICLHE classes as embarrassing:

I went the second day and I said, 'oh there are so many people [...] sixty, seventy, eighty people'. It was awful. I didn't go back to class, I stopped going after fifteen days, because of what they might ask me to do... if they made me speak, because they made me read one day and I died from embarrassment. I am not embarrassed to read in English, don't get me wrong, but there in front of everyone and people could laugh at me, I didn't feel like it. I said, 'I'm not going back to this class'.

As we can notice from MV's description, in terms of quality of contact, situations where there is a lot at stake, and which thus greatly involve the self, are particularly affected by the feelings that the learner experiences. For example, if the learner experiences contact with the L2 in an unpleasant manner, it is likely to lead to decreased L2 confidence and vice versa (Sampasivam & Clément 2014). In the case of MV, it meant that he stopped going to class, so he belongs to that group of students, who, as Coyle (2007) found, simply gave up. In other cases, such as MG (Economics, 2 ICLHE subjects), it was when he interacted with the teacher that he really felt he was learning: 'when you ask questions, you no longer ask a question about how to conjugate a verb, things related to grammar or such, but you ask a question about something you are studying, yet in English. So, I remember I learnt lots of vocabulary this way, in all truth'. DM has similar feelings of self-involvement: 'every time I ask a question, and I ask a lot of questions, I love it, I don't understand everything she [the teacher] says, and it's also in English [....] but I ask about the contents. Thus, I consider that I have improved a lot, as I ask questions better and I also understand the answers better'. These two students found taking ICLHE subjects a positive challenge that they were willing to embrace as it granted them the chance to establish meaningful communication.

6.2.3 Challenges and coping strategies

We will now explore the second part of the second research question, referring to the strategies participants used to overcome the difficulties they faced in the ICLHE context.

Most students mentioned the fact that their ICLHE classes were mentally exhausting and required greater levels of concentration in order to learn the content and the target language simultaneously. Our interviewees told us about the strategies they used to cope with these difficulties. For example, VC (History, 1-ICLHE subject) reported that she studied the theoretical aspects of the subject thoroughly beforehand, so that when she attended the class she already knew them and could concentrate on understanding the teacher. IR (History, 1-ICLHE subject) became quite confident mainly by working hard at home, taking responsibility for his own learning and preparing the classes well in advance. Towards the end, he recalls how he even met other peers, who struggled in class, and he offered to help them. MJG does not believe that the teachers used a different methodology in their ICLHE classes that would aid the students to cope with unknown vocabulary (e.g. using visual aids or glossaries). Students would rely on fellow students looking words up or did it themselves. Both VC and IM (History, 1-ICLHE subject) appreciated the teacher's positive attitude towards them: for instance, IM says 'the teacher was quite helpful. I used to often go to tutorials, in the run-up to the exam. The teacher would then talk to me in Spanish, but in the classroom, she only used English. It's the only way to learn'.

In terms of understanding the teachers' lectures, MJG found the teacher's accent difficult to follow because she had never come across a native English-speaking teacher before, while MG complained about the local teacher's pronunciation, and her lack of English knowledge, neither of which inspired confidence. Similar problems with lectures have been reported by previous studies and seem to remain unsolved (Flowerdew & Miller 1992; Hellekjaer 2010).

7 Conclusion

This study aimed at analysing at which point students' possible lack of self-confidence caused by the challenges associated with ICLHE starts to recede. A contribution of this research is the finding that both linguistic self-confidence and perceived level of English clearly increase by the time students have taken three ICLHE subjects. However, statistical differences were only observed after the students had taken more than four subjects.

This initial lack of confidence seems to be caused by a perceived insufficient level of English, which hinders WTC. This is not helped by overcrowded university classrooms. Two participants found the teacher's accent difficult to understand, in one case because the learner was confronted for the first time with a native English-speaking teacher, in the other because the local teacher's accent was not good enough and made her lose face.

Most students (except for one, who had a very negative attitude) found that their initial anxiety diminished as the course progressed or when they had taken at least three ICLHE subjects. At first, they were concerned about speaking in class and expressing themselves correctly, but they gained in confidence the more practice they got. Three of the students said that they felt from the outset that this was a rewarding challenge that motivated them even further.

As Wilkinson (2013) points out, students' complaints are common during the first years of instruction in English. However, these seem to decrease as students adapt to hearing different accents, studying and discussing in English. In our opinion, the students' language weaknesses need to be addressed early, so that they can start their ICLHE courses having an adequate English level allowing them to feel confident enough in their linguistic abilities to follow their lessons. Other solutions include collaboration between content and language teachers to address language deficiencies. Parallel courses could also be offered providing the necessary language support, such as traditional language courses or English for Academic Purposes (EAP).

Our results are in line with some researchers, who have found a correlation between increased exposure to richer forms of communication within ICLHE contexts and increased English proficiency (Wong 2010). Similarly, Coyle (2013) points out the opportunities that ICLHE courses offer for richer discussion, self-involvement and interaction, which helped develop confidence and feelings of achievement amongst students.

Limitations of this study include the small sample used (n=155), which hinders the generalisability of the study. Therefore, further studies should contemplate using bigger samples to analyse, also longitudinally, how linguistic self-confidence develops during the earlier and later stages of ICLHE.

Acknowledgements

We gratefully acknowledge funding from the Spanish Ministry of Economy and Competitiveness (FFI2013-48640-C2-2P, AEI/FEDER, EU).

References

Aguilar, Marta & Carmen Muñoz. 2014. The effect of proficiency on CLIL benefits in engineering students in Spain. *International Journal of Applied Linguistics* 24(1). 1–18.

Aguilar, Marta & Rosa Rodríguez. 2012. Lecturer and student perceptions on CLIL at a Spanish university. *International Journal of Bilingual Education & Bilingualism* 15(2). 183–197.

Airey, John & Cedric Linder. 2007. Disciplinary learning in a second language: A case study from university physics. In Robert Wilkinson & Vera Zegers (eds.), *Researching content and language integration in higher education*, 61–171. Maastricht: Maastricht University Language Centre.

Arnó-Macià, Elisabet & Guzman Mancho-Barés. 2015. The role of content and language in content and language integrated learning (CLIL) at university: Challenges and implications for ESP. *English for Specific Purposes* 37. 63–73. DOI:10.1016/j.esp.2014.06.007

Breeze, Ruth. 2014. Identifying student needs in English-medium university courses. In Ruth Breezes, Carmen Llamas Saíz, Concepción Martínez Pasamar & Cristina Tabernero Sala (eds.), *Integration of theory and practice in CLIL*, 143–159. Amsterdam, Netherlands: Rodopi.

Bruton, Anthony. 2013. CLIL: Some of the reasons why ... and why not. *System* 41(3). 587–597.

Cañado, María Luisa Pérez. 2010. Globalisation in foreign language teaching: Establishing transatlantic links in higher education. *Higher Education Quarterly* 64(4). 392–412.

Cenoz, Jasone, Fred Genesee & Durk Gorter. 2014. Critical analysis of CLIL: Taking stock and looking forward. *Applied Linguistics* 35(3). 243–262.

Clément, Richard. 1980. Ethnicity, contact and communicative competence in a second language. In Howard Giles, William Peter Robinson & Philip M. Smith (eds.), *Social psychology and language*, 147–159. Oxford: Pergamon.

Cohen, Jacob. 1988. *Statistical power analysis for the behavioral sciences*. Hillsdale, NJ.

Coleman, Jim. 2006. English-medium teaching in European higher education. *Language Teaching* 39(1). 1–14.

Coonan, Carmel. 2007. Insider views of the CLIL class through teacher self-observation–introspection. *International Journal of Bilingual Education and Bilingualism* 10. 625–646.

Cots, Josep Maria. 2013. Introducing English-medium instruction at the university of LLeida, Spain: Intervention, beliefs and practices. In Aintzane Doiz, David Lasagabaster & Juan Manuel Sierra (eds.), *English-medium instruction at universities: Global challenges*, 106–131. Bristol: Multilingual Matters.

Coyle, Do. 2007. Content and language integrated learning: Towards a connected research agenda for CLIL pedagogies. *International Journal of Bilingual Education and Bilingualism* 10(5). 543–562.

Coyle, Do. 2013. Listening to learners: An investigation into "successful learning" across CLIL contexts. *International Journal of Bilingual Education & Bilingualism* 16(3). 244–266.

Coyle, Do, Bernadette Holmes & Lid King. 2009. *Towards an integrated curriculum – CLIL national statement and guidelines.* http://www.rachelhawkes.com/PandT/CLIL/CLILnationalstatementandguidelines.pdf, accessed 2017-09-14.

Coyle, Do, Philip Hood & David Marsh. 2010. *Content and language integrated learning.* Cambridge: Cambridge University Press.

Csizér, Kata & Judit Kormos. 2009. Leaning experiences, selves and motivated learning behaviour: A comparative analysis of structural models for Hungarian secondary and university learners of English. In Zoltán Dörnyei & Ema Ushioda (eds.), *Motivation, language identity and the L2 self,* 99–119. Bristol: Multilingual Matters.

Dafouz Milne, Emma & Begoña Nuñez Perucha. 2010. Metadiscursive devices in university lectures: a contrastive analysis of L1 and L2 teacher performance. 213–231.

Doiz, Aintzane, David Lasagabaster & Juan Manuel Sierra. 2014. CLIL and motivation the effect of individual and contextual variables. *The Language Learning Journal* 42(2). 209–224. DOI:10.1080/09571736.2014.889508

Dörnyei, Zoltán. 2001. *Teaching and researching motivation. Applied linguistics in action.* Harlow: Pearson.

Dörnyei, Zoltán. 2005. *The psychology of the language learner: Individual differences in second language acquisition.* Mahwah, NJ: Lawrence Erlbaum.

Dörnyei, Zoltán. 2007. *Research methods in applied linguistics.* Oxford: Oxford University Press.

Dörnyei, Zoltán. 2010. *Questionnaires in second language research: Construction, administration, and processing.* London: Routledge.

Dörnyei, Zoltán & Ema Ushioda. 2011. *Teaching and researching: Motivation* Harlow: Pearson Education.

Eddy-U, Mary. 2015. Motivation for participation or non-participation in group tasks: A dynamic systems model of task-situated willingness to communicate. *System* 50. 43–55.

Falout, Joseph & Mika Maruyama. 2004. A comparative study of proficiency and learner demotivation. *The Language Teacher* 28(8). 3–9.

Feixas, Mónica, Eva Codó, Digna Couso, Mariona Espinet & Dolors Masats. 2009. Enseñar en inglés en la universidad: Reflexiones del alumnado y el profesorado en torno a dos experiencias AICLE. Investigar desde un contexto educativo innovador. In Rosabel Roig Vila (ed.), *Investigar desde un contexto educativo innovador.* 137–53. Alicante: Editorial Marfil.

Flowerdew, John & Lindsay Miller. 1992. Student perceptions, problems and strategies in second language lecture comprehension. *RELC Journal* 23. 60–80.

Gardner, Robert C. 1985. *Social psychology and second language learning: The role of attitudes and motivation.* London: Edward Arnold.

Gardner, Robert C. & Wallace E. Lambert. 1959. Motivational variables in second-language acquisition. *Canadian Journal of Psychology/Revue canadienne de psychologie* 13(4). 266–272.

Gené-Gil, Maria, Maria Juan-Garau & Joana Salazar-Noguera. 2015. Development of EFL writing over three years in secondary education: CLIL and non-CLIL settings. *The Language Learning Journal* 43(3). 286–303.

Graddol, David. 2006. *English next.* https://englishagenda.britishcouncil.org/sites/default/files/attachments/books-english-next.pdf.

Gregersen, Tammy & Elaine K. Horwitz. 2002. Language learning and perfectionism: Anxious and non-anxious language learners' reactions to their own oral performance. *The Modern Language Journal* 86(4). 562–570.

Hellekjaer, Glenn Ole. 2010. Language matters: Assessing lecture comprehension in Norwegian English-medium higher education. In Christine Dalton-Puffer, Tarja Nikula & Ute Smit (eds.), *Language use and language learning in CLIL classrooms,* 233–259. Amsterdam: John Benjamins.

Hood, Philip. 2010. Evaluating the impact of CLIL programmes. In Do Coyle, Philip Hood & David Marsh (eds.), *Content and language integrated learning,* 133–149. Cambridge: Cambridge University Press.

Horwitz, Elaine K., Michael B. Horwitz & Joann Cope. 1986. Foreign language classroom anxiety. *The Modern Language Journal* 70(2). 125–132.

Hunt, Marylin. 2011. Learner's perceptions of their experiences of learning subject content through a foreign language. *Educational Review* 63(3). 365–378.

Ivankova, Nataliya V. & Jennifer L. Greer. 2015. Mixed methods research and analysis. In Brian Paltridge & Aek Phakiti (eds.), *Research methods in applied linguistics,* 63–83. London: Bloomsbury.

Juan-Garau, Maria & Joana Salazar-Noguera. 2015. Learning English and learning through English: Insights from secondary education. In Maria Juan-Garau &

Joana Salazar-Noguera (eds.), *Content-based language learning in multilingual educational environments*, 105–123. Berlin: Springer.

Klaassen, Renate Gerarda. 2001. *The international university curriculum: Challenges in English-medium engineering education.* Delft: Delft University of Technology dissertation.

Lasagabaster, David. 2015. Different educational approaches to bi- or multilingualism and their effect on language attitudes. In Maria Juan-Garau & Joana Salazar Noguera (eds.), *Content-based language learning in multilingual educational environments*, 13–30. Berlin: Springer.

Leuven Communiqué. 2009. The Bologna Process 2020: The European Higher Education Area in the new decade. In *Conference of European Ministers Responsible for Higher Education*, 1–6.

MacIntyre, Peter D., Zoltán Dörnyei, Richard Clément & Kimberly A. Noels. 1998. Conceptualizing willingness to communicate in a L2: A situational model of L2 confidence and affiliation. *The Modern Language Journal* 82(4). 545–562.

MacIntyre, Peter D., Robert C. Gardner & Ian Richmond. 1994. The subtle effects of language anxiety on cognitive processing in the second language. *Language Learning* 44(June). 283–300.

Mearns, Tessa L. 2012. Using CLIL to enhance pupils' experience of learning and raise attainment in German and health education: A teacher research project. *Language Learning Journal* 40(2). 175–192.

Mercer, Sarah & Marion Williams. 2014. *Multiple perspectives on the self in SLA.* Bristol: Multilingual Matters.

Moratinos Johnston, Sofía. Forthcoming. *Influence of language learning contexts on the L2 selves of Spanish students in higher education.* University of the Balearic Islands dissertation.

Muñoz, Carmen. 2001. The use of the target language as the medium of instruction: University students' perceptions. *Anuari de Filologia. Secció A, Filologia anglesa i alemanya* 10. 71–82.

Ortega, Angeles & Susan Sheehan. 2016. *The core inventory for general English – resources – eaquals.* http://www.eaquals.org/resources/the-core-inventory-for-general-english/, accessed 2017-07-17.

Ozdener, Nesrin & H. Muge Satar. 2008. Computer-mediated communication in foreign language education: Use of target language and learner perceptions. *Turkish Online Journal of Distance Education* 9(2). http://files.eric.ed.gov/fulltext/ED501098.pdf, accessed 2017-07-07.

Pavlenko, Aneta. 2007. Autobiographic narratives as data in applied linguistics. *Applied Linguistics* 28(2). 163–188.

Pérez-Vidal, Carmen. 2013. Perspectives and lessons from the challenge of CLIL experiences. In Cristian Abello-Contesse, Paul M. Chandler, María Dolores López-Jiménez & Rubén Chacón-Beltrán (eds.), *Bilingual and multilingual education in the 21st century: Building on experience*, 59–82. Bristol: Multilingual Matters.

Pérez-Vidal, Carmen. 2015. Languages for all in education: CLIL and ICLHE at the crossroads of multilingualism, mobility and internationalisation. In Maria Juan-Garau & Joana Salazar-Noguera (eds.), *Content-based language learning in multilingual educational environments*, 31–50. Berlin: Springer.

Pihko, Marja-Kaisa. 2007. Foreign language anxiety in content and language integrated learning (CLIL) classes and in traditional language classes. In Seppo Tella (ed.), *From brawn to brain: Strong signals in foreign language education proceedings of the Vikipeda-2007*, 129–143. Helsinki: University of Helsinki.

Richards, Keith. 2003. *Qualitative inquiry in TESOL*. Basingstoke: Palgrave Macmillan.

Ruiz de Zarobe, Yolanda. 2011. Which language competencies benefit from CLIL? An insight into applied linguistics research. In Yolanda Ruiz de Zarobe, Juan Manual Sierra & Francisco Gallardo del Puerto (eds.), *Content and foreign language integrated learning: Contributions to multilingualism in European contexts*, 129–153. Frankfurt: Peter Lang.

Ryan, Stephen. 2009. Self and identity in L2 motivation in Japan: The ideal L2 self and Japanese learners of English. In Zoltán Dörnyei & Ema Ushioda (eds.), *Motivation, language identity and the L2 self*, 120–143. Bristol: Multilingual Matters.

Saldaña, Johnny. 2013. *The coding manual for qualitative researchers*. Los Angeles: SAGE Publications.

Sampasivam, Sinthujaa & Richard Clément. 2014. The dynamics of second language confidence: Contact and interaction. In Sarah Mercer & Marion Williams (eds.), *Multiple perspectives of the self in SLA*, 23–35. Bristol: Multilingual Matters.

Santos Menezes, Edleide & María Juan Garau. 2013. Análisis de la relación entre el modelo formativo de aprendizaje del inglés - AICLE y enseñanza formal- y la ansiedad. *Revista Española de Lingüística Aplicada* 26. 457–473.

Seikkula-Leino, Jaana. 2007. CLIL learning: Achievement levels and affective factors. *Language and Education* 21(4). 328–341.

Shao, Qing & Xuesong Gao. 2016. Reticence and willingness to communicate (WTC) of East Asian language learners. *System* 63. 115–120.

Spanish Ministry of Education. 2015. *Strategy for the internationalisation of Spanish universities.* http://www.mecd.gob.es/educacion-mecd/dms/mecd/educacion-mecd/areas-educacion/universidades/politica-internacional/estrategia-internacionalizacion/EstrategiaInternacionalizaci-n-ENGLISH.pdf%20(6%20May,%202017)..

Swain, Merrill. 2000. The output hypothesis and beyond: Mediating acquisition through collaborative dialogue. In James. P. Lantolf (ed.), *Sociocultural theory and second language learning*, 97–114. Oxford: Oxford University Press.

Sylvén, Liss Kerstin & Amy S. Thompson. 2015. Language learning motivation and CLIL: Is there a connection? *Journal of Immersion and Content-Based Language Education* 3(1). 28–50.

Taguchi, Tatsuya, Michael Magid & Mostafa Papi. 2009. The L2 motivational self system among Japanese, Chinese and Iranian learners of English: A comparative study. In Zoltán Dörnyei & Ema Ushioda (eds.), *Motivation, language identity and the L2 self*, 66–97. Bristol: Multilingual Matters.

Wächter, Bern & Friedhelm Maiworm (eds.). 2014. Bonn: Lemmens Medien GmbH.

Wilkinson, Robert. 2013. English-medium instruction at a Dutch university: Challenges and pitfalls. In Aintzane Doiz, David Lasagabaster & Juan Manuel Sierra (eds.), *English-medium instruction at universities: Global challenges*, 3–27. Bristol: Multilingual Matters.

Wong, Ruth M H. 2010. The effectiveness of using English as the sole medium of instruction in English classes: Student responses and improved English proficiency. *PORTA LINGUARUM* 13. 119–130.

Yashima, Tomoko. 2002. Willingness to communicate in a second language: The Japanese EFL context. *The Modern Language Journal* 86(1). 54–66.

Yashima, Tomoko. 2009. International posture and the ideal L2 self in the Japanese EFL context. In Zoltán Dörnyei & Ema Ushioda (eds.), *Motivation, language identity and the L2 self*, 144–163. Bristol: Multilingual Matters.

Chapter 5

Writing performance and time of exposure in EFL immersion learners: analysing complexity, accuracy, and fluency

Isabel Tejada-Sánchez

Universidad de los Andes

Carmen Pérez-Vidal

Universitat Pompeu Fabra

The present study explores the effects of two types of early-partial immersion programmes on writing performance in English as a Foreign Language (EFL). It examines adolescent learners (ages 12-17) in mainstream education in Colombia. The two programmes are similar as far as the learners' onset age (4) is concerned, but different with respect to the total amount of EFL exposure time and intensity: High Intensity plus (HI+) has a total of 8,760 accumulated hours by age 17, while High Intensity (HI) has a total of 7,002 hours. It has been prevalently hypothesized that the more time students dedicate to learning the L2, the higher their level of proficiency will be (Carroll 1962; Stern 1985), supporting the spread of instructed immersion and intensive programmes (Serrano et al. 2011; Lightbown 2012). One of the aims of this chapter is to further assess this hypothesis. The study examines a cross-sectional sample (N=188), adopting a between-groups design whereby programmes' performance is compared in terms of the effect of accumulated time. Analysis will focus on the domains of syntactic and lexical complexity, accuracy, fluency (CAF) (Housen et al. 2012) and on holistic ratings. Results indicate that learners' writing in HI+ and HI do not show to be significantly different in most domains of CAF examined, nor in the holistic ratings. This might be explained in the light of the prior high number of accumulated hours of English exposure and emphasis on literacy in the curriculum of both programmes, which has allowed

Isabel Tejada-Sánchez & Carmen Pérez-Vidal. Writing performance and time of exposure in EFL immersion learners: analysing complexity, accuracy, and fluency. In Carmen Pérez Vidal, Sonia López-Serrano, Jennifer Ament & Dakota J. Thomas-Wilhelm (eds.), Learning context effects: Study abroad, formal instruction and international immersion classrooms, 101–129. Berlin: Language Science Press. DOI:??

learners to reach a threshold level from which they do not regress (Bournot-Trites 2007; Williams 2012).

1 Introduction

Since the emergence of immersion programmes in Canada in the late 1960s (Lambert & Tucker 1972), much research has been carried out on the development of linguistic competence in an L2 in such settings (Genesee & Stanley 1976; Genesee 1978; Swain 2000). The majority of these studies, mostly in favour of immersion, have also addressed the limitations of immersion programmes, particularly in terms of the L2 competence attained and the risks involved in the development of the L1 (Genesee 1978; 2013; Lazaruk 2007). Despite these concerns, the immersion education model has developed rapidly, inspiring bi- and multilingual school programmes throughout the world (De Mejia 2002). The acknowledged success of immersion programmes may be due to a combination of factors that have been shown to positively affect L2 acquisition, such as onset age, the type of input made available and its quantity, that is, the amount of time allocated to L2 exposure, methodological flexibility (early, middle and late programmes) and teachers' backgrounds, among others (Genesee 2013; Johnson & Swain 1997; Lazaruk 2007).

This chapter is part of a larger study Tejada-Sanchez 2014 which examines the outcomes of immersion programmes in Colombia, focusing on EFL writing of L1-Spanish speakers. More specifically, it seeks to understand the relationship between the allocation of time in the programme and the resulting learners' written performance in their target language, English. This relationship has not been sufficiently addressed in studies on school immersion contexts outside Canada, and even less so in the Colombian context. Earlier studies and compilations have underscored the importance of addressing the effect of the time factor, and more specifically intensive exposure experiences, within L2 instructional settings (Muñoz 2012). Consequently, there remains a gap in the literature as to how language productive abilities benefit from such intensive instructional experiences. Undoubtedly, the number of uncontrollable variables within educational settings, such as individual differences, curriculum and context specifics, make this a particularly complex endeavour. For this study, data collection was conducted during class time in order to ensure the students' participation. It included written data and a background questionnaire which was used to control for individual variables such as age, L2 exposure and target language contact hours outside the school.

The chapter thus presents a descriptive study that evaluates the relative effect of different amounts of exposure to L2-English in two early partial immersion programmes in Colombia. We begin by reviewing the literature concerning time as an essential factor within immersion programmes, to then go on to discuss writing development in terms of the CAF triad, as well as the measurements adopted for profiling these dimensions. We then move on to present the methodology. Finally, results and analysis are outlined, followed by a discussion. Concluding remarks will focus on the implications of this study for L2 education and specifically curriculum allocation of languages within immersion programmes in non-English speaking contexts.

2 Literature review

2.1 Time as an intrinsic factor for immersion programmes

The question of the influence of the amount of target language exposure on language proficiency was raised quite early in the implementation of French immersion programmes in Canada. Carroll's contributions in the mid-sixties and seventies around the characteristics of immersion programmes were fundamental. Regarding the time-skill relationship, he asserted: "There are many factors which contribute directly to the effectiveness of French instructional programs (...) Organizationally, it is considered *that the key factor is the number of hours of instruction* in French (...) In other words, *the more hours a pupil spends in French, the higher level of achievement is likely to be*" (Carroll (1975: 8), cited in Swain (1981: 1-2): emphasis added). He identified a direct link between the volume of input made available to learners, quantified as time, and the overall L2 attainment. Stern (1985), in turn, referred to a threshold regarding the number of hours likely to ensure a *bilingual* competence in an immersion context: at least 5,000 hours, but this account did not determine the characteristics of the learner involved in the programme, and did not make explicit the distribution of exposure time or its intensity, in terms of hours per week/month. Currently, the publications which explore time as a factor in the development of an L2 emphasize its importance but at the same time its intricate complexity. The conclusions that can be drawn from Muñoz's (2012) compilation demonstrate that, depending on how and where time is operationalized in language education, it can lead to a myriad of effects, from cognitive to socio-pragmatic, from global language features to discrete ones such as those addressed by the CAF dimensions. In this study, we focus on the parameter of accumulated time of exposure. This parameter refers to the global amount of time, in terms of number of hours, dedicated to L2 learning (Stern 1985; Genesee 1978; 2013). It is usually required for the completion of a programme with a given target proficiency level, as defined for instance by the CEFR descriptors (Council of Europe 2001). Regarding the accumulated time of exposure, immersion programmes are those where L2-contact time, along with content integrated instruction, is deemed essential for the programme's functioning (Collins et al. 1999). Globally, immersion programmes have been traditionally described as beneficial for receptive skills (Day & Shapson 1988), while their limitations regarding writing and accuracy have been frequently reported in previous research (Lightbown 2012; Germain & Séguin 2004). In such respect, in written and oral expression, immersion learners often demonstrate a considerable influence of L1 grammar. Also, it has been repeatedly reported that learners would not start a conversation in the L2 spontaneously, unless when they are asked to do so (Harley 1992; Wesche 2002). Finally, it is suggested that even though productive skills appear to be distant from those of native speakers, learners in immersion programmes continue to make progress in the L2 (Harley 1992; Wesche 1989; Housen 2012).

Particularly in terms of writing, the main topic in this study, contributions by Bournot-Bournot-Trites (2007), Collins & White (2011),Turnbull et al. (1998) and Lightbown (2012) underscore learners' capability to communicate effectively but failing to reach native-like levels, for instance as regards lexical diversity and structural elaboration.

Summing up, it has been prevalently hypothesized that the more time students dedicate to learning the L2, the higher their level of proficiency will be (Stern 1985), thus supporting the spread of instructed immersion and intensive programmes (Serrano et al. 2011; Lightbown 2012). However, although the pioneer Canadian initiatives have been abundantly documented in the SLA literature, research is scarce as far as other countries are concerned. Hence, the current study seeks to shed light on the effects of EFL immersion in Colombia, by examining and comparing the effects on writing performance of students belonging to two programmes which differ in total number of hours and their distribution. Individual differences such as L2 exposure outside school, family bilingualism, and total amount of time in the school were also taken into consideration, but will not be discussed in this chapter.

2.2 L2 Written performance

Writing is a cognitively complex and multidimensional endeavour involving different stages and processes (Manchón 2013; Ortega 2012). In fact, this skill is understood as an 'interactive' process where various factors, such as genre awareness (stylistic organization and textual format) and mastery of content and language, are frequently activated and deactivated, according to writing pace and the needs of the composition process.

Creating a text comprises three main stages, namely, planning, formulation and revision (Manchón 2009; 2013; Silva & Matsuda 2005). In the case of an L2, this activity is complicated by additional demands such as the search for the appropriate lexicon, grammar, discourse and other peculiar dimensions of the target language and culture (Manchón 2009).

In this study, writing is seen as a genuine and meaningful way of communication in controlled L2 settings, such as the immersion school. Thus, in line with Harklau (2002), Ortega (2012) and Williams (2012), writing is a means of promoting permanent opportunities for practicing and revising L2 production in the classroom.

Two main approaches have been used to analyse writing in this study: quantitative measures for the three CAF dimensions and qualitative assessment using holistic ratings.

2.3 Complexity, accuracy, and fluency (CAF)

The quest for a developmental index to describe L2 performance has been a key issue in SLA research for decades now (among the first attempts, see e.g. Larsen-Freeman 1978). Building on models of L2 proficiency (Skehan 2009; Ellis & Barkhuizen 2005, among others), Housen et al's 2012 volume elaborates on the potential of CAF as complementary dimensions of language performance and as a reliable approach to gauging L2 proficiency, as the three dimensions encompass the major areas of performance in an interlanguage system.

In this study, we adopt the CAF triad to assess writing performance in immersion contexts. Several contributions (Bulté & Housen 2014; Housen & Kuiken 2009; Housen et al. 2012; Wolfe-Quintero et al. 1998), have discussed the operationalization of these measures in order to explain what makes a learner a *skilled* user of a language. Below we review those adopted for our study.

2.3.1 Complexity

Complexity is a construct that reflects the multidimensionality of the language learning process. It particularly poses numerous problems in the SLA field due to its polysemic nature, which can refer to structural, cognitive and developmental aspects (Pallotti 2015).

In this study, L2 complexity is analysed from the language structure point of view claimed by Housen et al. (2012) and Pallotti (2015). This implies looking at the properties of L2 constructions, forms, form-meaning mappings and their interrelationships.

Several accounts have discussed the multiple operationalisations of this construct and underscored its problematic nature (i.e. Wolfe-Quintero et al. 1998; Norris & Ortega 2009; Pallotti 2015; Housen et al. 2012; Skehan 2009). In this respect, a wealth of measurements have been applied, revealing relatively operationalization vagueness and 'low content validity' (Bulté & Housen 2014: 47). Its multicompositional nature implies that complexity operates based on major assumptions that include: 'the more content means more complex', or 'the longer', 'the most embedded' or the 'more varied', all imply more complexity. As Bulté & Housen (2014) emphasize when examining short-term changes in written complexity, L2 research needs to be cautious about the validity of such measures and their implications, as their predictions may vary depending on the context, the learner and the task.

In light of these observations, this study seeks to adopt complexity as an indicator of L2 performance at different stages of language instruction. The selection of measures for syntactic and lexical complexity takes into account the nature of the texts produced by different groups of learners, which, in our study are often rather short.

2.3.1.1 Syntactic complexity

Syntactic complexity is generally measured through the length, proportion, combination and interrelation of different elements within a text (Bulté & Housen 2014). Several elements or units have been taken into consideration such as the sentence, the clause and the T-Unit, among others. Following Pallotti (2015), this study examines L2 syntactic complexity by analysing structural properties at the sentential and the clausal level, as well as text organisation properties through the use of coordination and subordination. Following Torras et al. (2006) the measurements adopted for the study were independent and dependent clauses per sentence (IndepCS and DepCS), and, following Bulté & Housen (2014), the Coordinated Clause Ratio (CoordCR) calculated by dividing the number of coordinated clauses by the number of sentences was calculated. As argued by Bulté & Housen (2012; 2014) this type of calculation (CoordCR) highlights the use of coordination within a text and differs from the Coordination Index developed by Bardovi-Harlig (1992) in that the CI appears to be a measure of clause combination that entails subordination as well: "the score on this index depends on the amount of subordination produced" (Bulté & Housen 2012: 38).

2.3.1.2 Lexical complexity

Lexical complexity has been frequently analysed by looking at lexical diversity, density and sophistication (Housen et al. 2012; Bulté & Housen 2014). Diversity, also known as lexical range (Crystal 1982) or lexical variation (Read 2000), is measured through calculations which account for the variety of vocabulary items within a language sample (Malvern et al. 2004). Measurements of density and sophistication are mostly used either with larger text samples or to discriminate amongst text genres (Read 2000). Nonetheless, it has also been argued that these measures do not really operationalize structural complexity. As Pallotti (2015: 126) highlights, "indices of lexical sophistication, like the percentage of rare or difficult words, may be valid indicators of development, but they do not directly tap structural complexity; from a structural point of view, a rare word like *tar* is not in itself more complex than a common one like *car*." Today, there is a general consensus in that diversity, sophistication and density (and an additional dimension of lexical accuracy) allow us to profile vocabulary development. In addition, diversity has been frequently examined with shorter texts such as those in our data (Meara & Miralpeix 2017).This is then the measure we have adopted to assess lexical complexity in this study.

Thus, this study uses two measures of diversity to gauge learners' lexical repertoire. First, *Guiraud's Index,* which results from dividing the number of types by the square root of the tokens in order to limit text size effects. The second one is D, computed with the *vocd* tool in CLAN (MacWhinney 2000), which estimates lexical distribution in longer text samples (Malvern & Richards 2000). Both measures have been used used to gauge language diversity in general; however, consensus has not been reached over which index proves to be a better predictor of lexical diversity in a person's interlanguage (McCarthy & Jarvis 2010, in Pallotti 2015). Therefore, this study will report both measures, to provide a more comprehensive picture.

2.3.2 Accuracy

The accuracy domain refers to the appropriateness of grammatical, lexical, semantic and pragmatic choices with respect to L2 target parameters. It is one of the most observed traits in the language production of L2 learners and it has been frequently treated as a key aspect of interlanguage development (Housen et al. 2012). Accuracy is operationalised by counting the grammatical and lexical errors in a linguistic production. However, Polio (1997; 2001) remarks that the most commonly used measure for this domain is the quantity of units with no errors (Error-Free units), which poses problems for the analysis of short compositions or those by beginner learners. In this study, overall measures of specific errors such as total amount of errors per 100 words and grammar errors per 100 words (ToralErr/100 and GrErr/100) were calculated, as they capture the totality of errors produced as well as their structural category. Grammatical errors were predominant in most of the scripts, and they mainly corresponded to agreement phenomena and verb conjugations.

2.3.3 Fluency

This term is commonly associated with the speed of articulation, rhythm, and pausing in the production of oral language. In the case of written compositions, it refers to the length of units, that is, the quantity of words and structures produced within a given time (Bulté & Housen 2014). To account for written fluency, this study adopts the view whereby the proportion of words produced is observed in relation to a given amount of time (task time, which in our case was 20 minutes). Previous research employed measures such as the number of units produced per minute, or the number of units produced within a 'macro' structure such as the sentence; in the present study, measurements in this domain include words per minute and words per sentence (WM and WS). These measures provide an account of fluency in terms of quantity and rate of production. These were chosen over analogous proposals such as *words per burst,* defined as the number of written words produced between two pauses or other interruptions (Gunnarsson 2012), as the scripts analysed for this study were not collected using key-logging technologies.

2.4 Holistic ratings

Holistic approaches to the evaluation of L2 writing have frequently been used in SLA research. These can be operationalised through scoring carried out by trained raters following assessment rubrics. These instruments usually consist of descriptors of the language used by the learner as well as the degree of completion of a given task. For example, standardized tests' examination grids, (e.g. TOEFL) include various indicators that reflect a learner's L2 competence according to specific criteria, purpose and genre. In L2 research, these ratings often serve as complements to objective measurements of text quality (Weigle 2002).

Our study uses a scoring rubric for the qualitative assessment of learners' written composition (Friedl & Auer 2007). This scale examines the characteristics of beginner to high intermediate levels of expository and narrative composition, also including task completion criteria. It was originally designed for the evaluation of English-L2 written performance within CLIL school settings in Austria (Friedl & Auer 2007; Dalton-Puffer et al. 2010) and later on in Catalunya (Juan-Garau & Salazar-Noguera 2015; Roquet & Pérez-Vidal 2015). Four aspects are evaluated on a global scale of 0 to 20, which is in turn divided into four subscales ranging from 0 to 5: 1. Task fulfilment, 2. Text Organisation, 3. Grammar and 4. Vocabulary. In the current study this instrument has been adopted to profile learners' descriptive writing within content-based instruction contexts, which are highly comparable to the contexts for which it was originally developed (Pérez-Vidal 2013).

3 Research question

This study explores the relationship between L2 exposure time and writing performance in immersion learners, as measured through the CAF constructs and holistic ratings. Hence, the guiding research question is:

1. Does accumulated time of EFL exposure in two contrasting immersion programmes (HI and HI+) have a differential impact in the long run on the learners' writing performance, when assessed with a) CAF measures and b) holistic ratings?

On the basis of this question and our review of the literature we hypothesize that, at any given time that learners are measured in the respective programmes, the higher the number of accumulated hours of EFL exposure students receive, the higher their level of proficiency will be.

4 Method

4.1 Context and participants

Foreign language education is a central theme in Colombia's political agenda (Bonilla Carvajal & Tejada-Sánchez 2016). English plays a major role in a long-term education project entitled *Colombia Bilingüe*, which aims to rank Colombia as the highest provider of quality in education in Latin America.

Our study focussed on two immersion programmes with different total times of EFL exposure. We have named them High Intensity (N=52) and High Intensity *plus* (N=136) (HI and HI+) for the purpose of the study.[1] The difference in the number of participants in both programmes is due to a larger pool of students in the schools following the HI+ programme. Table 1 displays the number of participants per programme, age-group, and grade involved. Both programmes represent actual implementations of immersion models in the private sector of Colombia's educational system, with rather high amounts of L2 exposure compared to the average Colombian traditional EFL programmes. In the public sector, time of L2 instruction ranges in average from 2 to 4 hours per week, whereas in the private sector these amounts of L2-exposure are much higher, ranging from 7 to 20 hours per week, with L2 content-based instruction being predominant.

Table 1: Number of participants per programme.

Age-group	Grade	N HI+	N HI
12	6th	12	14
14	7th	34	8
15	8th	22	8
16	9th	20	5
17	10th	48	17
Total	11th	136	52

HI and HI+ follow an early partial EFL immersion model in an otherwise Spanish curriculum, the official language in Colombia. Schooling begins at the age of four in kindergarten. From this age onwards, courses are taught about 50% of the time in the L2 and the other 50% in the L1. The most significant exposure to the L2 is offered mainly through immersion instruction, that is through curricular content taught in English. In neither programme is English taught through a grammatical or metalinguistic approach. Interestingly, students seldom use the L2 outside the classroom or for non-academic activities, so there is little or none informal learning.

Figure 1 displays the mean L2-instruction hours per year in both programmes. Black refers to HI+ and light grey refers to HI. Primary school, which lasts five years (1st to 5th grade), is the most intense period in terms of L2 exposure, as most of the subject areas (Sciences, History, Arts, etc.) are taught in English in both programmes. In terms of time distribution in primary school, HI+ provides be-

---

[1]The designation of these programmes has been adopted from Collins et al. (1999); Bournot-Trites (2007), and Collins & White (2011).

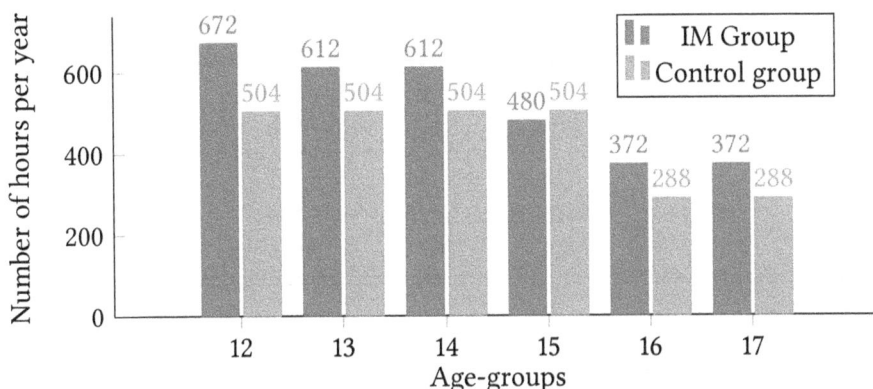

Figure 1: : Mean L2-instruction hours per school year for programmes HI and HI+.

tween 600 and 670 hours of L2-exposure per year, whereas HI provides 504 hours. High-school (6th to 11th grade) is characterized by a decrease in L2-instruction time in both programmes. The HI+ programme offers 372 hours of L2-instruction per year by the end of this stage, while the HI offers 288 hours.

Regarding the curriculum at higher stages, both the HI+ and HI programmes coincide in that the only subject areas taught in English during high school are *English Language Arts* or *Anglo-Saxon Literature*. These are offered in the L2 from 9th grade on in both programmes (around age 15). Opportunities for exposure to English at other locations in the schools, for example in the school cafeteria, the playground or common areas remains limited.

The HI+ programme gathers students from three schools. These offer the largest number of hours of L2 exposure-instruction time: **8760 accumulated hours** by the end of grade 11 (age 17). At the end of a school in the HI+ programme, a renowned international certification is provided.[2]

The HI programme involves students from one school. It offers a relatively lower number of hours of L2 exposure-instruction time, **7002 accumulated hours** by the end of grade 11 (age 17) A singular academic approach to literacy in the HI curriculum is underscored by the school's stakeholders (principals, coordinators and teachers), so students are frequently exposed to discourse and text analysis since primary school. Table 2 shows the distribution of hours per year and the accumulated hours in the two programmes.

---

[2]The *International Baccalaureate* certification (IB). In order to reach such a goal, these students from HI+ must follow the program for another year, grade 12, which was not considered in

Table 2: Number of hours of L2 accumulated per year per programme.

Grade	Mean accumulated L2 hours per programme					
	6th	7th	8th	9th	10th	11th
Age	12	13	14	15	16	17
HI	4914	5418	5922	6426	6714	7002
HI+	6312	6924	7536	8016	8388	8760

4.2 Design and procedure

Written data was collected from five different age-groups (ages 12, 14, 15, 16, and 17) in each programme. Age 13 was not taken into consideration since the data collection process could not be completed with the whole group in one of the programmes.

4.2.1 Data collection and trimming

Two main instruments were used to collect the data used for the present study: a linguistic background questionnaire and a written task consisting of a composition based on a silent film.

4.2.1.1 Linguistic background questionnaire

A general linguistic background questionnaire inspired by Grosjean (2010) was used to investigate participants' use of different languages, their learning habits, their L2 interaction and contact with target language speakers, as well as the average time spent in the immersion programme. This instrument was later used to make a selection of participants in the study. Students who had not been in the same school for their complete tuition (from primary years onwards), had lived in an English-speaking country or abroad, were binational or had English-speaking relatives, were excluded from the study. This left a final sample of 188 students including both programmes, as shown in Table 1.

4.2.1.2 The writing task: Retelling a story

In order to collect data on the participants' written abilities, they were asked to write a story retell on the basis of the silent film "College" (Horne & Keaton

---

this study.

1927), starring Buster Keaton. The choice for this task emerged from earlier analyses on task structure such as Skehan & Foster (1999), where narrative retellings tasks supported by visual prompts are used to elicit the three dimensions of CAF in comparable degrees. Likewise, silent films have frequently been used in SLA studies to elicit narratives in the L2 (e.g. Lambert 1997, who used Chaplin's *Modern Times*).

Participants watched a 3.30-minute scene of the film, which was played only once. Subsequently, they were allowed 20 minutes to complete the composition. They were asked to write as much as they were able to in the given time. They received the following instruction:

> Retell the story in writing while keeping in mind all the details. Use your current knowledge of English; do not use the dictionary.

4.2.2 Data coding and analysis

All the participants' compositions (N=188) collected through the written tasks were transcribed and coded using CLAN (MacWhinney 2000). A first streamlining was conducted to standardize coding procedures. L2 errors and spelling occurrences were identified and scripts were segmented into units. The errors that were not taken into account were those caused by phonology or graphical ambiguity (i.e. *the man say's*), misspelling (i.e. *he whent*), redundancy, or repetition of text content (i.e. *A **man** put a poster that says **Boy needed. And then** a **man** come and tell that he want the work*).

CAF measures and holistic ratings were employed to analyse the learners' writings. CAF analysis was carried out through manual coding of grammatical and lexical errors, segmentation of syntactic units and automatic calculations using CLAN and Excel. Holistic ratings were carried out by two external evaluators. In order to compare learners' performance in terms of the impact of the accumulated time of exposure in HI and HI+, descriptive statistics (means and SDs) were calculated on both CAF measures and holistic ratings for all the age groups combined (12, 14, 15, 16, and 17) in each programme, which allowed us to measure the effects throughout the programme. Between-groups comparisons were conducted using Welch's t-test.

4.2.2.1 The unit of analysis

The main unit of analysis in our study is the sentence. Our scripts resulted in an average of 32 words (see Table 3), which made an analysis based on T-Units

(Hunt 1965) too restraining, as this syntactic unit requires longer compositions to allow for a more substantive examination of how the units are conceived by the writer in terms of length and interrelations between clauses. Following Bardovi-Harlig (1992), this study adopts the sentence as the main syntactic unit in order to keep the author's original textual/syntactic segmentation.

We followed the criteria for defining the sentence and the clause established by Greenbaum & Quirk (1990),Bardovi-Harlig (1992), Vyatkina (2012) and Bulté & Housen (2014). We understand the sentence ('S') as a 'grammatically autonomous unit' (Quirk et al. 1985: 78) having a subject, at least one conjugated verb and possible complements. In written texts, sentences are identified as those stretches of writing enclosed between two full stops, or between a full stop and a colon or semi-colon. The clauses ('C') are the units which combined together form different types of sentences: simple, compound and complex. They contain a subject and predicate and can be independent or dependent (subordinate). Likewise, according to Bulté & Housen (2014) "a sentence can also include two or more coordinated independent clauses and become longer by adding more coordinated and/or subordinated clauses, when their constituent clause(s) contain more constituents and phrases, and when the phrases that make up these clauses contain more words" (p. 49). In contrast, a T-unit consists of one independent clause with all of its dependent (subordinate) clauses and they do not become longer when coordinated clauses are added.

The following excerpts are sentences derived from the data examined, and they serve to illustrate the segmentations applied for this study. T-Unit boundaries have also been marked (/). Sentence length differs between both subjects as does the amount of coordinated (Coord) and dependent clauses (DepC). L2-errors have been kept as in the original.

(1) Excerpt 1 (Grade 10, Age 16, HI):

a. Ronald passed throw [= through] the store and saw an announcement that says Boy Wanted, / so he decided to enter in the store and ask for the job.
(1 S, 2 T-Units, 2 Coord, 1 DepC).

b. When Ronald saw a beautiful girl in a table he was ashame of working as a clerk / so he went out of the bar and sat down as if he was a client.
(1 S, 2 T-Units, 2 Coord, 1 DepC).

(2)   Excerpt 2 (Grade 6, Age 12, HI+):

    a. There was a man that get by train to a new city.
       (1 S, 1 T-Unit, 1 DepC).

    b. he don't have the good cordination to do it /so he say* that he cannot do it again and he go*.
       (1 S, 2 T-Units, 2 Coord, 1 DepC).

Based on this analysis, the scripts examined for this study were fairly short, as shown in Table 3, with an average of 32 words, 5 sentences, and 11 clauses.

Table 3: Main descriptive statistics for the whole corpus

Words	Sentences	Coordination	Dependent clauses	Independent clauses
31.54	4.98	3.23	4.29	10.51

4.2.2.2 CAF measures

A total of nine measures, in the form of frequencies, means, and ratios, were examined in this study to account for complexity (syntactic and lexical), accuracy (use of L2 target parameters) and fluency (quantity of words). Table 4 presents the summary of the measures adopted.

Table 4: Summary of CAF measures applied in this study

Domain	Subdomain	Measures
Complexity	Syntactic	Independent clauses per sentence (IndepCS)
		Coordinated Clause Ratio (CoordCRatio)
		Dependent clauses (DepC)
	Lexical	Guiraud's Index
		D
Accuracy		Errors per 100 Words
		Grammar errors per 100 words (GrErr/100)
Fluency		Words per minute (W/M)
		Words per sentence (W/S)

4.2.2.3 Holistic ratings

About 55% percent of the scripts (100 in total, 10 per age-group and 50 per programme) was assessed by two evaluators from different backgrounds (Table 5). Rater 1 was a female EFL teacher in Colombia, she is originally from Cincinnati, Ohio (L1-English and L2-Spanish). Rater 2 was a female EFL teacher from Colombia (L1-Spanish and L2-English). Each evaluator scored all the narratives according to the chosen scale without knowing the authors' age or programme. Inter-rater reliability was examined by calculating the intra-class correlation (ICC) for the two programmes in each criterion of the rubric. Evaluators' agreement in scoring each immersion programme was moderate to strong on most of the rubric's criteria, except for Text Organisation. In this case, the ICC obtained for HI+ was 0.33 and for HI it was 0.66.

Table 5: Holistic ratings and Intra-class correlation for both evaluators and programmes

	HI+ (n=50)			HI (n=50)		
	Rater 1	Rater 2		Rater 1	Rater 2	
	Mean *(SD)*	Mean *(SD)*	ICCHI+	Mean *(SD)*	Mean *(SD)*	ICCHI
Task fulfillment	2.47 (0.80)	3.32 (0.81)	0.54	2.64 (1.14)	3.20 (0.87)	0.72
Text organisation	2.00 (0.62)	2.71 (0.69)	0.33	2.24 (1.02)	2.78 (0.76)	0.66
Grammar	2.57 (0.69)	2.66 (0.75)	0.58	2.62 (0.86)	2.64 (0.77)	0.78
Vocabulary	2.48 (0.73)	2.58 (0.76)	0.66	2.53 (0.92)	2.47 (0.79)	0.68
Total score	9.52 (2.32)	11.27 (2.76)	0.60	10.01 (3.44)	10.97 (2.91)	0.81

5 Results

5.1 CAF measures

The outcomes of CAF analysis for both programmes are shown in Table 6. Three measures are used for syntactic complexity: independent and dependent clauses per sentence, and the Coordinated Clause Ratio (IndepCS, DepCS and CoordCR). In terms of all these measures, the HI+ group has lower figures than the HI group, which appears to produce slightly more coordinations and subordinations throughout its scripts. Lexical complexity, as measured by D and the Guiraud index, proves to be similar in both groups, with relatively low values of D (between 42 and 43). As regards accuracy, the Errors per 100 words (Err/100) measure shows similar results for both programmes. Regarding grammar errors per 100 words (GrErrr/100), HI+ students produce an average of 9.09 errors per 100 words and the HI students produce 11.72. Lastly, fluency measured through the number of words per sentence (WS) appears higher in the HI group, while it his slightly higher in the HI+ group when measured in terms of words per minute (WM) (in a 20-minute task).

Table 6: Descriptive statistics for all CAF measures for programmes HI+ and HI

Measure	HI+				HI			
	mean	sd	Min.	Max.	mean	sd	Min.	Max.
Syntactic complexity								
IndepCS	2.68	0.76	1.2	7	3.26	1.03	1.86	7
CoordCR	0.59	0.37	0	10	0.68	0.53	1	10
DepCS	0.56	0.31	0	1.5	0.75	0.44	0.15	2.25
Lexical complexity								
Guiraud	1.52	0.27	0.76	2.35	1.46	0.19	1.06	1.8
D	42.69	13.21	19.33	98.21	41.78	8.65	26.08	72.42
Accuracy								
TotalErr	15.85	8.16	0	33.33	17.05	7.39	0	30
GRErrors100	9.09	5.48	0	20.83	11.72	6.80	0	26.78
Fluency								
WS	6.20	1.81	3.286	16	7.25	2.37	4	15
WM	2.24	0.81	0.47	4.07	2.07	0.73	0	0.41

Welch's t-tests were conducted to assess the statistical significance of between-group differences. Table 7 reports on the results of these tests as well as the effect sizes through Cohen's *d*, which were small to medium, according to Plonsky &

Oswald's (2014: 889) suggested criteria. In terms of Complexity, HI+ and HI prove to be significantly different as far as the production of independent clauses (IndepCS) (t=3.700, p < .001), with the HI + group producing fewer independent clauses than HI. Likewise, groups appeared to be significantly different concerning subordination (DepCS), where HI+ pupils appears again to write fewer dependent clauses than HI (t = 2.868 p < .05). Regarding both measures of lexical complexity (D and Guiraud index) no statistical differences were found.

Concerning accuracy, the calculation of grammar errors per 100 words (GrErr/100) yields significant differences between groups. The HI+ subjects seem to produce significantly fewer errors than their HI counterparts (t = 2.494, p < .05).

Finally, as per fluency, HI and HI+ learners significantly differ in terms of the words produced per sentence (WS), where the HI+ programme used around one word less per sentence when compared to HI (t = 2.887, p < .05). No significant differences were found as regards words per minute.

These results could be summarized by noting that HI+ learners produce fewer independent and dependent clauses, fewer words per sentence, but fewer grammar errors per 100 words than HI. That is, they are less complex and fluent, but more accurate. These findings could imply a trade-off effect. In terms of lexical complexity, both groups appear to perform similarly.

Table 7: Results for Welch's T-Test for between-group comparison of programmes HI and HI+

Domain	Measure	Statistical value (/t)	p	95% CI	d
Syntactic Complexiy	IndepCS	3.700	p < .001	0.267 0.890	0.60
	CoordCR	1.119	0.26	-0.070 0.249	0.18
	DepCS	2.868	p < .05	0.058 0.324	0.46
Lexical Complexiy	Guiraud	-1.834	0.068	-0.135 0.005	-0.3
	D	-0.553	0.58	-4.175 2.348	-0.09
Accuracy	TotalErr/100	0.969	0.34	-1.258 3.663	0.15
	GrErr/100	2.494	p < .05	0.530 4.726	0.40
Fluency	WS	2.887	p < .05	0.325 1.772	0.47
	WM	-1.387	0.16	-0.414 0.073	-0.22

5.2 Holistic ratings

Figure 2 shows two graphics with the two evaluators' scores for programmes HI and HI+ on the Total Score of the rubric. Rater 2's scores appear to be systematically higher than rater 1's. These discrepancies might be attributed to 1) the evaluators' different L1 backgrounds and 2) a differential judgement of text structure, grammar and lexical repertoires (raters might have judged learners' lexicons not only in terms of diversity but in terms of accuracy).[3]

Interestingly, the scores don't seem to change much across different age groups, except for a slight positive difference between initial (age 12) and final (age 17) levels. Both raters judged scripts produced at age 16 with the highest scores, with a rather surprising decrease at age 17.

Between-group comparisons using Welch's t-test did not reveal any statistical differences between the programmes, as shown in Table 8. The mean difference between raters' perception of HI+ and HI on various aspects of writing ability ranges from -0.17 to 0.03. These results suggest that neither programme is perceived as significantly different from the other, when it comes to the holistic rating of L2 writing performance.

Table 8: : Analysis of between-group differences in holistic ratings by two evaluators (Welch's T-Test)

	Group HI+ Mean (SD)	Group HI Mean (SD)	Mean difference between groups	t	p	95% CI	d
Task fulfillment	2.895 (0.69)	2.928 (0.93)	-0.033	0.191	0.84	-0.293 0.355	0.03
Text organisation	2.355 (0.51)	2.525 (0.82)	-0.170	1.15	0.253	-0.112 0.422	0.23
Grammar	2.615 (0.60)	2.628 (0.74)	-0.012	0.008	0.992	-0.264 0.266	0.001
Vocabulary	2.530 (0.64)	2.50 (0.74)	0.030	-0.334	0.738	-0.317 0.225	-0.06
Total score	10.395 (2.17)	10.520 (2.97)	-0.125	0.161	0.871	-0.939 1.106	0.03

[3]Open-ended questionnaires have been used in SLA research in order to explore raters' assumptions and beliefs (see for example by del Río et al. (2018 [this volume])), which could be a possibility for further research on our corpus.

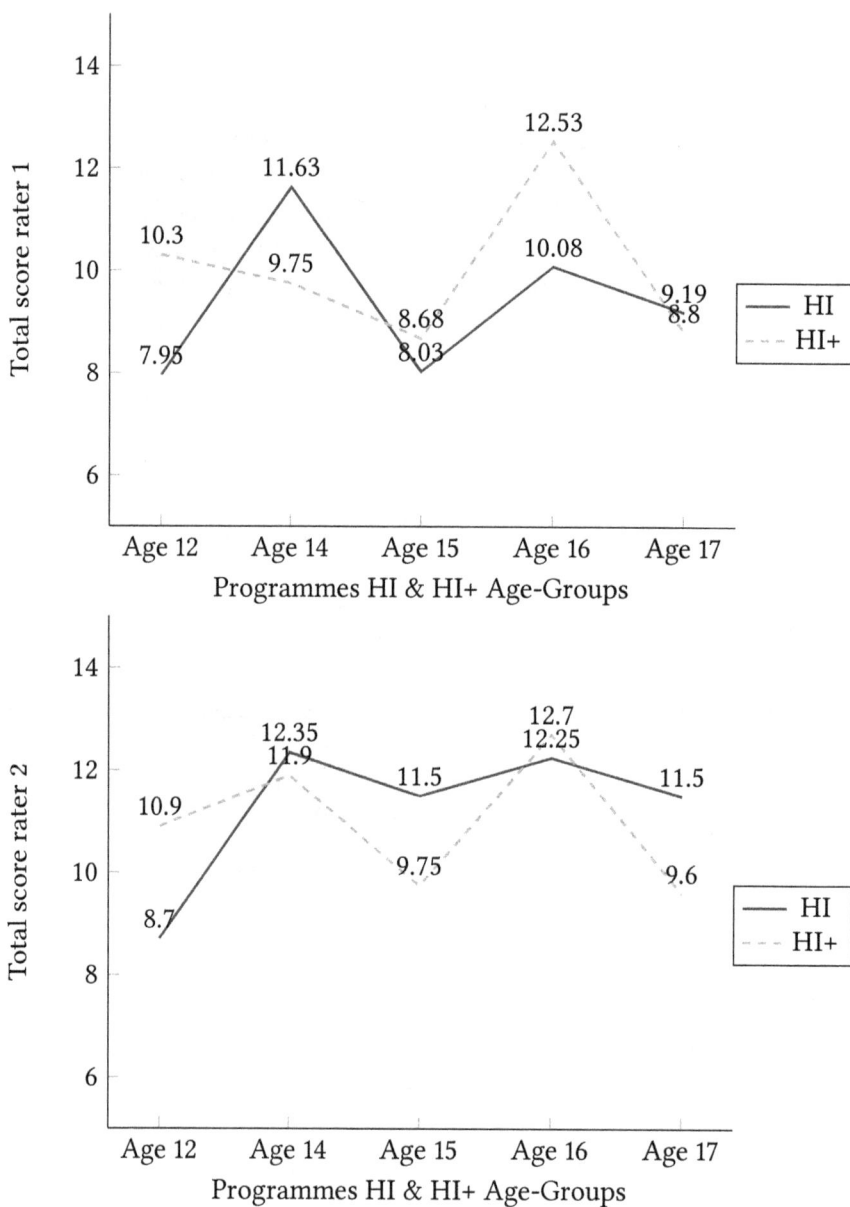

Figure 2: Rater 1 and Rater 2 Total Scores attributed to the scripts from HI and HI+ based on a 20-point scale rubric

6 Discussion and conclusions

This study has sought to understand whether the differential accumulated time of EFL-exposure (expressed in number of hours of L2 learning) has an impact on writing performance in two immersion programmes, HI+ and HI. They are different in the accumulated number of hours at all points throughout the programme, and clearly at the end, at learners' 17 years of age, when the HI+ programme has accumulated 8,760 hours, while the HI programme 7,002.

CAF measures and holistic ratings of writing samples were scrutinised with a cross-sectional design in which learners were measured throughout the programme, on a yearly basis, starting at age 12. Concerning CAF, four measures out of nine (IndepCS, CoordCR, DepCS, Guiraud, D, TotalErr/100, GrErr/100, WS, WM) were found to be statistically different between programmes but not all in favour of HI+. As regards complexity, IndepCS and DepCS were significantly lower for the HI+ group; for accuracy, GrErr/100 were statistically higher for the HI+ group; for fluency, WS, again, was statistically lower for the HI+ group. In terms of lexical complexity and the holistic ratings, no significant differences were found between the two programmes.

Overall, it would seem to be the case that the two programmes are not substantially different in terms of learners' outcomes in EFL written performance. However, it cannot be said that they are entirely the same either. Indeed, the HI+ programme reveals lower levels in the domains of syntactic complexity and fluency, but higher levels for accuracy, and equal levels for lexical complexity. This has been also found in studies on the effects of a CLIL course in English added to conventional formal instruction contrasted with a group only taking formal instruction, as the latter outperformed the former, although not significantly (Roquet & Pérez-Vidal 2015).

Consequently, given its mixed results, this study partly questions the early assertions made by Carroll (1962) and Stern (1985) in the direction that more L2-exposure time would directly lead to more skilled language use. Our approach to the interpretation of these findings is in terms of time distribution of each of the two programmes, between learners' ages 12 and 17, as presented in Table 2 and Figure 1. In the case of HI+, learners undergo a decrease of L2-exposure time which goes from 672 hours a year to 612, and then to 480 (see Figure 1). This is not the case for HI pupils, who receive fewer hours of target language exposure per year, 504, yet at a steady rhythm. Additionally, the reduction in exposure is placed one year earlier for the HI+ group, that is at age 15, than for the HI group, at age 16.

On the one hand, such a contrast in the distribution of L2 exposure time in the two programmes allows us to suggest that gradual exposure to the L2 (HI programme) might explain the similarity in results with HI+, with more accumulated amount of L2 exposure yet less consistent in its distribution.

However, such a constant exposure experienced by the HI learners may also have had a less positive consequence; that is, the HI learners' relative lower scores in terms of grammatical accuracy. In this sense, the notion of *stabilisation*, or *plateauing*, proposed by Long (2003) might be relevant. Indeed, a closer analysis of the learners' performance suggests a plateau effect mainly concerning grammatical accuracy, in the case of the HI programme predominantly observed in conjugation and agreement errors, a finding which has already been identified in immersion learners in the literature (Rifkin 2005; Hart & Swain 1991). HI's outcomes in accuracy could be interpreted as a level of "maintenance" achieved in this programme. These findings can be relative to the regular and steady amount of exposure for HI students in primary and between ages 12 and 15 in secondary school, as exposed in Figure 1.

On this note, Bournot-Trites's (2007) findings are only partially confirmed in our case. In her study, no significant differences in writing quality were found between two groups of secondary immersion students with different L2-French intensity. In addition, Bournot-Trites's (2007) study reveals a plateau effect in the field of grammar accuracy (particularly tense markers) and lexical diversity, where she observes: "it seems that after a certain threshold of competence in [L2], the increase in the time spent in this language in the class does not improve much the quality of the written production of pupils" (Bournot-Trites 2007: 20).

Likewise, the similarity of the two programmes in terms of lexical complexity could also be explained in terms of input exposure. It would seem that neither programme offers complementary hours of exposure outside of the classroom which would aid learners to make progress in such a domain.

Concerning the lower levels of fluency found in the HI+ group, they could be attributed either to the programme's didactic approach, or to task effects which remain to be explored in future research.

Some limitations of this study need to be acknowledged. First the unbalance in the sample size where the HI+ programme includes a larger number of subjects than HI, which is represented by fewer subjects. Second, task conditions as well as task variety (in terms of complexity and text genres) need to be reconsidered. Further research might include different types of tasks and writing genres with different cognitive demands. We should additionally underscore that the HI programme-related positive results, which refer to denser, richer texts, may be associated to the emphasis on literacy in the HI's curriculum described in section 4.1.1. The task might have been more familiar to HI students and therefore yielded to slightly more syntactically complex and organised texts.

To conclude, the present study has confirmed that the examination of the time factor in L2-acquisition in formal educational settings remains a rather complex endeavour due to a number of methodological constraints and issues. It is difficult to assess different programmes at exactly the same times (in terms of age, L2 exposure, curriculum years), and to control for programme features. Future research is needed to pursue research in bilingual schools or immersion programmes in non-English speaking contexts and to explore performance differences among different age groups, with a mixed methods approach including the holistic analyses suggested.

Acknowledgments

The authors are grateful to the anonymous reviewer as well as to Gabriele Pallotti for their insightful comments and contributions to this chapter. Also we would like to thank Cylcia Bolibaugh for her statistical advice. Isabel would like to thank Alejandra Plata and Alejandro Mejia from Uniandes for their help with earlier versions of this text.

References

Bardovi-Harlig, Kathleen. 1992. A second look at T-Unit analysis: Reconsidering the sentence. *TESOL Quarterly* 26(2). 390–395.

Bonilla Carvajal, Camilo Andrés & Isabel Tejada-Sánchez. 2016. Unanswered questions in Colombia's language education policy. *PROFILE Issues in Teachers' Professional Development* 18(1). 185–201.

Bournot-Trites, Monique. 2007. Qualité de l'écrit au niveau intermédiaire en immersion française: Effet d'un programme intensif et hypothèse d'un effet de plateau. *Canadian Journal of Applied Linguistics / Revue canadienne de linguistique appliquée* 10(1). 7–23.

Bulté, Bram & Alex Housen. 2012. Defining and operationalising L2 complexity. In Alex Housen, F. Kuiken & Ineke Vedder (eds.), *Dimensions of L2 performance and proficiency: Complexity, accuracy and fluency in SLA*, 21–46. Amsterdam/Philadelphia: Benjamins.

Bulté, Bram & Alex Housen. 2014. Conceptualizing and measuring short-term changes in L2 writing complexity. *Journal of Second Language Writing* 26. 42–65.

Carroll, John Bissell. 1962. The prediction of success in intensive foreign language training. In R. Glaser (ed.), *Training in research education*, 87–136. Pittsburgh: University of Pittsburgh Press. Reprint from Training Research and Education.

Carroll, John Bissell. 1975. *The teaching of French as a foreign language in eight countries*. New York: John Wiley.

Collins, Laura, Randall H. Halter, Patsy M. Lightbown & Nina Spada. 1999. *Time and the distribution of time in L2 instruction*.

Collins, Laura & Joanna White. 2011. An intensive look at intensity and language learning. *TESOL Quarterly: A Journal for Teachers of English to Speakers of Other Languages and of Standard English as a Second Dialect* 45(1). 106–133.

Council of Europe. 2001. *Common European framework of reference for languages: Learning, teaching, assessment*. Cambridge: Press Syndicate of the University of Cambridge.

Crystal, David. 1982. *Profiling linguistic disability*. London: Edward Arnold.

Dalton-Puffer, Christiane, Tarja Nikula & Ute Smit (eds.). 2010. *Language use and language learning in CLIL classrooms*. Amsterdam: John Benjamins.

Day, Elaine M. & Stan Shapson. 1988. A comparison study of early and late French immersion programs in British Columbia. *Canadian Journal of Education / Revue canadienne de l'éducation* 13(2). 290–305.

De Mejia, Anne-Marie. 2002. *Power, prestige and Bilingualism: International perspectives on elite bilingual education* (Bilingual Education and Bilingualism 344). Clevedon: Multilingual Matters.

del Río, Carmen, Maria Juan-Garau & Carmen Pérez-Vidal. 2018. Teachers' assessment of perceived foreign accent and comprehensibility in adolescent EFL oral production in Study Abroad and Formal Instruction contexts: A mixed-method study. In Carmen Pérez-Vidal, Sonia López-Serrano, Jennifer Ament & Dakota J. Thomas-Wilhelm (eds.), *Learning context effects: Study abroad, formal instruction and international immersion classrooms*, 179–211. Berlin: Language Science Press. DOI:10.5281/zenodo.1300632

Ellis, Rod & Gary Barkhuizen. 2005. *Analysing learner language, 404*. Oxford: Oxford University Press.

Friedl, Gabriele & Margit Auer. 2007. *"Assessment Scale for Writing." Erläuterungen zur Novellierung der Reifeprufungsverordnung fur AHS, lebende Fremdsprachen. Novelle der Reifeprufungsverordnung gütlig ab dem Sommertermin 2009*. Wien/St. Pölten. http : / / docplayer . org / 11483802 - Novelle - der -

reifepruefungsverordnung-2007-gueltig-ab-dem-sommertermin-2009-unter-beruecksichtigung-der-rpvo-novelle-2008.html.

Genesee, Fred. 1978. Scholastic effects of French immersion: An overview after ten years. *Interchange* 9(4). 20–29.

Genesee, Fred. 2013. Insights into Bilingual education from research on immersion programmes in Canada. In C. Abello-Contesse, P. M. Chandler, M. D. López-Jiménez & R. Chacón-Beltrán (eds.), *Bilingual and multilingual education in the 21st century: Building on experience (Bilingual education and Bilingualism)*, 24–41. Bristol: Multilingual Matters.

Genesee, Fred & M. H. Stanley. 1976. The development of English writing skills in French immersion school programs. *Canadian Journal of Education/ Revue canadienne de l'éducation* 1(3). 1–17.

Germain, Joan Netten, Claude & Serge Séguin. 2004. L'évaluation de la production écrite en français intensif: Critères et resultats. *The Canadian Modern Language Review* 60(3). 333–353.

Greenbaum, Sidney & Randolph Quirk. 1990. *A student's grammar of the English language.* Harlow: Longman.

Grosjean, François. 2010. *Bilingual: Life and reality.* Cambridge: Harvard University Press.

Gunnarsson, Cecilia. 2012. The development of complexity, accuracy and fluency in the written production of L2 French. In Alex Housen, Folkert Kuiken & Ineke Vedder (eds.), *Dimensions of L2 performance and proficiency: Complexity, accuracy and fluency in SLA*, 247–276. Amsterdam/Philadelphia: Benjamins.

Harklau, Linda. 2002. The role of writing in classroom second language acquisition. *Journal of Second Language Writing* 11(4). 329–350.

Harley, Birgit. 1992. Patterns of second language development in French immersion. *French Language Studies* 2(2). 159–183.

Hart, Sharon Lapkin, Doug & Merrill Swain. 1991. Secondary level immersion French skills: A possible plateau effect. In L. Malavé & G. Duquette (eds.), *Language, culture and cognition: A collection of studies in first and second language acquisition*, 250–265. Clevedon: Multilingual Matters.

Horne, James W. & Buster Keaton. 1927. *College.* Los Angeles: Joseph M. Schenck Productions.

Housen, Alex. 2012. Time and amount of L2 contact inside and outside the school - insights from European schools. In C. Muñoz (ed.), *Intensive exposure experiences in second language learning*, 111–138. Bristol: Multilingual Matters.

Housen, Alex & Folkert Kuiken. 2009. Complexity, accuracy, fluency (CAF) in second language acquisition. *Applied Linguistics* 30(4).

Housen, Alex, Folkert Kuiken & Ineke Vedder. 2012. Complexity, accuracy and fluency. Definitions, measurement and research. In A. Housen, F. Kuiken & I. Vedder (eds.), *Dimensions of L2 performance and proficiency: Complexity, accuracy and fluency in SLA*, 1–20. Amsterdam/Philadelphia: Benjamins.

Hunt, Kellog W. 1965. A synopsis of clause-to-sentence length factors. *The English Journal* 54(4). 300–309.

Johnson, Robert Keith & Merrill Swain. 1997. *Immersion education: International perspectives (the Cambridge applied linguistics series), 315*. Cambridge: Cambridge University Press.

Juan-Garau, Maria & Joana Salazar-Noguera. 2015. Learning English and learning through English: Insights from secondary education. In Maria Juan-Garau & Joana Salazar-Noguera (eds.), *Content-based language learning in multilingual educational environments*, 105–123. Berlin: Springer.

Lambert, Monique. 1997. *En route vers le bilinguisme*. Vol. 9. http:////aile.revues.org/732.

Lambert, Wallace E. & Richard G. Tucker. 1972. *The bilingual education of children. The st. Lambert experiment*. Rowley: Newbury House Publishers.

Larsen-Freeman, Diane. 1978. An ESL index of development. *TESOL Quarterly* 12(4). 439–448.

Lazaruk, Walter Andrew. 2007. Avantages linguistiques, scolaires et cognitifs de l'immersion française. *Canadian Journal of Education / Revue canadienne de l'éducation* 63(5). 629–654.

Lightbown, Patsy M. 2012. Intensive L2 instruction in Canada: Why not immersion? In C. Muñoz (ed.), *Intensive exposure experiences in second language learning*, 3–23. Bristol: Multilingual Matters.

Long, Michael H. 2003. Stabilization and fossilization in interlanguage development. In Catherine J. Doughty & Michael H. Long (eds.), *The handbook of second language acquisition*, 487–535. Oxford: Blackwell Publishing Ltd.

MacWhinney, Brian. 2000. *The CHILDES project: Tools for analysing talk*. 3rd edn. Mahwah, NJ: Lawrence Erlbaum.

Malvern, David D. & Brian J. Richards. 2000. Validation of a new measure of lexical diversity. In Mieke Beers, Beppie van den Bogaerde, Gerard Bol, Jan de Jong & Carola Rooijmans (eds.), *From sound to sentence: Studies on first language acquisition*, 81–96. Groningen: Centre for Language & Cognition.

Malvern, David D., Brian J. Richards, Ngoni Chipere & Pilar Duran. 2004. *Lexical diversity and language development (quantification and assessment)*. New York: Palgrave Macmillan.

Manchón, Rosa M. 2009. *Writing in foreign language contexts: Learning, teaching, and research.* Bristol: Multilingual Matters.

Manchón, Rosa M. 2013. The psycholinguistics of Bilingual writing: Mapping the terrain. In F. Grosjean & P. Li (eds.), *The psycholinguistics of bilingualism*, 102–116. Malden: Wiley-Blackwell.

McCarthy, Phillip M. & Scott Jarvis. 2010. MTLD, vocd-D, and HD-D: A validation study of sophisticated approaches to lexical diversity assessment. *Behavior Research Methods* 42. 381–392.   DOI:10.3758/BRM.42.2.381

Meara, Paul M. & Imma Miralpeix. 2017. *Tools for researching vocabulary.* Clevedon: Multilingual Matters.

Muñoz, Carmen. 2012. *Intensive exposure experiences in second language learning. Second language acquisition, 258.* Bristol: Multilingual Matters.

Norris, John M. & Lourdes Ortega. 2009. Towards an organic approach to investigating CAF in instructed SLa: The case of complexity. *Applied Linguistics* 30(4). 555–578.

Ortega, Lourdes. 2012. Epilogue: Exploring L2 Writing-SLA interfaces. *Journal of Second Language Writing* 21(4). 404–415.

Pallotti, Gabriele. 2015. A simple view of linguistic complexity. *Second Language Research* 31(1). 117–134.

Pérez-Vidal, Carmen. 2013. Perspectives and lessons from the challenge of CLIL experiences. In Cristian Abello-Contesse, Paul M. Chandler, María Dolores López-Jiménez & Rubén Chacón-Beltrán (eds.), *Bilingual and multilingual education in the 21st century: Building on experience*, 59–82. Bristol: Multilingual Matters.

Plonsky, Luke & Frederick L. Oswald. 2014. How big is "big"? Interpreting effect sizes in L2 research. *Methodological Review Article, Language Learning* 64(4). 878–912.

Polio, Charlene. 1997. Measures of linguistic accuracy in second language writing research. *Language Learning* 47(1). 101–143.

Polio, Charlene. 2001. Research methodology in second language writing: The case of text-based studies. In T. Silva & P. Matsuda (eds.), *On second language writing*, 91–116. Mahwah, NJ: Erlbaum.

Quirk, Randolph, Sidney Greenbaum, Geoffrey Leech & Jan Svartvik. 1985. *A comprehensive grammar of the English language.* London: Longman.

Read, John. 2000. *Assessing vocabulary.* Cambridge: Cambridge University Press.

Rifkin, Benjamin. 2005. A ceiling effect in traditional classroom foreign language instruction: Data from Russian. *The Modern Language Journal* 89(1). 3–18.

Roquet, Helena & Carmen Pérez-Vidal. 2015. The linguistic impact of a CLIL science programme: An analysis measuring relative gains. *System* 54. 80–90.

Serrano, Raquel, Àngels Llanes & Elsa Tragant. 2011. Analyzing the effect of context of second language learning: Domestic intensive and semi-intensive courses vs. Study abroad in Europe. *System* 39(2). 133–143.

Silva, Tony & Paul Kei Matsuda (eds.). 2005. *On second language writing*. Mahwah: Routledge.

Skehan, Peter. 2009. Modelling second language performance: Integrating complexity, accuracy, fluency, and lexis. *Applied Linguistics* 30(4). 510–532.

Skehan, Peter & Pauline Foster. 1999. The influence of task structure and processing conditions on narrative retellings. *Language Learning* 49. 93–120.

Stern, Hans H. 1985. The time factor and the compact course development. *TESL Canada Journal/Revue Tesl du Canada* 3(1). 13–29.

Swain, Merrill. 1981. Time and timing in bilingual education. *Language Learning* 31(1). 115.

Swain, Merrill. 2000. French immersion research in canada: Recent contributions to SLA and Applied Linguistics. *Annual Review of Applied Linguistics* 20. 199–212.

Tejada-Sanchez, Martha Isabel. 2014. *L'acquisition de l'anglais et l'exposition intensive en contexte d'immersion scolaire en colombie. Unpublished doctoral dissertation*. Barcelona/Paris: Universitat Pompeu Fabra - Université Paris 8 PhD Thesis.

Torras, María Rosa, Teresa Navés, Maria Luz Celaya & Carmen Pérez-Vidal. 2006. Age and IL development in writing. In Carmen Muñoz (ed.), *Age and the rate of foreign language learning*, 156–182. Clevedon: Multilingual Matters.

Turnbull, Miles, Sharon Lapkin, Doug Hart & Merrill Swain. 1998. Time on task and immersion graduates' French proficiency. In Sharon Lapkin (ed.), *French second language education in canada: Empirical studies*, 31–55. Toronto: University of Toronto Press.

Vyatkina, Nina. 2012. The development of second language writing complexity in groups and individuals: A longitudinal learner corpus study. *The Modern Language Journal* 96(4). 576–598.

Weigle, Sara (Cushing). 2002. *Assessing writing. 284*. Cambridge: Cambridge University Press.

Wesche, Marjorie Bingham. 1989. Les diplômés de l'immersion: Implications dans le domaine de l'enseignement du français. *The Canadian Journal of Higher Education* 19(3). 30–41.

Wesche, Marjorie Bingham. 2002. Early French immersion: How has the original Canadian model stood the test of time? In Petra Burmeister, Thorsten Piske & Andreas Rohde (eds.), *An integrated view of language development. Papers in honor of Henning Wode*, 23. Trier: WVT Wissenschaftlicher Verlag Trier.

Williams, Jessica. 2012. The potential role(s) of writing in second language development. *Journal of Second Language Writing* 21(4). 321–331.

Wolfe-Quintero, Kate, Shunji Inagaki & Kim Hae-Young. 1998. *Second language development in writing: Measures of fluency, accuracy, and complexity*. Manoa: National Foreign Language Resource Center - University of Hawaii at Manoa.

Chapter 6

Assessing learners' changes in foreign accent during Study Abroad

Pilar Avello

Universitat Pompeu Fabra

The present study aims to contribute to the field of Study Abroad (SA) research by exploring the under-investigated interface between SA and the measurement of pronunciation gains in terms of improvement in degree of foreign accent (FA). It is an exploratory study which analyzes changes in FA measures as a result of a short-term, 3-month SA program preceded by a Formal Instruction (FI) period. Data were collected from a group of non-native speakers (NNSs) consisting of 8 undergraduate, upper-intermediate learners of English as a second language (L2) with Catalan and Spanish as first languages (L1s), and from 3 undergraduate L1 English native speakers (NSs), who served as controls. Data from the NNSs were collected at the beginning of their degree (T1), after an 80-hour FI period (T2), and upon their return from SA (T3); data from the NSs were collected only once (T0). Thirteen L1 English listeners rated the speech samples from the NSs and the NNS for degree of FA by means of a rating experiment using a Likert scale. Analyses failed to yield a significant effect of SA on FA ratings and did not reveal a significant difference in FA ratings following SA as compared to FI. These findings are in line with the inconclusive and mixed results which are often reported for L2 pronunciation in short-term SA contexts.

1 Introduction

Over the last decades, Study Abroad (SA) programs have enjoyed increasing popularity worldwide, particularly at university level. The ever-growing popularity of SA is arguably linked to the widespread belief that an overseas program has substantial linguistic benefits for students. This belief is based on the assumption that immersion in the target language community is the best way to acquire the

Pilar Avello. Assessing learners' changes in foreign accent during Study Abroad. In Carmen Pérez Vidal, Sonia López-Serrano, Jennifer Ament & Dakota J. Thomas-Wilhelm (eds.), *Learning context effects: Study abroad, formal instruction and international immersion classrooms*, 131–154. Berlin: Language Science Press. DOI:10.5281/zenodo.1300622

language due to the opportunities for interaction and the amount and quality of the input available in this learning context.

Academic authorities and governments have played an active role in the promotion of SA programs, encouraging students to go abroad so as to improve their second language (L2) proficiency. One of the most popular examples is the interuniversity Erasmus program in the European Union. Hundreds of thousands of students from different European countries have received an Erasmus grant in order to pursue part of their university studies in a different European country, and Spain, where the present study has been conducted, is one of the countries which have benefited the most from this program, both in terms of outgoing and incoming students.

In this scenario, the need to empirically assess the actual benefits of SA on learners' L2 development has become evident. A growing body of research within the field of L2 acquisition has been devoted to this learning context in order to analyze the effects of SA on the different linguistic skills. Contributions to this body of research within a European perspective have been particularly called for, given the fact that an important part of SA research has been conducted from a North American perspective (Coleman 1998).

An overview of the existing SA literature does not indicate substantial SA gains for all the different linguistic skills across the board (cf. DeKeyser 2007). Results point to clear benefits in areas such as vocabulary growth, socio-pragmatic skills and overall oral proficiency, and especially regarding fluency, which has been one of the most extensively researched areas. However, the domain of phonology, which is the focus of the present study, has been the object of relatively little research within the SA literature, and findings so far are inconclusive as to the changes that can accrue in L2 speech perception and production during a period abroad. This is particularly remarkable, considering that one of the main aims of students going abroad is to improve their L2 pronunciation, which is normally far from native norms in the case of learners who have been exposed to foreign-accented input in formal instruction (FI) settings.

Research into L2 phonological acquisition in contexts of naturalistic, long-term immersion has shown that pronunciation is one area of L2 proficiency particularly resistant to change, even in an environment of massive and authentic L2 input exposure. Learners' difficulties in achieving native pronunciation norms are evidenced by a perceptible foreign accent, which is largely the reflection of the learners' first language (L1) phonology. In fact, research into L2 phonological acquisition, which has usually adopted a cross-sectional design, has established that one of the main causes underlying learners' difficulties in acquiring a new L2 phonology is the influence of the already existing L1 phonological system (Flege 1995; Best & Tyler 2007).

Given that the domain of L2 phonology within the SA literature remains under-investigated, we seek to further our understanding of the benefits that can be expected to accrue in this domain during a period abroad. We present the results of a longitudinal, pre-test/post-test design, which assesses the effects of a 3-month SA period preceded by an FI period on a group of L1 Spanish/Catalan undergraduate learners of L2 English.

2 Literature Review

2.1 L2 Speech Development & Foreign Accent

An important body of research in the field of L2 speech learning has been devoted to examining the phenomenon of foreign accent (FA), also referred to as accentedness in the literature. FA has been described, for instance, as "the extent to which an L2 learner's speech is perceived to differ from native speaker (NS) norms" (Munro & Derwing 1998: 160). It has also been characterized as "non-pathological speech produced by second language learners which differs in partially systematic ways from the speech characteristic of native speakers of a given dialect" (Munro 1998: 139). In his seminal work providing a full account of his Speech Learning Model for L2 phonological acquisition, Flege (1995: 233) noted that "[l]isteners hear foreign accents when they detect divergences from English phonetic norms along a wide range of segmental and suprasegmental (i.e. prosodic) dimensions".

FA is therefore a perceptual phenomenon related to the processing of L2 speech which results from listeners' perception of differences between specific properties of L2 speech and those that characterize native speakers' (NSs) norms. As such, a foreign accent is the perceptual correlate of objective acoustic-phonetic characteristics of L2 learners' pronunciation which, as pointed out by Flege (1995), can take place both at the segmental level (divergences from the range of native-like acoustic values, or number and severity of pronunciation errors), and at the suprasegmental level (stress, rhythm and intonation patterns which are found to differ from native norms).

Interest in the study of FA within L2 phonological acquisition research arises from its theoretical relevance regarding general theories of L2 acquisition and from its pragmatic dimension related to L2 teaching. From a theoretical perspective, research into the phenomenon of FA may shed light on the existence of age-related constraints that might influence L2 acquisition, as the domain of pronunciation very often evidences incomplete acquisition in adult and adolescent L2 learners. In this line of research, the study of FA has been strongly connected to what some authors have hypothesized as a 'critical' or 'sensitive' period for L2 acquisition (Lenneberg 1967; Scovel 1988; Long 1990). These authors posit biological and maturational constraints on L2 acquisition that would prevent native-like L2 phonological performance beyond the hypothesized critical or sensitive period, which is generally considered to end around puberty, leading to the emergence of a clearly perceptible foreign accent as a characteristic of L2 learner's speech.

From a pragmatic perspective, a better understanding of which specific features of L2 speech contribute more to a foreign accent may inform more efficient approaches in the teaching of L2 pronunciation (cf., for instance, Piske et al. (2001). In this sense, the study of FA has usually been related to research on other dimensions of L2 speech, such as speaking rate (Munro & Derwing 1998) and fluency, comprehensibility and intelligibility (Munro & Derwing 1995; Derwing & Munro 1997; 2013). The aim of these studies is to clarify the interaction between these different speech dimensions and how they affect listeners' processing of L2 speech, in order to shed light on the best teaching strategies that would facilitate the development of L2 learners' fluent and successful communication in the L2, which is usually the ultimate goal of the language learner in a context of immersion in the target language community.

Research in the field of FA has usually adopted the form of experimental studies with a cross-sectional design in which oral data are elicited at a single point in time. Many of these studies focus on immersion contexts in which the target language has been acquired usually without FI (e.g. immigrants from different backgrounds in an English-speaking country like the United States or Canada). Measures of FA are typically obtained by having a group of listeners rate L1 and L2 speech samples for degree of accentedness by means of Likert-type, equal-appearing interval scales. Most studies have analyzed the perception of accentedness by native listeners (NLs), who have been found to provide reliable FA ratings, although non-native listeners have also been found to assess accentedness reliably regardless of whether they share the same L1 with learners. Common data elicitation techniques include having the L2 learners read words, sentences or paragraphs aloud. Sometimes they may be asked to repeat a speech stimulus that has been produced by NSs. Samples of free or extemporaneous speech may also be obtained, for example, by asking the learners to describe a picture or tell a story.

Age of onset of learning (AOL), identified as age of first exposure to the L2, has been the most examined factor in the FA literature. Interest in the study of age effects on L2 pronunciation is related to the hypothesized critical or sensitive period for language acquisition (Lenneberg 1967; Scovel 1988). However, results from some studies have shown that adult learners may indeed be able to acquire native-like pronunciation (Bongaerts et al. 1995; Flege et al. 1995; Bongaerts et al. 1997). Conversely, some studies have also shown that an early age of L2 acquisition (as early as 3.2 years) does not guarantee accent-free pronunciation (Flege et al. 1997). Many studies have revealed a gradual increase in FA as AOL increases (Flege 1988; Flege & Fletcher 1992), a finding which points toward a linear relationship between AOL and degree of FA. In general, most research indicates that 'the earlier the better' for L2 pronunciation, but it seems that early L2 acquisition is not enough for mastery of the L2. This has led authors to assess the influence of other factors on degree of FA, most notably L2 experience, amount and quality of L2 input, or patterns of L1/L2 use (cf. Piske et al. 2001 for a review).

L2 experience has been the second most studied factor considered to influence degree of FA. Since most FA studies have been conducted in immersion contexts, L2 experience has been typically operationalized as length of residence (LOR) in the L2 country. Research assessing the effect of LOR on L2 pronunciation has yielded mixed results. Flege & Fletcher (1992) found that LOR had a significant correlation with FA, as did English-language instruction and AOL. An LOR effect has been usually found for early L2 learners, that is, learners who first encountered massive L2 exposure before the end of the hypothesized critical period (around puberty), whereas increased LOR does not seem to have an impact on late or adult L2 learners following an initial phase of improvement that takes place at the early stage of L2 learning (Flege 1988). Other studies suggest that LOR effects depend on learners' stage of L2 acquisition (Riney & Flege 1998; Meador et al. 2000).

Several studies have found that amount and quality of L2 input and language use patterns are also influential factors on L2 pronunciation (Flege et al. 1995; 1997; Piske et al. 2001). These studies make use of self-assessment questionnaires in which learners have to estimate, for instance, the amount of contact with NSs of the L2, the amount of time they spend using their L1 and L2 in different contexts, or L1 and L2 proficiency. Results in Flege et al. (1995) revealed that language use patterns constitute a significant predictor of FA ratings for Italian learners of L2 English, explaining 15% of the total variance. In a follow-up study (Flege et al. 1997), the role of L1 use was further explored by creating two groups of early Italian/English bilinguals who were AOL-matched (around 6 years old), but who differed in percentage of L1 use (3% vs. 36%). The authors reported an L1 use effect as the learners with higher L1 use were perceived to have a significantly stronger FA than the learners with lower L1 use. Results in Piske et al. (2001) showed that the L1 use effect observed for early bilinguals was also extended to late Italian/English bilinguals.

Results from these studies indicate that, although AOL has been found to be the most influential factor in the development of L2 pronunciation, differences in L2 pronunciation outcomes can also be the result of the interplay of other factors such as the amount and quality of the L2 input to which learners are exposed, as well as patterns of L1/L2 language use. However, as already noted, studies examining the phenomenon of FA have been mainly conducted in contexts of long-term immersion, rather than in shorter periods of immersion, such as those typical of SA learning contexts.

2.2 Study Abroad

SA is a context of L2 acquisition characterized by a combination of language-based and/or content-based classroom instruction together with out-of-class interaction in the native speech community (Freed 1995a: 5). SA programs have become very popular in Europe and North America due to the common sense and long-held assumption that immersion in the L2 community results in substantially enhanced L2 knowledge, as such immersion is assumed to offer plenty of opportunities for interaction with NSs and exposure to a great amount of high quality input. Consequently, SA programs have been encouraged by language instructors and academic administrators, and have come to play an important role in governments' L2 learning policies as a means to promote multilingualism in response to an increasingly globalized international context (cf. Kinginger 2009). A growing body of research has therefore been devoted to this learning context in order to account for the nature of the SA experience and empirically assess its impact on L2 learners' linguistic development (cf. overviews in Freed 1995a; DuFon & Churchill 2006).

For the most part, research has found evidence for a positive effect of the SA experience on learners' L2 development, yet actual linguistic gains appear to be related to individual and context variables such as contact patterns while abroad, L1 and L2 use, L2 exposure, initial level of L2 proficiency, and length of stay (LoS, operationalized as duration of the SA period), as well as to aspects of program design (see Pérez-Vidal & Juan-Garau 2011 for a characterization of SA). A complex picture results from the interaction of all these factors, with findings sometimes providing inconclusive or conflicting evidence, as the benefits of SA are not always clear for all language skills, or the gains reported may fall short of the high expectations arising out of the above-mentioned widespread belief in the substantial effects of SA immersion.

Research has analyzed the impact of SA on different linguistic domains, and usually in contrast with FI in at-home (AH) institutions. Results have provided consistent evidence of the beneficial effect of SA for lexical improvement (Collentine & Freed 2004; Llanes & Muñoz 2009), as well as for writing (Sasaki 2004; Pérez-Vidal & Juan-Garau 2011) and listening (Allen & Herron 2003; Llanes & Muñoz 2009). Sociolinguistic skills have been the object of considerable research with studies examining, for instance, communication strategies (Lafford 1995) and pragmatic competence (Barron 2006), which have also yielded results supporting the positive effect of SA on these areas. However, mixed results have been found for grammar; results reported by Collentine & Freed (2004) showed more grammatical improvement for AH learners as compared with those who went abroad, whereas the opposite was true in Howard (2005). Most SA research has focused on the development of oral skills, which has traditionally been considered the most likely linguistic domain to improve as a result of SA, and research findings in general have supported this view. Some studies have analyzed the impact of SA on overall L2 speaking proficiency (Brecht et al. 1995; Segalowitz & Freed 2004), and extensive research has also been carried out to analyze gains in L2 learners' fluency (Freed 1995b; Freed et al. 2004;Valls-Ferrer 2011).

However, studies focusing on specific aspects of phonological development in learners' L2 speech production during SA are scarce. The few existing studies generally focus on the differential effects of SA versus FI on L2 pronunciation, and have yielded mixed results. Díaz-Campos (2004) reported a positive effect of both learning contexts on the production of Spanish plosives in two groups of English students of Spanish, although development toward native-like patterns was found to be stronger in the FI group. In contrast, Díaz-Campos (2006) observed greater gains in the production of Spanish consonants for the SA group as compared with the FI group. Mora (2008) examined the production of voice onset time in English voiceless plosives by a group of L1 Spanish/Catalan bilingual learners after a two-term FI period at their home university and after a 3-month SA term abroad. He found no effect of FI on voice onset time duration, whereas a non-significant increase was observed after SA. However, in a study with a similar population analyzing English vowels, significant improvement in production was found after FI, but not after SA (Pérez-Vidal et al. 2011). Sanz et al. (2013) reported significant SA gains in the production of L2 plosives by L1 English learners of Spanish, whereas Simões (1996) did not find significant improvement in the production of Spanish vowels for L1 English learners following SA, but production at the segmental level for both vowel and segmental contrasts did not improve significantly. Avello (2010a) also failed to find improvement in the production of vowel contrasts following SA, although in Avello (2010b) the lack of improvement in vowel contrast production did not prevent considerable gains in FA scores. In contrast, Avello et al. (2012) reported significant gains in segmental production in terms of a reduction in error rate scores, but which were not accompanied by significant gains in FA scores.

The present study thus explores the under-investigated impact of SA on L2 learners' pronunciation development. It is an exploratory study which aims to analyze the interface between SA and FA by assessing the impact of a 3-month SA program on L2 speech production by a group of bilingual L1 Catalan/Spanish learners of L2 English by means of FA measures.

3 Research aims

1. To assess possible differential effects of type of instruction through time on global FA ratings by analyzing the impact of a 3-month SA period preceded by an 80-hour FI learning context.

2. To assess differences between native and non-native FA ratings and to assess whether a development through time toward native norms can be observed in L2 learners' FA ratings as a function of learning context.

4 Method

4.1 Design

The data presented in this paper are part of the Study Abroad and Language Acquisition (SALA) project. This is a large, state-funded project based at a University in Barcelona, Spain, which analyzes the development of linguistic proficiency in upper-intermediate learners of L2 English who experience an SA period preceded by an FI period (see full description in Pérez-Vidal & Juan-Garau 2011). This project has a longitudinal, pre-test/post-test design in order to assess possible differential effects of the FI period at the AH university versus the subsequent short-term SA period on the learners' L2 linguistic development. Data were collected at three different points in time covering a 15-month period:

- T1: at the beginning of the first academic year, to assess initial L2 proficiency.

- T2: after an 80-hour FI period, to assess the impact of this classroom learning context on the learners' L2 proficiency. Exposure to English in this learning context was basically limited to classroom language learning and was form-focused. The amount of input and communicative interaction was therefore rather limited. Students received no specific phonological training or pronunciation instruction.

- T3: after a compulsory 3-month SA period in an English-speaking country at the beginning of the second academic year, to assess the impact of the SA learning context on the learners' L2 development. In this context students were expected to receive a massive amount of out-of-class input and to benefit from opportunities for communicative interaction in real, everyday social situations.

4.2 Participants

Data were collected from a group of non-native speakers (NNSs, n = 8). They shared a similar AOL in AH institutions (AOL = 8 years), as established by the Spanish educational system. Their acquisition of English took place basically through classroom instruction (i.e. as a foreign language in their native speech community), with 700-800 hours of exposure to English. These learners had to certify an upper-intermediate English proficiency level (equivalent to a B2 in the Common European Framework of Reference, or CEFR) in order to be admitted into the AH university.

Speech samples from 3 NSs of American English served as baseline data to assess the learners' performance. These NSs were young university students enrolled in an L2 Spanish exchange program in Spain. Both groups of speakers had, therefore, a similar profile, and consequently their data were highly comparable. Data from the NSs was collected only once (T0).

A group of English NLs (n – 13) were recruited to assess the speech samples from the native and non-native groups for degree of FA; 6 of them were exchange students at a university in Spain and 7 were English teachers.

4.3 Speech samples

Speech samples from the NSs and the NNSs were elicited by means of a reading aloud task, which consisted of the rendition by the participants of the text "The

North Wind and the Sun". The International Phonetic Association (IPA) has encouraged the use of this short, 114-word text as a standard oral elicitation resource
to document the pronunciation of different languages and language varieties (cf.
IPA (1999), and it has been used to document differences characterizing English
pronunciation in different dialects and by L2 learners (see Schneider et al.).

   A member of the research team was present during the recordings to give
instructions to the participants on how to perform the reading aloud task and
to answer possible questions. Instructions were also provided on the test handout, which participants were asked to read carefully. Participants were recorded
individually. They were instructed to read the text twice, first silently on their
own in order to become familiar with it, and then out loud to be recorded. The
researcher told them that they would be asked a question about the text after
reading it the second time. This was done to draw the participants' attention to
the content with the aim of obtaining more natural-sounding data. Immediately
after reading the text aloud, they were asked the following question: "Was the
North Wind Stronger than the sun?", which they had to answer by merely stating
"yes" or "no".

   Data from the NNSs were recorded in sound-attenuated cabins using an analog
tape recorder and were subsequently digitized in .wav format at 22,050, 16 bit
monaural. Data from the NSs were recorded in sound-proof cabins using the Pro
Tools digital audio workstation platform for Microsoft Windows. The digital files
were saved in .wav format at 44,100 Hz (later downsampled to 22,050 Hz), 16 bit
monaural.

   A sentence extracted from the reading aloud task was used to create the stimuli
for the rating task (see §4.4. below).[1] This sentence presented several segmental
and suprasegmental properties that were likely to cause the L2 learners to produce pronunciation errors leading to accented L2 production. Some examples of
such pronunciation errors as produced by the NNSs are provided in (1-4):

(1) Deletions
         a. deletion of [l] in *warm(l)y*
         b. deletion of final syllable in *travel(er)*

(2) Insertions
         a. insertion of an extra vowel [e] in *immediat[e]ly*
         b. insertion of a velar consonant at the beginning of *[ɣ]warmly*

---

[1] *Then the sun shone out warmly, and immediately the traveler took off his cloak.*

(3) Substitutions

    a. substitution of bilabial approximant [β] for velar fricative [v] in *traveler*

    b. substitution of dental plosive [d] for dental fricative [ð] in *then*

    c. substitution of open vowel [a] for close back vowel [ɔ] in *warmly*

    d. substitution of dental fricative [ð] for alveolar plosive [d] in *immediately*

    e. substitution of velar fricative [x] for glottal fricative [h] in *his*

(4) Stress misplacement

    a. stress shift to the penultimate syllable in multisyllabic words: *tra'veler* for *'traveler, imme'diately* for *i'mmediately.*

4.4 Rating task

A rating task was conducted in order to obtain measures of changes in the learners' degree of FA through time. This experiment provided us with listeners' behavioral measures of global FA ratings regarding overall changes in the NNs' pronunciation as a result of FI and SA. As noted in §2.1 above, this methodology has been widely used in research on L2 speech production analyzing the construct of FA, as well as other dimensions of L2 speech such as intelligibility and comprehensibility.

The task was a self-paced task created and run with Praat software (Boersma & Weenink 2008, version 5.1) and displayed on PCs running Microsoft Windows XP OS. Stimuli consisted of speech samples extracted from the reading aloud task as produced by the 3 NSs (T0) and the 8 NNSs (T1, T2 and at T3). The resulting audio files were edited and saved in .wav format at 22,050 Hz, 16 bit monaural, and normalized for intensity at 70.0 dB.

At the beginning of the session, the NLs were given a handout with the description of the experiment, as well as with some instructions on how to run it with Praat. They rated the degree of FA in the oral samples by means of a 5-point equal-appearing Likert scale, where 1 = "native" and 5 = "heavy foreign accent" (see Figure 1 below).

A 9-point scale has been most commonly used in FA studies, since participants usually differ greatly in proficiency level, as well as in AOL and/or L2 exposure. However, a 5-point scale was deemed more appropriate for the data in the present study, taking into account the smaller degree of variability in our oral samples (NNSs with a similar age, AOL, L2 exposure and proficiency level).

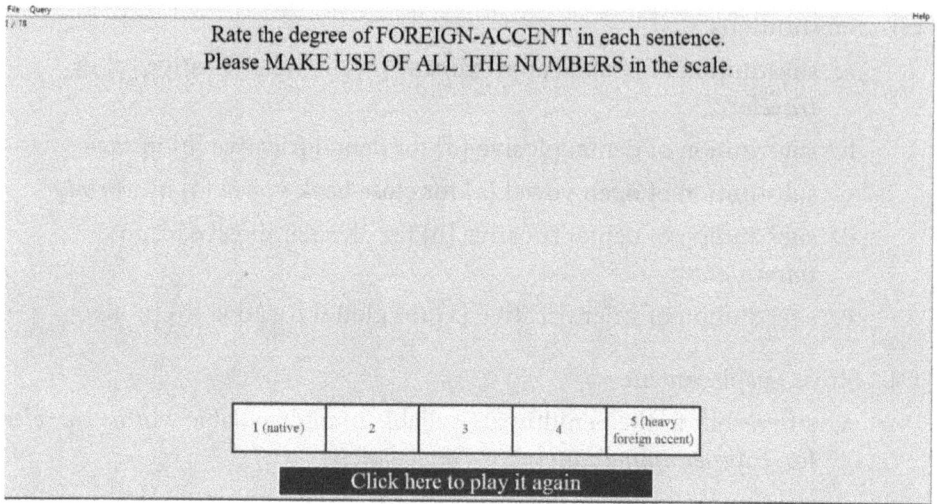

Figure 1: Initial Praat screen for the rating task

Listeners were instructed to focus on pronunciation and rate the degree of FA they perceived in the speech samples as produced by the NNSs and the NSs by making use of the whole scale. Each stimulus was repeated twice for a total of 54 test trials per listener (8 NNSs x 3 data collection times x 2 repetitions + 3 NSs x 2 repetitions), resulting in a total of 702 ratings (54 trials x 13 listeners). Each listener heard the stimuli in a different randomized order. Listeners could replay each trial twice before providing their answer. After rating a stimulus, they had to click on a "next" button to listen to the following stimulus. If the NLs made a mistake when rating a stimulus, they could click on an error button to listen to it again and change their answer (an answer could be changed only once). Listeners were presented with 16 practice trials (8 samples x 2 repetitions) before the test trials. During the test trials, there was the possibility of a pause after a block of 18 trials.

5 Results

Preliminary analyses were conducted to assess both intra-rater and inter-rater consistency in the NLs' ratings by means of Pearson correlations, which yielded both high intra-rater and inter-rater consistency coefficients.

Regarding intra-rater reliability, there was a strong correlation in the listener-based FA ratings assigned at each of the two rating repetitions ($r = .71$, $p = .007$), indicating that each listener's first and second repetition ratings were strongly correlated; that is, each listener assigned similar ratings to the same stimulus at both the first and second repetitions.

Similarly, strong correlations were found in the stimulus-based FA ratings assigned by the 13 listeners in all pair-wise combinations, with r coefficients ranging between .74 and .98 (in all cases $p < .05$), which indicates a high degree of agreement among listeners.

Table 1 and Figure 2 show the FA ratings assigned by the NLs to the baseline data provided by the NSs (T0) and to the NNSs through time (T1, T2 and T3). As expected, the ratings for the NSs were very close to 1 ($M = 1.06$), indicating that the listeners identified the English NSs and rated them accordingly. In contrast, the ratings assigned to the NNSs' were considerably outside the range of the NSs' ratings across all testing times.

Table 1: : Summary for FA ratings as assigned by the NLs (1 = native, 5 = heavy foreign accent)

Group	Time	n	Minimum	Maximum	Mean	SD
NS	T0	3	1.00	1.19	1.06	.11
NNS	T1	8	2.58	4.58	3.19	.68
	T2	8	2.62	4.23	3.47	.49
	T3	8	3.04	3.81	3.40	.31

An increase in FA ratings can be observed between T1 ($M = 3.19$) and T2 ($M = 3.47$), signaling no positive effect of FI on the NNSs' degree of FA. This is followed by a slight decrease in FA ratings between T2 ($M = 3.47$) and T3 ($M = 3.40$), which seems to suggest a positive trend of improvement in the NNSs' degree of FA during the SA period. A one-way repeated measures ANOVA was conducted with the FA ratings as dependent variable and time as within-subjects factor in order to assess the effect of the FI and SA learning contexts on the L2 learners' pronunciation development as measured by the FA ratings. This analysis yielded a non-significant effect of time on the FA ratings (Wilks' Lambda = .64, $F(2, 6)$ = 1.69, $p = .26$, $\eta^2 = .36$), indicating that the slight decrease observed in the FA ratings as a result of SA failed to reach significance.[2]

Indeed, as illustrated in Table 1 and Figure 2, the L2 learners' FA ratings remained similar through time. Independent samples t-tests showed significant

---

[2] Results pooled across all listeners are presented, as the same results pattern was observed in the exchange students and English teachers.

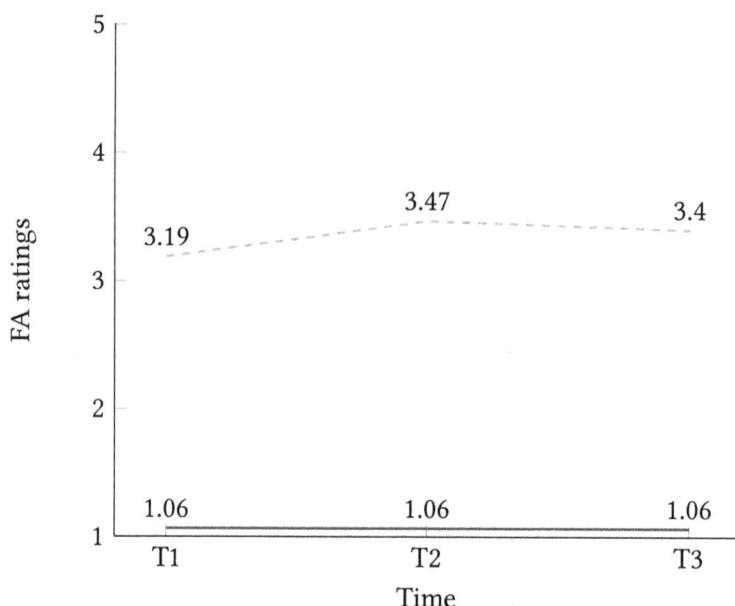

Figure 2: : Mean FA ratings for the NSs (represented by the horizontal line) and the NNSs at T1 (at the beginning of the academic year), T2 (after an 80-hour FI period prior to SA) and T3 (upon return from a 3-month SA).

differences between the ratings assigned by the listeners to the NSs' and to the NNSs' at T1 ($t(9) = -5.21$, $p = .001$, $\eta^2 = .75$), T2 ($t(9) = -8.17$, $p < .001$, $\eta^2 = .88$), and T3 ($t(9) = -12.42$, $p < .001$, $\eta^2 = .94$). However, no significant differences were found between the three testing times for NNSs, which indicates the lack of development toward NS patterns in terms of degree of FA. Taken together, these results yield no evidence of significant improvement in FA ratings during SA, although they seem to signal a positive trend of development toward less accented speech as a result of SA (as opposed to FI). This suggests that SA might have had some impact on reducing the NNSs' degree of accentedness, even though statistically non-significant.

6 Discussion

These results contrast with the findings reported in most studies assessing the effect of SA on L2 acquisition. As noted in §2.2, SA has been generally found to have a clear positive impact on L2 linguistic development, with results providing evidence of substantial SA gains in lexical development (Collentine & Freed 2004; Llanes & Muñoz), writing (Sasaki 2004; Pérez-Vidal & Juan-Garau 2011) and listening (Allen & Herron 2003; Llanes & Muñoz 2009). SA has been found to be particularly beneficial for the development of L2 oral skills, such as overall oral proficiency, enhanced accuracy and complexity, and most notably fluency (Brecht et al. 1995; Segalowitz & Freed 2004; Freed et al. 2004; Valls-Ferrer 2011). This is in line with the general assumption that oral production is one of the areas that can be expected to improve the most during SA, as it is assumed to be one of the most practiced skills while abroad and to specially benefit from the massive exposure to L2 input that SA offers.

However, these results are consistent with the scant existing research analyzing SA gains in L2 pronunciation, which has yielded inconclusive evidence regarding the effects of SA on this dimension. Whereas some studies have reported a positive effect of SA, for instance, on the production of consonantal segments (Díaz-Campos 2004; 2006; Mora 2008; Sanz et al. 2013), and rhythm metrics (Valls-Ferrer 2011), other studies have failed to find substantial SA gains in vowel production (Simões 1996; Avello 2010a; Pérez-Vidal et al. 2011), and in the production of both vowel and consonantal contrasts (Højen 2003). Avello (2010b) found that lack of improvement in vowel contrast production following SA did not however prevent considerable gains in FA scores. Conversely, results in Avello et al. (2012) showed significant improvement in phonetic measures of error rate scores during SA, whereas no significant improvement was found in FA ratings.

The lack of a stronger impact of SA on the FA ratings attributed to L2 learners in the present study may be related to the length of the SA program. LoS is one of the SA program features identified by Pérez-Vidal & Juan-Garau (2011) as influencing SA outcomes, since it determines amount of exposure to L2 input. LoS would thus be the SA equivalent to LOR, which is the variable that has traditionally been used as an index for amount of exposure to L2 input in FA studies analyzing the acquisition of L2 speech within long-term, naturalistic immersion contexts.

In his study addressing FA changes during SA by a group of L1 Danish undergraduate learners of English, Højen (2003) reported significant improvement in his participants' FA scores after their experience abroad. However, the participants in his study presented considerable variation in terms of LoS in the SA context. The mean LoS was 7.1 months (range = 3-11 months), which is considerably longer than the 3-month stay experienced by the learners in the present study. When analyzing these individual differences, Højen found a strong positive correlation between LoS and gains in FA scores ($r = .61$, $p < .05$). The learners who showed less improvement during SA were those with stays of only 3 to 4 months, which is in line with the results of the present study, whereas the greatest SA gains were obtained by the learners who stayed abroad up to 11 months. Højen interpreted these results as signaling the importance of LoS for SA gains in FA scores to accrue.

As indicated in §2.1 above, findings regarding the role of LOR on degree of FA in long-term immersion contexts have been mixed, with some studies reporting an effect of LOR on FA ratings while other studies have failed to do so. The impact of LOR seems to be influenced by L2 learners' age and stage of L2 learning. LOR seems to have an effect on L2 pronunciation for early learners, but not for late or adult learners (Flege 1988). It has been claimed that most L2 phonological learning for late or adult L2 learners would take place within the first year of massive exposure in the L2 context. Pronunciation would then fossilize, resisting further changes after this initial period of gains (Selinker 1972; Flege 1988; Scovel 1988; Flege & Fletcher 1992). More inexperienced late L2 learners (those at an early stage of L2 learning) could thus benefit from additional L2 exposure, whereas more experienced late L2 learners (those with higher proficiency) would be unlikely to benefit from further L2 exposure.

The results reported in the present study could be interpreted in the light of these general findings for LOR effects. Although the NNSs in this study had been learning English since childhood in FI settings at their AH institutions, opportunities for out-of-class exposure to conversational English input are rather limited in Spain. The SA experience allowed them to live in an English-speaking country and to have access to massive and authentic L2 English input. However, as stated above, a 3-month LoS might be too short to observe a significant improvement in these learners' FA ratings. Considering that there seemed to be a tendency toward a decrease in accentedness during SA, it is possible that the NNSs' degree of FA would have continued to gradually decrease with an increase in LoS up to, for example, the average 7.1 months or 11 months at which significant improvement in FA scores was reported by Højen (2003).

Improvement in FA ratings seems to be further influenced by other factors, such as the actual amount and quality of the L2 input learners receive. According to Piske et al. (2001: 197), the inconclusive findings of research on LOR effects can also be partly due to the fact that "LOR only provides a rough index of overall L2 experience". Following this line of thought, Højen (2003) created a composite measure which weighted LoS by self-reported English-language input while abroad, and found that the correlation between this composite measure and gains in FA scores ($r = .81$, $p < .001$) was stronger than the correlation between LoS alone and gains in FA scores as reported above. He interpreted this finding as an indication of the importance of having access to a substantial amount of high-quality L2 native input to improve FA scores, in line with previous findings (Flege & Liu 2001).

The learners in the present study reported a relatively high degree of contact with English NSs (an average of 3.6 on a 5-point scale, where 1 = 'never', 5 = 'very often'), but they also reported a higher degree of contact with other NNSs of English (an average of 4.5 on the same scale). Since these learners were Erasmus students, it is very likely that they were in contact with other Erasmus students from a variety of non-English speaking countries. Exposure to this poorer, foreign-accented L2 input could have thus contributed to the lack of significant improvement in their FA ratings. In terms of accommodation, only one learner reported sharing an apartment with English NSs, whereas the rest reported staying in a single room at a residence hall. The fact that this was the preferred type of accommodation for the learners in this study might also have had some bearing on the lack of significant FA gains, as this type of accommodation is more likely to limit opportunities for interaction with NSs as compared with other options, such as sharing a room or apartment with NSs or staying with a native family.

Another factor that has been found to influence FA gains is learners' patterns of L1 and L2 use during immersion in the L2 context. Results reported in previous research suggest that more frequent use of the L1 (which would entail less frequent use of the L2) is associated with higher degree of FA (Flege et al. 1997; Piske et al. 2001). As is normally the case with Erasmus programs, the learners in the present study traveled to their SA destination in small groups and reported spending some time with the other students from their AH university (an average of 1.5 on a 3-point scale, where 1 = 'most time', 3 = 'little'). The learners further reported a rather high degree of contact with their families back home while abroad by means of a scale from 'a' to 'e' ('a' = 'more than once a day' and 'e' = 'none'). Learners reported mostly 'b' ('a few times a week'), indicating frequent contact, whereas none reported 'd' or 'e'. These patterns of rather frequent L1 use could also have prevented the learners from obtaining greater gains in their FA ratings.

The lack of greater changes in the learners' FA ratings could also be related to the way in which listeners process speech samples and how this influences their FA ratings. Listeners seem to assess speech samples for overall degree of FA holistically (Magen 1998). This means that they pay attention to different speech features both at the segmental level (phonemic and subphonemic substitutions, insertions, deletions) and suprasegmental level (stress, pitch range, rhythm, speaking rate, connected speech phenomena, overall prosody, or intonation), and that different listeners may also weigh these features of speech differently for different L2 learners and proficiency levels. Some studies have reported a positive effect of a short SA program not exceeding 3 months on learners' segmental production (Díaz-Campos 2004; 2006; Mora 2008; Sanz et al. 2013). However, a 3-month SA program might not be long enough to trigger similar gains in other areas of pronunciation involving prosodic features of speech, which have also been found to considerably bear on the perception of FA (Anderson-Hsieh et al. 1992; Munro & Derwing 1999).

Another factor which could have influenced the outcome of the FA ratings is the rather homogeneous composition of the learner group in terms of L2 proficiency level. Although there were differences in pronunciation between the learners, they all shared a similar L1 background and L2 English language level (B2 or upper-intermediate). This could have made the rating task rather difficult for the listeners, who had to discriminate subtle FA changes between learners and across testing time. It is probably easier for listeners to rate speech samples from a pool of learners showing a wider range of proficiency levels, from low to advanced. This has typically been the case in the FA literature examining long-term immersion contexts, where differences in FA scores arise as a result of considerable inter-subject variation in terms of L2 proficiency, which in turn can be attributed to differences in AOL, as well as to other variables such as L2 exposure, L1/L2 use, etc. (see §2.1). It is also possible that the use of a scale wider than the 5-point scale used in the present study would have better captured the slight changes in pronunciation that the learners might have experienced.

7 Conclusion

To sum up, results in the present study showed no improvement in the NNSs' FA ratings as a result of FI and suggested, in contrast, a positive trend of development toward a decrease in FA following SA, although this decrease was not significant and the NNSs' FA ratings remained significantly different from the NSs' FA ratings through time. This outcome is in line with the mixed results that have been reported in the scarce research that has assessed the effect of SA as compared with FI on L2 pronunciation. Given the observed trend of development during SA, maybe an increased LoS could have resulted in continued gradual improvement leading to significant gains in the NNSs' FA ratings, as is suggested in previous research Højen (2003). Since general findings from research on L2 speech production suggest that most progress in pronunciation takes place during the first year of immersion in an L2 context, more studies are needed focusing on the effects of LoS on pronunciation outcomes for L2 learners with different proficiency levels.

Considering the holistic way in which listeners provide FA ratings, and the fact that different listeners may focus on different aspects of L2 speech, it is also possible that the FA ratings in the present study failed to reflect some gains that could have accrued in some specific features of the learners' L2 pronunciation. Such changes could have been captured by fine-grained phonetic or acoustic analyses, or could have been reflected in the FA ratings by means of the use of a scale with a wider range. Previous research has found that the relation between FA ratings and specific aspects of pronunciation is not always a straightforward one. For example, Avello et al. (2012) found significant SA gains in phonetic error rate scores, but not in FA scores. Conversely, in Riney & Flege (1998: 237), gains in global FA ratings did not coincide with improvement in segmental production regarding liquid identifiability and accuracy. The authors noted that it "appears not to be the case that improvement in global accent necessarily proceeds in parallel with improvement in any particular smaller components of pronunciation, such as segmental identifiability and accuracy". In this sense, in order to gain better insight into the types of changes that can be expected in L2 pronunciation as a result of SA, more research is needed with a multiple-measures approach that combines subjective FA scores as well as more objective acoustic and phonetic analyses that include acoustic measures and error rate scores.

Acknowledgements

This research was funded by grant FFI2010-21483-C02-01 awarded by the Spanish Government to the SALA project, and by grants BES-2008-010037 and EEBB-I-12-04294 awarded by the Spanish Government to the author within the FPI doctoral research program.

References

Allen, Heather W. & Carol Herron. 2003. A mixed-methodology investigation of the linguistic and affective outcomes of summer study abroad. *Foreign Language Annals* 36(3). 370–385.

Anderson-Hsieh, Janet, Ruth Johnson & Kenneth Kohler. 1992. The relationship between native speaker judgments of nonnative pronunciation and deviance in segmentals, prosody, and syllable structure. *Language Learning* 42(4). 529–555.

Avello, Pilar. 2010a. The effect of study abroad on Catalan/Spanish bilinguals' production of English /i- ɪ/ & /æ - ʌ/ contrasting pairs. Paper presented at the 6th International Conference on Language Acquisition - CIAL, Universitat de Barcelona, Spain.

Avello, Pilar. 2010b. *Study abroad and foreign accent: the production of /i- ɪ/ and /æ - ʌ/ by catalan/spanish bilinguals.* Paper presented at the 20th International Conference of the European Second Language Association - Eurosla, University of Modena and Reggio Emilia, Italy.

Avello, Pilar, Joan C. Mora & Carmen Pérez-Vidal. 2012. Perception of FA by non-native listeners in a study abroad context. *Research in Language* 10(1). 63–78.

Barron, Anne. 2006. Learning to say 'you' in German: The acquisition of sociolinguistic competence in a study abroad context. In Margaret A. DuFon & Eton E. Churchill (eds.), *Language learners in study abroad contexts*, 59–90. Clevedon, UK: Multilingual Matters.

Best, Catherine T. & Michael D. Tyler. 2007. Nonnative and second-language speech perception. In Ocke-Schwen Bohn & Murray J. Munro (eds.), *Language experience in second language speech learning: In honour of James Emil Flege*, 13–34. Amsterdam: Benjamins.

Boersma, Paul & David Weenink. 2008. *Praat: Doing phonetics by computer.* http://www.fon.hum.uva.nl/praat/.

Bongaerts, Theo, Brigitte Planken & Erik Schils. 1995. Can late starters attain native accent in a foreign language? A test of the critical period hypothesis. In David Singleton & Zsolt Lengyel (eds.), *The age factor in second language acquisition: A critical look at the critical period hypothesis*, 30–50. Clevedon, UK: Multilingual Matters.

Bongaerts, Theo, Chantal van Summeren, Brigitte Planken & Erik Schils. 1997. Age and ultimate attainment in the pronunciation of a foreign language. *Studies in Second Language Acquisition* 19(4). 447–465.

Brecht, Richard, Dan Davidson & Ralph Ginsberg. 1995. Predictors of foreign language gain during study abroad. In Barbara Freed (ed.), *Second language acquisition in a study abroad context*, 37–66. Amsterdam: Benjamins.

Coleman, James A. 1998. Language learning and study abroad: The European perspective. *Frontiers: The Interdisciplinary Journal of Study Abroad* 4(2). 167–203.

Collentine, John & Barbara F. Freed. 2004. Introduction: Learning context and its effects on second language acquisition. *Studies in Second Language Acquisition* 26(2). 153–171.

DeKeyser, Robert. 2007. Study abroad as foreign language practice. In Robert DeKeyser (ed.), *Practice in a second language: Perspectives from applied linguistics and cognitive psychology*, 208–226. Cambridge: Cambridge University Press.

Derwing, Tracey M. & Murray J. Munro. 1997. Accent, intelligibility, and comprehensibility: Evidence from four L1s. *Studies in Second Language Acquisition* 19. 1–16.

Derwing, Tracey M. & Murray J. Munro. 2013. The development of L2 oral language skills in two L1 groups: A 7-year study. *Language Learning* 63(2). 163–185.

Díaz-Campos, Manuel. 2004. Context of learning in the acquisition of Spanish second language phonology. *Studies in Second Language Acquisition* 26. 249–273.

Díaz-Campos, Manuel. 2006. The effect of style in second language phonology: An analysis of segmental acquisition in study abroad and regular-classroom students. In Carol A. Klee & Timothy L. Face (eds.), *Selected proceedings of the 7th conference on the acquisition of Spanish and Portuguese as first and second languages*, 26–39. Sommerville, MA: Cascadilla Proceedings Project.

DuFon, Margaret A. & Eton E. Churchill (eds.). 2006. *Language learners in study abroad contexts*. Clevedon, UK: Multilingual Matters.

Flege, James Emil. 1988. Factors affecting degree of perceived foreign accent in English sentences. *Journal of the Acoustical Society of America* 84(1). 70–79.

Flege, James Emil. 1995. Second language speech learning theory, findings, and problems. In Winifred Strange (ed.), *Speech perception and linguistic experience: Issues in cross-language research*, 233–277. Timonium, MD: York Press.

Flege, James Emil & Kathryn L. Fletcher. 1992. Talker and listener effects on degree of perceived foreign accent. *Journal of the Acoustical Society of America* 91(1). 370–389.

Flege, James Emil, Elaina M. Frieda & Takeshi Nozawa. 1997. Amount of native-language (L1) use affects the pronunciation of an L2. *Journal of Phonetics* 25(2). 169–186.

Flege, James Emil & Serena Liu. 2001. The effect of experience on adults' acquisition of a second language. *Studies in Second Language Acquisition* 23(4). 527–52.

Flege, James Emil, Murray J. Munro & Ian R. A. Mackay. 1995. Effects of age of second-language learning on the production of English consonants. *Speech Communication* 16(1). 1–26.

Freed, Barbara F. (ed.). 1995a. *Second language acquisition in a study abroad context.* Amsterdam: Benjamins.

Freed, Barbara F. 1995b. What makes us think that students who study abroad become fluent? In Barbara F. Freed (ed.), *Second language acquisition in a study abroad context*, 123–148. Amsterdam: Benjamins.

Freed, Barbara F., Dan P. Dewey, Norman Segalowitz & Randall Halter. 2004. The language contact profile. *Studies in Second Language Acquisition* 26(2). 349–356.

Højen, Anders Damgren. 2003. *Second-language speech perception and production in adult learners before and after short-term immersion.* Aarhus: University of Aarhus dissertation.

Howard, Martin. 2005. Second language acquisition in a study abroad context: A comparative investigation of the effects of study abroad and foreign language instruction on the L2 learner's grammatical development. In Alex Housen & Michel Pierrard (eds.), *Investigations in instructed second language acquisition*, 495–530. Berlin: Mouton de Gruyter.

IPA. 1999. *Handbook of the international phonetic association.* Cambridge: Cambridge University Press.

Kinginger, Celeste. 2009. *Language learning and study abroad. A critical reading of research.* Houndmills: McMillian.

Lafford, Barbara. 1995. Getting into, through and out of a survival situation: A comparison of communicative strategies used by students studying Spanish abroad and 'at home'. In Barbara Freed (ed.), *Second language acquisition in a study abroad context*, 97–122. Amsterdam: Benjamins.

Lenneberg, Eric H. 1967. *Biological foundations of language.* New York: John Wiley & Sons.

Llanes, Àngels & Carmen Muñoz. 2009. A short stay abroad: does it make a difference? *System* 37(3). 353–365.

Long, Michael H. 1990. Maturational constraints on language development. *Studies in Second Language Acquisition* 12(3). 251–285.

Magen, Harriet S. 1998. The perception of foreign-accented speech. *Journal of Phonetics* 26(4). 381–400.

Meador, Diane, James Emil Flege & Ian R. A. Mackay. 2000. Factors affecting the recognition of words in a second language. *Bilingualism: Language and Cognition* 3(1). 55–67.

Mora, Joan C. 2008. Learning context effects on the acquisition of a second language phonology. In Carmen Pérez-Vidal, Maria Juan-Garau & Aurora Bel (eds.), *A portrait of the young in the new multilingual Spain*, 241–263. Clevendon, UK: Multilingual Matters.

Munro, Murray J. 1998. The effects of noise on the intelligibility of foreign-accented speech. *Studies in Second Language Acquisition* 20. 139–154.

Munro, Murray J. & Tracey M. Derwing. 1995. Foreign accent, comprehensibility, and intelligibility in the speech of second language learners. *Language Learning* 45(1). 73–97.

Munro, Murray J. & Tracey M. Derwing. 1998. The effects of speaking rate on listener evaluations of native and foreign-accented speech. *Language Learning* 48(2). 159–182.

Munro, Murray J. & Tracey M. Derwing. 1999. Foreign accent, comprehensibility, and intelligibility in the speech of second language learners. *Language Learning* 49. 285–310.

Pérez-Vidal, Carmen & Maria Juan-Garau. 2011. The effect of context and input conditions on oral and written development: A study abroad perspective. *International Review of Applied Linguistics in Language Teaching* 49(2). 157–185.

Pérez-Vidal, Carmen, Maria Juan-Garau & Joan C. Mora. 2011. The effects of formal instruction and study abroad contexts on foreign language development: The SALA project. In Cristina Sanz & Ronald P. Leow (eds.), *Implicit and explicit conditions, processes and knowledge in SLA and bilingualism*, 115–138. Washington D. C.: Georgetown University Press.

Piske, Thorsten, Ian R. A. MacKay & James Emil Flege. 2001. Factors affecting degree of foreign accent in an L2: A review. *Journal of Phonetics* 29(2). 191–215.

Riney, Timothy & James Emil Flege. 1998. Changes over time in global foreign accent and liquid identifiability and accuracy. *Studies in Second Language Acquisition* 20. 213–243.

Sanz, Cristina, Alfonso Morales-Front, Charlie Nagle & Colleen Moorman. 2013. *Improvements in pronunciation in a 6 week study abroad program*. Learning without attention. Paper presented at the residence abroad, social networks and second language learning congress, University of Southampton, UK.

Sasaki, Miyuki. 2004. A multiple-data analysis of the 3.5-year development of EFL student writers. *Language Learning* 54(3). 525–582.

Schneider, Edgar W., Kate Burridge, Bernd Kortmann, Rajend Mesthrie & Clive Upton (eds.). 2004. *A handbook of varieties of English. Volume 1: Phonology*. Berlin: Mouton de Gruyter.

Scovel, Thomas. 1988. *A time to speak. A psycholinguistic inquiry into the critical period for human speech.* Cambridge, MA: Newbury House Publishers.

Segalowitz, Norman & Barbara F. Freed. 2004. Context, contact and cognition in oral fluency acquisition: Learning Spanish in at home and study abroad contexts. *Studies in Second Language Acquisition* 26(2). 173–199.

Selinker, Larry. 1972. Interlanguage. *International Review of Applied Linguistics in Language Teaching* 10(3). 209–231.

Simões, Antonio R. M. 1996. Phonetics in second language acquisition: An acoustic study of fluency in adult learners of Spanish. *Hispania* 79(1). 87–95.

Valls-Ferrer, Margalida. 2011. *The development of oral fluency and rhythm during a study abroad period.* Barcelona: Universidad Pompeu Fabra. (Doctoral dissertation.)

Chapter 7

The second time around: The effect of formal instruction on VOT production upon return from study abroad

Victoria Monje
Universitat Pompeu Fabra

Angelica Carlet
Universitat Internacional de Catalunya

The present study aims at assessing L2 phonological development, while controlling for proficiency level, as a result of a 2-month formal instruction (FI) period following a 3-month period spent abroad in a country where the learners' target language was spoken. It examines voice onset time (VOT) production of English voiceless stops in initial stressed position by Catalan/Spanish EFL learners. It is intended as a follow-up of Mora's (2008) study, which yielded no significant effects at the end of the stay abroad (SA) only. It is hypothesized that the FI period should allow students to focus on their phonology, away from the pressing demands of daily communication during SA. No explicit attention is paid to phonology in class. Speech samples were collected from 13 participants, through two tasks, upon their return from SA and immediately after a 2-month period of FI. No significant effect of the FI period preceded by a SA term on informants' VOTs was found. Proficiency level seems to have played a role in VOT production. Speaking style, vowel height and place of articulation were found to significantly affect VOT production of voiceless stops, in line with previous findings. A baseline group of natives showed the same numerical tendency. The lack of impact resulting from a FI period preceded by a SA term adds further support for the suggestion made by some authors (Darcy et al. 2012; Gordon & Darcy 2012; Calvo Benzies 2014) that explicit attention to phonology in FI should act as a potential factor to effectively improve L2 phonological development.

Victoria Monje & Angelica Carlet. The second time around: The effect of formal instruction on VOT production upon return from study abroad. In Carmen Pérez Vidal, Sonia López-Serrano, Jennifer Ament & Dakota J. Thomas-Wilhelm (eds.), Learning context effects: Study abroad, formal instruction and international immersion classrooms, 155–179. Berlin: Language Science Press.
DOI:10.5281/zenodo.1300624

1 Introduction

It is often assumed that L2 oral speech development will improve as a result of stay abroad (SA), whereas less improvement will be noted as a consequence of formal instruction (FI). However, there is little evidence to support this claim, as studies assessing second language (L2) phonological acquisition resulting from a SA are still scarce and results are conflicting. Importantly, phonological development seems to be one of the most challenging aspects of L2 acquisition for learners, a fact that is likely due to a lack of a consistent pedagogical methodology in teaching (Darcy et al. 2012).

Hence, this empirical study aims at continuing to fill the existing research gap in L2 speech production. The study has been carried out within the Study Abroad and Language Acquisition (SALA) project (see Pérez-Vidal 2014b), where linguistic and non-linguistic progress as a function of SA are analysed, including L2 phonological development. FI has also been examined in combination with SA within the project. However, FI periods preceded SA ones in the SALA studies. Our work seeks to provide a counterbalanced perspective by examining the impact of an FI period following a SA.

In order to obtain as thorough an understanding of L2 phonological development as possible, the interplay of three important connected aspects is explored in the literature review: (i) the teaching of pronunciation in the classroom, (ii) the linguistic outcomes obtained as a function of learning context, and (iii) voice onset time (VOT), which is the phenomenon under investigation in the present study.

2 Literature review

Pronunciation is often neglected in the English as a second language (ESL) classroom despite its importance and interconnection with the four linguistic skills (Darcy et al. 2012). Moreover, according to Calvo Benzies (2014; 2016), English pronunciation can be seen as one of the most difficult skills to acquire and develop for Spanish learners of English. First language (L1) interference, an incoherent relation between spelling and pronunciation and other non-linguistic factors such as motivation, age and amount of exposure have been identified as factors to which such difficulties can be ascribed (Darcy et al. 2012; Calvo Benzies 2014). The reasons that make the teaching of pronunciation complex are numerous: for instance, the lack of systematicity regarding content and lack of time devoted to it in the FL classroom (Derwing & Foote 2011), undertrained teachers (Derwing

2010; Foote et al. 2011) and paucity of teaching materials. Pronunciation is often neglected in syllabuses, which leads teachers to believe that spending time on it is unnecessary.

Darcy et al. (2012) and Calvo Benzies (2014) emphasize the need for pronunciation to be taught systematically at different levels of proficiency (from beginners to the most advanced learners). Additionally, Gordon & Darcy (2012) advocate for the usefulness of drawing explicit focus to form in pronunciation instruction. The lack of success in the acquisition of L2 pronunciation might partly be related to the little amount of attention it receives in the L2 classroom.

Due to the general lack of success of FI in L2 phonological development, SA is often considered a more appealing alternative to foster this linguistic skill. In fact, when SA and FI are compared, SA is said to be more advantageous regarding the quantity and quality of input it offers the learner. This constant exposure grounds the assumption that SA is more likely to lead learners to enhanced L2 knowledge than FI. However, this does not seem to be the case for L2 phonological development. In fact, there are reported cases of adults who, in spite of displaying a high command of their L2 due to a long length of stay abroad, still retain a distinct foreign accent revealing phonetic traits of their L1 (Dalton & Seidlhofer 1994; Flege & Frieda 1997).

Other factors that account for the (lack of) success in L2 phonological development are the characteristics of each learning context. According to Pérez-Vidal (2014b), SA is a naturalistic learning context in which exposure to the target language is constant, which can potentially provide massive amounts of input, output and interaction opportunities. The case of FI seems to be the opposite, due to its poorer input and limited opportunities for production. Therefore, one should expect different linguistic outcomes from SA and FI. SA spurs the enhancement of certain skills which are normally difficult to teach in FI. The latter, in turn, tends to focus on aspects such as metalinguistic awareness and grammar. Thus, from the point of view of skill acquisition theory, the classroom is the optimal environment for declarative knowledge to become procedural, whereas SA is ideal to reach automatization (DeKeyser 2007: 214).

In turn, success in L2 speech production is subject to inter-speaker variability due to the interplay of several factors (e.g. motivation and cognitive abilities) (Mora 2014). Mora suggests that having high motivation to learn the L2 makes learners more likely to interact with natives and hence gain access to richer input. The impetus for engaging in L2 encounters must then come from the learners themselves. Therefore, in-country residence does not guarantee quality input or interaction (Moyer 2009), just as context of learning per se does not grant enhanced L2 production. Learners must also process the comprehensible input they receive in order to benefit from it, a notion known as intake (Archibald 2005). This leads us to doubt the apparent superiority of the input received in SA over that obtained in FI.

The idea that input during a SA may be insufficient to reach success in L2 phonological acquisition might be linked to the fact that the processing demands learners have to face leave them with few resources to focus on form. As opposed to FI, SA is a meaning-oriented context. Other limitations to the quantity and quality of input in SA contexts are the (frequent) use of L1, fossilization and lack of feedback (Han 2004).

Lastly, the learner's initial proficiency level before the SA period also seems to play a role as far as L2 speech development is concerned. There is a fairly acceptable degree of agreement on the fact that the learners' initial L2 level might influence the accrued gains (if any) during their experience abroad (Collentine 2009). This phenomenon is known as *threshold level*. Learners at a lower level make greater progress during SA than their higher level counterparts (Brecht et al. 1995).

Hence, learning context is important, but it might not suffice to account for L2 speech development. Moreover, each learning context must be accurately defined to avoid misconceptions about the linguistic results they trigger. More specifically, given the SALA project's contradictory findings on different linguistic skills as a function of learning context, Pérez-Vidal (2014b: 29-30) concludes that skill development is not linear in a SA context, just as it is not in a FI context. For example, learners show substantial progress in oral skills after a SA period (López-Serrano 2010); however, research on L2 phonological development is scarce and has failed to show a clear superiority of SA over FI, yielding conflicting results (Díaz-Campos 2004; Avello 2010; Sanz et al. 2013).

A study within the SALA project which especially captured our interest was that of Mora (2008). He looked at the effects of a SA period preceded by a FI period on L2 phonological development and the subsequent retention effects measured 15 months upon return from the SA. As for the specific abilities on focus, L2 production was studied, with VOT of English voiceless plosive consonants used to measure it. In addition, he also dealt with phonemic contrasts to test for perception accuracy. He found slight non-significant positive effects of SA on VOT duration in voiceless stops by Catalan/Spanish speakers after a period of FI. That is to say, the positive effects were found only after the FI period. The SA period was reported to have had positive influence on the VOT production of those informants.

ESL learners with a Romance language as their L1 tend to produce intermediate VOT values that arise from cross-language influence in VOT studies (Flege 1987; Flege et al. 1998; Reis & Nobre-Oliveira 2007; Yavaş & Wildermuth 2006; Mora 2008; Schwartzhaupt & Kickhöfel 2014; Alves & Zimmer 2015). It could be the case that VOT does not take priority for learners, due to its allophonic character (Alves & Zimmer 2015). The Speech Learning Model (SLM) has provided so far the soundest basis to account for these results. It attributes L2 phonological errors mostly to incorrect perception, although other causes are not discarded. More specifically, Flege (1995) claims that the L1 and L2 categories coexist in a common phonological space, inevitably influencing each other, leading hence to a bidirectional interlanguage interaction. In this sense, the further apart an L2 sound is perceived to be from an L1 sound in that phonological space, the more likely it is to be discerned. In contrast, if the L1 and L2 sounds are close to each other, category assimilation is said to take place. However, if there are cues which differ from one language to the other, learners might be sensitive to them. This is explained through the notion of categorical perception, because "even if listeners perceive two speech sounds as belonging to the same category, they subconsciously perceive a difference, as stimuli that fit better into a given category are easier and faster to process" (Bach 2012: 25). This would ultimately lead to merged categories or intermediate values between the L1 and the L2. This is the case of VOT, which has hence been selected as an appropriate measure to shed light on L2 speech production in the present study. VOT has most generally been defined as "the interval between the release of the stop and the onset of glottal vibration, that is, voicing" (Abramson & Lisker 1964: 389). Interestingly, there is an overlap between English voiced stops and Spanish voiceless stops at the phonemic level Yavaş (2007), which might confuse Spanish learners of English. In contrast, English voiceless stops find no equivalent in the Spanish system. This explains the difficulty Spanish learners face when acquiring the long lag of English voiceless stops. They normally produce English voiceless stops without their characteristic aspiration. See Yavaş (2007) for a more detailed comparison between English and Spanish plosives.

Although there is no absolute value for each plosive, some authors (Kent & Read 1992; Toribio et al. 2005) indicate that the standard VOT patterns in English are 55ms for /p/, 70ms for /t/ and 80ms for /k/. Importantly, these values apply only to stressed syllables in word-initial position (Reis & Nobre-Oliveira 2007), as stress is a factor of variation in VOT production. Normally, stops in unstressed syllables display lower VOT values than their stressed counterparts (Abramson & Lisker 1967). In contrast, this value is of 30ms for the VOT of word initial

/p t k/ in Romance languages Yavaş (2007); Schwartzhaupt & Kickhöfel (2014). ESL learners with a Romance language as their L1 tend to produce English word-initial voiceless stops with a duration longer than 30ms, but shorter than typical native values.

Lastly, three independent factors have been found to affect VOT duration: speaking rate, place of articulation and height of the preceding vowel. Speaking rate has been found to be the most influential factor in VOT variation; the faster one speaks, the shorter one's VOT values are (Reis & Nobre-Oliveira 2007; Mora 2008; Bach 2012). Hence, speaking style has an effect on pronunciation, an idea which comes originally from Labov (1972). This can therefore pose challenges to VOT studies, given the difficulty to account for the variety in the speaking rate of informants. As for place of articulation, VOT has been reported to increase "as the place of articulation progresses farther back in the oral cavity" (Yavaş & Wildermuth 2006: 260), which explains that velar stop consonants have the longest average VOT (Cho & Ladefoged 1999). Lastly, the height of the vowel preceding the target stop might affect its VOT value, with longer VOT values found in the context of higher vowels than lower vowels (Flege et al. 1998; Yavaş & Wildermuth 2006).

3 The study

The present study aims to provide a complement to the SALA project. Whereas the SALA project examined the impact of an SA period following a FI period, in the current study, we focus on the effects of a FI period following a SA period on L2 oral production by a group of undergraduate Catalan/Spanish bilinguals. It is intended as a follow-up study based on Mora's (2008) SALA study, which measured the effects of a SA period preceded by a FI period on L2 phonological development[1]. Importantly, VOT constitutes the only phenomenon explored in our research, unlike in Mora (2008), who also looks at the perception of vowel contrasts. For this reason, VOT is more thoroughly analysed here.

With the purpose of offering a counterbalanced view of his results, Time 2 and Time 3 in the data collection of the SALA project have been reversed in our study, resulting in Time 2 (T2) and Time 1 (T1), respectively. T1 in our data collection corresponds to the beginning of the period of FI, and also the end of the SA period.

---

[1]Data collection times in Mora's (2008) research were those of the SALA project: upon students' enrolment (T1), after two terms of formal instruction (about 80 hours) (T2), after a SA term (T3) in an English-speaking country (this included about 40 hours of FI), and 15 months later, after a two-term period without instruction/exposure to English.

T1 data were collected immediately after participants' return from their SA. Then, after 2 months of FI, Time 2 (T2) data collection took place. The data collected allow us to test whether the VOTs produced at pre-test and post-test significantly differ as a result of the FI experience, preceded by a SA term. The impact of FI (with no explicit attention to pronunciation) is the independent variable and VOT duration of voiceless plosive English consonants is the dependent variable. Additional independent variables explored are (i) proficiency level, (ii) speaking style, (iii) vowel height and (iv) place of articulation.

Taking into account the difficulties for EFL learners with Spanish/Catalan as their L1 to produce the correspondent aspiration of English voiceless stops, this study seeks to answer the following research questions (RQ) and states the corresponding hypotheses (H):

RQ1. Does a 2-month FI period immediately following a 3-month SA period have an effect on the VOT production of voiceless plosive consonants by Spanish/Catalan EFL participants?

H1. The 2-month FI period preceded by a SA term will have a positive though not necessarily large impact on the duration of the VOT production of voiceless stops by the advanced Spanish/Catalan learners tested. More specifically, informants are expected to produce higher VOT values at T2 than at T1 but still not reaching native values, in line with the literature.

In addition, proficiency level (measured at T2) is addressed, as well as factors influencing VOT production such as task effect (i.e. speaking style), vowel height and place of articulation. In order to shed light on these issues, the research subquestions (SRQ) below and their corresponding hypotheses (HSRQ) have been identified:

SRQ1.1. Do results vary when proficiency level as measured through vocabulary size at T2 is taken into account?

HSRQ1.1. No significant differences in VOT values are expected as a function of proficiency level as tested both after the SA and the FI periods, in line with Alves & Zimmer (2015). Any differences found triggered by this variable are expected to result in larger improvement by low level learners than by more advanced ones, following Collentine's (2009) notion of *threshold level*.

SRQ1.2. Are there differences in the VOT values as a function of task type (i.e. speaking style) as measured through words produced in two different tasks (text reading-aloud task vs. carrier sentence task)?[2]

HSRQ1.2. The VOT values obtained from the read-aloud text are expected to be shorter than those gathered from the carrier phrase task, as VOT values tend to decrease in continuous speech in contrast with words uttered in isolation[3] (Labov 1972; Mora 2008; Bach 2012).

SRQ1.3. Are there differences in the VOT values as a function of the height of the vowel following the target voiceless plosive consonant?

HSRQ1.3. Longer VOT values are expected in the context of high vowels as opposed to low ones, according to Flege et al. (1998).

SRQ1.4. Does place of articulation have an effect on VOT duration?

HSRQ1.4. Higher VOT values will be obtained for /k/ than for the other stops as a function of place of articulation. In turn, the shortest VOT values are expected to be obtained for /p/, according to Yavaş & Wildermuth (2006).

4 Method

4.1 Participants

Thirteen undergraduate students from a university in Barcelona were recruited for the present study (11 females and 2 males[4], mean age = 19.1, *SD* = 0.49).

As for language dominance, all participants are Spanish/Catalan bilinguals. However, not all of them report feeling equally dominant in both languages (see Figure 1). More than a half feel Catalan-dominant, according to the answers they provided to the questionnaire they were administered.

Participants belong to the institution's intact groups, which are organized on the basis of an online entrance test pitched at a B2-C1 level. However, in order to check the real homogeneity of the group, an X/Y_lex vocabulary size test was

---

[2] A series of sentences containing target words to be elicited.

[3] Words elicited in the carrier-phrase task cannot be considered to be in complete isolation. See section 4.2 for a more detailed explanation of the purpose of each task.

[4] The fact that the vast majority of participants are females is due to the high number of females taking the degree informants were recruited from. As a consequence, it was not possible to have a balanced amount of males and females. This also prevented us from studying possible gender effects.

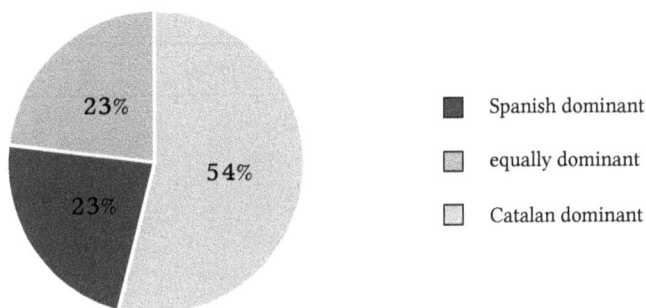

Figure 1: Self-reported language dominance

administered (see Meara 2005 and Meara & Miralpeix 2006 for thorough descriptions of this test), showing that our participants differed in their lexical competence. Making claims as to the informants' proficiency level by looking only at their lexical knowledge would result in oversimplification, since other areas such as grammatical and pragmatic knowledge, for instance, would be neglected. However, for the purpose of this investigation, vocabulary size was judged to be an adequate proxy for general linguistic proficiency (Milton 2010); considering that the main focus of the study is pronunciation, and that it has been shown to have a relatively weak correlation with general language proficiency, it was considered unnecessary to make participants undergo a time-consuming language proficiency test. Following previous studies that use X/Y lex vocabulary test as a proficiency measure (e.g. Meara 2005 and Meara & Miralpeix 2006), the test scores are divided into different ranges that correspond to the proficiency levels set by the Common European Framework of Reference for Languages (CEFR). See Table 1 for correspondences.

According to the vocabulary size test results, participants were placed into three different levels of CEFRL proficiency, A, B and C (see Figure 2). As it can be observed, 46% of the participants have a C level, four of which fall in the C2 range. The score of the other two participants corresponds to the C1 level. Of the 39% of learners who have a B level two learners fall in the B2 range and the other three at a B1 level. A learner scoring at an A1 level and another one at an A2 level constitute the 15% scoring within the A level range.

Three native speakers participated in the study as a baseline group (2 female, 1 male; mean age = 24.8, SD = 0.58). They all share a similar linguistic background, as they are linguistic majors and have a high command of two foreign languages,

Table 1: Vocabulary size following common European Framework for Reference: X_Lex Score equivalences

Vocabulary size	CEFR level
<1500	A1
1500-2500	A2
2750-3250	B1
3250-3750	B2
3750-4500	C1
4500-5000	C2

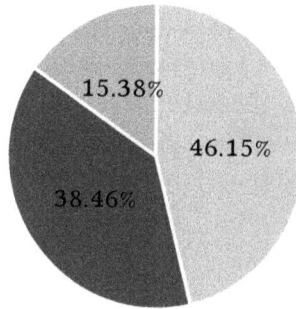

Figure 2: . CEFR proficiency level according to vocabulary size

namely Spanish and French. Two participants are speakers of American English and the third participant is a speaker of Hiberno-English. For the purpose of this investigation, it is considered that VOT values do not differ as a function of language variety among native speakers, as they produce native-like values (i.e. above 60ms) (Lowenstein & Nittrouer 2008).

4.2 Procedure, tasks and stimuli

The factors found to influence VOT production mentioned above are taken into account in the present study (i.e. speaking style, vowel height and place of artic- ulation). Speech samples were obtained for subsequent acoustic analysis. VOT was the segmental measure under scrutiny. Only voiceless stops in word-initial position and followed by a stressed vowel were included in the VOT analysis. Thirty-one word-initial voiceless stops produced three times by each of the 16 subjects (13 learners and three natives) at two data collection times were measured.

Participants were recorded in high quality sound-proof booths with the Audacity software and a *Rode NT-1AX* microphone. They were instructed to complete two tasks: a carrier sentence task (isolated target words embedded in a carrier sentence – i.e. *I say X, I say X now, I say X twice*) and a read aloud task (target words embedded in a text to be read continuously). The carrier-sentence/ read-aloud tasks were conceived to test participants' VOT production of word-initial stops in stressed syllables. Participants were instructed to articulate the stimuli as clearly as possible in both tasks, but especially the target words present in the carrier-sentence task.

Thirty-one monosyllabic words starting with a voiceless stop (/p, t, k/) were selected for the test. There were 29 distractors, resulting in a total of 60 words. Vowel height was taken into account, as it is an influencing factor in VOT production (Yavaş & Wildermuth 2006). Of the 11 words starting with /p/, the stop was followed by a high vowel in five of the items (*peach, pill, pear, pin, pig*) and by a low vowel in six of them (*pub, pan, park, pup, part, pun*). Of the ten words starting with /t/, the stop was followed by a high vowel in five instances (*tear, tip, two, ten, tent*) and by a low vowel in five of them (*tan, tuck, touch, tart, toss*). As for the ten words starting with /k/, the stop was followed by a high vowel in five cases (*key, could, kill, kilt, kit*) and by a low one in the remaining five (*cod, card, cot, cap, cut*). See Table 2 for a complete stimuli list. Distractors are presented in Table 3. The 60 items were randomized and displayed in a PowerPoint presentation for the carrier-sentence task.

Table 2: . Stimuli list for carrier sentence task

/p/		/t/		/k/	
HV	LV	HV	LV	HV	LV
peach	**pub**	tear	**tan**	**key**	cod
pill	pan	tip	tuck	could	card
pear	**park**	**two**	touch	kill	cot
pin	pup	**ten**	**tart**	kilt	cap
pig	part	tent	toss	kit	cut
	pun				

The second task was a text designed to be read aloud naturally with the purpose of taking into account the effect of speaking style. In order to do so, 12 items

Table 3: Distractors for carrier sentence task

bark	group	Bart	dart	beach	Dutch
duck	do	bun	ghee	grew	gap
God	big	dent	bear	dear	ban
Dan	den	got	doss	guilt	bin
Bill	good	guard	gut	dip	

starting with a voiceless stop were selected (in bold in Table 2), four of which begin with /p/ (*pill, peach, pub, park*), four with /t/ (*two, ten, tan, tart*) and four with /k/ (*keys, could, cod, card*). In 6 items, the stop was immediately followed by a high vowel (*key, ten, could, pill, two, peach*) and in the other 6, the stop was immediately followed by a low vowel (*tan, park, pub, cod, tart, card*). The text was printed and physically handed to the participants for them to read aloud.

The tasks were administered in two different orders with the purpose of counterbalancing task effects. In Order 1 the carrier sentence task was performed first, whereas in Order 2, participants started by reading the text. They were asked to read the text as naturally as possible. Additionally, at T1 the learners completed the Carlet-SALA questionnaire, a language background questionnaire that resulted from the combination of the questionnaire used in Carlet (2017) and the SALA questionnaire on SA conditions. They did so once they had performed the task. Lastly, they performed the vocabulary size test (Meara 2005; Meara & Miralpeix 2006) at T2.

5 Results and discussion

5.1 Research question 1

Given the sample size, Wilcoxon signed-rank nonparametric tests for related samples were performed. As shown in Table 4 and Figure 3, participants displayed slightly longer VOT values at T2 than at T1. However, the 2-month FI period immediately following a 3-month long SA period was found to have no statistically significant effect on the VOT production of voiceless plosive consonants ($z = 0.384$, $N = 13$, $p = .3505$, one-tailed).

Similar results were also obtained when analysing the two tasks separately. As can be seen in Table 4 and Figure 3, participants displayed slightly longer VOT values at T2 than at T1 for both tasks. A further Wilcoxon-test was run in order to reveal whether this difference reached statistical significance. Again, the 2-month FI period immediately following a 3-month long SA term was found to have no statistically significant effect on the VOT production of voiceless plosive consonants in either the text (z = 0.314, N = 13, p = .3765, one-tailed) or the carrier sentence task (z = 0.454, N = 13, p = .325, one-tailed).

Table 4: Mean VOT measurements (ms) at both testing times (T1, T2)

	Non-native speakers				Native English speakers	
	T1 ms	(sd)	T2 ms	(sd)	ms	(sd)
Both tasks	51.05	(20.39)	51.54	(18.13)	65.47	(24.94)
Words	54.93	(23.55)	55.07	(20.13)	67.96	(29.87)

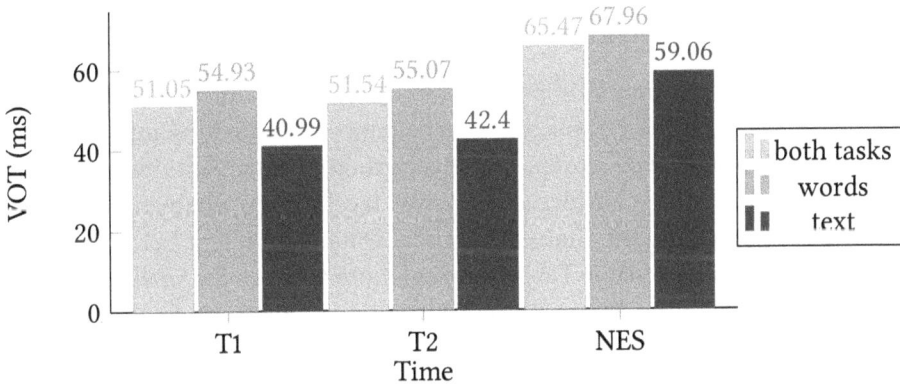

Figure 3: Mean VOT measurements (ms) at both testing times (T1, T2)

These results may be interpreted as follows: The lack of explicit focus on L2 phonology in the FI participants received might account for the fact that the slight lengthening of VOT values displayed at T2 failed to reach statistical significance. This view is supported by those studies stressing the need for explicit attention to L2 phonology in FI for the improvement of L2 production accuracy (Darcy et al. 2012; Gordon & Darcy 2012; Calvo Benzies 2014).

Hence, the answer to our research question is that a 2-month FI period preceded by a 3-month long SA term has no statistically significant effect on the VOT production of voiceless plosive consonants. Our hypothesis has not been confirmed as results are not significant. However, we have obtained a numerical tendency towards the native-like model in the VOTs of plosive consonants in initial position. Importantly, the native group always produced longer VOTs than the non-native participants. The shorter VOT found for non-NES confirmes the SLM's prediction and finding that EFL learners produce intermediate VOT values between their L1 and their L2 (Flege 1987; 1995; Flege et al. 1998; Reis & Nobre-Oliveira 2007; Yavaş 2007; Mora 2008; Wrembel 2011; 2013; Schwartzhaupt & Kickhöfel 2014; Alves & Zimmer 2015). As explained by the SLM, learners perceive the L2 sounds in relation to their pre-existing L1 categories. Therefore, this model accounts for the intermediate VOT values produced by our participants, whose interlanguage is in the process of moving towards the target language values. Importantly, the SLM does not predict that learners can completely attain native-like VOT values. It must be noted, however, that no statistical tests were run comparing both groups due to the low number of participants. For this reason, the native speakers served the present investigation solely as a baseline group.

5.2 Sub-research question 1.1

In order to assess whether VOT productions differed as a function of proficiency level (assessed with the lexical test), participants were divided into two proficiency groups (high level group, low level group). Participants with A and B proficiency levels were considered the lower level group, whereas participants with a C level made up the high-level group. Data gathered at both times were averaged and are displayed in Table 5 and in Figure 4. Given the small sample size of each individual group, the results concerning this sub-research question were not submitted to statistical analyses. Group differences will thus be discussed in terms of numerical differences in the descriptive statistics.

Table 5: Mean VOT measurements (ms) as a function of proficiency level

Participants	T1 ms	(sd)	T2 ms	(sd)
Native English speakers		65.47 (24.94)		
High level group	60.11	(21.26)	55.83	(16.56)
Low level group	43.27	(20.12)	47.87	(18.96)

Interestingly, it can be observed in Table 5 that the high-level group obtained numerically higher and more native-like VOT values than the low-level group at the outset of the study, that is, after the SA period. This result might point

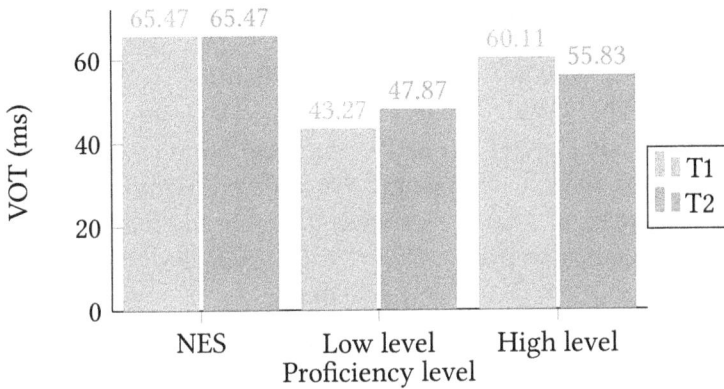

Figure 4: Mean VOT measurements (ms) as a function of proficiency level

towards a tendency of language experience to have a potential impact on L2 phonological category learning, as predicted by the SLM. Along these lines, the more advanced group experienced stronger effects of category learning than the least experienced group, as a result of the SA period.

Looking more closely at the performance of both groups over time, the lower level group shows the largest improvement (43.27% to 47.87%). In fact, the higher proficiency group experiences a slight numerical decrease in VOT (60.11% to 55.83%). These results point to a tendency for improvement for the lower level group, while the tendency points in the opposite direction for the high-level group. These results, even though drawn from a small sample, may suggest that the high-level group had reached their ceiling VOT values during the SA period, whereas the lower level group still had room for improvement. A potential reason for this is that the likely L2 categories formed by the high-level group for the target segments are more robust than those of the low-level group. Therefore, the FI period following the SA might have been more effective in enhancement of L2 VOT production for the low-level group than for their more advanced counterpart. This numerical tendency found in our data is in line with Collentine's (2009) notion of a *threshold level.*

Thus, it can be said that proficiency level seems to play a significant role in the VOT production of English plosive consonants in initial stressed position by Catalan/Spanish EFL learners, at least as far as the effects of an FI period following a SA period are concerned. However, given the small sample size and the lack of inferential statistical analysis, this study should be seen as mainly exploratory.

5.3 Sub-research question 1.2.

In order to explore whether the VOT values obtained significantly differ as a function of task type, a Wilcoxon-test was performed on the non-native data. As shown in Table 6 and Figure 5, for both the non-native and the native groups, the VOT durations produced when reading the text were significantly shorter than those obtained during the carrier sentence task at both times ($z = 2.830$, $N = 13$, $p = .0025$, one-tailed) as well as at T1 ($z = 2.621$, $N = 13$, $p = .0045$, one-tailed) and at T2 ($z = 2.900$, $N = 13$, $p = .002$, one-tailed).

Table 6: Mean VOT measurements (ms) as a function of task (text vs. words)

| | Non-native speakers | | | | | | Native English speakers | |
| | T1 | | T2 | | T1+T2 | | | |
	ms	(sd)	ms	(sd)	ms	(sd)	ms	(sd)
Words	54.93	(23.55)	55.07	(20.13)	55.00	(20.91)	67.96	(29.87)
Text	40.99	(14.55)	42.40	(13.98)	41.69	(13.28)	59.06	(13.54)

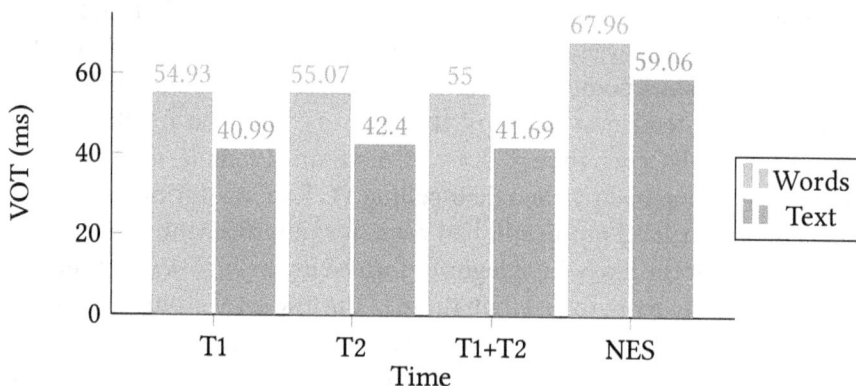

Figure 5: Mean VOT measurements (ms) as a function of task (text vs. words)

The results presented here suggest that speaking style significantly affects the VOT production of Catalan/Spanish learners of English, answering sub-research question 1.2. Despite the lack of statistical differences between the native and non-native groups, the numerical values obtained from the natives suggest that speaking style affected both our groups of participants similarly. Our hypothesis is thus confirmed. Our data support Labov's (1972) original idea that speaking style does have an effect on pronunciation and more specifically on VOT production, as also found by Mora (2008) and Bach (2012), confirming that in continuous speech, VOT values tend to decrease, whereas they tend to increase when produced in (quasi-)isolation.

5.4 Sub-research question 1.3.

With the purpose of determining whether there are differences in the VOT values as a function of the height of the vowel, another Wilcoxon-test was conducted. As observed in Table 7 and Figure 6, VOTs produced preceding a high vowel were longer than those followed by a low vowel both for the native and the non-native speakers. The test on the non-native speaker data revealed that this difference did reach statistical significance between the VOT values of high and low vowels (z = 3.180, N = 13, p= .0005, one-tailed).

Table 7: Mean VOT measurements (ms) as a function of vowel height averaged across time (T1+T2).

	Non-native speakers		Native English speakers	
	ms	(sd)	ms	(sd)
High vowel	56.52	(18.04)	71.51	(25.75)
Low vowel	46.25	(18.96)	59.72	(24.18)

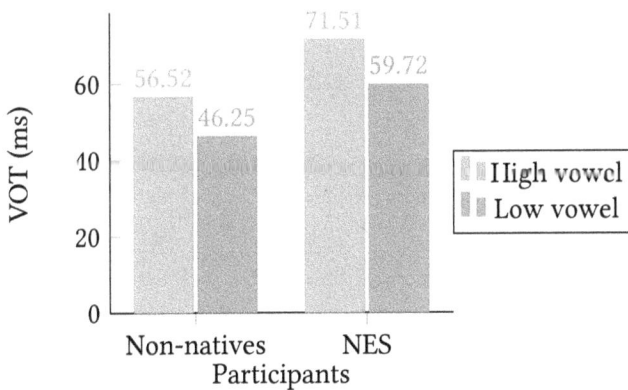

Figure 6: Mean VOT measurements (ms) as a function of vowel height averaged across time (T1+T2).

These results suggest that vowel height does have a significant effect on VOT production of Catalan/Spanish learners of English, answering sub-research question 1.3. Interestingly, a similar pattern was observed for the native speakers. The hypothesis formulated regarding this sub-RQ is confirmed by the data and in line with Flege et al. (1998) and Yavaş & Wildermuth's (2006) findings that vowel height does influence VOT production.

5.5 Sub-research question 1.4.

To determine whether VOT values differed as a function of place of articulation, three Wilcoxon-tests were run on the data obtained from non-native speakers. As shown by Table 8 and Figure 7, /k/ displayed the longest VOT values, with /t/ in the second place and /p/ having triggered the shortest durations for the non-native group. However, natives produced slightly longer VOTs for /t/ than for /k/. In turn, VOT values for /p/ were the shortest for this group.

Table 8: Mean VOT measurements (ms) as a function of place of articulation averaged across time (T1+T2).

	K		T		P	
	ms	(sd)	ms	(sd)	ms	(sd)
Non-native speakers	61.62	(20,17)	57.50	(22.09)	35.78	(15.26)
Native English speakers	70.44	(24.68)	72.79	(22.81)	54.01	(27.28)

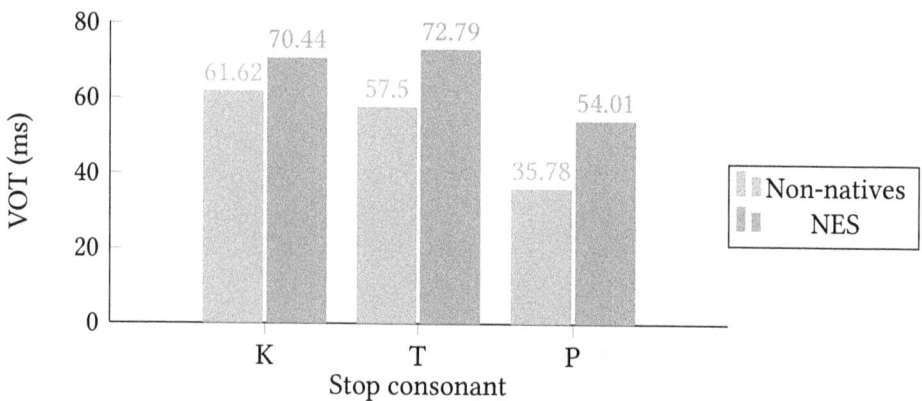

Figure 7: Mean VOT measurements (ms) as a function of place of articulation averaged across time (T1+T2).

The test revealed that VOT values obtained for /p/ were significantly different from those obtained for /k/ (z = 3.180, N = 13, p = .0005, one-tailed) and for /t/ (z = 3.180, N = 13, p = .0005, one-tailed), respectively. However, VOT values obtained for /k/ and /t/ were not significantly different from one another (z = 1.223, N = 13, p = .1105, one-tailed).

The relative similarity of VOT values for /k/ and /t/ might be explained by the fact that they are quite similar in native speakers as well. Moreover, according to Alves & Zimmer (2015), aspiration is a cue that learners pay attention to, which might explain why the VOT values for /k/ and /t/ did not to reach statistical significance in the present study. Specifically, it is more salient in some places of articulation than in others. This seems to indicate that our participants are in the process of creating L2 categories for the target segments, as their performance shows certain similarities with that of the baseline group. Although their VOT durations never reach those produced by the natives, as predicted by the SLM, the initial hypothesis that place of articulation affects VOT (Yavaş & Wildermuth 2006) is confirmed.

6 Summary and conclusions

The present study aimed at making a contribution to the SALA project by providing a study not undertaken before. Moreover, it sought to reduce the present research gap in the field of L2 phonology acquisition during SA in combination with a subsequent FI period. It sought to examine and measure the effects of a 2-month FI period, with no specific training in the learners' L2 phonological abilities, preceded by a 3-month long SA term, on the VOT production by Catalan/Spanish EFL learners.

Results revealed that a 2-month FI period preceded by a 3-month long SA term undergone by our participants had no statistically significant effects on their VOT production of English voiceless plosive consonants, although a tendency towards improvement was observed. Such findings might be due to the limited statistical power of this exploratory study, but they may also lead one to reflect on the absence of explicit instruction on L2 phonology which characterises most FI. We are thus led to wonder whether an FI with explicit instruction on L2 phonology would have a positive effect on L2 phonological acquisition in EFL learners.

Moreover, proficiency level might play a role on VOT production, given that the high level group displayed higher values than the low level one, although this was not statistically confirmed. In addition, ceiling effects were found in the advanced group, whereas the lower level group seemed to have more room for improvement. These findings must tentatively be taken as tendencies. On the other hand, speaking style, vowel height, and place of articulation do significantly affect VOT production of voiceless plosives by Catalan/Spanish learners. The native group displayed a similar numerical pattern, which indicates that these three independent factors affect both groups in a similar way. However, natives always produce higher VOT values for English voiceless stops, confirming that EFL learners tend to produce intermediate VOT values between their L1 and their L2 for the same consonants. As for speaking style, words in (quasi-)isolation (carrier sentence task) displayed significantly higher values than those produced in continuous speech (read aloud task). We might interpret these results by stating that the more attention is paid when uttering words, the more likely the sounds produced are to be clearly articulated. As for vowel height, VOT values produced before a high vowel were significantly longer than those produced preceding a low vowel. Finally, concerning place of articulation, VOTs for /k/ displayed the highest values, with /t/ in the second place and values for /p/ being the shortest. It must be stressed that only the /k/ vs. /t/ comparison failed to reach statistical significance. The results concerning place of articulation can be understood through the SLM. Our participants seem to be in the process of creating L2 categories for voiceless stops, as they performed similarly to the native group regarding the lack of difference between /k/ and /t/. This suggests that aspiration is more salient in some places of articulation than in others Alves & Zimmer (2015).

7 Limitations and directions for prospective research

In this final section, we identify some of the limitations of the current study and highlight directions for future research. When work on this study started, it was no longer possible to test participants prior to their experience abroad, and thus VOT measurements before SA could not be obtained. The reason is that informants were already abroad by data collection T1. Hence, all collected data were gathered only after the SA period, so the obtained VOTs cannot be contrasted against those prior to SA, which would presumably have provided valuable information as for the learners' VOT departure values.

One other issue is the measurement of proficiency level. Testing should have been conducted at both data collection times, and not only at T2. Time constraints prevented this from happening.

In addition, the number of participants was low, both for the non-native and the native groups. This prevented us from drawing general conclusions and accentuates the fact that conclusions related to our population must be taken with caution. Finally, the native speakers who served as a baseline group are not mono-lingual, so their VOT values might have been influenced by other languages. However, all of them are late bilinguals.

Despite the lack of statistical reliability for some of the tendencies we found, they leave a door open to prospective research, namely with a larger population so that more robust claims can be made. A further study should measure the effects of a post-stay-abroad FI period including either explicit instruction on L2 phonology or L2 phonetic training and focusing either on the VOT of English stops or on other relevant acoustic cues.

References

Abramson, Arthur S. & Leigh Lisker. 1964. A cross-language study of voicing in initial stops: Acoustical measurements. *Word* 20. 384–422.

Abramson, Arthur S. & Leigh Lisker. 1967. The voicing dimension: Some experiments in comparative phonetics. In *Proceedings of the 6th international congress of phonetic sciences*, 9–15. Prague: Academia.

Alves, Ubiratã Kickhöfel & Márcia Cristina Zimmer. 2015. Perception and production of English VOT patterns by Brazilian learners: The role of multiple acoustic cues in a DST perspective. *Alfa: Revista de Lingüística (São José do Rio Preto* 59(1). 157–180.

Archibald, John. 2005. Second language phonology as redeployment of L1 phonological knowledge. *The Canadian Journal of Linguistics* 50. 285–314.

Avello, Pilar. 2010. The effect of study abroad on Catalan/Spanish bilinguals' production of English /i- ɪ/ & /æ - ʌ/ contrasting pairs. Paper presented at the 6th International Conference on Language Acquisition - CIAL, Universitat de Barcelona, Spain.

Bach, Ocke-Schwen. 2012. *Coexistence of phonetic systems in Danish/English bilinguals: A study of the production of VOT categories*. Aarhus: University of Aarhus. (M.A. dissertation.)

Brecht, Richard, Dan Davidson & Ralph Ginsberg. 1995. Predictors of foreign language gain during study abroad. In Barbara Freed (ed.), *Second language acquisition in a study abroad context*, 37–66. Amsterdam: Benjamins.

Calvo Benzies, Yolanda Joy. 2014. The teaching of pronunciation in Spain: Students' and teachers' views. In Tania Pattison (ed.), *IATEFL 2013 Liverpool Conference Selections*, 106–108. Faversham, UK: IATEFL.

Calvo Benzies, Yolanda Joy. 2016. *The teaching and learning of English pronunciation in Spain. An analysis and appraisal of students' and teachers' views and teaching materials.* Santiago: University of Santiago de Compostela. (Doctoral dissertation.)

Carlet, Angélica. 2017. *L2 perception and production of English consonants and vowels by Catalan speakers: The effects of attention and training task in a cross-training study.* Barcelona: Universitat Autònoma de Barcelona. (Doctoral dissertation.)

Cho, Taehong & Peter Ladefoged. 1999. Variation and universals in VOT: Evidence from 18 languages. *Journal of Phonetics* 27. 207–229.

Collentine, Joseph G. 2009. Study abroad research: Findings, implications and future directions. In Michael H. Long & Catherine J. Doughty (eds.), *The handbook of language teaching*, 218–233. Malden, MA: Blackwell.

Dalton, Christiane & Barbara Seidlhofer. 1994. *Pronunciation.* Oxford: Oxford University Press.

Darcy, Isabelle, Doreen Ewert & Ryan Lidster. 2012. Bringing pronunciation instruction back into the classroom: An ESL teachers' pronunciation "toolbox". In John Levis & Kimberly LeVelle (eds.), *Proceedings of the 3rd pronunciation in second language learning and teaching conference*, 93–108. Ames, IA: Iowa State University.

DeKeyser, Robert. 2007. Study abroad as foreign language practice. In Robert DeKeyser (ed.), *Practice in a second language: Perspectives from applied linguistics and cognitive psychology*, 208–226. Cambridge: Cambridge University Press.

Derwing, Tracey M. 2010. Utopian goals for pronunciation teaching. In John Levis & Kimberly LeVelle (eds.), *Proceedings of the 1st pronunciation in second language learning and teaching conference*, 24–37. Ames, IA: Iowa State University.

Derwing, Tracey M. & Jennifer Ann Foote. 2011. 2010 national survey of pronunciation teaching: Deja vu. Paper presented at the American Association for Applied Linguistics, Chicago, IL.

Díaz-Campos, Manuel. 2004. Context of learning in the acquisition of Spanish second language phonology. *Studies in Second Language Acquisition* 26. 249–273.

Flege, James Emil. 1987. The production of 'new' and 'similar' phones in a foreign language: Evidence for the effect of equivalent classification. *Journal of Phonetics* 15. 47–65.

Flege, James Emil. 1995. Second language speech learning theory, findings, and problems. In Winifred Strange (ed.), *Speech perception and linguistic experience: Issues in cross-language research*, 233–277. Timonium, MD: York Press.

Flege, James Emil & Elaina M. Frieda. 1997. Amount of native-language (L1) use affects the pronunciation of an L2. *Journal of Phonetics* 25. 169–186.

Flege, James Emil, Elaina M. Frieda, Amandas C. Walley & Lauren A. Randazza. 1998. Lexical factors and segmental accuracy in second language speech production. *Studies in Second Language Acquisition* 20(2). 155–187.

Foote, Jennifer Ann, Amy K. Holtby & Tracey M. Derwing. 2011. Survey of pronunciation teaching in adult ESL programs in Canada, 2010. *TESL Canada Journal* 29(1). 1–22.

Gordon, James. & Isabelle Darcy. 2012. *Effects of explicit pronunciation instruction on segmentals and suprasegmentals: The development of comprehensible speech in L2 learners.* Paper presented at American Association for Applied Linguistics, Boston, MA.

Han, Zhaohong. 2004. *Fossilization in adult second language acquisition.* Clevedon, UK: Multilingual Matters.

Kent, Raymond D. & Charles Read. 1992. *The acoustic analysis of speech.* San Diego: Singular.

Labov, William. 1972. The social stratification of (r) in New York city department stores. In William Labov (ed.), *Sociolinguistics patterns*, 43–54. Philadelphia: University of Pennsylvania Press.

López-Serrano, Sonia. 2010. Learning languages in study abroad and at home contexts: A critical review of comparative studies. *Porta Linguarum* 13. 149–163.

Lowenstein, Joanna H. & Susan Nittrouer. 2008. Patterns of acquisition of native voice onset time in English-learning children. *The Journal of the Acoustical Society of America* 124(2). 1180–1191. . http://doi.org/10.1121/1.2945118.

Meara, Paul M. 2005. *X_Lex: The swansea vocabulary levels test* (Version 2.05.). Swansea: Lognostics.

Meara, Paul M. & Imma Miralpeix. 2006. *Y_Lex: The Swansea advanced vocabulary levels test* (Version 2.05.). Swansea: Lognostics.

Milton, James. 2010. The development of vocabulary breadth across the CEFR levels. In Inge Bartning, Maisa Martin & Ineke Vedder (eds.), *Communicative proficiency and linguistic development: Intersections between SLA and language testing research* (Eurosla Monographs Series 1), 211–232. European Second Language Association.

Mora, Joan C. 2008. Learning context effects on the acquisition of a second language phonology. In Carmen Pérez-Vidal, Maria Juan-Garau & Aurora Bel (eds.), *A portrait of the young in the new multilingual Spain*, 241–263. Clevendon, UK: Multilingual Matters.

Mora, Joan C. 2014. Inter-subject variation in L2 speech perception and cognitive abilities. In Raquel Casesnoves, Montserrat Forcadell & Núria Gavaldà (eds.), *Ens queda la paraula. Estudis de lingüística aplicada en honor de M. Teresa Turell*, 83–101. Barcelona: Institut Universitari de Lingüística Aplicada.

Moyer, Alene. 2009. Input as a critical means to an end: Quantity and quality of experience in L2 phonological attainment. In Thorsten Piske & Martha Young-Scholten (eds.), *Input Matters in SLA*, 159–174. Clevedon, UK: Multilingual Matters.

Pérez-Vidal, Carmen. 2014b. Study abroad and formal instruction contrasted: The SALA project. In Carmen Pérez-Vidal (ed.), *Second language acquisition in study abroad and formal instruction contexts*, 17–57. Amsterdam: John Benjamins.

Reis, Mara Sliva & Denize Nobre-Oliveira. 2007. Effects of perceptual training on the identification and production of English voiceless plosives aspiration by Brazilian EFL learners. In *Proceedings of the 5th International symposium on the acquisition of second language speech* (New Sounds 5), 398–407. Florianopolis: UFPR.

Sanz, Cristina, Alfonso Morales-Front, Charlie Nagle & Colleen Moorman. 2013. *Improvements in pronunciation in a 6 week study abroad program*. Learning without attention. Paper presented at the residence abroad, social networks and second language learning congress, University of Southampton, UK.

Schwartzhaupt, Bruno Moraesa & Alves Ubriatã Kickhöfel. 2014. A influência do contexto fonético-fonológico nos valores de voiceonsete time: Verificação de dados des três sistemas lingüísticos. *Fórum Linguístico* 11(1). 51–68.

Toribio, Almeida Jacqueline, Barbara E. Bullock, Christopher G. Botero & Kristopher Allen Davis. 2005. Perseverative phonetic effects in bilingual code-switching. In Randall Gess & Edward J. Rubin (eds.), *Theoretical and experimental approaches to Romance linguistics*, 291–306. Amsterdam: Benjamins.

Wrembel, Magdalena. 2011. Cross-linguistic influence in third language acquisition of voice onset time. In *Proceedings of the 17th international congress of phonetic sciences*, 2157–2160. Hong Kong.

Wrembel, Magdalena. 2013. *Cross-linguistic influence in the acquisition of VOT in a third language*. Paper presented at the 7th international symposium on the acquisition of second language speech (New Sounds), Concordia University.

Yavaş, Mehmet. 2007. Factors influencing the VOT of English long lag stops and interlanguage phonology. In Andréia S. Rauber, Michael A. Watkins & Barbara O. Baptista (eds.), *New sounds 2007: Proceedings of the 5th international symposium on the acquisition of second language speech*, 492–498. Florianópolis: UFPR.

Yavaş, Mehmet & Renée Wildermuth. 2006. The effects of place of articulation and vowel height in the acquisition of English aspirated stops by Spanish speakers. *International Review of Applied Linguistics in Language Teaching* 44(3). 251–263.

Chapter 8

Teachers' assessment of perceived foreign accent and comprehensibility in adolescent EFL oral production in Study Abroad and Formal Instruction contexts: A mixed-method study

Carmen del Río
Universitat Pompeu Fabra

Maria Juan-Garau
University of the Balearic Islands

Carmen Pérez-Vidal
Universitat Pompeu Fabra

Research on second language acquisition has long been interested in analyzing different learning contexts that language learners experience when trying to improve their target languages (Collentine & Freed 2004) such as formal instruction (FI), study abroad (SA), and, more recently, different types of immersion (Pérez-Vidal 2017). The aim of the present study is to examine two of these contexts, SA and FI at home, in the case of English as a foreign language adolescent learners having Catalan and Spanish as their first languages, an age band which has received comparatively less attention than others (but see Llanes 2012; Llanes & Muñoz 2013). We focus on the learners' foreign accent and comprehensibility, as judged by a group of non-native listeners, with the objective of assessing progress and the relationship between both dimensions, following Trofimovich & Isaacs (2012). Most centrally, we are interested in analyzing the aspects of each speech dimension of focus which have reportedly affected the judges' ratings. In order to do that, speech

Carmen del Río, Maria Juan-Garau & Carmen Pérez-Vidal. Teachers' assessment of perceived foreign accent and comprehensibility in adolescent EFL oral production in Study Abroad and Formal Instruction contexts: A mixed-method study. In Carmen Pérez Vidal, Sonia López-Serrano, Jennifer Ament & Dakota J. Thomas-Wilhelm (eds.), *Learning context effects: Study abroad, formal instruction and international immersion classrooms*, 181–213. Berlin: Language Science Press.
DOI:10.5281/zenodo.1300632

samples were collected longitudinally for the SA (N = 25) and the FI (N = 31) groups of learners, respectively, with a pre-test/post-test design. Listeners were asked to rate and report on the aspects which affected their ratings. Our results reveal that the aspect which most influenced the judges was pronunciation. This places pronunciation at the center of the search for better practices in instructed second language acquisition in line with recently published studies (Van Loon 2002; Darcy et al. 2012; Gordon & Darcy 2012; Saito & Lyster 2012; Grant 2014).

1 Introduction

Within the communicative approach to language teaching, many second language (L2) researchers and teachers would agree that intelligibility is the main aim in oral communication and L2 pronunciation instruction, rather than a native-like accent. Indeed, the main objective of L2 learners in most cases is to be able to communicate and be understood, rather than accent reduction (Pennington & Richards 1986; Derwing & Munro 1997; Jenkins 2000; Munro 2008). The abilities linked to communication have been described on the basis of two constructs, intelligibility and comprehensibility. In previous studies a distinction between these two has been made (Munro & Derwing 1995; 1999; Derwing & Munro 1997; 2009. Intelligibility has been defined as the extent to which a given utterance is understood by a listener, and comprehensibility has been used to refer to the listeners' own perception of how easily they understand an utterance. However, in the present study, we have chosen the term 'comprehensibility' to refer to the construct which some studies have identified as 'intelligibility', in line with Isaacs & Trofimovich (2012).

All in all, both in authentic communication and in the interaction which takes place with teachers in classrooms, accentedness may play a role which, to some extent, may eventually account for the felicitious accomplishment of interactions. This is the focus of our study, which seeks to disentagle the issue of the degree to which speech accentedness may count more than comprehensibility when teachers evaluate learners. More specifically, we first want to examine the correlation between these two speech dimensions based on the ratings provided by the teachers/listeners in our study in relation to the pronunciation of two groups of English as a foreign language (EFL) adolescent learners: one group experiencing a 3-month study abroad (SA) programme, and another group experiencing conventional formal instruction in the at home (AH) institution. In a previous research study (del Río 2013) we compared gains in those two dimensions by each group respectively. Results indicated that SA participants obtained significantly greater gains in FA than the AH group. The findings also suggested that the SA context was more beneficial than the AH context in terms of comprehensibility development, since the percentage of learners improving their comprehensibility scores during SA was significantly larger than the percentage of learners improving their scores in the AH context, and SA learners obtained larger comprehensibility gains than AH learners, although such improvement was not significant (see del Río 2013: 139–164). Second, we want to explore the aspects which listeners consider when evaluating foreign accent and comprehensibility in SA learners' speech samples when completing a perception task. We aim at identifying and drawing comparisons across the different factors underlying the judges' accentedness and comprehensibility ratings (following the analyses conducted by Trofimovich & Isaacs 2012). As pointed out by Isaacs (2010), knowledge of the factors influencing comprehensibility in L2 speech can help teachers to set instructional objectives, integrate pronunciation with the teaching of other skills, and take these questions into account in their assessment practice in the EFL classroom, and when preparing learners for SA experiences.

2   Literature review

Two main principles have traditionally led the discussion about the objectives of pronunciation instruction: the *nativeness principle* versus the *intelligibility principle* (Levis 2005), i.e. comprehensibility. The *nativeness principle* aims at native-like pronunciation for L2 speakers, whereas the *intelligibility principle* considers intelligibility. , That is, how easily messages can be understood (what we refer as comprehensibility in this article)as the primary objective.

Following the latter principle, most L2 pronunciation research does not consider accent reduction to be the goal for communicative teaching and claims that pronunciation teaching should aim at language intelligibility (Kenworthy 1987; Pennington 1996; Derwing 2008; Thomson 2013). Thus, the interest when teaching pronunciation is not centred on the nuances of particular speech sounds, but on getting the L2 learners up to a level of competence which should allow them to deal with everyday communication situations (Gimson 1994).

In this study we have chosen to adopt the construct of 'intelligibility' and not that of nativelikeness in line with Isaacs & Trofimovich (2012), who adopted Levis' (2006) distinction between broad and narrow definitions of intelligibility. In its narrow sense, intelligibility refers to listeners' actual understanding of L2 speech (Munro & Derwing 1999). It is often measured by examining listeners' accuracy in providing orthographic transcriptions of L2 speech, although other methods have also been used (e.g. comprehension questions, true-false statements, reaction times). In its broad sense, intelligibility is defined as listeners' ability to understand speech.

However, the story does not end here, as two other concepts have also been the focus of attention when discussing pronunciation in formal instruction: *foreign accent* and *comprehensibility*. The former reflects how far from target-like standards learners' speech is, the latter, how easy it is for listeners to perceive the information contained in learners' messages (Isaacs 2010). As far as accentedness is concerned, we understand this concept as the listeners' perception of how closely the pronunciation of an L2 utterance resembles that of a NS of English (Munro & Derwing 1995; 1999; Derwing & Munro 1997; 2009. Although L2 learners do not necessarily consider having a native-like pronunciation as a priority, there might be L2 learners who aim at achieving it for different reasons (e.g. professional reasons, building up a certain 'self-image', integrative motivation, etc.). In contrast, we may find L2 learners preferring to retain something of their first language (L1) accent when speaking in an additional language (Porter & Garvin 1989). Dalton & Seidlhofer (1994: 7) note that "pronunciation is so much a matter of self-image that students may prefer to keep their accent deliberately, in order to retain their self-respect or to gain the approval of their peers." This is indeed what we often find as teachers in the foreign language classroom when our students tend to avoid sounding 'English', since this can result in their peers joking about their 'native like accent' (Fisher & Evans 2000). As for comprehensibility, according to Levis (2006: 252), intelligibility "is not usually distinguished from closely related terms such as comprehensibility" and has been typically measured through listeners' ratings of how easily they understand speech (Munro & Derwing 1999). As Isaacs & Trofimovich (2012) pointed out, it is actually comprehensibility (not intelligibility) that is being assessed when listeners rate how easily they understand the information contained in a message. Therefore, in line with Trofimovich & Isaacs (2012), in this study, instead of intelligibility, we have adopted the construct of comprehensibility, which falls under Levis' broad sense of intelligibility and reflects a common approach to assessing intelligibility in oral proficiency scales.

Finally, and most importantly for this study, it must be pointed out that the two constructs, foreign accent and comprehensibility, have been claimed to constitute two partially independent dimensions. Regrettably, this may not be reflected in some assessment rubrics and actual assessment practices, which very often conflate these two different, albeit partially overlapping, dimensions of speech production. As Munro & Derwing (1995: 92) note, we may find pronunciation assessment scales ranging from "not accented, perfectly comprehensible at one endpoint to accented and difficult to understand at the other." Given the possible overlap between different dimensions in popular assessment practices, our research study precisely aims at analyzing whether teachers are aware of these two different constructs currently included in the analysis of speech production. In other words, the aim of this study is to examine the extent to which teachers bear in mind the distinction between foreign accent and comprehensibility when they rate their learners' speech productions.

In this respect, results reported by previous studies examining the relationship between foreign accent and comprehensibility posit that heavily accented speech can often be perfectly understood (Munro & Derwing 1995; 1999; Derwing & Munro 1997; Gallardo del Puerto et al. 2007; Munro 2008; Hayes-Harb & Watzinger-Tharp 2012). Producing comprehensible speech is more than a matter of pronunciation. While it is true that some errors in pronunciation may affect speech comprehensibility, foreign-accented speech does not necessarily impede comprehensibility. Thus, if comprehensibility is the main objective of pronunciation instruction, the degree of foreign accent in L2 learners' oral productions should be of minor concern, and accent reduction should not be a priority. Rather, those aspects of L2 speech that appear to interfere with listeners' comprehension of the learners' production should be the focus. The question is: which aspects do seem to affect comprehensibility?

A research priority is to distinguish the aspects of L2 speech that hinder comprehensibility from those that, while noticeable or irritating, do not impede understanding the message (Munro 2008; Isaacs & Trofimovich 2012). Little empirical research has examined the particular aspects of foreign-accented speech which affect comprehensibility (Munro & Derwing 1995, Munro & Derwing 1999; Zielinski 2008; Isaacs & Trofimovich 2012; Trofimovich & Isaacs 2012). Moreover, opinions of a particular L2 speaker's pronunciation problems may vary from listener to listener since familiarity with accented speech and individual differences in the ability to comprehend L2 speech may influence foreign accent and comprehensibility perception (Gass & Varonis 1984; Munro & Derwing 1999).

In line with Derwing & Munro (2009), we believe it is appropriate to work on those aspects of accent which may affect comprehensibility. Some studies have indicated that pronunciation training can help L2 speakers produce more comprehensible speech. Derwing et al. (1998) examined perceived accentedness, comprehensibility and fluency in the oral productions of L2 learners of English. The learners were assigned to one of these conditions: (1) no specific pronunciation instruction group; (2) global instruction group, who received instruction with a focus on features such as speaking rate, intonation, rhythm, projection, word stress, and sentence stress; and (3) segmental instruction group, who received instruction to improve their production of individual sounds. Their research concluded that even though the two groups receiving instruction in pronunciation showed significant improvement in accentedness and comprehensibility on the sentences, only the group receiving global instruction showed improvement in comprehensibility and fluency in the narratives.

In line with these results, Munro & Derwing (1999: 285) reported that "prosodic errors appear to be a more potent force in the loss of intelligibility than phonetic errors." These findings are in opposition with the actual situation in the EFL classroom, where much pronunciation practice and error correction focuses on the segmental level.

More recently, Trofimovich & Isaacs (2012) and Isaacs & Trofimovich (2012) explored the linguistic aspects which affect foreign accent and comprehensibility. In the former study, Trofimovich & Isaacs (2012) concluded that both dimensions were related to many speech measures, but that "four categories uniquely distinguished accent from comprehensibility, with all categories specific to the dimension of phonology (i.e. vowels and consonants, syllables, sounding native-like, and rhythm)", whereas comprehensibility was additionally linked to grammatical accuracy and lexical richness. Although it is true that speaking involves pronunciation, it is worth highlighting that L2 speech comprehensibility was found to be linked to vocabulary and grammar. In the second study, Isaacs & Trofimovich (2012) studied the construct of comprehensibility in greater depth, and explored the aspects of speech that affected L2 comprehensibility at different ability levels. Based on the analyses of 19 quantitative speech measures, and listeners' judgments and introspective reports, the authors identified five speech measures that distinguished between L2 learners at different comprehensibility levels: "lexical richness and fluency measures differentiated between low-level learners; grammatical and discourse-level measures differentiated between high-level learners; and word stress errors discriminated between learners of all levels" (Isaacs & Trofimovich 2012: 476). Thus, it is interesting to highlight that not only pronunciation features of foreign-accented speech, but also other language aspects affect speech comprehensibility (e.g. vocabulary, grammar, and discourse measures).

The studies mentioned above included English native speakers (NSs) as listeners of L2 learners' oral production. It has been claimed that work on perceived accentedness and comprehensibility with non-native listeners is still insufficient (Derwing & Munro 2011; Isaacs & Trofimovich 2012). What for example some of these studies have suggested is the possibility of a speech comprehensibility benefit in those situations where non-native speakers (NNSs) and listeners share the same L1 background (Gallardo del Puerto et al. 2007). However, further evidence is necessary to strengthen this argument. Thus, the present study provides data regarding perceived foreign accent and comprehensibility, with data from a group of adolescent EFL learners who have experienced a period of residence in the target language country (United Kingdom) and formal instruction (FI) in their home country, Spain, and from a group of Spanish L1 non-native listeners, who are EFL teachers, allowing for comparisons with previous studies including native listeners to be made to see if our results agree with previous findings.

Concerning the specific focus of this study, there is a bulk of research focusing on accentedness and comprehensibility with a similar population, namely FI EFL learners in Spain, sometimes contrasting them with Content and Language Integrated Learning (CLIL) learners (García Lecumberri & Gallardo del Puerto 2003; Gallardo del Puerto et al. 2007; Rallo & Juan-Garau 2011). However, to our knowledge, none of them has included a group participating in a SA context of learning, and examined the possible differences which may result (but see Llanes 2012; Llanes & Muñoz 2012). In sum, no previous study exists focusing on the issues of accentedness and comprehensibility, from the perspective of the raters, in the case of adolescent SA EFL learners.

3 The present study

The current study aims at probing the constructs of foreign accent and comprehensibility as understood and used by listeners when asked to rate EFL learners' speech production. Learners experience two different learning contexts, FI and SA. The fact that listeners were asked to judge at the same time speech from learners who had experienced either a SA learning context or a FI context of learning strengthens the robustness of the data.

Our study examines a sample of oral narratives from a group of adolescent EFL learners completing their secondary education. The speech samples were collected longitudinally before (pre-test) and after (post-test) the SA period experienced by the first group of learners, and before and after the AH period experienced by the other group of learners, respectively. The oral productions from both groups of participants were grouped together and presented to the listeners for their evaluation in terms of perceived foreign accent and comprehensibility by non-native listeners. We also included speech samples collected from NSs as baseline data to assess listeners' ratings.

The main objectives of this study are: (a) to explore the relationship between the constructs of foreign accent and comprehensibility, and (b) to identify the aspects influencing non-native listeners' accentedness and comprehensibility ratings. These objectives led us to formulate the following general research question: In the case of a group of EFL learners experiencing a SA period, and another group experiencing a FI period at home, to what extent are their foreign accent and comprehensibility related speech dimensions when judged by non-native listeners, and which aspects do the latter take into account for their ratings? More specifically, two sub-questions were formulated to guide the analysis and discussion presented in the following sections:

1. To what extent do degree of foreign accent and comprehensibility correlate, in the case of a group of EFL learners experiencing a SA period, and another group experiencing FI period at home?

2. Which aspects do listeners report as affecting their foreign accent and comprehensibility ratings when analysed together?

4 Method

The methodological approach taken in this research study involves production and perception tasks from two different groups of participants, L2 learners and listeners, respectively, and uses a mixed-method approach with both quantitative and qualitative data (Dörnyei 2007).

4.1 Design

Data from an oral production task were collected from participants at two different times over 7 months. The first data collection (T1 or pre-test) took place in May before finishing the academic year previous to a SA period, which part of the participants undertook. SA and AH participants were tested again after their return from a 3-month SA or after an equivalent AH period (T2 or post-test). The SA or AH period covered the first term of the academic year (September-December). A group of NSs of English was also recruited to provide baseline data.

The speech samples obtained from these three groups of participants served as the stimuli for the perception task the listeners completed. The objective of the perception task was to examine and understand perceived foreign accent and comprehensibility by a group of non-native listeners.

4.2 Participants

The participants in this study included a group of Spanish adolescent learners of L2 English, some of them having experienced a period of SA ($n = 25$), and the rest AH instruction ($n = 31$), hence NNSs ($n = 56$). Moreover, a group of adolescent English NSs ($n = 15$) was also used in the perception task to provide baseline data. The total number of participants in the three speaker groups (SA, AH, NS) was 71. Additionally, the listeners ($n = 12$) constituted one final group of NNSs.

4.2.1 EFL NNS group

The EFL participants were 56 adolescent learners of English who were native Spanish speakers (40 females, 16 males). They were from Valencia, Spain, and studied at a semi-private school in this city. All of them were between 12 and 15 years old at pre-test ($M_{age\ T1} = 12.96$ years), and between 13 and 15 years old at post-test ($M_{age\ T2} = 13.52$ years). All participants had started learning English at school in their third year of primary education (i.e. at the age of 7-8) on a 60-minute weekly basis, and had received up to 3 hours per week of subsequent EFL instruction at school. They reported normal hearing, and none had any detectable speech disorder. Thirty-one learners were experiencing FI during the experimental period, and 25 had joined an optional SA programme in a British or Irish school.

4.2.2 NS group

This group was formed by 15 English NSs (10 females, 5 males) attending a state school in Majorca (Spain). Two of these participants were born in England and had arrived in Majorca 5-6 years before time of testing. The rest of students in this group were early English-Spanish bilinguals. All speakers in this group were between 13 and 14 years old at data collection time.

4.2.3 Listeners

The speech samples were rated by 12 native speakers of Spanish/Catalan teaching EFL in mainstream secondary education in Spain (males = 1; females = 11). They ranged in age from 29 to 46 years ($M_{age} = 36.75$). All listeners reported normal hearing. They were all EFL mainstream secondary education instructors in Spain, who are proficient NNSs of English, with no specific training in phonetics, but a long-standing professional career as EFL instructors in mainstream education. As for their linguistic profile, seven listeners reported Spanish as their mother tongue, four considered both Catalan and Spanish as their mother tongue and one listener reported that his mother tongue was Catalan. They also reported familiarity with British and American accents, and were highly familiar with the Spanish/Catalan-accented speech they had to assess, as they shared the learners' L1 background. They were fully qualified for teaching at secondary education levels. Their EFL teaching experience ranged from 4 to 25 years ($M_{\text{teaching experience}}$ = 12.6). They rated their own knowledge of phonetics/phonology in English on a scale from 1 to 5, and the results indicated a mean self-rated knowledge of 3.8. The same result was obtained when they were asked to rate their own pronunciation of English (M = 3.8).

4.3 Data collection: Instruments and procedure

The participants were asked to tell an oral narrative from a picture story. The speakers' extemporaneous speech was elicited using a six-frame picture story about a bank robbery. The speakers first studied the picture story for about one minute and then were recorded individually. High quality digital recordings were made at the learners' schools on different days.

A short excerpt (M_{duration} = 20.4 seconds) was extracted from the middle-end part of each narrative. Therefore, the content of the speech samples was kept relatively consistent across speakers. The first few seconds of the excerpt were excised from the recordings by eliminating all dysfluencies (e.g. false starts) and by using natural pauses to demarcate the end of each excerpt. The preparation of speech samples for the perception task was conducted with Praat software. The excerpts from the two time periods (T1 and T2) for the SA and AH participants, and from T0 in the case of the NS group, were then normalized for peak intensity and randomized for presentation to the listeners. This procedure is consistent with previous studies using ratings of speech samples from the same task (Rossiter 2009; Trofimovich & Isaacs 2012; Derwing & Munro 2013).

A total of 127 speech samples were obtained from the three groups of participants in the study. The SA and the AH group recorded the story at two data collection times (56 x 2 = 112 speech samples), and the group of baseline NSs (n = 15) produced the speech samples once (15 speech samples).

Measures of perceived degree of foreign accent and comprehensibility were obtained from 12 listeners who performed a rating task. The rating task was created and presented to the listeners using the e-learning platform Moodle. The listeners read an introduction to the online rating task providing information about the context of the experiment and the procedure. They were instructed to view the cartoon story on which the oral narratives were based to minimize familiarity effects.

Next the listeners heard the speech samples produced by the SA group (*n* = 25) and the AH group (*n* = 31) at pre-test and post-test, and by the group of baseline NSs (*n* = 15), who had been recorded once. Listeners heard the 127 stimuli in randomized order and assigned ratings using separate seven-point Likert-type scales for accentedness (1 = heavy foreign accent, 7 = native-like accent) and comprehensibility (1 = extremely difficult to understand, 7 = extremely easy to understand), respectively. A 9-point scale has been most commonly used in this type of study, in which participants usually differed greatly in proficiency level. However, a 7-point scale was deemed more appropriate for the data in the present study, taking into account the smaller degree of variability in our speech samples (SA and AH participants with a similar age and proficiency level), as compared to other FA and comprehensibility studies. As indicated in the instructions for the listeners, accentedness was defined as how different they thought the speaker sounded from a NS of English, if at all; and comprehensibility as how easy or difficult the sample was to understand. Listeners were instructed to use the whole scale over the course of the experiment. In line with previous research (Derwing & Munro 2013), the mean foreign accent scores for native participants in our research (*M* = 6.71, *SD* = 0.41) indicated that listeners had recognized them during the rating task, and had assigned them high scores on the 7-point rating scale.

The listeners were also asked to comment on the aspects of speech that had influenced their comprehensibility ratings for 20 of the speech samples, excluding the NS samples from this portion of the task. They were instructed to write their comments on the aspects of speech that they had found most striking and that they had taken into account when rating comprehensibility. They could use bullet points and report their impressions in English, Spanish and/or Catalan. Listeners were also asked to rank the top three aspects that they felt had most influenced their accentedness ratings.

The whole rating experiment was a self-paced task. The listeners could play each speech sample as many times as needed and rate either the accentedness or the comprehensibility dimension first. After rating a sample, they had to click on the "Next page" button to listen to the following speech sample. Four samples were provided as rating practice at the beginning of the rating experiment so as to allow listeners to become familiar with the procedure.

The 127 speech samples were organised in 15 parts (with 8 or 9 speech samples each). Given that this was an online rating task, listeners could pace themselves. The only restriction was that once they started whichever part of the experiment, they had to carry it out until the end. They could have a break or stop the experiment after finishing any part.

After completing the rating experiment, the listeners were asked to summarize their listening experience by answering a short online questionnaire. The main objective of this questionnaire was to gain insight into the aspects of speech that had affected listeners' ratings for accentedness and comprehensibility, the main focus of this study.

In the online questionnaire that the listeners had to complete after the rating experiment, listeners were shown a list of 12 factors and were asked to select those that had most influenced their foreign accent and comprehensibility ratings. They were asked to select as many as they wanted. These 12 aspects were chosen in an attempt to accommodate the various factors that can influence such ratings. In so doing, we followed Kennedy & Trofimovich (2008), who reported that semantic context affected listeners' ratings for accentedness and intelligibility, and Isaacs & Trofimovich (2012), who found that not only the pronunciation features of foreign-accented speech, but also other language aspects, affect speech comprehensibility (e.g. vocaburary, grammar, and discourse measures).

4.4 Data analysis

Two types of analyses were conducted, quantitative and qualitative. On the one hand, the quantitative analyses measured the listeners' ratings which were extracted from the online rating experiment and transferred to an SPSS data editor. We also examined the relationship between the participants' degree of foreign accent and comprehensibility. Correlations between foreign accent scores and comprehensibility scores were run in order to check for the existence of a relationship between the two dimensions and its strength.

On the other hand, the qualitative analyses dealt with the comments reported by the listeners in the online questionnaire completed after the rating experiment, stating the aspects of foreign accent and comprehensibility which they took into account. They sought to determine which aspects of the learners' utterances had influenced their foreign accent ratings and which ones had affected their comprehensibility ratings. To gain insight into the comprehensibility dimension, further qualitative analyses were undertaken examining the data reported by the listeners in the rating experiment on Moodle, where they were instructed to type in their comments for 20 of the speech samples.

5 Results

This section presents the results for the research question and its corresponding subquestions. The main research question addressed the strength of a potential relationship between foreign accent and comprehensibility when judged by non-native listeners, in the case of a group of EFL learners experiencing a SA period, and another group experiencing a FI period at home. The two sub-questions of the study provide the data which will allow us to address the main question and which are presented below.

5.1 Foreign accent and comprehensibility ratings

In order to answer research sub-question 1, correlations between foreign accent scores and comprehensibility scores were run to check for the existence of a relationship between the two dimensions and its strength at the two testing times, for each of the groups examined before and after FI and SA, respectively. A strong correlation between foreign accent and comprehensibility for the two groups at the two testing times was found. That is, the more native-like the accent, the greater the comprehensibility, both before and after FI at home and SA (Table 1).

Table 1: Pearson correlations between foreign accent scores and comprehensibility scores at pre-test and post-test for SA and FI groups.

		SA ($n = 25$)	FI ($n = 31$)
T1	Pearson	.849	.789
	Sig.	<.001	<.001
T2	Pearson	.814	.741
	Sig.	<.001	<.001

In the following sections we examine the aspects that listeners reported as affecting their foreign accent and comprehensibility ratings (research sub-question 2) and explore whether listeners' foreign accent and comprehensibility ratings were based on similar aspects of the learners' oral productions.

5.2 Aspects influencing listeners' foreign accent and comprehensibility ratings

This section tackles sub-question number 2 with the qualitative data on aspects influencing the listeners' ratings for both foreign accent and comprehensibility.

5.2.1 Aspects influencing listeners' foreign accent ratings

In order to find out the aspects influencing the listeners' accentedness scores, and address the first part of sub-question 2, as mentioned above, listeners were given a list of 12 aspects and were asked to choose those which had most affected their foreign accent ratings. It included the following items: grammar, vocabulary, pronunciation, word stress, rhythm, intonation, repetition of words, number of filled pauses with 'ums' and similar items, number of silent pauses, speakers' story telling abilities, lack of thematic content, and lack of content organization (adapted from Isaacs & Trofimovich 2012; Trofimovich & Isaacs 2012). Figure 1 shows the list with the 12 aspects and the raw number of listeners who selected each aspect:

Factors from the domain of phonology seemed to contribute the most to listeners' perception of foreign accent. Both segmental and suprasegmental aspects of speech were selected by most listeners. Pronunciation of individual sounds was selected by 92% of the listeners, followed by word stress (reported by 83% of the raters), and rhythm and intonation (75% each). The next aspect selected by most teachers was "the number of 'ums' and 'uhs'" (42%), with a considerably lower percentage, however.

As mentioned above, listeners were also asked to rank the top three aspects that they felt had most influenced their accentedness ratings. As illustrated in Figure 2, the three most selected aspects influencing listeners' foreign accent ratings were pronunciation of individual sounds, intonation, word stress, and rhythm. Other aspects which were reported by the listeners' are shown in this figure (e.g. grammar, vocabulary, number of pauses and number of 'uhms' and 'uhs'):

5.2.2 Aspects influencing listeners' comprehensibility ratings

As regards the second part of sub-question two, that is, the analysis of the aspects influencing listeners' comprehensibility scores, listeners were given a list of 12 aspects and were asked to choose those which had most affected their comprehensibility ratings. The list was identical to the one used for foreign accent and

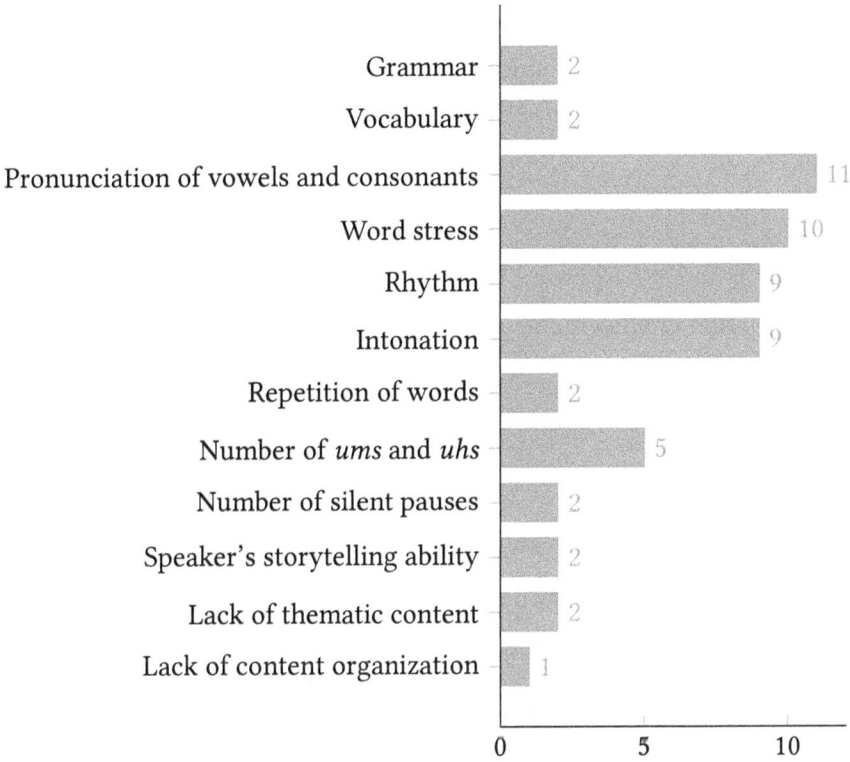

Figure 1: Aspects affecting foreign accent ratings

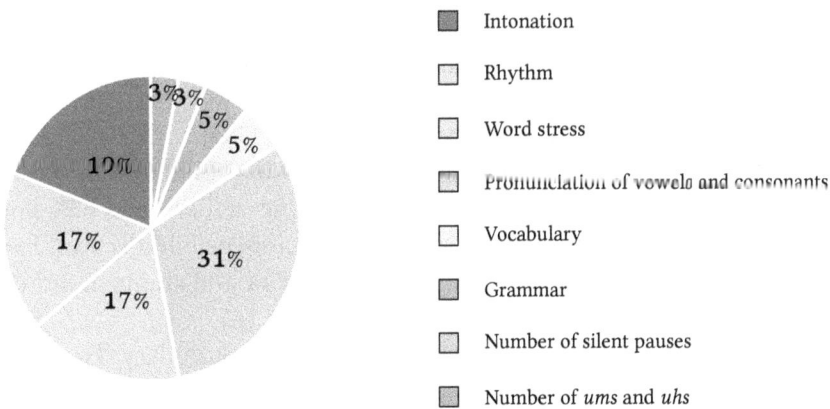

Figure 2: Aspects affecting listeners' foreign accent ratings most (%)

included: grammar, vocabulary, pronunciation, word stress, rhythm, intonation, repetition of words, number of filled pauses with 'ums' and similar items, number of silent pauses, speakers' story telling abilities, lack of thematic content, and lack of content organization. A summary of the results is presented in Figure 3.

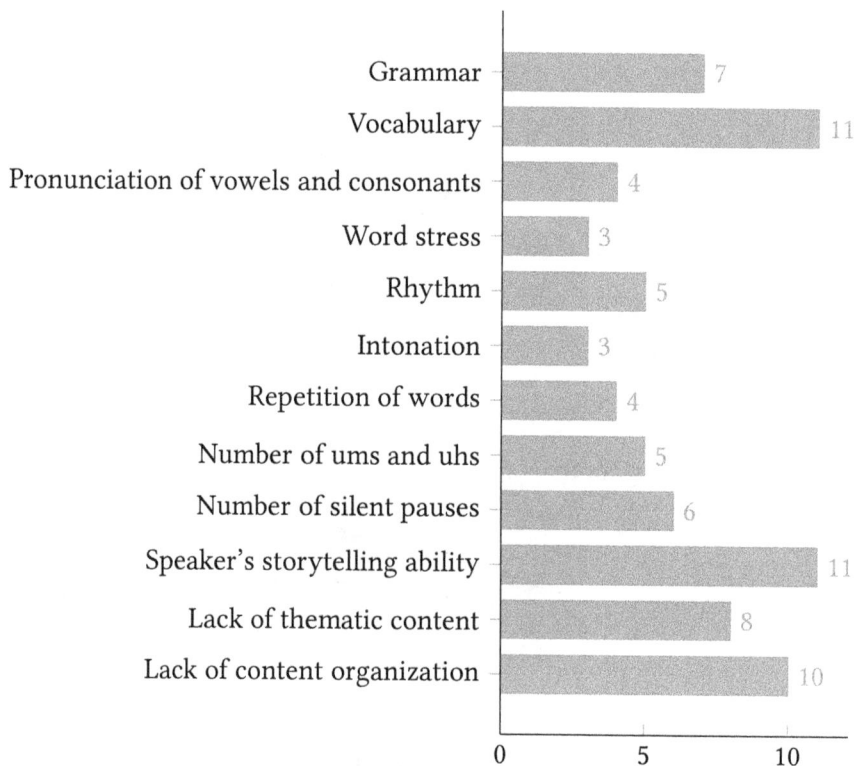

Figure 3: Aspects affecting comprehensibility ratings

Unlike accent, comprehensibility was mostly associated with vocabulary and discourse (storytelling and content organization). More than 90% of the listeners selected 'vocabulary' and 'speaker's storytelling ability', and 83% bore in mind 'content organization' when assigning comprehensibility scores. Lack of thematic content was important for 67% of the listeners, and grammar influenced the ratings of 60% of the listeners.

Seventy-five percent of these comments referred to vocabulary. Two listeners pointed out the use of L1 vocabulary as interfering with comprehensibility. The lack of vocabulary was stressed by one of the raters especially. Interestingly, one of the listeners highlighted that speaker's attitude had also affected her comprehensibility ratings.

Listeners were also asked to rank the top three aspects that they felt had most influenced their comprehensibility ratings. The three most cited aspects were vocabulary, lack of content organization and speakers' storytelling ability (followed by grammar and pronunciation of individual sounds). Figure 4 illustrates the results.

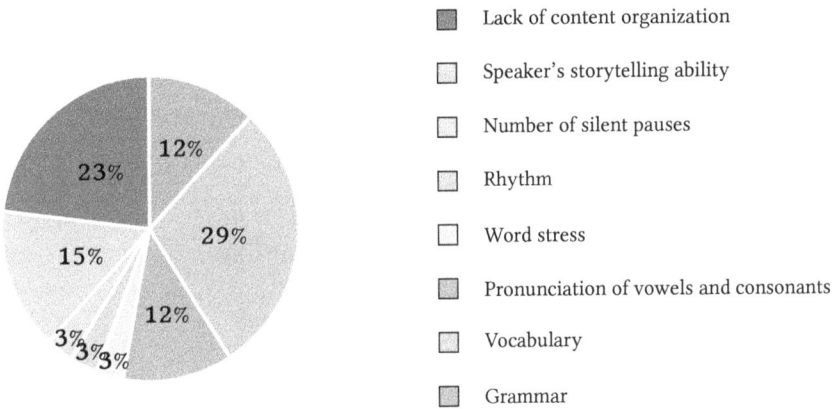

Figure 4: Aspects affecting listeners' comprehensibility ratings most (%)

In order to delve into the comprehensibility construct, we asked listeners to type in their comments immediately after rating the comprehensibility of 20 speech samples scattered throughout the rating experiment. We obtained 688 comments about comprehensibility from the text entry boxes which were filled in by the listeners during the rating experiment. The listeners' descriptive comments were first classified as *indicating a positive or negative remark on the comprehensibility of the sample*. There were 426 negative comments and 262 positive comments. Then the comments were thematically coded, and re-coded to eliminate overlapping ones (e.g. 'L1 word', 'invented word' and 'wrong word' were combined under a 'vocabulary' category).

We found that some listeners were more specific than others regarding their comments. Whereas some listeners made general comments about comprehensibility such as "grammar errors," other listeners specified in their reports the type of grammar errors they found in the participants' speech (e.g. "no subject," "wrong verb tense," etc.). Table 2 shows all the categories obtained from the listeners' comments indicating whether they were considered as negative (N), or positive (P) evaluations, or both (B). The initial number of comments is provided together with the final number of comments obtained, once double references to the same category made by the same listener were identified (number of comments deleted are indicated in brackets). The percentage of each category over the total number of final comments is indicated in the % column.

Table 2: Frequency of coded categories for comprehensibility from teacher reports (initial raw number, final raw number, and %)

Category	Considered as negative, positive or both	Initial number of comments	Final number of comments after re-coding	%
Ambiguous[a]	B	10	10	1.67
Attitude	B	19 (-3)	16	2.68
Listener's teaching profile	P	2	2	0.33
Communicative strategies	B	10	10	1.67
Content	B	37 (-1)	36	6.04
Discourse	B	61 (-12)	49	8.22
English proficiency	N	1	1	0.16
Familiarity with the story	P	4	4	0.67
Fluency	B	97 (-11)	86	**14.42**
Grammar	B	99 (-12)	87	**14.59**
L1 familiarity	B	16 (-2)	14	2.34
L1 influence (general comment)	N	3	3	0.50
Listener's attitude	P	4	4	0.67
Low voice	N	3	3	0.50
Pronunciation	B	194 (-39)	155	**26**
Self-correction	P	4	4	0.67
Style	B	3 (-1)	2	0.33
Vocabulary	B	121 (-11)	110	**18.45**

[a]There were a number of comments which were categorized as 'Ambiguous'. They were included in this category when it was not clear what the listeners were considering. For instance, for comments such as "I can't understand some words," it was not clear whether there was a pronunciation problem on the part of the speaker or if the speaker had invented a word which the listener could not understand (vocabulary). Given that we were not sure whether this was a comment referring to pronunciation or vocabulary, we assigned it to the 'Ambiguous' category.[2] The data collection procedure comprised 3 academic years since data was collected from two consecutive cohorts of students at the same home institution.[3] Data from NSs was collected by researchers at the *Universitat de les Illes Balears* participating in the SALA and COLE research projects, coordinated by *Universitat Pompeu Fabra* (Barcelona, Spain).

As can be observed, 26% of the comments referred to pronunciation (including segmental and supra-segmental aspects). Vocabulary was the second most frequent aspect considered by listeners in their comments (18.45%), followed by grammar (14.59%) and fluency (14.42%).

Further analyses explored whether the above-mentioned aspects were also taken into account to a similar extent in negative and positive comprehensibility ratings. Therefore, we examined the 426 negative comments and the 262 positive ones separately.

As for the comments identifying negative evaluations of comprehensibility, pronunciation, vocabulary and grammar were reported as the categories that most frequently affected listeners' scoring decisions. Twenty-six percent of the comments referred to segmental and supra-segmental aspects of participants' speech, 22.71% dealt with vocabulary items, and 19.11% with grammar. Fluency was mentioned in almost 15% of the comments. Table 3 shows the results of this analysis.

Table 3: Frequency of coded categories for negative comments on comprehensibility from teacher reports (initial raw number, final raw number, and %).

Category	Initial number of comments	Final number of comments	%
Ambiguous	7	7	1.93
Attitude	10	8	2.21
Communicative strategies	1	1	0.27
Content	19	19	5.26
Discourse	20	19	5.26
English proficiency	1	1	0.27
Fluency	62	53	**14.68**
Grammar	80	69	**19.11**
(No) L1 familiarity	3	1	0.27
L1 influence (general comment)	3	3	0.83
Low voice	1	3	0.83
Pronunciation	126	94	**26.03**
Style	2	1	0.27
Vocabulary	91	82	**22.71**
Total	426	361	

Table 4: Pronunciation aspects reported by listeners as negatively influencing their comprehensibility ratings of participants' speech

Pronunciation aspect	%
Pronunciation of individual sounds and words	55.55
Foreign accent	17.46
Intonation	11.11
Rhythm	3.96
Stress	2.3
Native-like pronunciation	4
Other[a]	5.55

[a]Comments regarding pronunciation in general and speech clarity were categorized under the 'Other' category.

To have a better idea of the pronunciation features, we classified the comments according to the aspect of speech they were more specifically referring to. Table 4 shows this classification and the percentage of comments assigned to each pronunciation category.

Half of the comments regarding pronunciation problems referred to the pronunciation of individual sounds or words. It is worth remarking that specific reference was made to foreign-accented speech as an aspect affecting comprehensibility (17% of the comments referred to foreign accent). However, 'L1 interference' was mentioned when considering other pronunciation factors such as pronunciation of individual sounds or words, and intonation. Comments such as "Spanish intonation," "L1 influence on pronunciation" and "typical pronunciation mistake (from their L1)" were collected.

Having a native-like pronunciation was regarded as hindering comprehensibility to some extent by some of the listeners when rating native participants' speech. Comments such as those in (1) were collected from listeners' evaluations:

(1)   EMLE: "after listening to so many recordings with the same type of syllable-timed speech, it was hard to readjust my ear to connected speech"

As regards the comments referring to aspects positively affecting comprehensibility ratings, pronunciation was also considered the most influential aspect. As shown in Table 5, fluency, discourse and vocabulary were aspects reported in more than 10% of the comments.

Table 5: Frequency of coded categories for positive comments on comprehensibility from teacher reports (initial raw number, final raw number, and %)

Category	Initial number of comments	Final number of comments	%
Ambiguous	3	3	1.23
Attitude	9	8	3.29
Being a teacher	2	2	0.82
Communicative strategies	9	9	3.70
Content	18	17	7
Discourse	41	31	12.75
Familiarity with the story	4	4	1.64
Fluency	35	34	14
Grammar	19	19	7.81
L1 familiarity	15	13	5.34
Listener's attitude	4	4	1.64
Pronunciation	68	63	26.33
Self-correction	4	4	1.64
Style	1	1	0.41
Vocabulary	30	30	12.34
Total	262	242	

As with the pronunciation comments identifying negative aspects of participants' speech comprehensibility, we analyzed listeners' reports on positive evaluations in further depth and found that listeners did not identify any particular aspects of pronunciation as positively affecting their comprehensibility ratings, but rather they referred to pronunciation in general. About 40% of the comments were similar to the following ones: "quite good pronunciation that facilitates comprehensibility," "pronunciation is OK," and "pronunciation is not that bad". Having a native-like pronunciation or imitating native-like pronunciation was the second most frequently cited aspect (22% of the comments). Moreover, general comments on accent were reported in 15% of the listeners' comments (e.g. "good accent"). Table 6 shows the percentage of comments assigned to each pronunciation aspect reported by the listeners as positively affecting their comprehensibility ratings.

Table 6: Pronunciation aspects reported by listeners as positively influencing their comprehensibility ratings of participants' speech

Pronunciation aspect	%
Pronunciation of individual sounds and words	2.94
Accent (general comment)	14.7
Intonation	10.29
Rhythm	7.35
Pronunciation (general positive comment)	41.17
Native or imitating native-like pronunciation	22.05
Being familiar with L1 accent	1.47

While language aspects such as pronunciation, vocabulary, grammar or fluency were most frequently reported by listeners as affecting comprehensibility, other aspects were mentioned which will be discussed in more detail in the following section. Reference to a NS model or the importance of native-like speech, L1 familiarity and the speaker's and listener's attitude were points made by the listeners which will also receive special attention in the next pages so as to provide further answers and comments in the context of English pronunciation teaching today.

6 Discussion

The main research question in this study enquired as to whether or not and to what extent foreign accent and comprehensibility are related speech dimensions when judged by non-native listeners, in the case of a group of EFL learners experiencing a SA period, and another group experiencing a FI period at home, and what aspects affected their decisions.

Our results have revealed significant strong positive correlations between the two speech dimensions at the two testing times, that is before and after both FI and SA, for both groups of participants, indicating that the more native-like the accent, the greater the comprehensibility, and vice-versa. These results contrast with those reported in previous studies positing that heavily accented speech can often be perfectly intelligible, which, in contrast had mostly naïve (that is, non-language professionals) NSs as listeners (Munro & Derwing 1995; 1999; Derwing & Munro 1997; Gallardo del Puerto et al. 2007; Hayes-Harb & Watzinger-Tharp 2012). One possible interpretation of these findings is that the sample is rather homogeneous, both in the speakers and in the listeners: The learners who provided the speech samples have been attending the same FI class during their former education prior to data collection, and the listeners are non-native EFL teachers, who train their students to try and achieve native-like standards. For them, accent may actually indeed interfere with comprehension. Another interesting result was the fact that none of the participants were assigned a high foreign accent rating and a low comprehensibility score. In other words, participants who were assigned high comprehensibility scores were also given good ratings in foreign accent.

Given these three results – that is, (1) positive correlations between foreign accent and comprehensibility, (2) learners' approximation to native-like accent always associated with good comprehensibility ratings, and (3) a contrast with the extant literature regarding the link established by listeners between accent and comprehensibility – our sub-question 2, which taps into the aspects which influenced listeners' foreign accent and comprehensibility ratings, gained more relevance. Qualitative analyses were thus conducted of listeners' comments gathered from the questionnaires they completed after finishing the rating task, and from 20 reports which were typed in at the same time that they provided their ratings during the rating task.

Concerning the aspects affecting foreign accent ratings, factors from the domain of phonology were selected from the list by most listeners (see Figure 1). Pronunciation of vowels/consonants, word stress, rhythm and intonation were reported in this order as mainly affecting their foreign accent assessment. This finding was confirmed when listeners were asked which three aspects had influenced their foreign accent ratings most (see Figure 2). Pronunciation of vowels/consonants, intonation, word stress and rhythm were considered in this order. In fact, these phonological dimensions altogether represented 84% of the factors selected by the listeners as mostly influencing their foreign accent ratings. These results confirmed the findings in Trofimovich & Isaacs (2012) indicating that accent was mainly associated with aspects of phonology (e.g. rhythm, segmental accuracy, and syllable structure).

On the other hand, comprehensibility was mostly related to vocabulary and discourse aspects, such as storytelling and content organization (see Figure 3). Lack of thematic content and grammar were also selected by more than half of the listeners. When asked to identify the three most influential aspects on their comprehensibility ratings (Figure 4), vocabulary (29%), lack of content organization (23%) and speaker's storytelling ability (15%) were reported in this order, followed by grammar (12%) and pronunciation of individual sounds (12%).

If we now consider the last part of sub-question 2, which tapped into whether listeners' foreign accent and comprehensibility ratings were based on similar aspects of the learners' oral productions, it is worth noting that even though none of the phonological factors were as important individually for the comprehensibility ratings as in the case of the foreign accent ratings, pronunciation of vowels and consonants represented 12% of the comments, word stress 3% and rhythm 3%. All these phonological factors taken together represented 18% of the comments related to comprehensibility ratings, a higher percentage than, for instance, speaker's storytelling ability, which was ranked third in the list presented above of the most influential factors affecting listeners' assessment of comprehensibility.

These results are in line with Trofimovich & Isaacs' (2012) findings, which indicated that comprehensibility was mainly linked to grammatical accuracy and lexical richness. As seen in the literature review, Trofimovich & Isaacs (2012) identified five speech aspects which differentiated between L2 learners at different comprehensibility levels: lexical richness and fluency distinguished between low-level learners, grammatical and discourse-level measures differentiated between high-level learners, and word stress errors discriminated between learners of all levels. Overall, results in our study suggest that listeners regarded vocabulary and also discourse aspects (lack of content organization and speaker's storytelling ability) as the most important factors related to comprehensibility, factors which were also indicated in Trofimovich & Isaacs' (2012) research. However, findings in our research do not support Trofimovich & Isaacs' conclusion pointing out that "four categories uniquely distinguished accent from comprehensibility, with all categories specific to the dimension of phonology (i.e. vowels and consonants, syllables, sounding native-like, and rhythm)" (p. 912). As we have seen, pronunciation aspects (e.g. pronunciation of individual sounds) were also taken into account by the listeners in our study when assessing comprehensibility. As suggested above, the differences in listeners' profiles in both studies, non-native language specialists in the current study versus naïve NSs in prior works, might be the reason for this discrepancy.

It is worth mentioning other aspects (different from the ones provided in the list) which some of the listeners reported as having influenced their comprehensibility ratings. Almost all comments referred to vocabulary, and some of them stressed the use of L1 items as hampering comprehensibility, as in (2) and (3).

(2)   INCA: "Use of Spanish words maybe"[1].

---

[1]L1 lexical interference was confirmed to negatively affect INCA's comprehensibility ratings, as she reported other comments throughout the perception task such as, "use of words translated from Spanish ('senior', from Spanish word "señor" -meaning 'man').

(3)   MOLO: "The use of L1 words in some cases which shows the lack of ability of the student to make the message be understood"

The fact that these listeners considered the use and transfer of L1 words as negatively affecting comprehensibility does not necessarily contradict findings in previous studies suggesting the speech comprehensibility benefit for NNSs and non-native listeners sharing the same L1 background (Hayes-Harb et al. 2008; Gallardo del Puerto et al. 2009), mentioned previously. However, the analysis of all the comments gathered from listeners, including those in (4)–(6), showed that L1 lexical interference was not positively considered in many instances.

(4)   COGA: "The use of Spanish words makes it confusing."

(5)   INCA: "Usa vocabulario 'traducido' de la lengua materna." ('He "translates" words from his L1.')

(6)   MAGU: "Clara influencia de la lengua materna. Adapta claramente vocabulario al inglés. Es difícil de comprender por el vocabulario." ('Clear influence of his L1. He adapts lexical items from his L1. It's difficult to understand because of the vocabulary.')

So far, our results partly support those reported by recent research indicating that foreign accent and comprehensibility are linked to different language aspects. On the one hand, we can conclude that aspects of phonology affected foreign accent ratings more than aspects related to other domains such as grammar or vocabulary. On the other hand, although results confirmed that vocabulary and discourse factors, as well as grammar, were the main contributors to variation in comprehensibility ratings, reports from the listeners in our study suggested that factors related to pronunciation also had some influence on their assessment of comprehensibility, when considering the data from the two learning contexts together.

The listeners were also asked to type in the aspects of speech which they were taking into account when providing their comprehensibility ratings. Responses for 20 of the speech samples were analyzed. The analyses of these comments helped us to elucidate whether pronunciation was actually involved (or not) in listeners' comprehensibility ratings.

When analyzing all the comments provided by the listeners we found that 26% of the comments regarding their comprehensibility ratings considered aspects of pronunciation, 18.45% of the comments referred to vocabulary, 14.59% to grammar, and 14.42% to fluency. Therefore, a new distribution of the aspects affecting this speech dimension was obtained (compared to the 12-item classification from the final questionnaires presented above). Vocabulary was considered a key aspect for comprehensibility in many of the comments, but pronunciation was even more frequently highlighted.

The comments from the reports were classified as affecting negatively or positively the listeners' ratings. With regard to the aspects hindering comprehensibility, 26% of the comments were related to pronunciation, 22.71% associated with vocabulary, and 19% linked to grammar. Pronunciation was also regarded as the variable enhancing comprehensibility most. Twenty-six percent of the comments providing reasons for good comprehensibility had to do with pronunciation, 14% were related to fluency, 12.75% to discourse, and 12.34% were associated with vocabulary.

Therefore, according to these analyses, comprehensibility was related to pronunciation to a considerable degree. In order to gain a better understanding of the pronunciation aspects promoting (or hampering) comprehensibility, we classified the comments according to the pronunciation features which the listeners were particularly referring to. The top three pronunciation features which were mentioned in negative evaluations of comprehensibility were pronunciation of individual sounds and words (55.5%), foreign accent (17.42%), and intonation (11.1%). As for the pronunciation aspects which were identified in positive comments on comprehensibility, listeners cited pronunciation in general (41.1%), imitation of native-like pronunciation (22%), and degree of accentedness (14.7%), followed by intonation (10.29%).

Therefore, according to the reports on comprehensibility provided by the listeners while carrying out the perception task, pronunciation was found to be the most relevant aspect in their assessment of comprehensibility of L2 learners' speech. The fact that pronunciation was not ranked within the top three aspects affecting comprehensibility in the data obtained from the questionnaires may potentially be explained in two ways. First, since we presented the questions about the factors influencing foreign accent and comprehensibility ratings in the same questionnaire, we could have implicitly motivated the distinction between the two constructs. Second, as already remarked, while it is true that specific pronunciation features (e.g. pronunciation of individual sounds, intonation, stress, etc.) did not greatly affect comprehensibility when considered separately, pronunciation aspects taken as a whole did have a considerable impact on the listeners' comments. On the other hand, we may consider the comments made by the listeners during the rating experiment as more reliable and ecologically valid than the comments collected at the end of the experiment, as the former were reported when listeners were actually rating the speech samples for comprehensibility.

According to these data, non-native listeners in our study took into account pronunciation aspects when assessing L2 learners' comprehensibility of English, both after FI and SA. First, strong positive correlations between foreign accent and comprehensibility were found for data from both contexts, in spite of the fact that these contexts might have affected learners differently. Second, listeners in our study did pay attention to aspects related to accent or native-like pronunciation when providing their comprehensibility ratings with data from both contexts, in contrast with previous research involving native listeners of English (Trofimovich & Isaacs 2012). Against such backdrop, further research is needed to gain a better understanding of the aspects affecting comprehensibility as reported by native and non-native listeners.

7 Conclusion

In this research study we have examined foreign accent and comprehensibility ratings assigned by English non-native instructors, who are frequently responsible for teaching FI EFL courses in the AH context in Spain, so as to determine the relationship between these two speech dimensions, in the case of a group of EFL learners experiencing a SA period, and another group experiencing a FI period at home. Contrary to previous findings (Munro & Derwing 1999; Derwing & Munro 2009), a strong correlation has been found between foreign accent and comprehensibility, indicating that those learners with better accent obtained higher comprehensibility ratings, and learners with heavier foreign accent were also perceived as less comprehensible. Furthermore, we have explored the aspects that listeners took into account when assessing foreign accent and comprehensibility. Results showed that the foreign accent dimension was mainly associated with pronunciation aspects, which also affected comprehensibility ratings assigned by the non-native listeners in our research. Confirming previous research (Trofimovich & Isaacs 2012), aspects such as vocabulary and grammar were taken into account when rating L2 learners' speech comprehensibility but, contrary to previous findings in studies involving native listeners of English, pronunciation was the aspect that listeners heeded most when assigning comprehensibility scores.

It remains unclear whether the aspects reported by the group of non-native listeners of our study are specific to our participants, or can be generalized to learners from different L1 backgrounds, or experiencing other learning contexts besides FI and SA, such as, for example, immersion classrooms. In addition, it would be advisable to validate our findings with English native and non-native listeners from other L1 backgrounds and profiles. Likewise, when considering the

12 factors that influence foreign accent and comprehensibility ratings the most, the preponderance of aspects that concern phonetics should guide our analyses in future, paired with a more careful weighting of the factors included in the list. In these respects further research is necessary to throw more light on this area of speech production abilities, in the case of EFL adolescent learners.

One of the findings in our study is the difference between ratings given by listeners who are language specialists, sharing their L1 with the learners' whose samples they are rating, as opposed to naïve NSs. More research seems necessary in order to add further evidence to allow us to disentangle those two variables which now seem to be conflated and tackle the issue of listerners' profile under this new light. Finally, although it is widely accepted that the objective of L2 pronunciation teaching should be to help L2 learners be understandable for their interlocutors, classroom teachers have received little guidance on the pronunciation features on which they should focus during lessons (Derwing & Munro 2009). Nonetheless, teaching pronunciation should be even more important in the case of EFL learners facing a period of residence abroad, during which issues of comprehensibility and accentedness may impinge on the efficacy learners display in establishing interaction with target language speakers, and being seen as possible interlocutors in communicative encounters. The fact that pronunciation tends to suffer from neglect may not be due to teachers' lack of interest in the subject but rather to a feeling of doubt as to how to teach it. Another factor affecting the teaching of pronunciation these days may be the popular idea that one learns it best while being in the target language country, hence during SA programmes. Even if this may be partially true, current research on SA emphasizes the need for preparation before departure as it has been observed to correlate very highly with progress made while abroad (Paige et al. 2002). Lack of knowledge of phonetics and lack of formal preparation to teach pronunciation are two of the most cited problems, which have been corroborated in our research. The urgent need for specific pronunciation training for teachers in Spain has been called for frequently (Levey 1999; Levey (2001)Donovan 2001; Pavón Vázquez 2001; Pavón Vázquez & Rosado García 2003). In this regard, it is worth highlighting the willingness reported by listeners to benefit from pronunciation training programs and participation in studies like this one, which have provided them with food for thought.

In sum, the current study has sought to make several contributions to the field of speech production studies. Firstly, it hopes to contribute to the field by offering an analysis of the L2 speech dimensions of accentedness and comprehensibility in the case of SA EFL learners. By having done so we have increased the number of studies examining these dimensions in the speech production of adolescent EFL learners, who experience the two learning environments mentioned above, FI and SA, a clearly underresearched population. Secondly, we sought to contribute to bridging the gap between research and language teaching practice in the face of the number of learning contexts which learners can experience, such as FI and SA, to name but two. Although further studies need to be conducted in order to confirm and generalize our findings, ours is a modest but ecologically valid contribution to empirical-based research aiming at exploring what really happens with regard to the assessment of pronunciation.

References

Collentine, Joseph G. & Barbara F. Freed. 2004. *Studies in second language acquisition 26 (2)*. Cambridge: Cambridge Core.

Dalton, Christiane & Barbara Seidlhofer. 1994. *Pronunciation*. Oxford: Oxford University Press.

Darcy, Isabelle, Doreen Ewert & Ryan Lidster. 2012. Bringing pronunciation instruction back into the classroom: An ESL teachers' pronunciation "toolbox". In John Levis & Kimberly LeVelle (eds.), *Proceedings of the 3rd pronunciation in second language learning and teaching conference*, 93–108. Ames, IA: Iowa State University.

del Río, Carmen. 2013. *Perceived foreign accent and comprehensibility in the oral production of adolescent learners of English: Study abroad vs. At home learning contexts*. Barcelona: Universidad Pompeu Fabra. (Doctoral dissertation.)

Derwing, Tracey M. 2008. Curriculum issues in teaching pronunciation to second language learners. In Jette G. Hansen Edwards & Mary L. Zampini (eds.), *Phonology and second language acquisition*, 347–369. Amsterdam: John Benjamins Publishing Company.

Derwing, Tracey M. & Murray J. Munro. 1997. Accent, intelligibility, and comprehensibility: Evidence from four L1s. *Studies in Second Language Acquisition* 19 1–16.

Derwing, Tracey M. & Murray J. Munro. 2009. Putting accent in its place: Rethinking obstacles to communication. *Language Teaching* 42(4). 476–490.

Derwing, Tracey M. & Murray J. Munro. 2011. Second language accent and pronunciation teaching: A research-based approach. *TESOL Quarterly* 39(3). 379–397.

Derwing, Tracey M. & Murray J. Munro. 2013. The development of L2 oral language skills in two L1 groups: A 7-year study. *Language Learning* 63(2). 163–185.

Derwing, Tracey M., Murray J. Munro & Grace Wiebe. 1998. Evidence in favor of a broad framework for pronunciation instruction. *Language Learning* 48. 393–410.

Donovan, Patrick J. 2001. Making pronunciation a priority for EFL teachers and learners. In David T. Levey, María Araceli Losey León & Miguel Ángel González Macías (eds.), *English language teaching changing perspectives in context*, 245–249. Cádiz: Universidad de Cádiz (Servicio de Publicaciones).

Dörnyei, Zoltán. 2007. *Research methods in applied linguistics.* Oxford: Oxford University Press.

Fisher, Linda & Michael Evans. 2000. The school exchange visit: Effects on attitudes and proficiency in language learning. *Language Learning Journal* 22. 11–16.

Gallardo del Puerto, Francisco, Esther Gómez Lacabex & María Luisa García Lecumberri. 2009. Testing the effectiveness of content and language integrated learning in foreign language contexts: The assessment of English pronunciation. In Yolanda Ruiz de Zarobe & Rosa Maria Jiménez Catalán (eds.), *Content and language integrated learning. Evidence from research in Europe*, 63–80. Clevedon: Multilingual Matters.

Gallardo del Puerto, Francisco, Eugenia Gómez Lacabex & María Luisa García-Lecumberri. 2007. *Proceedings of the Phonetics Teaching and Learning Conference, London, August 2007.*

García Lecumberri, María Luisa & Francisco Gallardo del Puerto. 2003. English FL sounds in school learners of different ages. In María del Pilar García-Mayo & María Luisa García-Lecumberri (eds.), *Age and the acquisition of English as a foreign language*, 115–135. Clevedon, England: Multilingual Matters.

Gass, Susan M. & Evangeline Varonis. 1984. The effect of familiarity on the comprehensibility of nonnative speech. *Language Learning* 34. 65–89.

Gimson, Alfred Charles. 1994. *Gimson's pronunciation of English. Revision by Alan Cruttenden.* London: Edward Arnold.

Gordon, James. & Isabelle Darcy. 2012. *Effects of explicit pronunciation instruction on segmentals and suprasegmentals: The development of comprehensible speech in L2 learners.* Paper presented at American Association for Applied Linguistics, Boston, MA.

Grant, Linda (ed.). 2014. *Pronunciation myths: Applying second language research to classroom teaching.* Ann Arbor: University of Michigan Press.

Hayes-Harb, Rachel, Bruce L. Smith, Tessa Bent & Ann R. Bradlow. 2008. The interlanguage speech intelligibility benefit for native speakers of Mandarin: Production and perception of English word-final voicing contrasts. *Journal of Phonetics* 36. 664–679.

Hayes-Harb, Rachel & Johanna Watzinger-Tharp. 2012. Accent, intelligibility, and the role of the listener: Perceptions of English-accented German by native German speakers. *Foreign Language Annals* 45. 260–282.

Isaacs, Talia. 2010. *Issues and arguments in the measurement of second language pronunciation*. McGill University dissertation.

Isaacs, Talia & Pavel Trofimovich. 2012. "deconstructing" comprehensibility: Identifying the linguistic influences on listeners' L2 comprehensibility ratings. *Studies in Second Language Acquisition* 34. 475–505.

Jenkins, Jennifer. 2000. *The phonology of English as an international language*. Oxford: Oxford University Press.

Kennedy, Sara & Pavel Trofimovich. 2008. Intelligibility, comprehensibility, and accentedness of L2 speech: The role of listener experience and semantic context. *Canadian Modern Language Review* 64. 459–489.

Kenworthy, Joanne. 1987. *Teaching English pronunciation*. London: Longman.

Levey, David Trevor. 1999. Half truths and white lies: A practical pronunciation guide for Spanish speakers. In Tony Harris & Inmaculada Sanz Sainz (eds.), *ELT: Through the looking glass*, 215–226. Granada: Greta.

Levey, David Trevor. 2001. Stressing intonation. In Tony Harris, María Inmaculada Roldan Miranda, Inmaculada Sanz Sainz & Montserrat Torreblanco Sojo (eds.), *ELT2000: Thinking back, looking forward*, 35–45. Granada: Greta.

Levis, John M. 2005. Changing contexts and shifting paradigms in pronunciation teaching. *TESOL Quarterly* 39. 369–377.

Levis, John M. 2006. Pronunciation and the assessment of spoken language. In Rebecca Hughes (ed.), *Spoken English, TESOL and applied linguistics: Challenges for theory and practice*, 245–270. New York: Palgrave Macmillan.

Llanes, Àngels. 2012. The short and long-term effect of a short study abroad experience. *System* 40. 179–190.

Llanes, Àngels & Carmen Muñoz. 2012. Age effects in a study abroad context: Children and adults studying abroad and at home. *Language Learning* 64(1). 1–28.

Llanes, Àngels & Carmen Muñoz. 2013. Age effects in a study abroad context: Children and adults studying English abroad and at home. *Language Learning* 63(1). 63–90.

Munro, Murray J. 2008. Foreign accent and speech intelligibility. In Jette G. Hansen Edwards & Mary L. Zampini (eds.), *Phonology and second language acquisition*, 193–218. Amsterdam: John Benjamins Publishing Company.

Munro, Murray J. & Tracey M. Derwing. 1995. Foreign accent, comprehensibility, and intelligibility in the speech of second language learners. *Language Learning* 45(1). 73–97.

Munro, Murray J. & Tracey M. Derwing. 1999. Foreign accent, comprehensibility, and intelligibility in the speech of second language learners. *Language Learning* 49. 285–310.

Paige, R. Michael, Andrew D. Cohen & Rachel L. Shiveley. 2002. Assessing the impact of a strategies-based curriculum on language and culture learning while abroad. *Frontiers: The Interdisciplinary Journal of Study Abroad* 10. 253–276.

Pavón Vázquez, Víctor. 2001. El Papel del profesor en la enseñanza de la pronunciación. In David T. Levey, Losey León, María Araceli & Miguel Ángel González Macías (eds.), *English language teaching changing perspectives in context*, 289–300. Cádiz: Universidad de Cádiz (Servicio de Publicaciones).

Pavón Vázquez, Víctor & Ángel José Rosado García. 2003. *Guía de fonética y fonología para estudiantes de filología inglesa en el umbral del siglo XXI*. Granada: Comares.

Pennington, Martha C. 1996. *Phonology in English language teaching*. London: Longman.

Pennington, Martha C. & Jack C. Richards. 1986. Pronunciation revisited. *TESOL Quarterly* 20(2). 207–225.

Pérez-Vidal, Carmen. 2017. Study abroad and ISLA. In Shawn Loewen & Masatoshi Sato (eds.), *The Routledge handbook of instructed second language acquisition*, 339–361. New York: Routledge.

Porter, Don & Sue Garvin. 1989. Attitudes to pronunciation in EFL. *Speak Out!* 5. 8–15.

Rallo, Lucrecia & Maria Juan-Garau. 2011. Assessing FL pronunciation in a semi-immersion setting: The effects of CLIL instruction on Spanish-Catalan learners' perceived comprehensibility and accentedness. *Poznań Studies in Contemporary Linguistics PSiCL* 47. 96–108.

Rossiter, Marian. 2009. Perceptions of L2 fluency by native and non-native speakers of English. *The Canadian Modern Language Review* 65(3). 395–412.

Saito, Kazuya & Roy Lyster. 2012. Effects of form-focused instruction and corrective feedback on L2 pronunciation development of /ɹ/ by Japanese learners of English. *Language Learning* 62(2). 595–633.

Thomson, Ron I. 2013. Accent reduction. In Carol A. Chapell (ed.), *The encyclopedia of applied linguistics.* Hoboken, NJ: Wiley-Blackwell. DOI:10.1002/9781405198431.wbeal0004

Trofimovich, Pavel & Talia Isaacs. 2012. Disentangling accent from comprehensibility. *Bilingualism: Language and Cognition* 15. 905–916.

Van Loon, John. 2002. Improving pronunciation of adult ESL students. *TESL Canada Journal* 20(1). 83–88.

Zielinski, Beth W. 2008. The listener: No longer the silent partner in reduced intelligibility. *System* 36. 69–84.

Chapter 9

International posture, motivation and identity in study abroad

Leah Geoghegan

Portsmouth University

In the context of Study Abroad (SA) researchers have called for a more refined analysis of students' personal language learning motivations (Mitchell et al. 2015). Furthermore, the spread of English as a Lingua Franca (ELF) has led to an exponential increase in learners of English, and has consequently changed the learners' motivations for learning, as well as the way they identify with the language (Jenkins et al. 2011; Isabelli-García 2006). With this in mind, the present study draws on Yashima's (2009) international posture as a more fruitful alternative to the concept of integrative motivation. The study investigates the motivation and identity of undergraduate Spanish-Catalan bilinguals, learning English, as well as either German or French. Using quantitative tools, the study compares students cross-sectionally prior to and at the end of a SA period, and contrasts those spending a SA in an English-speaking country with those in a German- or French-speaking country. The results suggest that there is a partial effect of a three-month SA on the language learning motivation and identity of higher education students. Significant differences were found between pre- and end of SA participants in areas such as international posture, willingness to communicate and interest in foreign languages. Furthermore, when comparing those in an English-speaking country with a French or German-speaking country, differences arose regarding the ideal L2 self and intended learning effort. It is suggested that due to the generally high levels of motivation across all participants, a more detailed, qualitative investigation is required in order to gain a more thorough understanding of the development and negotiation of the learners' ongoing motivational process (Kim 2009).

1 Introduction

Within the field of Second Language Acquisition (SLA) and Study Abroad (SA), there has been a recent increase in interest regarding research examining indi-

Leah Geoghegan. International posture, motivation and identity in study abroad. In Carmen Pérez Vidal, Sonia López-Serrano, Jennifer Ament & Dakota J. Thomas-Wilhelm (eds.), *Learning context effects: Study abroad, formal instruction and international immersion classrooms*, 215–253. Berlin: Language Science Press. DOI:10.5281/zenodo.1300634

vidual factors such as identity (e.g. Jackson 2008b; Kinginger 2013; Brown 2013) and motivation (e.g. Isabelli-García 2006; Allen 2010; Hernández 2010; Sasaki 2011; Irie & Ryan 2014), an unsurprising fact given that "ethnographic and post-structuralist thinking have become increasingly influential within SLA theorising" in recent decades (Mitchell et al. 2015: 8). The international role of English as a Lingua Franca (ELF) in SA and higher education contexts has also seen increasing attention in research over the last decade (e.g. Smit 2010; Jenkins 2011; Coleman 2015), in part due to the increase in English medium instruction in tertiary education outside English-speaking countries.

What has been called for in this field of research, is a more refined investigation into students' personal language learning motivations (Mitchell et al. 2015). This analysis is particularly necessary as a result of the spread of ELF, which has changed the learners' motivations for learning as well as the way they identify with the language (Jenkins et al. 2011; Isabelli-García 2006). As Melitz (2016: 2) points out, "there has never been in the past a language spoken more widely in the world than English is today." What is more, in 2013 the number of people actively learning English at a useful level was estimated at 1.75 billion people worldwide, and this figure is predicted to reach 2 billion by 2020 (British Council 2013). However, the importance of the language does not only affect the number of people who learn it, but also the way in which it is taught and learned. The emergence of concepts such as World Englishes (WE) and ELF have challenged the traditional English language teacher paradigm (Pakir 2009), wherein the ultimate objective was often the unrealistic ideal of native-like competence (Ke & Cahyani 2014). It has been suggested that concepts such as ELF may lead to a reconsideration of these traditional native speaker models (Seidlhofer 2001), in that the language learner, rather than aspiring towards native-like proficiency, could instead aim towards becoming a proficient, international English speaker (Majanen 2008). This approach seems appropriate, given that native-speaker norms and usages are often not relevant in the context of an international ELF exchange (Ke & Cahyani 2014), as individuals may be more concerned with being understood rather than speaking like a native speaker.

This alternative approach will evidently affect the language learner, both in how they identify with their target language (TL), as well as their motivation to learn. Regarding identity, it has been suggested that ELF may offer a more attractive identity to the non-native speaker, given that "instead of perpetual *learners* of English, they can now regard themselves as legitimate English *users* in the international world" (Majanen 2008: 2). As for motivation, there are at least two repercussions as a result of ELF (Dörnyei & Ushioda 2013). Firstly, given that speaking English is increasingly viewed as a basic educational skill crucial to economic and professional advancement, a learner's motivation for learning English is likely different from that of learning other languages. This issue is highlighted by Block & Cameron (2002) who discuss how language learning and communication skills that are demanded by globalisation influence the learners' motivation towards instrumentality. Secondly, Gardner & Lambert (1972: 135) highlight the importance of integrative motivation, stating that a motivated learner "must be willing to identify with members of another ethnolinguistic group and take on very subtle aspects of their behaviour." However, this concept of integrative motivation makes little sense when discussing ELF learners, who may instead focus on communication with speakers of different linguistic backgrounds (Breiteneder 2005). In such a context, traditional concepts in motivation research such as integrativeness and attitudes toward the TL community become increasingly obscure, given that it becomes more and more difficult for ELF learners to identify with a clear target group or culture (Yashima 2009). Consequently, when it comes to ELF, it may make more sense to evaluate students' motivation based on their international posture, that is, the "tendency to see oneself as connected to the international community" (Yashima 2009: 3), rather than a specific second language (L2) group. For example, in the context of a European SA, native Spanish speakers studying abroad in the UK can interact in English with both native English speakers, as well as other non-native speakers using ELF. In such a context, these students may not (solely) be motivated to improve their language skills in order to become integrated in the native speaker community. Their language motivation may also be driven by a desire to become integrated into a community of ELF users in an Erasmus "community of practice" (Wenger 1998). As Kaypak & Ortaçtepe (2014) point out, due to the growing number of Erasmus students studying abroad in such ELF communities, what is needed is a closer look into the use of English in these communities.

With this in mind, this study takes a cross-sectional approach, using quantitative research tools to investigate the identity and motivation of the language learners in the context of SA, by exploring the differences between pre- and end-of SA students, and between language learning in an English-speaking country compared to a French/German-speaking country. The participants in the study are Spanish-Catalan bilinguals, learning English, as well as either German or French as part of their undergraduate degree, and who spent a semester abroad in an English-, German- or French-speaking country.

2 Literature review

The following three sections provide an overview of the relevant literature for this study: the fields of SA, identity and motivation.

2.1 Study Abroad

Since the second half of the twentieth century, there has been an exponential development of a global market in international education (Mazzarol et al. 2003). This surge of internationalisation naturally has also included the encouragement and increase of SA programmes (Jackson 2008a). For example, within the European context, one of the key features of the European linguistic policy towards multilingualism "has been the promotion of student mobility across Europe" (Pérez-Vidal 2011: 103).

As Jackson (2008b) points out, much of SA research to date has been dominated by statistical studies that have focused on linguistic outcomes and grammatical development, while, according to Coleman (1998), essential components of proficiency, such as sociocultural and intercultural competence, have been largely neglected. Collentine & Freed (2004: 165) also point to this issue, highlighting the need to better define "the social conditions surrounding, affecting and perhaps impeding learner gains."

This call has led SA research to change its trajectory from "identifying and quantifying linguistic gains (or lack of) to exploring the experience of SA from an ethnographic perspective" (Devlin 2014: 6). Recent research has thus seen an increase in introspective techniques such as diary studies, first-person narratives and interviews, as well as case studies and ethnographies, in an effort to better understand the processes involved in language learning (Jackson 2008b). As Devlin (2014) points out, this "learner-centric" approach has allowed researchers such as Isabelli-García (2006), Jackson (2008b) and Kinginger (2004) to underscore the specific factors which aid or inhibit a learner's language acquisition and access to native speakers. More recently, Mitchell et al. (2015: 134) have called for a "more refined analysis of students' personal motivations and characteristics, multilingual language practices, and emerging social relations" with the aim of explaining the variation in the L2 development of SA participants. This learner-centric approach reflects the "social turn" in SLA (Block 2003), and may aid in deciphering why there is "no evidence that one context of learning is uniformly superior to another for all students" Collentine & Freed (2004: 164).

2.2 Identity

One facet of the above mentioned learner-centric approach is the issue of identity. According to Oxford Dictionaries, the term identity can be used to describe "the fact of being who or what a person or thing is' (Identity [Def.1] 2016), and also 'a close similarity or affinity" (Identity [Def.2] 2016). Many researchers now define identity as a process, due to the fact that individual identities are not fixed states, but rather "are negotiated, or performed, in the interplay of the relationships between individuals and their social contexts" (Stockton 2015: 11). As regards SLA, both an L2 learner's individual identity and also how they identify with the culture of the TL are of particular interest. L2 motivation researchers "have always believed that a foreign language is more than a mere communication code [...] and have therefore typically adopted paradigms that linked the L2 to the individual's personal 'core', forming an important part of one's identity" (Dörnyei & Ushioda 2009: 9).

Many researchers have highlighted the importance of the degree to which the learner identifies with the TL, finding that in many cases a positive identification with the TL and target culture results in successful language acquisition (e.g. Regan 2013; Norton 2000; Nestor & Regan 2011; Nestor et al. 2012), while negative identification results in unsuccessful language acquisition (e.g. Norton 2000; Block 2006). Informal language learning and its impact on the learner's identity is thus of particular interest, given that "the sustained immersion in a new cultural and linguistic milieu seemingly cannot but impact on the individual's sense of self" (Block 2007: 109).

The learning context of SA is one such environment that may challenge the learner's identity. Having been taken out of their 'comfort zone', and thrown into an entirely different linguistic milieu, learners often struggle with their sense of identity (Jackson 2008b). According to Kinginger (2009: 202), the value of SA as a learning environment depends on "whether [the student's] encounters lead to frustration or to the desperate, creative longing to craft a foreign language-mediated identity." It is possible that the way in which students manage this impact on their sense of self will ultimately determine the success of their language acquisition. Thus, by investigating these individual experiences, researchers may be able to interpret the varying results of SA students' lives.

2.3 Motivation

As with identity, research has also shown that motivation is a key factor in students' learning (Keblawi 2009). As pointed out by Dörnyei (2014), even language learners with the most remarkable abilities will be unable to accomplish long term goals if they lack the motivation to do so.

According to Ushioda & Dörnyei (2012), there have been four different stages in the history of motivation research in foreign language teaching and learning, as summarised in Table 1.

Table 1: Four stages in the history of motivation research, adapted from Ushioda & Dörnyei (2012).

Stage	Timeline	Characteristics
(1) The social psychological period	1959-1990	Proposes two kinds of motivational orientation: integrative and instrumental.
(2) The cognitive-situated period	During the 1990s	Draws from cognitive theories in educational psychology
(3) The process-oriented period	Turn of the century	Focuses on motivational change
(4) The socio-dynamic period	Current	Concerned with dynamic systems and contextual interactions

The current stage, the socio-dynamic period, which has developed over the last decade, has given rise to three new conceptual approaches (Ushioda & Dörnyei 2012), namely (i) Ushioda's (2009) person-in-context relational view of L2 motivation, (ii) motivation from a complex dynamic systems perspective (Waninge et al. 2014), and (iii) Dörnyei's (2009) L2 motivational self system, which will be central to the current study. This system is influenced by two key psychological concepts, namely Markus & Nurius' (1986) theory of *possible selves* and Higgins' (1987) theory of *ought selves*. The L2 motivational self system fuses aspects of these two concepts and draws on the idea that an individual's motivation is made up of the following three key parts:

1. The *Ideal L2 Self*: the image one has of their future self as an L2 user according to their own wishes. This component typically fosters integrative

and internalised motives (e.g. 'I am motivated to learn Spanish because I see myself being surrounded by lots of Spanish friends.').

2. The *Ought-to L2 Self:* the image one has of their future self as an L2 user according to external expectations. This facet deals with attributes which the learner believes they *ought to* possess in order to meet expectations and avoid negative outcomes. This component reflects more extrinsic types of instrumental motivation (e.g. 'I need to work hard at learning my L2 so that I don't disappoint my parents.').

3. The *L2 learning experience:* concerned with volition, or 'executive' motives, that is, "motivational influences that operate during task engagement, facilitating or impeding goal-directed behavior." (Dörnyei & Ottó 1998: 45). Such influences may include the impact of the language teacher, curriculum, peer group, experience of success or failure, etc. (e.g. 'I don't want to learn French because my teacher is not very nice and I always get bad grades.').

Within this motivational self system, both instrumental motivation (i.e. wanting to learn a language for some practical purpose such as economic or educational advancement) and integrative motivation (i.e. the desire to learn a language in order to communicate with the language's speakers and out of an interest in the language's culture) play a key role. However, regarding ELF, the role of integrative motivation may undergo a drastic change given that learners of English are perhaps less inclined to see themselves integrating with native speakers than with other non-native English speakers, as discussed above. This issue has been highlighted by Dailey (2009: 7), who states that "due to the change in global languages, there is no model community to identify with, consequently leading to a broader classification of integrative motivation." This implies that in a context of international students using English as a common language, it makes little sense to gauge the extent to which these students wish to integrate with a native English-speaking community. To resolve this issue, international posture has been offered as an alternative to integrative motivation (Yashima 2009), a concept which captures the learners' tendency to relate themselves to an international community rather than a specific L2 group. In other words, it captures "a tendency to see oneself as connected to the international community, have concerns for international affairs and possess a readiness to interact with people [of different nationalities]" (Yashima 2002: 3). Yashima introduced this term in relation to Japanese students learning English in Japan. The context at hand, however, differs in that students studying abroad may have both the option of integrating with native English speakers, and/or with other non-native English users, with one situation at times appearing more attractive, for varying reasons.

A final concept that is important here is that of Willingness to Communicate (WTC), that is, the willingness of students to actively seek out opportunities to communicate in their TL. WTC has been linked to both motivation and international posture. For example, a study by Yashima (2002) found that motivation affected self-confidence in L2 communication, which in turn led to increased WTC in the L2. In addition, a significant link was found between International Posture (IP) and WTC in a L2.

With the increasing dominance of socio-dynamic approaches in L2 motivation research, it is becoming increasingly evident that the dynamic individuality of the learners needs to be taken into account, as well as the fact that the students' identities, and their motivation, are in constant change (Guerrero 2015). Given that research to date has proven the Ideal L2 Self and the L2 learning experience to be important components of the L2 motivational self system (e.g. Taguchi et al. 2009; Islam et al. 2013; Kim & Kim 2014), while the ought-to self has been shown to be the least contributing factor (Islam et al. 2013; Papi 2010 as quoted in Tort Calvo 2015), the current work will focus only on the two former components of the L2 motivational self system. IP will also be investigated, in order to determine its effect on the participants' motivation. To this effect, the fourteen categories chosen for this study will reflect these issues, focusing on the Ideal L2 Self, L2 Learning Experience, WTC and IP.

3 The study

The current study was carried out for two main reasons. Firstly, in order to begin to answer Mitchell et al.'s (2015) call for more a refined analysis of students' personal motivations during SA. Secondly to investigate what Kinginger (2009) highlights as one of the most pressing issues for SA researchers: the effect of intensified globalization on language learning. In order to do so, the study has two objectives. Firstly, it compares two groups of students cross-sectionally, prior to and at the end of a SA period. Secondly, focusing only on the second group of students who have completed their SA, this study contrasts those spending a SA in an English-speaking country with those in a German- or French-speaking country. The study puts forth the following research questions and hypotheses:

RQ1. Is there an effect of a three-month SA on the motivation and identity of higher education students who are sojourning in English, French- and German-speaking countries?

H1. It is expected that there will be a difference between the identity and motivation of these students and those who have not spent a three-month period of SA.

RQ2. Is there an effect of a three-month SA on the motivation and identity of higher education students who are sojourning in an English-speaking country as compared with a French- or German-speaking country?

H2. It is expected that there will be a difference between the motivation and identity of students sojourning in English-speaking countries compared to French- or German-speaking countries, given that students studying English may be more instrumentally motivated.

4 Methodology

4.1 Research approach and design

The original design of the study aimed to capture the identity and motivation of SA students by means of quantitative data collections.

Table 2: Design of the study.

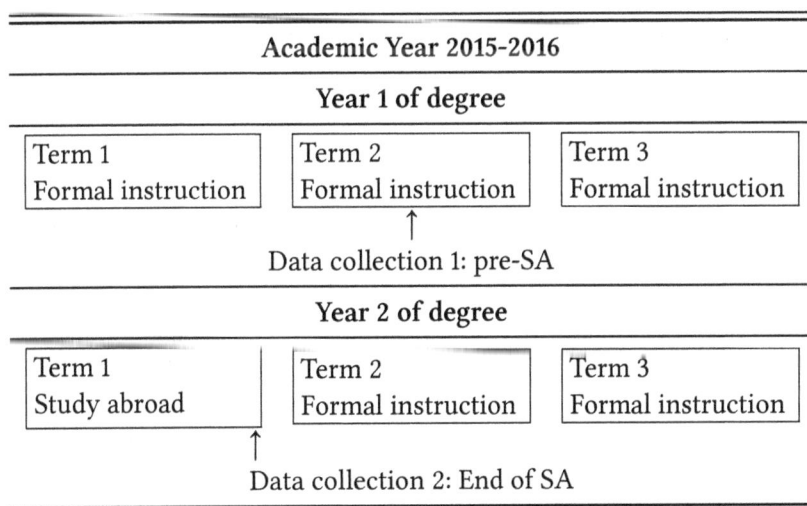

Academic Year 2015-2016		
Year 1 of degree		
Term 1 Formal instruction	Term 2 Formal instruction	Term 3 Formal instruction
	Data collection 1: pre-SA	
Year 2 of degree		
Term 1 Study abroad	Term 2 Formal instruction	Term 3 Formal instruction
Data collection 2: End of SA		

The design of this study, outlined in Table 2, spanned across one academic year and was conducted with two groups of students in the first and second year of the same undergraduate degrees in order to collect data on motivation and identity from students before and after SA[1]. More specifically, data collection took place in term 2, year 1 (Group 1, pre-SA), and in term 1, year 2 (Group 2, end of SA).

4.2 Participants

The participants in this study were Spanish-Catalan bilinguals (N=68) studying in the first or second year of their undergraduate degree. All participants were learning English as a major language, as well as either French or German as a minor language in their undergraduate degree. As part of their curriculum, the students completed one year of formal instruction, followed by a compulsory three-month SA in a TL country. The sojourn was organised by the university at the beginning of the second year of their degree and counted towards ECTS credits in their home university. The majority of the students were between 18 and 22 years old (*M*=19.7) and were primarily female (10 male, 58 female), reflecting a demographic trend in language degrees.

Group 1 (N=25) was made up of first year, pre-SA students. Group 2 (N=43) was made up of second year students of the same degree who were at the end of their SA at the time of the data collection. Both Group 1 and Group 2 completed the questionnaire concerning language background, motivation and identity.

4.3 Data collection

4.3.1 Instruments: The questionnaire

A questionnaire was used as the main instrument for data collection in this study (see Appendix 1). It was made up of a total of 116 questions: seven open questions concerning background information and the rest regarding issues concerning identity, motivation and WTC, with a five-level Likert scale format, offering five choices for each item ranging from 'strongly agree' to 'strongly disagree', or 'absolutely true' to 'not true at all' (Table 3). The questionnaire was written in English given that the faculty of the participants' degree programmes set a minimum standard of a B2.2 level in English for admission, because students are expected to achieve a C1.1 by the end of their first year of formal instruction and a C1.2 by the end of their second year (Beattie 2014). This level of En-

---

[1]Due to the time restrictions, it was not possible for a two-year longitudinal sample to be collected, and thus a cross-sectional design had to be adopted for the purposes of this study.

glish was a requirement for all students including those who would SA in a non-English-speaking country. The Likert scale format was chosen, rather than a simple yes/no answer format, to allow room for manoeuvre, while at the same time maintaining control over the possible responses (Bloomer 2010).

Table 3: Sample questionnaire item using a five-level Likert scale format.

	absolutely true	mostly true	partly true partly untrue	not really true	not true at all
33. In the future, I would like to participate in a volunteer activity to help foreigners living in the surrounding community. (155)	☐	☐	☐	☐	☐

The questionnaire was based on Ryan's (2009) and Yashima's (2009) questionnaires, which were used to investigate the Ideal L2 Self of English learners in tertiary educational institutions. These questionnaires were chosen for two main reasons. Firstly, they investigated the Ideal L2 Self while also incorporating elements that were relevant to the current study, including International Posture and Willingness to Communicate. Secondly, variables had been piloted and were shown to have high internal reliability.

The questionnaire, which consisted of a total of 14 categories, was divided into three sections: the first section dealt with personal details and general information. The second dealt with the categories WTC in the native language (NL) and TL, which was given its own section due to the large number of questions it contained, and the third with the remaining twelve. As discussed by Dörnyei & Csizér (2012: 76), the notion of multi-item scales, that is, the use of more than one item to address each identified content area, "is the central component in scientific questionnaire design." With this in mind, the categories in the questionnaire were made up of multi-item scales of between three to eighteen items. Furthermore, items and scales were mixed throughout the questionnaire to create variety and prevent participants from simply repeating previous answers (Dörnyei & Csizér 2012).

Initial piloting of the item pool, which took the form of a think-aloud protocol, was carried out with three students in order to test the questionnaire. This process involved having the individuals answer the items in the questionnaire and provide feedback, after which the questionnaire was further revised prior to administration[2].

The original questionnaires by Ryan (2009) and Yashima (2009) were revised for the purposes of the current study in three main ways. Firstly, several categories were eliminated given that they were "only of peripheral interest but not directly related to the variables and hypotheses that the questionnaire has been designed to investigate" (Dörnyei & Csizér 2012: 76). Secondly, several questions were re-worded in order to create additional questions for §3, which contained two distinct parts: 'While Abroad' (WA) and 'In General' (IG). In the section WA of the questionnaire, students were asked to specifically reflect on how they felt while abroad. These questions were used for comparison purposes with the original question found in §3 IG, where the students were asked to reflect on their feelings in general. An example of this can be seen as follows:

(1) WA, Question 15: Using English/French/German in front of people on Erasmus makes me feel like I will be thought of as less Spanish.
IG, Question 37: Using English/French/German in front of people in Spain makes me feel like I will be thought of as less Spanish.

Thirdly, newly created questions were introduced in the section on 'WA', asking students to reflect on their linguistic improvement and ease of learning while abroad. The questionnaires for Group 1 and 2 were identical except for the fact that Group 2's questionnaire included the additional 'WA' segment of §3, which dealt with reflection after time spent studying abroad. As Group 1 had not yet been abroad, this section was excluded from their questionnaire. Furthermore, Group 1 was instructed to indicate in which country they planned to do their SA, and to answer the questionnaire thinking specifically about the language spoken in that country, while Group 2 focused on the language of the country they were studying in at the time. Other than these two differences, the questionnaire and the order of the questions were the same for both groups.

---

[2] Given the timeline of this study, the think-aloud protocol was considered the best piloting scenario available to the researcher, as a full piloting with the specific population it was intended for was not possible.

In order to determine the appropriateness of the scales, reliability analyses were carried out following the study. Post hoc item analysis revealed that a number of items (six questions in total) did not work in the particular category, and were consequently removed in order to increase the scales' internal reliability. Despite these exclusions, it was found that the Cronbach alpha values of some categories were not as high as they were in the source questionnaires, with five categories above .75, and nine ranging between .60 and .67 (see Appendix 2). As Dörnyei & Taguchi (2009: 95) pointed out, "if the Cronbach alpha of a scale does not reach .60, this should sound warning bells". Given that all categories were not below this figure, they were deemed acceptable for the purposes of the current study.

4.3.2 Procedure

The main criterion for taking the questionnaire was that the students must have been partaking in a SA, a compulsory component of the students' undergraduate degrees. To this effect, convenience sampling was used in this study (Dörnyei 2007), as the students who took the questionnaire all possessed the key characteristic relevant to the study: having spent an academic semester abroad (Aiken 1997). Statistical consideration was also taken into account, with the sample including more than 30 people (Hatch & Lazaraton 1991). During the last month of their SA (Year 2, Term 1), the 44 participants that made up Group 2 answered the questionnaire via the online survey platform Qualtrics. The students were contacted via email to introduce the study and were send a hyperlink to complete the online questionnaire, which took about fifteen to twenty minutes to complete. The students were also contacted at a later date in order to have them sign a consent form, indicating that they gave their approval for their data to be used in the study. The students were also informed that the results would be fully confidential, and that their personal data would not be used by or distributed to other parties. The 25 Group 1 students were invited to take part in the questionnaire at the end of one of their university classes (Year 1, Term 2). All students signed the consent form at this time, and were then sent the hyperlink to complete the questionnaire.

4.4 Data analysis

The data gathered by means of the questionnaire were analysed using SPSS, version 23. When coding the questionnaire data, each response on the Likert scale was assigned a consecutive number, as suggested by Dörnyei & Csizér (2012):

numerical value 1 was assigned to 'strongly disagree', 2 to 'disagree', 3 to 'somewhat agree/somewhat disagree', 4 to 'agree', and 5 to 'strongly agree'. Before analysis, data cleaning and data manipulation were carried out. Negatively-worded items were re-coded by being reversed before analysis. For the first and second research questions, non-parametric, independent-samples Mann-Whitney U tests were carried out, given that the results of two independent groups (Group 1 pre-SA versus Group 2 end of SA, as well as students on SA in an English-speaking country versus students on SA in a French- or German-speaking country) were being compared, and the data were not normally distributed (Dörnyei 2007). Non-parametric, paired samples Wilcoxon signed-rank tests were also carried out on the second year's 'While abroad' and 'In General' comparison pairs, given that two sets of scores obtained from the same group were being compared, and the data were not normally distributed (Dörnyei 2007). Alpha level was set to be at α =.05, as is typical in the SLA literature (Larson-Hall 2012).

5 Results

5.1 RQ1: SA vs. at home

The first research question in this study aimed to answer whether there was an effect of a three-month study abroad on the motivation and identity of higher education students sojourning in English-, French- or German-speaking countries. Results of Mann-Whitney U tests comparing the pre-SA Group 1 with the end of SA Group 2 showed a statistical difference in only 2 out of the 14 categories, along with 2 individual questions. These results are to be interpreted with caution, given the risk of obtaining significant results by chance when running multiple statistical tests. However, they point to some interesting trends in the data that merit discussion here and further investigation in future research. Table 4 below shows the descriptive statistics with the means, the standard deviation and the statistics for the categories as well as the individual questions, which yielded significant results. In interpreting results, it should be borne in mind that higher numerical values correspond to 'agree' and 'strongly agree', while lower values correspond to low agreement. Three categories were relevant, namely (i) interest in foreign languages (IFL), (ii) international posture: having things to communicate in the world (IPHTCW) and (iii) WTC in the individual's native language (WTCN).

The results revealed that Group 1 was significantly more likely to want to learn the foreign language of the country they were visiting (IFL_31), and that their

Table 4: Results of RQ1.

Question	M		SD		U	z	p	n²	d
	G1	G2	G1	G2					
WTCN_- Mean: Mean of 9 statements on "Willingness to Communi- cate' in the students' L1	3.81	3.3	.824	1.01	304.500	2.063	.039	0.07	0.547
IFL_Mean: Mean of 4 statements on 'Interest in Foreign Languages'	5	4.3	.000	.1.28	387.500	2.874	.004	0.054	0.476
IFL_31: If I were visiting a foreign country I would like to be able to speak its language.	5	4.7	.000	.513	387.500	2.885	.004	0.054	0.476
IPHTCW_34: I have thoughts that I want to share with people from other parts of the world.	3.76	4.23	.779	.996	724.000	2.514	.012	0.083	0.601

overall interest in foreign languages was higher than that of Group 2 (IFL_Mean). I presume that given that Group 2 was immersed in a context where it was the norm to use their TL, and possibly other languages as well, it is suggested that they were less conscious of having to *learn* the language but instead *use* it as a normal part of their day. That is to say, their foreign language may have become less foreign to them as they became more accustomed to using it. With regards to IP, results showed that Group 2 was significantly more likely to have thoughts they wished to share with others of different nationalities (IPHTCW_-34). This makes sense, given that Group 2 was likely to have spent a lot of time with international students while abroad. Finally, Group 1 appeared to have a significantly higher level of WTC in their native language (WTCN_Mean), but not their foreign language.

In order to investigate this further, Wilcoxon signed-rank tests were carried out, which showed that there was a significant difference between Group 1's WTC in their native language (M=3.8, SD=.824) compared to their WTC in their foreign language (WTCF) (M=3.12, SD=.857), with students being more willing to communicate in their native language (WTCN) (T =53.500, z = 2.759, p = .006). No such difference was found for WTCN (M = 3.27, SD = 1.01) and WTCF (M = 3.38, SD = .854) among Group 2 (T = 292.500, z = .086, p = .932). It appeared that while both groups had similar WTC scores in their foreign language, Group 2, at the end of their SA, experienced a reduced WTC score in their native language. This is perhaps due to using it less while abroad and the fact that the students may have felt less dependent on it while they were abroad. Figure 1 displays these results visually.

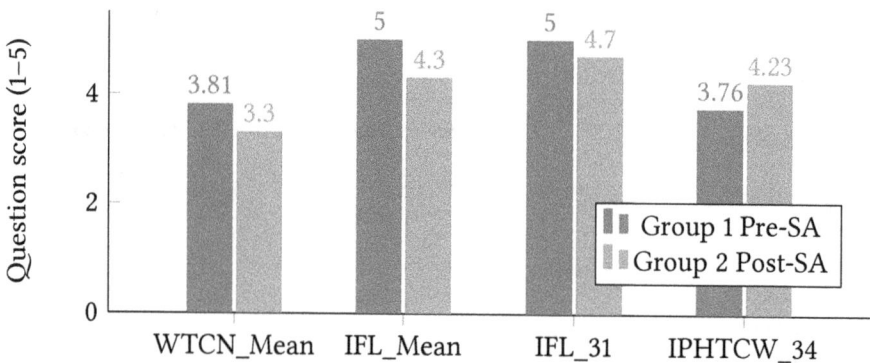

Figure 1: Results of RQ1.

In addition to comparing them to the Group 1 pre-SA students, the Group 2 end of SA students were also assessed using the comparison pairs 'In General' (IG) and 'While Abroad' (WA), wherein students reflected on how they felt about issues in general and specifically while abroad, as outlined in the methodology section. Results of Wilcoxon signed-rank tests showed that, out of the 14 comparison pairs divided between 'IG' and 'WA', 4 pairs were statistically different (Table 5).

Pair 1 indicated that students felt they would be thought of as less Spanish when using their L2 in Spain as compared to during thier Erasmus. This suggests that students may perceive themselves to be more self-conscious about speaking their TL in their home country, given that they will not be presenting themselves as having a uniquely Spanish identity. On the other hand, in an international setting, students may perceive themselves as being free to exhibit their multilingual identity without any threat of loss of face. Pair 2 suggested that, while reflecting on being abroad, students were less inclined to believe speaking their L2 well was needed to communicate with people from other countries, which seems counterintuitive. This could be explained by the fact that WA, students may be exposed to more situations in which they could use their TL, meaning that they did not need to seek out such situations to the extent they would at home. In other words, simply being abroad provided more opportunities to interact in the target language. This may have resulted in the students being less concerned with needing a high L2 proficiency level in order to meet people from other countries: simply being abroad would lead to these opportunities. Pair 3 indicated that in the future, students saw themselves working abroad more than simply living abroad. This suggests that students may have been more instrumentally motivated in this regard, thinking practically about their opportunities for economic advancement in the future. Pair 4 suggested that students were overall more anxious speaking to a native speaker while abroad, as opposed to any other speaker in the TL. This finding is consistent with what is suggested in the literature (e.g. Woodrow 2006).

5.2 RQ2: English vs. other languages

The second research question in this study aimed to investigate whether there was an effect of a three-month study abroad on the motivation and identity of higher education students sojourning in an English-speaking country as compared with a French- or German-speaking country. In order to investigate this, Mann-Whitney U tests were also carried out in order to compare students who had sojourned, or planned to sojourn, in an English-speaking country with those

Table 5: Comparison Pairs.

Pair	In General	While Abroad	T	z	p	n^2
1	37. Using Eng/Fr/Ger in front of people in Spain makes me feel like I will be thought of as less Spanish.	15. Using Eng/Fr/Ger in front of people on Erasmus makes me feel like I will be thought of as less Spanish.	713.500	5.032	.000	11.788
2	53. If I could speak Eng/Fr/Ger well, I could get to know more people from other countries.	26. If I could speak Eng/Fr/Ger well, I could get to know more people from other countries while on my Erasmus.	41.000	3.624	.000	11.596
3	21. In the future, I would rather have a job in my home country than abroad.	9. I would rather stay in my home country than live abroad.	352.500	4.041	.000	8.036
4	16. I think I often feel anxious and ill at ease when I have to speak to someone in Eng/Fr/Ger.	25. I think I often feel anxious and ill at ease when I have to speak Eng/Fr/Ger with a native speaker.	313.000	3.044	.002	8.297

in a German- or French-speaking country. Only 1 of the 14 categories, namely the Ideal L2 Self, and 4 individual questions, were found to be significantly different when comparing the two factors, which once again demands caution in interpreting the results. Table 6 below shows the descriptive statistics with the means, the standard deviation and the test statistics for the category and questions which yielded significant results. Two categories were relevant, namely the Ideal L2 Self (IL2S) and intended leaning effort (ILE). Again, it should be borne in mind that higher values correspond to 'strongly agree' and 'agree' while lower values imply less agreement.

Most importantly, the results show that the English group scored higher overall with regards to Ideal L2 Self (IL2S_Mean), suggesting that those students focusing on learning English could better visualize themselves as the L2 user they wished to be than those in the Fr/Ger group. One reason for this could be the fact that the English group may simply believe that the English language is more important for their future given its role as an international language. Within this category, it was found that those in the English group could imagine themselves using English in their future career (IL2S_42) to a greater extent than the French/German group. This element of instrumental motivation is not surprising given the importance that is placed on speaking English for economic advancement, as mentioned above and discussed by Block & Cameron (2002). Results also showed that while the English group was more likely to take classes elsewhere if it was not possible to learn their TL in their home university (ILE_4), the French/German group was more likely to take a language course if it was offered in the future (ILE_54). Finally, it was found that the English group was significantly more likely to think that it was extremely important for them to learn their target language (ILE_24), again highlighting the importance placed on learning English. Figure 2 displays the values above in order to offer a visual presentation of the results, where higher values correspond to more agreement with the proposed statements.

6 Discussion

Regarding RQ1, the results of the questionnaire pointed to a difference between Group 1 and 2 in two of the fourteen categories, and a difference between the English and French/German subgroups of Group 2 in just one of the fourteen categories. Results showed that the pre-SA Group 1 was significantly more likely to want to learn the foreign language of the country they will be visiting and that their overall mean for interest in foreign languages was greater than that

Table 6: Results of RQ2.

Question	M Eng	M Fr/Ger	SD Eng	SD Fr/Ger	U	z	p	n^2	d
IL2S_Mean	4.57	3.58	1.05	1.60	216.000	2.597	.009	0.057	0.49
IL2S_42: In my future career, I imagine myself being able to use English/French/German.	4.92	4.69	.269	.480	260.000	2.248	.025	0.025	0.321
ILE_24: It is extremely important for me to learn English/French/German.	4.69	4.38	.643	.650	239.000	2.040	.041	0.041	0.411
ILE_4: If English/French/German were not taught in my home university, I would try to go to classes somewhere else.	4.71	4.23	.457	.927	238.500	1.977	.048	0.041	0.413
ILE_54: If an English/French/German course was offered in the future, I would like to take it.	4.04	4.69	1.120	.480	453.000	2.044	.041	0.055	0.481

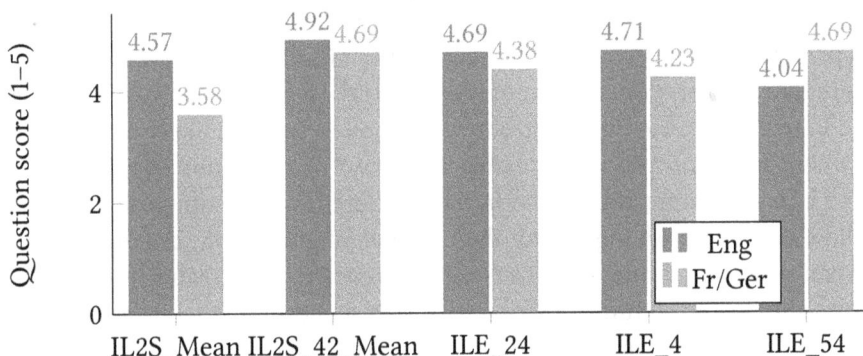

Figure 2: Results of RQ2.

of end of SA Group 2. Group 2, however, was significantly more likely to have thoughts they wish to share with others of different nationalities, suggesting a higher level of international posture in this regard. Finally, it was found that the pre-SA students were significantly more willing to communicate in their native language than in their target language, whereas the end-of SA group was equally as likely to communicate in both languages. These findings are in accordance with the idea that SA offers a potential boost to the learner's willingness to communicate, as well as a consequential development of a sense of belonging within an international community (Juan-Garau et al. 2014). Notably, regarding the remaining categories, no statistical difference was found, which suggests that a period of SA may have little or no effect on dimensions such as fear of assimilation, instrumentality, language anxiety, L2 self confidence, international vocation or activities, interest in international news and WTC in the TL. At this point, it should again be noted that in order to address this research question, a cross-sectional approach was taken. It is important to take this into consideration when discussing the results, and highlight the benefit of carrying out a similar study with a longitudinal approach in order to determine whether similar findings would arise. As for RQ2, comparing Group 2 students sojourning in an English-speaking country with those in a German- or French-speaking country, it was found that the English group considered learning their TL to be extremely important, and that students could imagine themselves using this language in their future careers to a significantly greater amount than the other groups. In other words, as suggested in the literature, there is a tendency for those learning a lingua franca such as English to be increasingly instrumentally motivated (Block & Cameron 2002). In addition, this group appeared to be better able to visualise themselves as the L2 users they wished to be than the French/German group, having a statistically higher score in the Ideal L2 Self mean. Finally, while the French/German group was more likely to take a language course if it was offered in the future, the English group was found to be more likely to take classes elsewhere (e.g. in a private language academy) if it was not possible to learn their TL in their home university. In these different ways, both groups appeared to show an interest in improving their formal language learning outside of the university setting. Again, despite these differences, a far greater number of categories showed no significant difference. This suggests that while students who study in an English compared with a non-English speaking country may differ in particular with regards to the Ideal L2 Self, this appears not to be the case for the remaining dimensions. The results of the questionnaire thus allow us to partially confirm our hypothesis, as only some categories resulted in a significant effect of a three-month SA on the language learning motivation and identity of higher education students, in particular regarding categories such as WTC in the native language and interest in foreign languages comparing pre-SA and end-SA (research question 1), and the ideal L2 self comparing the English group and the French/German group, (research question 2).

The results suggest that those questions which did not reach a statistical difference may not have done so due to two main reasons (besides the obvious possibility that our sample was not large enough to achieve sufficient statistical power). Firstly, it is possible that the instrument itself was unable to capture the subtle changes in the individuals' motivation and identity during study abroad or across groups. As is suggested by DeKeyser (2014: 318), "much more detailed documentation is needed of how individual students are motivated for acquiring advanced language proficiency" and "how this motivation increases or decreases during their stay abroad". Secondly, it is possible that there simply was no difference between the two groups, given that students in each group generally achieved very high scores in each section. As the students were all enrolled in specialised language learning degrees it may be that the majority were just very highly motivated language learners, with no noticeable differences among the groups. This issue is also addressed in DeKeyser (2014: 314) who points out that these language students who go on SA "are also quite motivated because language learning is what they are all about as translators/interpreters". That is to say, there is a certain ceiling effect at hand, typical of learners at a more advanced stage (Meara 1994). It should also be pointed out that participation was entirely voluntary, meaning that it is possible that only those students who were more motivated participated in the study. Thus, while the findings of the study reveal some interesting differences among the various groups, what is perhaps more noteworthy is this lack of differences found in the majority of the categories. Categories such as fear of assimilation, instrumentality, language anxiety, L2 self confidence, international vocation or activities, interest in international news and WTC in the TL showed no statistical difference both overall and in the individual questions. This is to say that neither the period of SA, nor the country which they studied in, affected these issues. Future research would benefit from investigating whether similar results would be found in a longitudinal study, and from exploring the specific factors that affect, or do not affect, students regarding the categories addressed in this study.

7 Conclusions

This study aimed to investigate the effect of SA on the motivation and identity of higher education students. The results show only a partial difference between the two groups who completed the questionnaire, perhaps, as suggested above, due to the overall high levels of motivation across the students, indicating that a more detailed investigation is required in order to discern significant differences between the groups, if they do exist.

Concerning the limitations of the study (besides the sample type), a further issue was the sample size of students focusing on learning French or German. It was hoped that the groups would contain an equal number of students studying in each country. However, given the demand by students, the majority of placements were in English-speaking countries.

While individually the fields of SA, identity, motivation and ELF, as well as the theory of the L2 motivational self system, have been studied extensively, relatively little has been done so far to investigate how these elements interact. This study has taken the initial steps towards understanding the effect of SA, on an array of factors pertaining to motivation and identity, investigating in particular elements from the L2 motivational self system, while also aiming to gain a preliminary understanding of the effect of ELF on these issues. It has been suggested that while a period of SA may have a positive impact on learners' WTC in the NL and interest in FL, it may have no effect on the other issues that were investigated. Furthermore, when comparing those studying abroad in an English/non-English-speaking country, differences were found in particular with regards to the category of the Ideal L2 Self, with participants showing similarities in the other categories.

As highlighted above, a more detailed investigation is needed alongside the quantitative analysis in order to fully understand and discern the similarities and differences between the groups. With this in mind, in order to gain a more thorough understanding of the development and negotiation of the learner's on-going motivational process during SA (Kim 2009), in Geoghegan & Pérez-Vidal (forthcoming), a follow-up study is carried out, adopting quantitative tools in order to provide this more detailed investigation.

Appendix 1: Questionnaire content

We would like to ask you to help us by answering the following questions concerning language learning in Study Abroad, and people's feelings about languages and communication in general. This is not a test so there are no 'right' or 'wrong' answers. We are interested in your personal opinion. Please give your answers sincerely as only this will guarantee the success of the investigation. Thank you very much for your help!

Section 1

First, would you please answer a few personal details and general information – we need this information to be able to interpret your answers properly.

1. What is your name?

2. What is your age (in years)?

3. What degree are you studying?

4. What foreign languages are you studying as part of your degree? Please write the language, how old you were when you started learning, and your level. e.g. English (6, B2.2) = (I am learning English. I started learning English when I was 6 years old. My level is B2.2) French (11, B1.1) = (I am learning French. I started learning French when I was 11 years old. My level is B1.1)

5. In what country are you doing your Erasmus?

6. Why did you choose this country/language to do your Erasmus?

7. Before this Erasmus, had you ever spent a period of time in a foreign country? If yes, where and for how long (in weeks)? Please include all trips e.g.

1. England (2 weeks) summer 2010, 2. England (4 weeks) summer 2011, 3. Germany (1 week) summer family trip 2011, etc.

Section 2

In this section, there are going to be questions concerning interpersonal communication in everyday and classroom situations, using your native language, or the language you are learning. In some questions, you will be given the option English/French/German. Please answer ONLY with regards to the language of the country where you are abroad (i.e. French if you are in France, German if you are in Germany or English if you are in an English-speaking country).

Q1. How likely would you be to initiate communication in your native language in the following situations?

1. Talking with an acquaintance while waiting for the bus. (2)

2. Talking with a salesperson in a store. (3)

3. Talking in a small group of strangers. (4)

4. Talking with a friend while waiting for the bus. (5)

5. Talking with a stranger while waiting for the bus. (6)

6. Talking in a small group of acquaintances. (7)

7. Volunteering to make a presentation in front of a large group. (8)

8. Being the first one to speak while doing group work. (9)

9. Asking the teacher a question in front of the class. (10)

Q2. How likely would you be to initiate communication in English/French/German in the following situations?

1. Talking with an acquaintance while waiting for the bus. (2)

2. Talking with a salesperson in a store. (3)

3. Talking in a small group of strangers. (4)

4. Talking with a friend while waiting for the bus. (5)

5. Talking with a stranger while waiting for the bus. (6)

6. Talking in a small group of acquaintances. (7)

7. Volunteering to make a presentation in front of a large group. (1)

8. Being the first one to speak while doing group work. (8)

9. Asking the teacher a question in front of the class. (9)

Q3. This section is about the importance and usefulness of languages in the world.

1. How much do you think knowing English/French/German would help you to become a more knowledgeable person? (1)

2. How much do you think English/French/German would help you if you travelled abroad in the future? (2)

3. How much do you think English/French/German would help your future career? (3)

4. To what extent do you think English/French/German is important in the world these days? (4)

Section 3.1

Finally, in this last section, we would like to know to what extent the statements included describe your own feelings or situation. After each statement you'll find five options. Please select the option which best expresses how true the statement is about your feelings or situation. For example, if the first statement was "I like skiing" and you like skiing very much, select the first option. Remember: In some questions, you will be given the option English/French/German. Please answer ONLY with regards to the language of the country where you are abroad (i.e. French if you are in France, German if you are in Germany or English if you are in an English-speaking country). First, think about how you feel while you are studying abroad and answering this questionnaire.

1. While abroad, I take every opportunity I can to speak English/French/ German with international friends. (66)

2. I'm not very good at volunteering answers in my classes in English/French/German. (67)

3. I often read newspapers and watch tv news in the language of the country I am staying. (68)

4. I think that my writing ability has improved the most during this Erasmus. (88)

5. When I first arrived, I found it more difficult to learn English/French/German while on Erasmus than while at home. (69)

6. When I first arrived, I found it more difficult to learn English/French/German than halfway through my Erasmus. (93)

7. I am worried that other speakers of English/French/German would find my English/French/German strange. (70)

8. I try to avoid talking with native English/French/German speakers if I can. (71)

9. I would rather stay in my home country than live abroad. (72)

10. I would not like to live with someone of a different nationality than me. (73)

11. Halfway through my Erasmus, I thought it was easier to learn English/French/German abroad than at home. (74)

12. I think I would be studying English/French/German even if it weren't compulsory. (75)

13. I worry that native speakers will laugh at me when I speak English/French/German. (76)

14. I think that my reading ability has improved the most during this Erasmus. (92)

15. Using English/French/German in front of people on Erasmus makes me feel like I will be thought of as less Spanish. (77)

16. I think I often feel anxious and ill at ease when I have to speak to someone in English/French/German. (78)

17. I would get tense if someone asked me for directions in English/French/German. (79)

18. I think that my speaking ability has improved the most during this Erasmus. (89)

19. Whenever I think of my future career, I imagine myself being able to use English/French/German. (80)

20. I think that my listening ability has improved the most during this Erasmus. (90)

21. I'm interested in the news of the country where I'm staying. (81)

22. In the future, I want to work in a foreign country. (82)

23. I get nervous and confused when I am speaking in my English/French/German classes. (83)

24. I think that my pronunciation has improved the most during this Erasmus. (91)

25. I can honestly say that I am really doing my best to learn English/French/German while on my Erasmus. (84)

26. If I could speak English/French/German well, I could get to know more people from other countries while on my Erasmus. (85)

27. English/French/German ability would help me get a better paying job. (86)

28. Now that I'm at the end of my Erasmus, I think it is easier to learn English/French/German at home than abroad. (87)

29. Now that I'm at the end of my Erasmus, I think that it is more difficult to learn English/French German than I did halfway through. (94)

30. I am more eager to return home now than I was halfway through my Erasmus. (95)

Section 3.2

Now, think about how you feel IN GENERAL about each of these statements.

1. 1. I often read newspapers and watch TV news about foreign countries (123)

2. If I made the effort, I could learn a new foreign language. (124)

3. I would feel somewhat uncomfortable if a foreigner moved in next door. (125)

4. If English/French/German were not taught in my home university, I would try to go to classes somewhere else. (126)

5. I can imagine speaking English/French/German with international friends in my home country. (127)

6. I'm not very good at volunteering answers in our English/French/German language class in my home university. (128)

7. When I hear a song in English/French/German, I listen carefully and try to understand all the words. (129)

8. Learning a foreign language is a difficult task for me. (130)

9. I have ideas about international issues, such as environmental issues and north-south issues. (131)

10. I would like to be able to use English/French/German to get involved with people from other countries. (132)

11. In the future, I would like to make friends with international students studying in my home country. (133)

12. As a part of international society Spanish people must preserve the Spanish language and culture. (134)

13. I have issues to address with people from different parts of the world. (135)

14. I am sure I will be able to learn English/French/German to a high level. (136)

15. Learning English/French/German is necessary because it is an international language. (137)

16. Studying English/French/German will help me get a good job. (138)

17. I always feel that my classmates speak English/French/German better than I do. (139)

18. I don't think what's happening overseas has much to do with my daily life. (140)

19. As internationalization advances there is a danger of losing the Spanish language and culture. (141)

20. When I think about my future, it is important that I use English/French/German. (142)

21. In the future, I would rather have a job in my home country than abroad. (143)

22. I think that English/French/German will help me meet more people. (144)

23. I would like to be able to use English/French/German to communicate with people from other countries. (145)

24. It is extremely important for me to learn English/French/German. (146)

25. I feel uneasy speaking English/French/German with a native speaker. (147)

26. I have a strong interest in international affairs. (148)

27. The things I want to do in the future require me to speak English/French/German. (149)

28. If my dreams come true, I will use English/French/German effectively in the future. (150)

29. I wouldn't mind sharing an apartment or room with an international student. (151)

30. As a result of internationalization, there is a danger Spanish people may forget the importance of Spanish culture. (152)

31. If I were visiting a foreign country I would like to be able to speak its language. (153)

32. Studying English/French/German will give me more opportunities. (154)

33. In the future, I would like to participate in a volunteer activity to help foreigners living in the surrounding community. (155)

34. I have thoughts that I want to share with people from other parts of the world. (156)

35. I think I would study a foreign language even if it weren't compulsory. (157)

36. I worry that the other students will laugh at me when I speak English/French/German. (158)

37. Using English/French/German in front of people in Spain makes me feel like I will be thought of as less Spanish. (159)

38. A knowledge of English/French/German would make me a better educated person. (160)

39. I would like to learn a lot of foreign languages. (161)

40. I would talk to an international student if there was one in my class in my home university. (162)

41. When I meet a speaker of English/French/German, I feel nervous. (163)

42. In my future career, I imagine myself being able to use English/French/German. (164)

43. I often imagine myself as someone who is able to speak English/French/German. (165)

44. I'm not much interested in overseas news. (166)

45. If I could have access to TV stations in English/French/German, I would try to watch them often. (167)

46. I am the kind of person who makes great efforts to learn English/French/German. (168)

47. I'm interested in an international career in the future. (169)

48. For me to become an educated person, I should learn English/French/German. (170)

49. I have no clear opinions about international issues. (171)

50. I want to work in an international organization such as the United Nations. (172)

51. I often talk about situations and events in foreign countries with my family and/or friends. (173)

52. I can honestly say that I am really doing my best to learn English/French/German. (174)

53. If I could speak English/French/German well, I could get to know more people from other countries. (175)

54. If an English/French/German course was offered in the future, I would like to take it. (177)

55. I am working hard at learning English/French/German. (178)

56. In the future, English/French/German ability would help me get a better paying job. (179)

Appendix 2: Cronbach alpha values

Category	Number of items	Cronbach Alpha (original study)	Number of items	Cronbach Alpha (this study)
Fear of assimilation	4	0.67	4	0.651
Ideal L2 self	6	0.85	4	0.761
Instrumentality	6	0.87	6	0.759
Intended learning effort	8	0.86	8	0.760
Interest in foreign languages	4	0.70	3	0.629
International contact	4	0.87	4	0.609
Language anxiety	3	0.81	3	0.670
L2 self confidence	4	0.57	3	0.625
Willingness to communicate in native language	9	0.87	9	0.881
Willingness to communicate in target language	9	0.87	9	0.916
International posture:				
Intergroup approach-avoidance tendency	4	0.80	4	0.625
International vocation or activities	4	0.79	4	0.624
Interest in international news	5	0.76	5	0.676
Having things to communicate to the world	4	0.78	3	0.614

Leah Geoghegan

References

Aiken, Lewis. 1997. *Questionnaires and inventories: Surveying opinions and assessing personality.* New York: John Wiley.

Allen, Heather W. 2010. Language-learning motivation during short-term study abroad: an activity theory perspective. *Foreign Language Annals* 43(1). 27–49.

Beattie, John. 2014. The 'ins and outs' of a study abroad programme: The SALA exchange programme. In Carmen Pérez-Vidal (ed.), *Language acquisition in study abroad and formal instruction contexts,* 59–87. Amsterdam: John Benjamins Publishing.

Block, David. 2003. *The social turn in second language acquisition.* Washington, DC: Georgetown University Press.

Block, David. 2006. *Multilingual identities in a global city: London stories.* London: Palgrave.

Block, David. 2007. *Second language identities.* London/New York: Continuum.

Block, David & Deborah Cameron. 2002. Introduction. In David Block & Deborah Cameron (eds.), *Globalization and language teaching,* 1–10. London: Routledge.

Bloomer, Aileen. 2010. Designing a questionnaire. In Susan Hunston & David Oakley (eds.), *Introducing applied linguistics concepts and skills (vol. 13),* 145–150. London: Routledge.

Breiteneder, Angelika. 2005. *Exploiting redundancy in English as a European lingua franca: The case of the 'third person -s'.* Vienna: University of Vienna. (Master's Thesis.)

British Council. 2013. *The English effect: The impact of English, what it's worth to the UK and why it matters to the world.* London: British Council.

Brown, Lucien. 2013. Identity and honorifics use in Korean study abroad. In Celeste Kinginger (ed.), *Social and cultural aspects of language learning in study abroad,* 269–298. Amsterdam: John Benjamins.

Coleman, James A. 1998. Language learning and study abroad: The European perspective. *Frontiers: The Interdisciplinary Journal of Study Abroad* 4(2). 167–203.

Coleman, James A. 2015. Social circles during residence abroad: What students do, and who with. In Rosamond Mitchell, Nicole Tracy-Ventura & Kevin McManus (eds.), *Social interaction, identity and language learning during residence abroad* (EUROSLA monographs series 4), 33–51. Amsterdam: European Second Language Association.

Collentine, Joseph G. & Barbara F. Freed. 2004. Learning context and its effects on second language acquisition: introduction. *Studies in second language acquisition* 26(02). 153–171.

Dailey, Aja. 2009. *Key motivational factors and how teachers can encourage motivation in their students.* Birmingham: University of Birmingham. (Master's Thesis.)

DeKeyser, Robert. 2014. Research on language development during study abroad: Methodological considerations and future perspectives. In Carmen Pérez-Vidal (ed.), *Language acquisition in study abroad and formal instruction contexts,* 313–327. Amsterdam/Philadelphia: John Benjamins.

Devlin, Anne Marie. 2014. *The impact of study abroad on the acquisition of socio-pragmatic variation patterns: The case of non-native speaker English teachers. Intercultural studies and foreign language learning 13.* Oxford: Peter Lang.

Dörnyei, Zoltán. 2007. *Research methods in applied linguistics.* Oxford: Oxford University Press.

Dörnyei, Zoltán. 2009. The L2 motivational self system. In Zoltán Dörnyei & Ema Ushioda (eds.), *Motivation, language identity and the L2 self,* 9–42. Bristol: Multilingual Matters.

Dörnyei, Zoltán. 2014. *The psychology of the language learner: Individual differences in second language acquisition.* London: Routledge.

Dörnyei, Zoltán & Kata Csizér. 2012. How to design and analyze surveys in second language acquisition. In Alison Mackey & Susan M. Gass (eds.), *Research methods in second language acquisition: A practical guide,* 74–94. Oxford: Wiley-Blackwell.

Dörnyei, Zoltán & Istvan Ottó. 1998. Motivation in action: A process model of L2 motivation. *Working Papers in Applied Linguistics* 4. 43–69.

Dörnyei, Zoltán & Tatsuya Taguchi. 2009. *Questionnaires in second language research: Construction, administration, and processing.* London: Routledge.

Dörnyei, Zoltán & Ema Ushioda. 2009. Motivation, language identities and the L2 self: A theoretical overview. In Zoltán Dörnyei & Ema Ushioda (eds.), *Motivation, language identity and the L2 self,* 1–8. Bristol: Multilingual Matters.

Dörnyei, Zoltán & Ema Ushioda. 2013. *Teaching and researching: Motivation.* London: Routledge.

Gardner, Robert C. & Wallace E. Lambert. 1972. *Attitudes and motivation in second-language learning.* Rowley: Newbury House Publishers.

Geoghegan, Leah & Carmen Pérez-Vidal. Forthcoming. English as a lingua franca, motivation and identity in Study Abroad. In Martin Howard (ed.), *Study abroad, second language acquisition and interculturality: Contemporary perspectives.* Bristol: Multilingual Matters.

Guerrero, Mario. 2015. Motivation in second language learning: a historical overview and its relevance in a public high school in Pasto, Colombia. *HOW* 22(1). 95–106.

Hatch, Evelyn Marcussen & Anne Lazaraton. 1991. *The research manual: Design and statistics for applied linguistics.* New York: Newbury House Publishers.

Hernández, Todd A. 2010. Promoting speaking proficiency through motivation and interaction: The study abroad and classroom learning contexts. *Foreign Language Annals* 43(4). 650–670.

Higgins, E. Tory. 1987. Self-discrepancy: A theory relating self and affect. *Psychological Review* 94(3). 319–340.

Irie, Kay & Stephen Ryan. 2014. Study abroad and the dynamics of change in learner L2 self-concept. In Zoltán Dörnyei, Peter D. MacIntyre & Alastair Henry (eds.), *Motivational dynamics in language learning*, 343–366. Bristol: Multilingual Matters.

Isabelli-García, Christina. 2006. Study abroad social networks, motivation and attitudes: Implications for second language acquisition. In Margaret A. Dufon & Eton Churchill (eds.), *Language learners in study abroad context*, 231–258. Clevedon, UK: Multilingual Matters.

Islam, Muhammad, Martin Lamb & Gary Chambers. 2013. The L2 motivational self-system and national interest: A Pakistani perspective. *System* 41(2). 231–244.

Jackson, Jane. 2008a. Globalization, internationalization, and short-term stays abroad. *International Journal of Intercultural Relations* 32(4). 349–358.

Jackson, Jane. 2008b. *Language, identity and study abroad: Sociocultural perspectives.* London: Equinox.

Jenkins, Jennifer. 2011. Accommodating (to) ELF in the international university. *Journal of Pragmatics* 43(4). 926–936.

Jenkins, Jennifer, Alessia Cogo & Martin Dewey. 2011. Review of developments in research into English as a lingua franca. *Language Teaching* 44(3). 281–315.

Juan-Garau, Maria, Juana Salazar-Noguera & José Igor Prieto-Arranz. 2014. English L2 learners' lexico-grammatical and motivational development at home and abroad. In Carmen Pérez-Vidal (ed.), *Language acquisition in study abroad and formal instruction contexts*, 235–258. Amsterdam: John Benjamins.

Kaypak, Eda & Deniz Ortaçtepe. 2014. Language learner beliefs and study abroad: a study on English as a lingua franca (ELF). *System* 42. 355–367.

Ke, I-Chung & Hilda Cahyani. 2014. Learning to become users of English as a lingua franca (ELF): how ELF online communication affects Taiwanese learners' beliefs of English. *System* 46. 28–38.

Keblawi, Faris. 2009. A review of language learning motivation theories. *Jameea* 12. 23–57.

Kim, Tae-Young. 2009. The dynamics of L2 self and L2 learning motivation: A qualitative case study of Korean ESL students. *English Teaching* 64(3). 49–70.

Kim, Tae-Young & Yoon-Kyoung Kim. 2014. A structural model for perceptual learning styles, the ideal l2 self, motivated behavior, and English proficiency. *System* 46. 14–27.

Kinginger, Celeste. 2004. Alice doesn't live here anymore: Foreign language learning and identity construction. In A. Pavlenko & A. Blackledge (eds.), *Negotiation of identities in multilingual contexts*, 219–242. Cleveden: Multilingual Matters.

Kinginger, Celeste. 2009. *Language learning and study abroad. A critical reading of research.* Houndmills: McMillian.

Kinginger, Celeste. 2013. Identity and language learning in study abroad. *Foreign Language Annals* 46(3). 339–358.

Larson-Hall, Jenifer. 2012. How to run statistical analyses. In Alison Mackey & Susan M. Gass (eds.), *Research methods in second language acquisition: A practical guide*, 245–274. Oxford: Wiley-Blackwell.

Majanen, Silke. 2008. *English as a lingua franca: Teachers' discourses on accent and identity.* Helsinki: University of Helsinki. (Master's Thesis.)

Markus, Hazel & Paula Goodstein Nurius. 1986. Possible selves. *American Psychologist* 41(9). 954–969.

Mazzarol, Tim, Geoffrey Norman Soutar & Michael Sim Yaw Seng. 2003. The third wave: future trends in international education. *International Journal of Educational Management* 17(3). 90–99.

Meara, Paul M. 1994. The year abroad and its effects. *Language Learning Journal* 10(1). 32–38.

Melitz, Jacques. 2016. English as a global language. In Victor Ginsburgh & Shlomo Weber (eds.), *The Palgrave handbook of economics and language*, 583–615. Houndmill: Palgrave Macmillan UK.

Mitchell, Rosamond, Nicole Tracy-Ventura & Kevin McManus (eds.). 2015. *Social interaction, identity and language learning during residence abroad* (Eurosla Monographs Series 4). Amsterdam: The European Second Language Association.

Nestor, Niamh, Caitríona Ní Chasaide & Vera Regan. 2012. Discourse 'like' and social identity – a case study of poles in Ireland. In Bettina Migge & Máire Ní Chiosáin (eds.), *New perspectives on Irish English*, 327–354. Amsterdam: John Benjamins.

Nestor, Niamh & Vera Regan. 2011. The new kid on the block. A case study of young Poles, language and identity. In Merike Darmody, Naomi Tyrrell & S. Song (eds.), *The changing faces of Ireland: Exploring the live of immigrant and ethnic minority children*, 35–52. Rotterdam: Sense Publishers.

Norton, Bonny. 2000. *Identity and language learning*. London: Longman.

Pakir, Anne. 2009. English as a lingua franca: analyzing research frameworks in international English, world Englishes, and ELF. *World Englishes* 28(2). 224–235.

Papi, Mostafa. 2010. The L2 motivational self system, L2 anxiety, and motivated behavior: A structural equation modeling approach. *System* 38(3). 467–479.

Pérez-Vidal, Carmen. 2011. Language acquisition in three different contexts of learning: Formal instruction, stay abroad and semi-immersion (CLIL). In Yolanda Ruiz de Zarobe, Juan Manuel Sierra & Francisco Gallardo del Puerto (eds.), *Content and foreign language integrated learning: Contributions to multilingualism in European contexts*, 103–128. Bern/Berlin: Peter Lang.

Regan, Vera. 2013. The bookseller and the basketball player: Tales from the French polonia. In David Singleton, Vera Regan & Ewelina Debaene (eds.), *Linguistic and cultural acquisition in a migrant community*, 28–48. Bristol: Multilingual Matters.

Ryan, Stephen. 2009. Self and identity in L2 motivation in Japan: The ideal L2 self and Japanese learners of English. In Zoltán Dörnyei & Ema Ushioda (eds.), *Motivation, language identity and the L2 self*, 120–143. Bristol: Multilingual Matters.

Sasaki, Miyuki. 2011. Effects of varying lengths of study-abroad experiences on Japanese EFL students' L2 writing ability and motivation: A longitudinal study. *TESOL Quarterly* 45(1). 81–105.

Seidlhofer, Barbara. 2001. Closing a conceptual gap: the case for a description of English as a lingua franca. *International Journal of Applied Linguistics* 11(2). 133–158.

Smit, Ute. 2010. *English as a lingua franca in higher education: A longitudinal study of classroom discourse (vol. 2)*. Berlin: Mouton de Gruyter.

Stockton, Heather Lynn. 2015. *Identity-focused second language acquisition : A systematic review of classroom applications*. St.Paul: Hamline University. (Master's Thesis.)

Taguchi, Tatsuya, Michael Magid & Mostafa Papi. 2009. The L2 motivational self system among Japanese, Chinese and Iranian learners of English: A comparative study. In Zoltán Dörnyei & Ema Ushioda (eds.), *Motivation, language identity and the L2 self*, 66–97. Bristol: Multilingual Matters.

Tort Calvo, Elizabet. 2015. *Language learning motivation: The L2 motivational self system and its relationship with learning achievement.* Universitat Autònoma Barcelona MA thesis. https://ddd.uab.cat/pub/tfg/2015/137854/TFG_elisabettort.pdf.

Ushioda, Ema. 2009. A person-in-context relational view of emergent motivation, self and identity. In Zoltán Dörnyei & Ema Ushioda (eds.), *Motivation, language identity and the L2 self*, 215–228. Bristol: Multilingual Matters.

Ushioda, Ema & Zoltán Dörnyei. 2012. Motivation. In Susan M. Gass & Alison Mackey (eds.), *The Routledge handbook of second language acquisition*, 396–409. New York: Routledge.

Waninge, Freekien, Zoltán Dörnyei & Kees De Bot. 2014. Motivational dynamics in language learning: Change, stability, and context. *Modern Language Journal* 98(3). 704–723.

Wenger, Etienne. 1998. *Communities of practice: Learning, meaning, and identity.* Cambridge: Cambridge University Press.

Woodrow, Lindy. 2006. Anxiety and speaking English as a second language. *RELC Journal: A Journal of Language Teaching and Research* 37(3). 308–328.

Yashima, Tomoko. 2002. Willingness to communicate in a second language: The Japanese EFL context. *The Modern Language Journal* 86(1). 54–66.

Yashima, Tomoko. 2009. International posture and the ideal L2 self in the Japanese EFL context. In Zoltán Dörnyei & Ema Ushioda (eds.), *Motivation, language identity and the L2 self*, 144–163. Bristol: Multilingual Matters.

Chapter 10

An exploration of life experiences during Study Abroad: A case study of bilingual students and their process of intercultural adaptation

Iryna Pogorelova
Universitat Pompeu Fabra

Mireia Trenchs
Universitat Pompeu Fabra

This qualitative case study investigates intercultural adaptation during a study abroad (SA) of undergraduate bilingual Catalan/Spanish students, focusing specifically on life experiences which resulted in inflection points in that process of adaptation. Data were collected through a pre-departure questionnaire, individual interviews conducted before and after SA, and narrative diaries collected during the sojourn. The results point to the complexity and the nuances of the adaptation process, the diversity of life experiences that may affect adaptation (Bennett 1993) and the need to expand existing explanatory theoretical models.

1 Introduction

Over the last two decades, European policies aiming at promoting European citizenship have reduced border-crossing formalities for EU citizens with legislation reforms facilitating and promoting free mobility. To prepare undergraduate students for such a common space, study abroad (SA) programmes have become more accessible, and an increasing number of universities establish a compulsory stay abroad in the curriculum. The logic for higher education administrators behind such policy is clear: the SA experience, even of short duration, may help

Iryna Pogorelova & Mireia Trenchs. An exploration of life experiences during Study Abroad: A case study of bilingual students and their process of intercultural adaptation. In Carmen Pérez Vidal, Sonia López-Serrano, Jennifer Ament & Dakota J. Thomas-Wilhelm (eds.), *Learning context effects: Study abroad, formal instruction and international immersion classrooms*, 255–282. Berlin: Language Science Press. DOI:10.5281/zenodo.1300636

students not only improve their foreign language ability, but also develop their intercultural competence (IC), namely, knowledge, skills and attitudes needed to communicate effectively (Byram 1997; Deardorff 2006) and behave appropriately in a foreign context.

Academic mobility has been on the rise in Europe at the same time as increasing numbers of sojourners grow up in diverse linguistic and cultural backgrounds. They are often bilingual, trilingual or even multilingual and are used to sharing globalized classrooms and neighbourhoods with people from other cultures (Trenchs-Parera & Newman 2015). While abroad, they are supposed to adjust to a different culture and to speak a foreign language, both within and outside the host university, and use it for demanding academic purposes.

Academic and social interest in the consequences of this growing phenomenon has triggered much research in the last decades (for reviews, see Williams 2005; Behrnd & Porzelt 2012). Much of it focuses on L2 acquisition (Mitchell et al. 2015) since SA experience has been seen as an opportunity for immersion in the target culture and, thus, a key for linguistic improvement. Research has been predominantly, though not exclusively, quantitative and it has scarcely focused on bilinguals who come from multicultural and multilingual backgrounds (but see Pérez-Vidal 2014b). Although there have been longitudinal studies investigating personal and academic experiences of students (for instance, Isabelli-García 2006), few have explored how such experiences relate to students' adaptation to a new culture and their development of intercultural competence (but see Beaven 2012 and Vande Berg et al. 2009).

This longitudinal multi-case study seeks to shed further light on personal and academic experiences during SAs by tapping into how a group of bilingual undergraduate students from a multicultural and multilingual society adapt to a new environment during a short- or mid-term SA programme. We specifically focus on those life experiences that influence the most their adaptation to the host country (Bennett, 1993). In this study, such experiences —whether having a positive or negative impact— are therefore either positive or negative "inflection points" in their expected process of adaptation to the host culture.

We were interested in focusing on bilingual sojourners to explore the common assumption that they are more responsive to and faster in adapting to a new country just because they are used to switching from one language to another in their everyday lives (Bialystok 2001; Vedder & Virta 2005). Furthermore, we wanted to choose sojourners that, besides being bilinguals, had lived in a context as multilingual and multicultural as possible and, consequently, had already gone through intercultural experiences before their SA. Present-day Catalonia seemed to be an ideal context because of its high immigrant population and its histori-cal, institutional bilingualism – Catalan and Spanish have been co-official since 1983 and are spoken everywhere whereas Aranese Occitan, Catalonia's third co-official language, is of preferential institutional use in the Pyrenean Valley of Aran (Newman et al. 2008; Trenchs-Parera & Newman 2015).

2 Literature review: intercultural adaptation and study abroad

Various scholars have used different terminology to define people's reactions to intercultural contacts (Berry 1997; Ward 2004; Masgoret & Ward 2006). The con-cepts such as adjustment, adaptation, acculturation, assimilation, and integration are often used to describe changes in how people respond to cultural differences and act in a new milieu. Kim (2005) refers to adaptation as a broad concept that includes all the above-mentioned terms. She defines the process itself as "the en-tirety of the phenomenon of individuals who, upon relocating to an unfamiliar sociocultural environment, strive to establish and maintain a relatively stable, reciprocal and functional relationship with the environment" (p.380). Whatever term is adopted, change (for instance, changes in attitudes, motivations or beliefs) and personal transformation are two core constituents of the process of "fitting" into a new social and cultural environment.

In an attempt to explain how people react to changes and behave in a new cul-tural setting, some theoretical models have emerged. Synthetically, the U-curve hypothesis model (Lysgaard 1955) points at the existence of a period of excite-ment, followed by culture shock and a final recovery from the crisis. The W-curve model (Gullahorn & Gullahorn 1963) adds a possible shock upon return. The culture-learning model of cross-cultural adjustment (Ward 2004; Masgoret & Ward 2006) posits that sojourners adapt well if they acquire culture-specific skills, including the knowledge of the language spoken in the host culture; in this case, the model is represented with an upward learning curve. Ward (2004) further suggests that adjustment operates on two different levels, psychological and sociocultural, which are predicted by different factors. Hence, such factors as personality, expectations and social support might have an influence on psycho-logical adjustment, whereas cultural knowledge, cultural distance, previous ex-perience abroad, language fluency, length of stay abroad, amount of contact with host nationals, and the quality of this contact might affect sociocultural adjust-ment. The integrative model proposed by Kim (2005) focuses on a deculturation-acculturation process depicted in a form of a spiral that develops in an upward direction in a "draw-back-to-leap" pattern. Finally, Bennett's (1993) Developmental Model of Intercultural Sensitivity (DMIS) describes adaptation as a stage towards effective intercultural communication and ethnorelativism. Although this model is a general framework to describe people's reactions to cultural differences and does not address mobility, it may appropriately be applied to a SA context since it posits that adaptation entails the acquisition of necessary skills for intercultural communication and the final display of either empathy or cultural pluralism.

The aforementioned models explaining adaptation in a variety of contexts have been used in empirical studies that explore intercultural adaptation. However, they have been put largely into question and continue to be debated. With a longitudinal perspective, Beaven (2012) carried out qualitative research to find out the effect of Erasmus mobility on Italian university students' adaptation. Having explored students' personal and academic life experiences, the scholar concludes that adaptation is not the linear process most early models (Bennett, 1993) described and can be affected by different external and internal factors, such as students' motivation and expectations, personality traits, coping strategies, social and linguistic abilities, and stay abroad conditions.

Some studies have explored students' motivation as a crucial factor in the culture-learning process. Sojourners' attitudes towards the host society, openness to other cultures, and willingness to take part in social communication with host nationals contribute to what Gardner (1985) calls "integrativeness." Accordingly, the level of integrativeness is considered to be a predictor for host language acquisition, which in turn has influence on the amount of interaction with hosts and is correlated with a decrease in social adaptation difficulties (Ward 2004). More recently, Badstübner & Ecke (2009) have acknowledged the importance of considering, not just the amount of interaction with host nationals, but also the quality and depth of those interactions.

A number of studies have attempted to correlate students' expectations regarding SA experience with their adjustment. Some scholars report that sojourners whose experiences exceed initial expectations demonstrate a higher level of adaptation than those whose pre-departure expectations are unfulfilled (Ward 2004). Apart from expectations, research also highlights the role of social support during cross-cultural transitions. Pitts's (2009) ethnographic study revealed that everyday talk with co-nationals helped students reconsider their expectations, which in turn contributed to their gradual adjustment and to the development of an intercultural identity. Friendships with co-nationals during SA, however, are not always reported as being a facilitator of adaptation. Instead, the results of Blake et al.'s (2011) survey-based study align with the studies that emphasize the importance of building a network of friends from the host country during the sojourn. The implications of their study highlight the importance of receiving intercultural and social support training before departure, finding housing with locals and using the classroom as a platform for building friendships with hosts.

SA research informs, though, about other facilitators of adaptation. Thus, Van de Berg and his colleagues (2009) investigated the extent to which SA contributed to American university students' intercultural learning and host language acquisition. Their findings indicated that prior language study in high schools and colleges, the length of the mobility programme, blended class composition and the amount of time spent with host nationals were the best predictors of their students' intercultural development. Some scholars report that sojourners who had studied or had lived abroad demonstrated a higher degree of adjustment in further intercultural encounters (Ward 2004), while other scholars cannot confirm this correlation (Vande Berg et al. 2009). Finally, an increasing number of studies have found that SA experience alone does not guarantee the improvement of intercultural communication skills. Pre-departure intercultural training and cultural mentoring during SA are shown to play an important role for students' awareness, as well as for adjustment (Williams 2005; Jackson 2008a; Vande Berg et al. 2009).

Most existing research into such issues is quantitative with a pre- and post-test group design. On the contrary, few studies (Jackson 2008b; Bown et al. 2015; Campbell 2015; Plews 2015) involve the analysis of students' narratives of daily experiences both during and after the sojourn. At the same time, little is still known about the effect of SA on intercultural adaptation of bilingual sojourners accustomed to multilingual and multicultural backgrounds at home, even though bilingual and multilingual citizens have become the norm rather than the exception in today's Europe. To contribute to these gaps, Pogorelova (2016) conducted a longitudinal study combining quantitative and qualitative methods. By collecting participants' self-assessment of experiences during a SA, she was able to construct graphs with curves representing their individual adaptation processes for both their personal and academic lives abroad. These representations resembled trends described in two previous models, the U- and the learning-shaped curves, but the individual curves displayed fluctuations of various intensities, suggesting that participants' adaptation process was not always smooth. In fact, some trajectories differed from those models to a large extent and pointed at the need to further explore possible explanations for inflection points in their adaptation curves, which is what the present study intends to do.

3 Research questions

The current study seeks to extend research on the effect of SA university programmes on bilingual students' intercultural adaptation by answering the following questions:

RQ1. What life experiences during study abroad have an impact on bilingual university students' intercultural adaptation to the country of stay?

RQ2. To what extent are those life experiences similar or different to those identified in previous literature in relation to monolingual students on SA?

4 Method

4.1 Design

This study took the form of a longitudinal, qualitative, multi-case study with data collected during an academic year from a group of 12 undergraduate students from a university in Catalonia (Spain). We chose this context because we wanted to collect data from a group of bilingual students whose previous schooling had taken place in a de facto multilingual and multicultural society, as Catalonia actually is due to recent international immigration (Trenchs-Parera & Newman 2015). This university also had its own language policy which preserved the use of three working languages —Catalan, English and Spanish— both for administrative and academic purposes in all graduate and undergraduate degrees; therefore, our participants would go on an SA after having experienced academic life in more than one language. The study, as further explained below, includes the use of three different instruments — a profile questionnaire, two interviews and a series of narrative diaries for each participant— used at three different times: before, during and after the participants' sojourn abroad.

4.2 Participants

The participants of this study were 12 undergraduate students, 11 females and 1 male, with an age range between 20 and 25 (M=22.3). They were volunteers from four faculties—Health and Life Sciences, Political and Social Sciences, Humanities and Communication—and were enrolled in a non-compulsory SA programme. Their host destinations spread over Europe, North-America, South-America, China, and Australia. The length of the sojourns varied from one and a half to six months. To maintain confidentiality, all the participants were offered to adopt the pseudonyms used in the present study. Table 1 summarizes the participants' profile data.

Table 1: *Participants' profile data*

Participant	Gender	Age	Acad year	Faculty	Destination	Length of SA (months)
Maria	f	23	4th	Health and Life Sciences	Germany	4
Cristina	f	23	4th	Health and Life Sciences	Argentina	4
Virginia	f	21	2nd	Political and Social Sciences	Canada	4
Daniel	m	25	3rd	Political and Social Sciences	USA	1,5
Sara	f	22	2nd	Humanities	Australia	6
Elizabeth	f	22	3rd	Humanities	Brazil	6
Angela	f	26	3rd	Humanities	China	6
Anna	f	22	3rd	Humanities	USA	6
Kira	f	22	3rd	Humanities	Netherlands	6
Lola	f	21	2nd	Communication	Netherlands	6
Ares	f	20	2nd	Communication	Netherlands	6
Natalia	f	21	3rd	Communication	China	4

Regarding the participants' linguistic background, all of them were Catalan/Spanish bilinguals and had attended compulsory education in Catalonia. Ten of them had previously attended foreign language courses abroad which did not exceed two months. Besides, all had made short sojourns abroad involving school trips, work and summer camps, and tourism, but not with academic purposes.

In order to participate in the SA programme, the students had to meet a number of foreign language requirements. Nine out of twelve participants selected universities where English was the language of instruction and their linguistic abilities varied between B2 and C1 levels of the CEFR. The other two students (Virginia and Elizabeth) enrolled on courses taught in a foreign language other than English. Thus, Virginia attended her courses in French, Elizabeth in Portuguese. One student, Cristina, did medical practices in Spanish-speaking Argentina and did not need any foreign language accreditation.

4.3 Data collection procedures

The current study adopted a longitudinal design with data collected at three different times —before, during and after the participants' sojourn abroad. First, volunteers were asked to fill in a profile questionnaire and send it back by e-mail. Second, we organized an informative, individual session to get to know each student personally, to explain the procedures adopted in the study, to inform them that their participation was voluntary and anonymous, and to conduct a pre-departure interview. To collect data during the SA, four virtual Moodle classrooms were created for each of the faculties. In these virtual classrooms, every two weeks, the participants submitted a narrative diary entry. After returning from the SA, another interview was conducted with each of the participants.

When participating in the interviews and completing the narrative diaries, the participants were free to use the three work languages at the university. However, during the interviews, the great majority expressed the desire to practice their foreign language and communication between the interviewer and the participants took place in English.

4.4 Instruments

The pre-SA individual profile questionnaire was adapted from the linguistic profile survey used in the SALA research project[1]. The adapted version comprises 16 questions investigating the participants' cultural and linguistic background, and includes questions inquiring into prior SA experiences, frequency of interactions with Erasmus exchange students or language tandems at their home university, and estimated target language proficiency.

Two semi-structured interviews were conducted with each of the participants before departure and upon return (Isabelli-García 2006). The pre-departure interview aimed at completing the data provided in the profile questionnaire, while collecting further data on students' motives for going abroad, destination choice, and expectations. Moreover, each participant was asked a number of personalized questions depending on his or her answers to the profile questionnaire. The post-SA interview aimed at collecting reflections on their adaptation to the new cultural and academic environment and on life experiences which might have influenced that adjustment.

During the SA, the participants completed narrative diaries biweekly, adapted from the ones used by Beaven (2012). First, students were asked to self-evaluate

---

[1]IRIS is an open-access digital repository (Marsden et al. 2016) accessible at http://www.iris-database.org).

their personal and academic lives on a Likert scale from 1 (very bad) to 5 (very good) according to the degree of difficulty they had experienced during the corresponding two-week period. As in previous literature, responses to these Likert scales would be used to graphically represent adaptation. After that, they were required to leave explanatory comments on their self-assessment. Thus, these narratives served to provide an insight into what experiences influenced their self-assessment during their stays.

The narratives were guided by ten thematic strands, five of them were adopted from Beaven's (2012) weekly diary tables, and the other five were motivated by previous research on the effect of personal characteristics, SA conditions and social networks (Vande Berg et al. 2009; Pitts 2009; Coleman 2015). We separated the ten thematic strands into two broad categories –Personal Life and Academic Life– also used by Beaven since, according to her results, the personal and academic experience may evolve differently. The Personal Life category included six subcategories: (a) relationships with native friends; (b) relationships with friends of other nationalities; (c) relationships with host nationals; (d) daily life; (e) foreign language for social interaction; and (f) culture, custom and habits of the host country. In turn, the Academic Life category involved four subcategories: (a) educational system; (b) classes (teachers, classmates, etc.); (c) foreign language for academic purposes; and (d) academic support for administrative issues. We are aware that other classifications might have yielded slightly different results. To counterbalance this limitation, we introduced face-to-face interviews which could open the possibility for the emergence of other relevant issues in the students' lives abroad.

4.5   Data analysis

As in previous literature (see §2), we wanted to construct graphs representing individual adaptation curves. To do so, we averaged the mean values of the students' intercultural adaptation biweekly self-assessments. For every student, the mean of his or her responses on a five-point Likert scale was calculated separately for every two-week period and per thematic strand. Upon those mean values, we constructed a set of ten graphs representing ten single adaptation curves for each participant, one for each thematic strand. In these graphs, we set out to detect inflection points in the curves and, therefore, in their stay abroad: that is, either a negative change (a "shock", "difficulty" or "crisis" in the previous explanatory model seeing intercultural adaptation as a U-curve, e.g. Lysgaard 1955) or a positive change (also called previously a moment of "excitement") in these self-assessments of intercultural adaptation. As inflection points, we considered only curve variations that were higher with respect to a previous value, that is, in the curve displaying, e.g. +1 followed by +3, the latter indicator was counted as a positive inflection. Negative inflections were counted in the same way.

Since our main intended focus was to find out possible explanations for those positive and negative inflection points, we turned to the participants' written and oral narratives obtained from the narrative diaries and the interviews. These narratives were subjected to an in-depth thematic analysis (Lichtman 2012). We employed a directed approach to content analysis in which initial coding is guided by relevant theories and previous research findings. With this approach, excerpts in interview transcripts or diary entries appearing either to transmit affective reactions to life experiences or to include factors influencing adjustment were assigned a predetermined category from previous studies (Ward 2004; Williams 2005; Vande Berg et al. 2009; Beaven 2012). Any excerpt that did not fall into initial coding categories was assigned a new code. This thematic recursive analysis, similar to Beaven's (2012), allowed us to identify issues triggering inflection points in students' stays.

In the following section, we explore the categories relating to personal and academic life experiences that emerged from the data and illustrate them with excerpts from the participants' comments. The quotes that were originally produced in Catalan and Spanish have been translated into English, but the original versions are left in footnotes. Whenever no Catalan or Spanish version is presented, the comments were originally provided in English. Original punctuation and orthography have been preserved.

5 Results

5.1 Personal life

In this section (see Table 2), we present the main themes related to inflection points in the students' adaptation curves for their Personal Life. Table 2 below includes the number of participants for whom a life experience related to a given personal issue resulted in either a positive or negative inflection point in their stays.

Friends from home and family provided what Beaven (2012) calls "emotional support." Communication with them was made mostly through Skype and social networks. Nevertheless, relatives' and friends' visits were not uncommon either and influenced the participants' biweekly assessments positively. A few students, however, found it challenging to keep in touch with friends left home and noted

Table 2: Main themes relating to inflection points in participants' personal life

Personal issues	# of participants (n=12)
Emotional support from family and friends from home	7
Relationships with friends prior to the SA over distance	2
Social and emotional support from co-nationals	9
Making new friendships with international students	7
Building friendships with host nationals	8
Difficulties in interacting in the foreign language either with hosts or internationals	8
Feeling improvement in the foreign language	7
Leisure activities in gatherings and trips	11
Combining studies with work outside the university	2
Adapting to a new social environment (host transport system, timetable, sanitary conditions, accommodation, food, weather etc.)	9

that distance had had an impact on their relationships, and that they did not feel their best friends at their side when they needed to share SA experiences (Coleman & Chafer 2010). Apart from friends back home, a great majority maintained close relationships with Spanish students from their home university and other co-nationals who were in the same location. These friendships were considered to be helpful without being overbearing and were related to significant, positive inflection points in their adaptation curves, as in the case of Angela, who arrived in Beijing and, from the very beginning, made friends with two other Catalan girls who stayed in the same residence hall. In her first narrative, she wrote:

"Luckily we are becoming more than exchange students mates. We are building something like a real friendship. We are always checking upon each other but we are also letting ourselves private moments to do some things on our own." Angela's data showed clearly such positive impact several times throughout the sojourn, coinciding with the moment when she felt overwhelmed by her university studies and work; she was very grateful to her friends for being at her side:

> Narrative diary (at week 8)
>
> This month has been quite hard, to be honest. I went to job interviews, and I've got one. We have the exams very soon and I've been up and down in this huge city, taking the underground every day for more than three hours. I arrived exhausted at night, but I was glad to know that I could talk to the girls, disconnect with them even if it lasted only a moment.

There were also participants who hardly kept in touch with co-nationals during their SA. For Sara, for instance, her relationships with Spanish students met in the host country featured mostly the so-called instrumental friendship. These friends were approachable occasionally in terms of basic needs and functional problems (like to help each other to send a suitcase or get university papers) but, as Virginia did in Quebec, some of our participants tried to set themselves apart from co-nationals during their sojourn. Departing for Canada, Virginia aimed at improving her French and meeting as many host and exchange students as possible. Therefore, she was not interested in interacting with Spanish students, which was reported in her narrative diary at week 2: "I try not to interact too much with Spanish people because that is certainly NOT what I look for in an exchange program."

Besides the co-nationals, the participants spent their time with other international students. Orientation sessions and events organized by the host university's mobility office or Erasmus Students Network (ESN) were the starting point for building a network of international friends. After having made first acquaintances, the students usually joined a group on Facebook or WhatsApp so as to coordinate joint events or just stay in touch. When compared to a decade ago, this is a fairly recent phenomenon in SAs that allows for more common shared spaces of interaction, albeit virtual, with acquaintances from other countries (Coleman & Chafer 2010). Most of such friendships were made in residence halls and shared apartments. The majority assessed their relationships with other exchange students positively and considered these friendships as being beneficial for their foreign language and cultural learning. The main difficulty reported here was the language barrier which made some students feel embarrassed or even refrain from interacting, especially in the initial period.

As regards host nationals, only a small number of students managed to build meaningful friendships with them throughout the sojourn. In fact, the greater part of the participants experienced difficulties in this respect. The reasons mentioned were linguistic difficulties, reluctance on the part of hosts to build friendships, and the Erasmus context itself. Angela, for instance, chose to limit her relationships with Chinese at the university almost from the very beginning, as, from her viewpoint, they were only interested in practising their English. After university hours, she however communicated more closely with her Chinese colleagues at the school where she had a part-time job. Although she was well-received at work, Angela considered these relationships with co-workers superficial as they were not interested in building a friendship, but rather wanted to take advantage of the opportunity to talk in English with a foreigner. Beyond the university, Natalia managed to meet some local people in Hong Kong thanks to friends, but the contacts with host nationals were not frequent. The language barrier also complicated communication as, contrary to her expectations, very few local people spoke English and she could only speak a bit of Mandarin and no Cantonese. Sara was one of the students who pointed to the difficulty of meeting hosts in the Erasmus international environment. Most of her time, she was surrounded by people from other countries either at the university or in the apartment where she stayed:

> Narrative diary (at week 8)
>
> I don't know, here in Australia, it is quite hard to meet people from here being on the Erasmus programme. Most of them are international. I have a bit of relationship with two Australians, but not like very deep relationship. I'm basically with people from all over the world but not from here.

Assessing their relationships either with hosts or internationals, students verbalised linguistic difficulties in their interactions although none had anticipated significant problems communicating with other students before departure. Such beliefs were underpinned mainly by the students' prior experiences abroad. As can be judged by their comments, the recognition of their own linguistic limitations on-campus and off-campus came later during the sojourn, which then caused disappointment and sometimes even led to what Beaven (2012) calls "foreign language exhaustion." In these moments of fatigue, some students were willing to find a refuge among their co-national friends with whom they could speak

Spanish or Catalan, and there was no need to make an effort explaining every-thing in a foreign language. Lack of fluency, vocabulary limitations, the diffi-culty of understanding jokes and a strong local accent were among the reasons for negative inflection points. In her narrative diary at week 4, Sara verbalizes her feelings as ". . . many times I do not understand what they're talking about ... and it's a little bit frustrating." At the end of the SA, however, most felt that their overall foreign language had been considerably enhanced and were satis-fied with the experience that allowed them to practise the target language in different contexts.

One word also needs to be said about Cristina's experience in Spanish-speak-ing Argentina. Despite being a native speaker of Spanish, she faced linguistic problems when trying to make friends with hosts at the start of her sojourn. She reported that the use of some words in Argentina was considerably different from their use in Barcelona and she needed to select words carefully:

> Narrative diary (at week 2)
>
> In spite of the same language during the first days I did not understand a lot of words. And the most important thing is the forbidden word "coger," we use it to say to catch a flight or to catch something ... and there it means going to bed with someone, so I have to constantly think about what I have to say in order not to use completely different words to say the same things.[2]

In the participants' daily life, tourism and leisure activities triggered a great deal of positive emotions. The great majority travelled around the area or even outside the host country at the weekends, on days off and on holiday. These experiences allowed them to leave their international on-campus environment and to see the host country in a new perspective, as well as to explore other cultures beyond its borders. For instance, Ares, who was studying in Groningen, explored her host city and also visited Berlin with her new international friends during a week-off. Natalia, who studied in Hong Kong, visited other Chinese provinces. She also had the opportunity to visit other Asian countries, such as Malaysia, Japan, and Korea. Daniel, who stayed in Los Angeles, made a five-day road trip with his Catalan friends in the States. Virginia, who stayed in Quebec, made a road trip with a group of her new French friends around Canada. Later at the end of her exchange programme, she also went to Mexico with the same

---

[2] Original quote in Spanish: "Todo y ser el mismo idioma los primeros días no entendía muchas palabras. Y lo más importante la palabra prohibida "coger", para nosotros es coger un vuelo, coger algo... y ahí significa ir a la cama con alguien, así que he de pensar constantemente que he de decir por no hablar de palabras completamente diferentes para decir las mismas cosas."

people. All these experiences translated into positive inflection points in their adaptation curves.

Accommodation, food and weather were sometimes among the reasons that affected negatively their stay, at least initially. Some students, for instance, had to get used to sharing showers and kitchens in residence halls and others lived in small apartments which made them miss their room back home. However, these hurdles did not incite them to leave their SA programmes and, in the end, some participants even reported that such shared facilities made them feel integrated into the community and contributed to their adaptation to customs and habits from other countries. Besides, the experience of living alone was considered enriching in terms of personal growth, as it made the majority feel like real adults. Completing errands and chores on their own, such as going shopping, cooking, or doing the laundry, made them feel more independent and self-sufficient.

A few students, who were working during their residence, had difficulty balancing work commitments and university studies, and this combination resulted in stress, especially in the period of exams. Nevertheless, the overall assessment of working experience was positive as these participants reported that working had contributed to their maturity and independence. Sara's quote illustrates the positiveness of such personal experiences that seems to trigger a sense of self-discovery and feeling of readiness to confront new cultural challenges:

Narrative diary (at week 12)

Super good, feeling of total freedom! I had never lived away from home and had never earned my own salary, so explosive mixture of freedom! […] I feel much more mature, independent, sure of myself, with more strengths.

Interestingly, many found their host culture to be similar to their own and felt they did not need to step outside of their comfort zone. However, it should be noted that the greater part of the participants lived in the dorms on campus or apartments associated with a host university, and had little contact with a "real host life". In the post-SA interviews, the majority admitted that they had spent most of their time in an international academic environment and, consequently, felt adapted to the "international students' life", rather than to the "real life" of hosts. Lola's comment drawn from the post-SA interview is representative: "Well, I didn't have a real Dutch life, because I didn't work. Probably I have adapted well to the Erasmus life in Holland, not to the Dutch life." When comparing the trajectories of those who lived on-campus and off-campus, the latter ones show more negative inflection points. These students felt at times more distressed at such inconveniences, in their point of view, as poor public transport, unhealthy eating habits, inconvenient local timetable, and insufficient sanitary arrangements. The excerpt below illustrates Daniel's feelings in the US:

> Narrative diary (at week 2)
>
> I knew that Americans weren't much healthy in food terms but now I have understood it on my own flesh why it is so, and it shocks me that such a developed country has such bad habits. [...] Apart from that, distances are a problem if you don't have a car, since public transportation is not as good as it is in Barcelona.

As we have seen, personal life is tied intrinsically to the participants' academic life and, therefore, in the following section, we present those vital experiences that have been identified by the participants as relevant during their academic stay.

5.2 Academic life

In this section (see Table 3), we present the main themes related to inflection points in the students' adaptation curves for their Academic Life. Table 3 below includes the number of participants for whom a life experience related to a given academic issue resulted in either a positive or negative inflection point in their stays. It is important to notice that the students' curves built for their Academic Life experiences showed more fluctuations than the curves for Personal Life.

As regards academic support, the majority of participants were satisfied with the service they had received from administrative staff at their host universities. The participants assessed positively, not only welcome events and other activities organized by the mobility office for exchange students, but also the instructors who had been assigned to settle their queries in the academic sphere, as in the case of Anna, who highlighted the role of her international assistant (IA) during her stay in Boston. Her IA was an American master student who helped her resolve her doubts not only about academic aspects, but also about basic needs (e.g. where to buy winter clothes). Negative inflection points occurred in initial stages of the SA and were mostly due to a slow process of enrolment upon arrival in the host university and bureaucratic delays in paperwork procedures.

When describing the host educational system, the participants compared their home and host universities in terms of facilities, requirements, schedule, curriculum, and teaching approaches. In the first few weeks, the majority evaluated positively their host university's campus facilities, such as libraries, computer

Table 3: Main themes relating to inflection points in participants' academic life

academic issues	# of participants (n=12)
Academic support and enrolment process upon arrival in the host university	5
Host university's welcome events and services for integration	8
Instructors and assistants assigned to resolve doubts in the academic sphere	6
University facilities	6
Curriculum	6
High demanding requirements for assignment submissions and exams	2
Distribution of workload	2
Teaching methodology and working pace in class	7
Expectations regarding academic experiences	6
Working jointly on projects with groupmates	4
Participating in classroom activities	8
Relationships with lecturers	2
Feedback from teachers	6
Feeling improvement in the foreign language	8

labs and sporting clubs, as well as the curriculum, which was often characterized as being well organized and efficient with a wide range of courses available. However, for some, coinciding with the U-curve explanatory model, their initial excitement with the host university was followed by difficulties adjusting to new rules and requirements for assignment submissions and exams. The distribution of the workload differed from what they were used to at their home university and, as a result, final papers and projects required much more commitment. Some students ended up disliking the host educational system as a whole, which, for instance in the case of Angela, was too structured and did not allow for flexibility:

> Narrative diary (at week 8)
>
> I don't like the way they teach in China. It is very repetitive and sometimes childish: they work with merits and if you show that you have done your homework, if you are always on time and never miss class... then you will pass the course with higher marks. It's totally contrary to that in Europe, when you are supposed to be more independent, more curious and it is always better if you make your own questions related to your personal interests.

Some had trouble adjusting to working pace in class and felt disappointed with the teaching approaches customary at the host university. For instance, Anna, whose host destination was Boston, found the teaching methodology to be of regular quality and classes as "light". It is worth noting that participants' initial disappointment was often caused by their very high pre-departure expectations concerning the academic experience. In fact, six out of twelve participants reported their dissatisfaction with the academic experience as the sojourn proceeded, and related their negative self-assessment to the unfulfillment of their pre-departure expectations, as illustrated in the following extract drawn from Anna's diary:

> Narrative diary (at week 4)
>
> Maybe it is because I expected so much and from there [*Barcelona*] people 'venerate' the American system (without having been here I think) ... Classes are not bad but I expected much more level. Teachers are not really teachers. They comment the subject matters - not teach them.

Another issue raised by several participants was the difficulty of building closer relationships with lecturers. Sara, for instance, pointed out that her university was extremely huge, seminars were overcrowded and lecturers often changed within the same subject. She believed that such organization had affected negatively the overall atmosphere of classes and did not contribute to learning:

> Interview (after SA)
>
> It is not that I don't like the university, but I think that the price Australian people pay for this education is really high. [...] The good thing about it is

that it has many subjects to choose from, which we don't have here. But then subjects too easy, low-level and, well, ordinary. Education at [*name of the home university*] is, in some things, much better. It is a good university and it's small, while in Sydney it was a big university. Here I have very close contacts, I know the teachers. There with the professor of philosophy yes, but with others not. They give huge classes, in one subject the teacher was changed every week and the topic was explained so badly. I don't know, it doesn't motivate me.

When it came to group work, the main difficulty was related to working jointly on projects and presentations with their mates. Some students found that hosts were avoiding collaboration with exchange students. Others faced a similar problem with international teammates, and reported that those were reluctant to fulfil their duties and act in concert with other group members, which forced them to take on extra work. Natalia's comment reflects her negative feeling:

Narrative diary (at week 12)

I am so pissed off in one of my projects as the host nationals really didn't do anything, lots of free riders. I am supposed to be the one partying around and having fun as I am the exchange, but, on the contrary, I am doing the work of others. TOO BAD!

It is worth noting that the foreign language used in the academic sphere presented a considerable obstacle for most of the students despite their high linguistic proficiency, which resulted in negative inflection points in their curves. The participants articulated difficulties in contributing to classroom discussions, completing writing tasks, giving oral presentations, understanding lecturers, and reading academic literature. For instance, Ares felt initial anxiety, because she could not contribute actively to classroom discussions and her teachers showed her their dissatisfaction:

Narrative diary (at week 4)

The worst thing I had to face is that lecturers want us to talk, ask and comment during the class. This is very new for me, because in my home university this is something completely optional and at any case mandatory, just positive. So, I had to deal with the fact that a professor was disappointed because I didn't express my opinion during the class.

Anna and Daniel reported that their speaking skills had been their weakest point. When required to participate in classroom debates, they felt unable to develop their ideas properly due to vocabulary limitations. Natalia realized that she was not as confident as she expected when giving oral presentations. Ares faced the same problem, and she felt particularly flustered when she needed to speak in front of students with a higher level of English or native speakers. Lola experienced difficulties understanding some of her lecturers and found completing writing tasks linguistically challenging. Similarly, Virginia found writing in French difficult and had to invest extra time correcting her French handouts. Similar to Lola and Virginia, Sara had difficulties writing essays and, as she lacked academic vocabulary, spent a lot of time translating assigned articles. The excerpt below illustrates Sara's feelings of anxiety:

> Narrative diary (at week 6)
>
> Now I understand almost everything the professors say but I am a little bit "crushed" because for the next week I have to write an essay in philosophy of about four pages and my English is still regular for writing about philosophy. I feel very childish when writing, I know that I make mistakes and I get frustrated![3]

As can be judged from their narratives, most students felt a great improvement in their language skills as the sojourn proceeded. They often appreciated extensive feedback from their teachers on their assignments and considered it as being beneficial for their learning, especially in terms of their academic language use. Following classes, submitting written tasks, giving presentations, reading assigned articles and, most importantly, passing exams in a foreign language not only contributed to the development of the corresponding skills, but also to the students' linguistic confidence and pride in accomplishments, similarly to Beaven's (2012) Italian participants. Therefore, the positive inflection points in the adaptation curves for the academic life resulted from good grades, encouraging comments from teachers on their exams, and satisfaction with achieved outcomes.

All in all, these results point to the diversity and complexity of both life experiences and individual, social, linguistic and academic abilities that may affect adaptation during an academic stay.

---

[3]Original quote in Spanish: "Ahora entiendo casi todo lo que dicen los profes pero estoy un poco "rallada" *[sic]* porque para la semana que viene tengo que hacer un ensayo de filosofía de unas cuatro páginas y mi inglés ya es regular como para encima escribir filosofía. Me siento muy infantil cuando escribo, sé que hago muchas faltas y me frustro!"

6 Discussion

This chapter has attempted to shed light onto those vital experiences that may influence the adaptation process of bilingual undergraduate students during a SA.

As regards personal experiences, friends from home and family provided emotional support and their sporadic visits positively influenced the participants' personal lives, confirming Beaven's (2012) results. The relationships with co-nationals who were in the same location also had a positive influence, especially during stressful moments. Pitts (2009) also argues that co-national support plays an important role for adjustment in the context of short-term mobility, a phenomenon further confirmed by Coleman (2013, 2015). Since in this study these experiences always coincided with significant, positive changes in their self-assessment, we would rather go beyond the concept of "emotional support" and argue that, in terms of language and daily cultural habits, co-nationals provide a "zone of familiar comfort" which acts as a fulcrum for the students to confront the new milieu with self-assurance and strength.

Meeting people from the host country was one of the main motives for going abroad and it turned out a key issue in the adaptation process. In fact, most participants felt more satisfied with the relationships they could build with other exchange students and considered them as beneficial for their intercultural awareness. In contrast, the greater part of the students had trouble in establishing friendly relationships with hosts, with linguistic difficulties being a major hurdle, at least initially. Even Cristina, who did medical practices in Spanish-speaking Argentina and needed to speak neither English nor other foreign languages, reported difficulties understanding the local dialect at the beginning of her SA. In fact, such correlation between linguistic fluency and increased intercultural interactions has already been explored and reflected in the culture-learning model (Ward 2004). Despite the fact that SA programmes are developed to bring students in closer contact with a host society, the Erasmus context itself may complicate contact with host nationals both at the university and in the residence halls. Reluctance on the part of host nationals was mentioned by our participants as an impediment to building friendships with them. Similarly, Ward (2004: 190) claims that such intercultural friendships tend to be infrequent due to various factors, "including the willingness of host nationals to interact across cultural boundaries and their perceptions of newcomers." In our view, if students on an SA are not prepared before their departure to expect such attitudes, their unfruitful efforts towards building a network of host friends may lead precisely to such negative experiences as feeling homesick —experiences which that network is supposed to prevent (Blake et al. 2011)— or little empathic towards the host culture, in the terms of Bennett's (1993) Developmental Model of Intercultural Sensitivity (DMIS). For the purpose of supporting and helping Erasmus students benefit from their intercultural encounters, the IEREST[4] (2015) offers a wide range of teaching resources and practical guidelines that span the three stages (before, during and after) of the SA experience.

Given the positive effect on adaptation of intercultural friendships, we pose that the definition of the term "intercultural adaptation" in the SA context should be extended by moving from the restricted meaning of "adaptation to a host culture" (as if the sojourner was just encountering one new culture in the SA context) to the wider meaning of "adaptation to foreign cultures," a definition that would include, not only the host culture, but also those brought to the SA context by other international students. By reconsidering the concept of adaptation, we could claim that SA nowadays could be preparing students for life afterwards in increasingly multicultural societies, whether in their own home country or in another country of residence. For students who have shared primary and secondary classrooms with people from culturally different backgrounds, the context of a university SA would reinforce pre-existing, if any, intercultural abilities and act as a springboard for adult life beyond the academic sphere.

Accommodation during the sojourn is one more important characteristic that needs to be considered (Vande Berg et al. 2009). In their daily life, those participants who lived on campus did not find their new environment to be much different from their hometown and seemed to experience no trouble adjusting to it. However, as was mentioned earlier, they had little contact with other social domains/environments in the host culture. Residing either in apartments or dorms, which were normally situated on the outskirts of a city and fully equipped, often made it unnecessary for them to leave this comfortable academic/international area. Thus, it would be appropriate to say that they adjusted to the international student lifestyle and their successful adaptation processes can be discussed only in the particular on-campus context.

The relevance of context in the adaptation process resulted, in fact, in two quite different SA experiences: what we may call "predominantly on-campus SA" (i.e. when residing in residence halls and apartments with other university, mostly international, students) and a "predominantly off-campus SA" (i.e. when residing outside the university). For our participants, the off-campus residence revealed daily difficulties, not felt by those living on campus, when adjusting to

---

[4]Intercultural education resources for Erasmus students and their teachers. Koper: Annales University Press. Retrieved from http://ierest-project.eu/humbox

certain inconveniences, such as poor public transport, unhealthy food, bad sanitary conditions, and local timetable. Such difficulties translated into negative inflection points in their adaptation cycle. In fact, this is coherent with Beaven's participants and the difficulties they faced when moving from on-campus to off-campus facilities; in their case, Beaven observed that "the adaptation cycle may start all over again as the changed environment makes new demands on the sojourner" (2012: 286). Beyond the mere location of the residence and the existence or not of the network of local friends, at least two other SA conditions would be at play to make the on-campus SA similar to a more "real" —in the participants' terms— off-campus one: 1) work experience off-campus and 2) extensive travelling, which allowed our participants to see the host destination under a different light. All in all, such difficulties highlight the necessity of pre-departure preparation sessions in which students should be briefed on possible challenges linked to different SA conditions.

If we now turn to academic life, the results show that academic experiences triggered inflection points in the participants' adaptation curves more often than personal ones. Linguistic difficulties often translated into negative self-assessment, especially during the first half of the sojourn. However, most participants eventually perceived they had improved their foreign language skills, especially their listening, reading and writing. This lends support to previous research studies that report the beneficial effect of the SA context on the development of such skills (Pérez-Vidal 2014b). In fact, both Bennett's and Ward's models point at the acquisition of necessary communication skills for effective intercultural communication. As a result of the SA, some participants felt that they had become even more willing to learn foreign languages, which is in line with research that reports a positive effect of SA on motivation towards language learning (Trenchs-Parera & Juan-Garau 2014). The connection between reduced anxiety and increased linguistic confidence found by Trenchs-Parera and Juan-Garau in their quantitative study was confirmed in ours, as the initial anxiety that some participants experienced decreased.

Nevertheless, when commenting on their academic outcomes, only half of the participants felt that they had benefited from the chosen courses, contradicting previous studies that report the overall academic improvement of their participants after the stay (Teichler 2004). The other half expressed disappointment with the academic side of their SA experience. As main reasons, they mentioned (a) strictness and inflexibility of the host educational system, (b) repetitive and easy classes that lacked deep analysis, and (c) unexceptional teaching methodology that did not correlate with the host university's prestige and tuition fees.

This frustration points at a gap between reality and very high pre-departure expectations, as also documented by Ward (2004). Our participants' expectations were mostly based on the assumption that foreign universities were much better, but the experience taught them to value their home university higher. Therefore, confronting a foreign academic environment had a positive "boomerang effect" and triggered a positive, conscious re-assessment of their own academic culture.

Relationships with professors abroad also hindered adaptation to the new environment for some students who often blamed it on the number of students in seminars and the changing of teachers within subjects, as several of Beaven's participants (2012) had reported. A possible explanation to such a reaction may lie in the fact that our participants' home university is far smaller than some of the host universities and registers fewer people in classes. Besides, the degree of formality between teachers and students in Catalan universities is less strict than in other countries, and students are accustomed to behaving more informally with their professors. It should be noted that, even though we are reporting this phenomenon in the context of SA, it could also take place locally, for instance when changing universities. Thus, an SA during undergraduate studies may be serving an unexpected academic goal: namely, preparing students for better adjustment when facing academic differences in local, supposedly familiar contexts.

All in all, these experiences point to the complexity of the adaptation process, to interactions among a large number of aspects —such as pre-departure expectations, co-national support, or individual academic and linguistic abilities— and to the beneficial effects of pre-departure preparation.

7 Conclusion

Although the current study is based on a small sample of participants, the findings are highly informative for study abroad administrators and instructors. In such societies as Catalonia, it is believed that bilingual and multilingual people adapt easily to new cultural environments because of their linguistic flexibility and, often, because internationalized secondary schools provide a kind of preparatory context for encounters with other cultures. However, the inflection points in our participants' life experiences during SA and their effect on their intercultural adaptation do not reveal major differences between our bilingual Catalan participants and monolingual ones in previous —both quantitative and qualitative— studies (Williams 2005; Vande Berg et al. 2009; Beaven 2012). As a token, the foreign language used in the academic sphere presented a considerable obstacle for most of our participants, even if their linguistic abilities varied between B2 and C1 levels. What our study has revealed is more nuances in already identified phenomena, such as the role of co-nationals as an emotional fulcrum, simultaneous adaptation to a multiplicity of cultures, the role of different lodgings as triggers of varied SA experiences, the unexpected difficult adaptation to the variety of one's native language spoken in the host culture, and difficulties to adapt to a different academic culture that may also occur in the home country and not be exclusive of an SA.

Acknowledgements

We gratefully acknowledge our twelve participants who provided us with rich data for this study as well as the Deans and Mobility Coordinators in the Faculties of Health and Life Sciences, Political and Social Sciences, Humanities and Communication of the Catalan university for facilitating contacts with outgoing students. We would also like to thank the technical staff for their help in creating Moodle classrooms and Roberto Molowny-Horas for his help with statistical analysis. The present work has benefitted from funding from UPF's research group GREILI and from the research project FFI2014-52663-P (Spain's Ministry of Economy and Competivity). Finally, special thanks go to this volume's editors and the anonymous reviewer for their feedback on earlier versions of this chapter.

References

Badstübner, Tina & Peter Ecke. 2009. Student expectations, motivations, target language use, and perceived learning progress in a summer study abroad program in Germany. *UP* 42(1). 41–49.

Beaven, Ana. 2012. *An exploration of cross-cultural adaptation in the context of European student mobility.* Warwick: University of Warwick. (Doctoral dissertation.)

Behrnd, Verena & Susanne Porzelt. 2012. Intercultural competence and training outcomes of students with experiences abroad. *International Journal of Intercultural Relations* 36. 213–223.

Bennett, Milton J. 1993. Towards ethnorelativism: A developmental model of intercultural sensitivity. In R. Michael Paige (ed.), *Education for intercultural experience*, 21–71. Yarmouth, ME: Intercultural Press.

Berry, John W. 1997. Immigration, acculturation and adaptation. *Applied Psychology: An International Review* 46. 5–34.

Bialystok, Ellen. 2001. *Bilingualism in development: Language, literacy, and cognition.* Cambridge: Cambridge University Press.

Blake, Hendrickson, Devan Rosen & R. Kelly Aune. 2011. An analysis of friendship networks, social connectedness, homesickness, and satisfaction levels of international students. *International Journal of Intercultural Relations* 35(3). 281–295.

Bown, Jennifer, Dan P. Dewey & R. Kirk Belnap. 2015. Student interactions during study abroad in Jordan. In Rosamond Mitchell, Nicole Tracy-Ventura & Kevin McManus (eds.), *Social interaction, identity and language learning during residence abroad*, 199–221. Amsterdam: The European Second Language Association.

Byram, Michael. 1997. *Teaching and assessing intercultural communicative competence.* Bristol, UK: Multicultural Matters.

Campbell, Rikki. 2015. Life post study abroad for the Japanese language learner: Social networks, interaction and language usage. In Nicole Tracy-Ventura Rosamond Mitchell & Kevin McManus (eds.), *Social interaction, identity and language learning during residence abroad*, 241–262. Amsterdam: The European Second Language Association.

Coleman, James A. 2015. Social circles during residence abroad: What students do, and who with. In Rosamond Mitchell, Nicole Tracy-Ventura & Kevin McManus (eds.), *Social interaction, identity and language learning during residence abroad* (EUROSLA monographs series 4), 33–51. Amsterdam: European Second Language Association.

Coleman, James A. & Tony Chafer. 2010. Study abroad and the internet: Physical and virtual context in an era of expanding telecommunications. *Frontiers: The interdisciplinary journal of study abroad* 29. 151–167.

Deardorff, Darla K. 2006. Identification and assessment of intercultural competence as a student outcome of internationalization. *Journal of Studies in Intercultural Education* 10(3). 241–266.

Gardner, Robert C. 1985. *Social psychology and second language learning: The role of attitudes and motivation.* London: Edward Arnold.

Gullahorn, John T. & Jeanne E. Gullahorn. 1963. An extension of the U-curve hypothesis. *Journal of Social Issues* 19. 33–47.

Isabelli-García, Christina. 2006. Study abroad social networks, motivation and attitudes: Implications for second language acquisition. In Margaret A. Dufon & Eton Churchill (eds.), *Language learners in study abroad context*, 231–258. Clevedon, UK: Multilingual Matters.

Jackson, Jane. 2008a. Globalization, internationalization, and short-term stays abroad. *International Journal of Intercultural Relations* 32(4). 349–358.

Jackson, Jane. 2008b. *Language, identity and study abroad: Sociocultural perspectives*. London: Equinox.

Kim, Young Yun. 2005. Adapting to a new culture. An integrative communication theory. In William B. Gudykunst (ed.), *Theorizing about intercultural communication*, 375–400. Thousand Oaks, CA: Sage Publications.

Lichtman, Marilyn. 2012. *Qualitative research in education: A user's guide*. Thousand Oaks, CA: SAGE Publications, Ince.

Lysgaard, Sverre. 1955. Adjustment in a foreign society: Norwegian fulbright grantees visiting the United States. *International Social Science Bulletin* 7. 45–51.

Marsden, Emma, Mackey Alison & Luke Plonsky. 2016. The IRIS repository: Advancing research practice and methodology. In Alison Mackey & Emma Marsden (eds.), *Advancing methodology and practice: The IRIS repository of instruments for research into second languages*, 1–21. New York: Routledge.

Masgoret, Anne-Marie & Colleen Ward. 2006. Culture learning approach to acculturation. In David L. Sam & John W. Berry (eds.), *Cambridge handbook of acculturation psychology*, 59–77. Cambridge: Cambridge University Press.

Mitchell, Rosamond, Nicole Tracy-Ventura & Kevin McManus (eds.). 2015. *Social interaction, identity and language learning during residence abroad* (Eurosla Monographs Series 4). Amsterdam: The European Second Language Association.

Newman, Michael, Mireia Trenchs-Parera & Shukhan Ng. 2008. Normalizing bilingualism: The effects of the catalonian linguistic normalization policy one generation after. *Journal of Sociolinguistics* 12(3). 306–333.

Pérez-Vidal, Carmen. 2014b. Study abroad and formal instruction contrasted: The SALA project. In Carmen Pérez-Vidal (ed.), *Second language acquisition in study abroad and formal instruction contexts*, 17–57. Amsterdam: John Benjamins.

Pitts, Margaret J. 2009. Identity and the role of expectations, stress, and talk in short-term student sojourner adjustment: An application of the integrative theory of communication and cross-cultural adaptation. *International Journal of Intercultural Relations* 33. 450–462.

Plews, John L. 2015. Intercultural identity-alignment in second language study abroad, or the more-or-less Canadians. In Rosamond Mitchell, Nicole Tracy-Ventura & Kevin McManus (eds.), *Social interaction, identity and language learning during residence abroad*, 281–304. Amsterdam: The European Second Language Association.

Pogorelova, Iryna. 2016. *A study of intercultural adaptation and the development of intercultural sensitivity of Catalan/Spanish university students during study abroad*. Barcelona: University Pompeu Fabra. (Doctoral dissertation.)

Teichler, Ulrich. 2004. Temporary study abroad: The life of ERASMUS students. *European Journal of Education* 39(4). 395–408.

Trenchs-Parera, Mireia & Maria Juan-Garau. 2014. A longitudinal study of learners' motivation and beliefs in at home and study abroad contexts. In Carmen Pérez-Vidal (ed.), *Language acquisition in study abroad and formal instruction contexts*. 259–282. Amsterdam: John Benjamins.

Trenchs-Parera, Mireia & Michael Newman. 2015. Language policies, ideologies, and attitudes in catalonia. Part 2: International immigration, globalization and the future of Catalan. *Language and Linguistics Compass* 12(9). 491–501.

Vande Berg, Michael, Jeffrey Connor-Linton & R. Michael Paige. 2009. The Georgetown consortium project: Interventions for student learning abroad. *Frontiers: The Interdisciplinary Journal of Study Abroad* 18. 1–75.

Vedder, Paul & Erkki Virta. 2005. Language, ethnic identity, and the adaptation of Turkish immigrant youth in the Netherlands and Sweden. *International Journal of Intercultural Relations* 29. 317–337.

Ward, Colleen. 2004. Psychological theories of culture contact and their implications for intercultural training and interventions. In Daniel Landis, Janet M. Bennett & Milton J. Bennett (eds.), *Handbook of intercultural training*, 185–216. Thousand Oaks, CA: Sage Publications.

Williams, Tracy Rundstrom. 2005. Exploring the impact of study abroad on students' intercultural communication skills: Adaptability and sensitivity. *Journal of Studies in International Education* 9(4). 356–371.

Chapter 11

Acculturation and pragmatic learning: International students in the United States

Ariadna Sánchez-Hernández
Leuphana University Lüneburg

The present study explores the relationship between acculturation and the development of second language (L2) pragmatic competence during a semester-long study abroad (SA) program in the United States (US). Drawing on Schumann's (1978) Acculturation theory of L2 acquisition, it was hypothesized that the degree to which SA participants acculturate socially and psychologically to the target language community would be related to the extent to which they acquire L2 pragmatic competence. Twelve international students of three different nationalities – Brazilian, Turkish, and Spanish – in their first semester of study at an American university completed a pre-test and a post-test version of a discourse completion task that measured their ability to produce speech acts and a sociocultural adaptation scale Ward & Kennedy (1999) that measured their acculturation. Additionally, they participated in semi-structured interviews at the beginning and at the end of the stay that provided insights into their SA adaptation experiences. An exploration of individual trajectories indicated that gains in pragmatic competence were promoted by acculturation development. On the one hand, pragmatic gains were related to social variables that included the integration strategy adopted and academic pressure. On the other hand, they were associated with affective factors such as social support from home-country peers. The reported findings bring new insights to the field of L2 pragmatics by examining the effects of acculturation. Ultimately, the results emphasize the importance of enhancing L2 learners' social and affective adaptation during SA programs, so as to maximize their acculturation experiences and their subsequent L2 pragmatic learning.

Ariadna Sánchez-Hernández. Acculturation and pragmatic learning: International students in the United States. In Carmen Pérez Vidal, Sonia López-Serrano, Jennifer Ament & Dakota J. Thomas-Wilhelm (eds.), *Learning context effects: Study abroad, formal instruction and international immersion classrooms*, 283–309. Berlin: Language Science Press. DOI:10.5281/zenodo.1300638

Ariadna Sánchez-Hernández

1 Introduction

A main consequence of globalization is the increase of study abroad (SA) programs all over the world, which have even become mandatory for many university students. However, the traditional view that SA programs are the optimal context for learning[1] a second language (L2) is being challenged by studies reporting cases of unsuccessful adaptation experiences by international students (for a review, see Mitchell et al. 2015; 2017) and limited acquisition of some pragmatic features (for a review, see Taguchi & Roever 2017). This is not surprising if one considers that SA participants not only have to focus on improving their L2 proficiency, but also have to face the multiple challenges involved in the process of adapting to a new and unknown setting, while being expected to interact with people of diverse sociocultural backgrounds. Drawing on this idea, recent research (e.g. Taguchi et al. 2016; Sykes 2017; Taguchi 2017; Taguchi & Roever 2017) points out that a problem in understanding SA outcomes is that there is a scarcity of empirical support for the relationship between intercultural and pragmatic competences, areas that have traditionally belonged to different domains (psychology and linguistics, respectively).

To address this problem, the present study explores the extent to which SA participants' acculturation experiences are related to the development of their pragmatic competence in the SA context. Drawing on Schumann's (1978; 1986) Acculturation theory of L2 acquisition, the study is based on the premise that the degree to which an individual acculturates to the target language society will determine his/her acquisition of the L2. According to Schumann (1978), in the process of adapting to a new environment, different social variables (e.g. integration strategies, attitude towards the host culture) and affective factors (e.g. culture shock, motivation) are at play. While the Acculturation model has commonly been used in the general field of L2 acquisition (e.g. Hansen 1995; Lybeck 2002), its application in the field of L2 pragmatics still represents a research desideratum. There is no conclusive evidence as to whether acquisition of pragmatic ability during a stay abroad is related to students' acculturation experiences.

---

[1]Acknowledging the difference between the terms *acquisition* and *learning* pointed out by Krashen (1985) - i.e., natural acquisition vs. acquisition that involves formal instruction respectively – the present study follows the mainstream use of both terms as synonyms to refer to language development.

2 Literature review

2.1 Study abroad programs as a context for learning pragmatics

Study abroad programs – that is, temporary educational sojourns in which a target language is used by the members of the community (Taguchi 2015a) – have typically been referred to as the optimal context for the acquisition of pragmatic competence. Mastering pragmatic competence in a L2 involves learning how to the use language appropriate in the context, the situation and with the interlocutors – in other words, knowing "*when* and *where* to say something, *what* to say, [and] to *whom* to say it in a given social and linguistic context" (García 1989: 314). Pragmatic ability mainly involves the ability to perform speech acts, such as suggestions, requests, refusals, apologies, and compliments, among others. In addition, it concerns the mastery of pragmatic features like implied meaning, pragmatic routines (i.e., formulaic language recurrently used by native speakers (NSs) in given situations), and managing interaction (i.e., turn-taking or conversation openings). While studying abroad, learners are likely to acquire these features as they have the potential to have rich exposure to the L2 outside of class and plenty of opportunities to use the language in diverse social situations, with different interlocutors and for real-life purposes. Moreover, they continuously witness interactions among users of the L2 that provide them with valuable and authentic input. Taguchi (2015a: 4) summarizes the main elements that make the SA context potentially optimal for pragmatic learning as given in (1).

(1) a. Opportunities to observe local norms of interaction;
  b. contextualized pragmatic practice and immediate feedback on that practice;
  c. real-life consequences of pragmatic behavior; and
  d. exposure to variation in styles and communicative situations.

There is a burgeoning of studies in the field of interlanguage pragmatics (ILP) that have pointed out the advantage of the SA context for the development of different pragmatic features. These have typically involved cross-sectional investigations, that is, comparing pragmatic ability among groups of L2 learners or comparing NSs and non-native speakers (NNSs), or, to a lesser extent, longitudinal studies that examine pragmatic development over time (see Alcón-Soler 2014 for a review of cross-sectional and longitudinal ILP findings in the SA context). All in all, these studies have reported that during SA, learners improve their pragmatic awareness, their production of speech acts, their use of pragmatic routines and their comprehension of implied meaning.

Nevertheless, longitudinal ILP studies have shown that the advantage of the SA context for pragmatic development is not straightforward. The process of acquiring L2 pragmatic competence is variable and non-linear, as it depends on (1) the pragmatic feature under study and (2) different factors associated with the SA setting. For instance, SA seems to be beneficial for the acquisition of pragmatic routines, but there are mixed findings on its benefits for the ability to comprehend implied meaning and to produce certain speech acts (Taguchi & Roever 2017). Indeed, not all speech acts present the same degree of difficulty. For instance, greetings, leave-takings, and offers are acquired more quickly, and students thus learn them at earlier stages of immersion, while appropriate use of requests, refusals, and invitations is achieved at a slower pace and is thus more common in longer SA sojourns (Barron 2003; Félix-Brasdefer 2004; Hassall 2006).

ILP scholars have commonly classified predictors of pragmatic learning during SA into two main categories: external factors related to the context, and internal ones related to learners' individual differences. The main external factors investigated in ILP research are length of stay and intensity of interaction with users of the L2, with studies reporting that amount of interaction is a better predictor of pragmatic development than length of stay (e.g. Bardovi-Harlig & Bastos 2011; Bella 2011). That is, spending more time in the target language setting is not enough on its own to fully develop pragmatic competence, as L2 learners need to be willing to take advantage of the opportunities for interaction offered by the context. Nevertheless, a focus on the role of external factors does not seem to be enough to explain L2 pragmatic acquisition, since internal factors often interfere with the effect of contextual variables. Evidence of this fact is provided, for example, by Eslami & Ahn (2014), who explored how pragmatic development (measured in terms of the ability to respond to compliments) by Korean students in the US was influenced by two external factors, namely length of stay and intensity of interaction and one internal variable, namely motivation, reporting that only motivation had a positive impact on pragmatic development. All in all, proficiency has been the most investigated internal predictor of pragmatic acquisition, with most research findings indicating that having a certain proficiency level enhances the acquisition of most pragmatic features, although lower-level students at times outperform higher-level ones depending on the pragmatic feature and on the context (for a review, see Xiao 2015).

In sum, although most ILP investigations have revealed positive gains in pragmatic ability during SA, they have also reported that such pragmatic development is variable and non-linear, as it is influenced by different factors. Drawing on this idea, some scholars (e.g. Taguchi 2015a) have expressed the need for ILP studies to focus on the processes – rather than merely on the outcomes – of SA. This implies a call for more longitudinal research on the factors that influence the development of pragmatic ability over time. More particularly, in a recent monograph, Taguchi & Roever (2017) call for ILP studies to investigate new variables that have gained importance in the current era of globalization, such as intercultural competence, an umbrella term that encompasses the concept of acculturation.

2.2 Acculturation and pragmatic learning

The present study aims to bridge the gap between internal and external factors that affect L2 pragmatic learning by focusing on the variable of acculturation. Acculturation is a multifold phenomenon that is defined as "the process of cultural change that occurs when individuals from different cultural backgrounds come into prolonged, continuous, first-hand contact with each other" (Redfield et al. 1936: 146). It has been operationalized in terms of three main constructs: acculturation conditions (antecedent factors such as the characteristics of the sojourning and host cultures, of the sojourning group, and of the individuals), acculturation orientations (strategies of integration in the host society, such as assimilation, marginalization, or separation), and acculturation outcomes, which include sociocultural adaptation (implying behavioral aspects, skills, attitudes, and cultural knowledge) and psychological adaptation (sojourners' well-being and satisfaction) (see Arends Tóth & Van de Vijver 2006).

Different models have been proposed in an attempt to explore the influence of acculturation on the acquisition of an L2. Three major frameworks include the Inter-group model by Beebe & Giles (1984), the Socio-Educational model by Gardner (Gardner et al. 1983), and the Acculturation model by Schumann (1978; 1986) (see Ellis 1994: Chapter 3). The present study takes Schumann's model as a reference to understand acculturation, as it accounts for acculturation conditions, orientations and outcomes. Moreover, it is the only model that has generated empirical evidence concerning the relationship between acculturation and pragmatic learning (Schmidt 1983; Dörnyei et al. 2004; Schmitt et al. 2004).

In the first seminal book that provides a comprehensive review of L2 pragmatic development, Kasper & Rose (2002) present Schumann's (1978) Acculturation model as the first theoretical framework that explains pragmatic development. According to Schumann, the degree to which an L2 learner acculturates to the new sociocultural community will influence the extent to which he/she learns the target language, acculturation being the first (but not the only one) in a list of factors that determines L2 acquisition. A key point of Schumann's theory is that acculturation is determined by the proximity of the sojourner to the target language group in terms of sociocultural and psychological adaptation. Sociocultural adaptation refers to the degree to which a language learner achieves contact with the L2 group and becomes part of it; it thus depends on the individual's skills with respect to integration and management of everyday situations. Psychological adaptation involves the degree to which a student is comfortable with the learning and adaptation processes and therefore implies emotional well-being and personal satisfaction. To determine the extent of acculturation with respect to these two aspects, Schumann (1986) distinguishes two sets of factors. Firstly, seven social factors, provided in (2), shape sociocultural adaptation:

(2)   a. Social dominance of the target language group, in terms of political, cultural, technical, and economic status, as perceived by the sojourning group.

   b. Integration strategy: assimilation, preservation or adaptation of sociocultural values.

   c. Enclosure: the degree to which the two cultural groups share the same social facilities.

   d. Cohesiveness and size of the sojourning group.

   e. Cultural congruence between the two groups regarding religion, general social practice, and other beliefs.

   f. Attitude towards the host culture.

   g. Intended length of stay in the target language context.

Secondly, the four affective factors in (3) determine psychological adaptation:

(3)   a. Language shock: fear of appearing ridiculous when speaking the L2.

   b. Culture shock: feelings of rejection, anxiety, and disorientation by the sojourners while living amongst members of the target community.

   c. Motivation: according to Schumann, an integrative motivation is more likely to assist in SLA than an instrumental one.

   d. Ego permeability: the extent to which identity is flexible and can adapt.

A few studies have drawn on Schumann's (1978) assertion that the degree to which individuals acculturate will determine the extent to which they learn the L2. Most of them suggest that L2 acquisition, especially in terms of oral proficiency, is benefited by the learners' process of acculturation (Hansen 1995; Lybeck 2002; Jiang et al. 2009). In the field of pragmatics, Schmidt's (1983) and

Dörnyei et al. (2004), to the best of my knowledge, that have applied Schumann's model to explain L2 pragmatic development.

Schmidt (1983) conducted a case study of Wes, a 33-year-old Japanese male who immigrated to the US (Hawaii) without having previous formal instruction in English. Wes's development with respect to acculturation and L2 acquisition was tracked over 3 years. With the optimal sociocultural and psychological orientations, he increased his pragmatic ability but did not improve his grammatical competence. To assess pragmatic competence, Schmidt focused on directives, which include speech acts used to incite action on the part of the interlocutor, such as orders, requests, and suggestions. At earlier stages of pragmatic development, Wes's use of directives was characterized by a reliance on a small number of speech formulas that he only used in specific situations (for example, *shall we go?*), and by transfer from Japanese sociopragmatic norms. Over time, he improved the appropriateness of meanings, reduced pragmatic transfer, became aware of differences between languages, and developed significant control of speech act strategies and formulas used in social interactions. Schmidt (1983) thus confirmed that acculturation leads to increased L2 pragmatic competence.

Schmitt et al. (2004) analyzed quantitatively how acculturation affected the use of formulaic language learning. They quickly realized that acculturation was a complex phenomenon that demanded a qualitative in-depth analysis, which led them to conduct semi-structured interviews with a subset of seven of the participants. This second investigation, conducted by Dörnyei et al. (2004), was a case study of seven international students having spent seven months in a British university, in which the authors explored the participants' acculturation development in terms of sociocultural adaptation, measured through the social factors outlined in Schumann's (1978) model[2]. Four of the participants showed positive gains in their ability to use formulaic language, while three of them did not experience such gains. Research findings indicated a strong relationship between sociocultural adaptation and pragmatic learning. In particular, acquisition of formulaic language was mainly influenced by the variables of enclosure and the integration strategy adopted, as evidenced in the participants' development of social networks. Indeed, most of the participants found it extremely hard to have meaningful contact with the L2 speakers outside of class. Successful learning of formulaic language depended on whether they could "beat the odds" and

---

[2]Dörnyei et al. (2004: 88) take Schumann's (1978) Acculturation theory as a base, but they focus on the social aspects of the process. They define acculturation as "the extent to which learners succeeded in settling in and engaging with the host community, thereby taking advantage of the social contact opportunities available".

come out of the "international ghetto" (Dörnyei et al. 2004: 105). This was evident in two of the participants, who scored higher in a formulaic language test. The other two successful students had extraordinary motivation and language aptitude. These two aspects therefore also played a key role in pragmatic learning.

Schumann's (1978) Acculturation theory, however, has received little further empirical support, and it has faced some criticism (Ellis 1994; Zaker 2016). The main critique has been that it is difficult to assess some of the variables proposed by Schumann. Moreover, the framework disregards additional factors that may be better predictors of L2 learning, such as individual differences (e.g. cognitive abilities, learning style) and instruction (Mondy 2007; cited in Zaker 2016). According to Mondy 2007 learners may acculturate successfully despite not having favorable conditions in the social and affective variables proposed by Schumann.

Other studies have explored the role of acculturation factors on pragmatic development without drawing on Schumann's (1978) model. Overall, they have reported that pragmatic competence is determined by specific aspects such as identity (Siegal 1995), motivation (Eslami & Ahn 2014), and cultural similarity (Bardovi-Harlig et al. 2008). Additionally, a recent line of studies has addressed the role of intercultural competence on the development of pragmatic ability (Taguchi 2015b; Taguchi et al. 2016). Nevertheless, the question still remains as to whether the development of pragmatic competence is determined by students' sociocultural and psychological adaptation during SA. The current study directly addresses this question and in doing so fills in the existing gap between studies on acculturation and on L2 pragmatic acquisition.

3 Research questions

This investigation sheds new light on the development of L2 pragmatic competence in the SA context by exploring the influence of acculturation on the development of speech act performance by students in their first semester of participation in a SA program in the US. Two research questions guide the study:

RQ1. Does a semester of study abroad afford gains in pragmatic competence in terms of speech act production?

RQ2. To what extent, if any, are gains in pragmatic competence related to students' acculturation development, measured in terms of sociocultural and psychological adaptation?

4 Method

4.1 Research design

To address these research questions, a mixed-method case study approach was employed. This methodology differs from purely qualitative case-study ethnography as it integrates a quantitative research component, which in this case provided an objective assessment of pragmatic competence and of sociocultural adaptation. Additionally, both sociocultural and psychological adaptation were measured qualitatively through semi-structured interviews. Moreover, the current investigation was longitudinal and involved two data-collection points: at the beginning and at the end of a semester.

4.2 Participants

Twelve international students at a public university in the US Midwest participated in the study. The sample was drawn from a larger-scale study that involved 122 international students. The group of 12 was selected as they had volunteered to take part in interviews. Table 1 summarizes the demographic information about the 12 informants.

Table 1: Demographic information about case-study informants

Pseudonym	Age	Gender	Nationality	Proficiency	Living situation
David	23	M	Brazilian	Beginner	With NNSs (Brazilian)
Emma	26	F	Spanish	Advanced	With NNSs (Spanish)
Sean	25	M	Turkish	Advanced	Change: NSs to NNSs (diverse nationalities)
Lisa	24	F	Spanish	Intermediate	With NNSs (Spanish)
Jeff	20	M	Brazilian	Advanced	With NNSs (Brazilian)
William	22	M	Brazilian	Advanced	With NNSs (Brazilian)
Steven	26	M	Turkish	Advanced	With NNSs (diverse nationalities)
Jason	26	M	Brazilian	Intermediate	With NNSs (Brazilian)
Ethan	29	M	Spanish	Advanced	With NSs
Michelle	29	F	Turkish	Intermediate	With NSs
Mark	27	M	Turkish	Intermediate	With NSs

The group consisted of three females and nine males, their mean age was 24.4 (ranging from 20 to 29), and they were of three different nationalities: Brazilian

(n = 5), Turkish (n = 4), and Spanish (n = 3). All of them were in their first semester of study in the US, and their living arrangements varied: eight of them were living with NNSs, three of them were living with NSs, and one student changed from living with NSs to living with NNSs. The amount of English instruction they received during the semester depended on their proficiency level, which was measured by scores on the Test of English as Foreign Language (TOEFL). Beginner students (n = 1) enrolled in full-time English classes, intermediate students (n = 4) took part-time classes (and therefore combined them with content classes), and advanced (n = 7) learners took occasional and specialized English courses in addition to content classes.

4.3 Instruments

Three main instruments were used in the study: a written discourse completion task (DCT) that measured students' pragmatic knowledge quantitatively, a modified Sociocultural Adaptation Scale (SCAS; Ward & Kennedy 1999) that assessed their sociocultural adaptation, and semi-structured interviews that revealed qualitative information about students' acculturation in the US in terms of sociocultural and psychological adaptation. Additionally, a background questionnaire was administered to collect demographic information and to control for variables such as age, proficiency, previous experience abroad, and nationality.

The written DCT was developed to elicit participants' production of speech acts in high-imposition and low-imposition situations. The choice of the instrument was based on the suitability of DCTs for the elicitation of information about speech act production, as they allow the researcher to control the given conditions and to obtain simulated oral data (Félix-Brasdefer & Hasler-Baker 2017). The selected speech acts were requests and refusals, chosen because of the importance of their appropriate use by L2 learners for successful communication with NSs. Requests and refusals are considered "face-threatening acts" (Brown & Levinson 1987); inappropriate production of these could therefore lead to unintended offense by the interlocutor. Table 2 displays the classification of the speech act situations included in the DCT.

To determine the high- and low-imposition categories, Brown & Levinson's (1987) framework was employed by considering the social distance between the speaker and hearer, the social power of the interlocutors, and the degree of imposition. High-imposition situations included formal interactions between a student (the speaker) and a professor (the hearer), where the social distance is large, and the social power of the hearer is higher. Low-imposition scenarios involved informal interactions between two students, where the social distance is small,

Table 2: Description of the situations included in the DCT

High-imposition situations	
1. Request	Asking a professor for an extension of the deadline for an assignment
2. Request	Asking a professor to have the test on a different day
3. Refusal	Refusing to take summer classes
4. Refusal	Refusing to help a lecturer carry some books to his/her office

Low-imposition situations	
5. Request	Asking a friend for a pen
6. Request	Asking a friend for a ride to the supermarket
7. Refusal	Refusing an invitation to a party
8. Refusal	Refusing to lend your notes to a classmate

and the social power of the interlocutors is equal. The selection of the situations was made on the basis of previous studies that have used DCTs to explore the production of requests and refusals (Alcón-Soler 2008; Taguchi 2006; 2011; 2013; Martínez-Flor & Usó-Juan 2011). The DCT was validated through a pilot study conducted in the previous academic semester with eight NSs and with 21 international students enrolled at the same university. This preliminary study aimed to check whether the situations were understood correctly and whether they elicited the corresponding speech act.

Regarding the assessment of acculturation, a modified version of the Sociocultural Adaptation Scale[3] (SCAS; Ward & Kennedy 1999) was used to measure participants' sociocultural adaptation in the US. Drawing from Berry (2003), I focused the quantitative analysis on sociocultural – rather than on psychological – adaptation, considering that affective factors are to some degree responsible for students' sociocultural adaptation. The SCAS is a five-point Likert scale in which students are asked to rate from 1 (= very difficult) to 5 (= no difficulty) their level of adaptation to 29 items. In the original instrument, high scores had been associated with higher levels of difficulty (that is, less degree of acculturation). In this study, items were reversed from the original scale so that higher scores corresponded with a positive adaptation. These items included 21 behavioral situations such as *finding food you enjoy* and *making friends*, and seven cognitive aspects such as *seeing things from an American point of view*.

---

[3] The SCAS has been widely used in empirical studies given its strong psychometric properties (Celenk & Van de Vijver 2011). In this study, the calculation of Cronbach alpha coefficient in the entire sample of 122 participants revealed a strong internal consistency of the scale (α = 0.937).

Additionally, acculturation was measured qualitatively through semi-structured interviews at the beginning and at the end of the semester, which revealed reasons for individual trajectories of sociocultural and of psychological adaptation during SA. The interviews were conducted in English in the principal researcher's office and lasted between 25 and 35 minutes. The questions formulated were related to students' acculturation experiences following Schumann's (1978) proposal of social and psychological acculturation variables (c.f. §2.2). Moreover, the semi-structured format of the interviews was advantageous for the elicitation of relevant topics that could explain acculturation but were not included in Schumann's proposal. More particularly, the following themes were pre-selected: educational background and English experience in the home country; SA program goals and expectations; SA outcomes; academic and sociocultural adjustment; overall well-being; English use (interaction with English speakers); pragmatic awareness; and influence of instruction.

4.4 Data collection

This is a longitudinal study that employed a pre-test–post-test design. Data collection took place during the 2014 fall semester. For the pre-test, a day and time were established during the second week of the semester, during which participants were asked to complete the written instruments (the background questionnaire, the DCT, and the SCAS) and to participate in the interviews. Completion of the written instruments took place during L2 English classes and lasted for approximately 30 minutes, during which participants read and signed the consent form (5 minutes), completed the background questionnaire (5 minutes), the SCAS (10 minutes), and the pragmatic test (10 minutes). The interview sessions were held at the main researcher's office, each lasting between 25 and 35 minutes, and they were recorded with the software Audacity. The post-test data collection sessions followed the same protocol used for the pre-test and took place during the week before the end of the semester.

4.5 Data analysis

The first type of data coded was quantitative information about pragmatic competence. Pragmatic knowledge was operationalized in terms of appropriateness of speech act production, and it was evaluated by means of NSs' ratings in a holistic appropriateness scale designed by Taguchi (2011). The instrument is a 5-point Likert scale that ranges from (1) very poor to (5) excellent. It assesses an answer to a DCT situation in terms of 3 aspects of pragmatic competence: level of politeness, level of directness, and level of formality. Table 3 shows the rating scale used.

Table 3: Appropriateness rating scale developed by Taguchi (2011: 459)

Excellent	Almost perfectly appropriate and effective in the level of directness, politeness and formality.
Good	Not perfect but adequately appropriate in the level of directness, politeness, and formality. Expressions are a little off from target-like, but pretty good.
Fair	Somewhat appropriate in the level of directness, politeness, and formality. Expressions are more direct or indirect than the situation requires.
Poor	Clearly inappropriate. Expressions sound almost rude or too demanding.
Very poor	Not sure if the target speech act is performed.

Five NSs were trained in the rating of pragmatic appropriateness. The training contained information about the purpose of the data collection, the coding criteria, some examples of previous studies that have used the appropriateness scale of the study (Taguchi 2011; 2013), and practice with data from the pilot study (N = 21). Drawing from Hudson et al. (1995), who proposed the use of an appropriateness rating scale to assess pragmatic production, the NSs were instructed not to consider grammaticality. Inter-rater reliability was r = 0.83. The disagreements (17% of the data) were discussed and resolved during a meeting.

The second type of data coded was quantitative information about the students' sociocultural adaptation. Answers from the SCAS were analyzed, revealing scores that ranged from 1, which indicated poor sociocultural adaptation, to 5, meaning high levels of adaptation.

Thirdly, the content of the semi-structured interviews was analyzed by eliciting different themes that allowed for the establishment of participant profiles based on the development of their sociocultural and psychological adaptation. Following Schumann's (1986) proposal of acculturation variables, comments in the interviews were coded into 5 main sociocultural themes and 4 psychological ones. Sociocultural adaptation aspects included the integration strategy adopted (which involved the development of social networks), enclosure, cohesiveness and size of the sojourning group, cultural congruence, and changes in attitude towards US culture. Intended length of residence and social dominance were not included in the analysis as there was homogeneity across the participants in these two aspects. Psychological adaptation aspects included culture shock, language shock, motivation, and ego permeability. Additionally, I considered that the semi-structured interviews could reveal further factors that accounted for students' adaptation, especially psychological factors (Schumann 1986). Finally, accultur-ation profiles of students were established by discerning whether sociocultural and psychological adaptation increased or decreased from the beginning to the end of the semester. To do so, I focused on answers given during the final inter-view, as well as on the change in answers given across time.

Once the three types of data were coded, the next step was to analyze them to answer the two research questions of the study. Firstly, gains in pragmatic production were calculated by means of a series of Wilcoxon Signed-Ranks tests. This non-parametric test, selected given the small sample size of participants, al-lowed for comparisons of average scores from the rating scales in the pre-test and the post-test. Secondly, gains in sociocultural adaptation were calculated through an additional Wilcoxon Signed-Ranks test, and the relationship between sociocultural adaptation and pragmatic development was measured through the non-parametric Spearman rho correlation. To analyze the qualitative data, dif-ferent individual trajectories of sociocultural and psychological adaptation were discerned, and they were compared against individual trajectories of pragmatic learning. This allowed for the presentation and interpretation of case studies that illustrate patterns of associations between acculturation and pragmatic compe-tence.

5 Results

5.1 RQ1: Does a semester of study abroad afford gains in pragmatic competence, in terms of speech act production?

The first research question of the study asked whether students improved their pragmatic competence in the SA context, pragmatic ability being operationalized in terms of appropriateness of speech act production, which was measured on a 5-point scale. To determine whether there were statistical differences between pre-test and post-test pragmatic performance, Wilcoxon Signed-Ranks tests were conducted for speech act production in high- and low-imposition situations, both including requests and refusals. Moreover, gains in overall speech act production were calculated. Table 4 displays pre-test and post-test means (M), standard devi-ations (SD), and differences – which indicate gains – for each of the three aspects. Differences were considered significant at $p < 0.05$.

Table 4: Descriptive statistics of production of speech acts

	Pre-test		Post-test		Difference	
	M	SD	M	SD	Score	%
High-imposition situations	3.12	0.74	3.56	0.79	0.44	10.94
Low-imposition situations	2.80	0.63	3.35	0.64	0.56*	14.06*
Overall production of speech acts	2.96	0.47	3.45	0.55	0.50*	12.50*

*Significant at $p < 0.05$

The statistical analysis revealed that participants improved their overall pragmatic competence during the first semester of immersion in the US ($Z = 2.31$; $p = .021$). More particularly, they significantly improved their appropriateness in the production of requests and refusals in low-imposition situations ($Z = 2.41$; $p = .016$), although they did not experience statistically-significant pragmatic gains in high-imposition situations ($Z = 1.69$; $p = .09$). To illustrate these findings, example (4) illustrates positive gains in pragmatic production in a low-imposition situation, and example (5) shows no gains in a high-imposition context. Both examples include answers in the pre- and post-tests to request situations by the same participant, Lisa, and they also show the agreed assessment of the responses by the raters in the appropriateness rating scale.

(4)   You are in class and you need to write something down, but you realize you forgot your pen at home. You tell the classmate sitting next to you:

   a.   Pre-test: *I was wondering if you have a pen I could maybe borrow*
Evaluation: (3) fair. Somewhat appropriate in the level of directness, politeness, and formality. Expressions are more direct or indirect than the situation requires.

   b.   Post-test: *Do you have a pen I could borrow? Please?*
Evaluation: (5) excellent. Almost perfectly appropriate and effective in the level of directness, politeness and formality

(5)   You need to ask a professor for an extension of a deadline for turning in a paper. At the end of a class session you tell him:

   a.   Pre-test: *Sorry, could I have an extension of the deadline for the Biology paper?*
Evaluation: (3) fair. Somewhat appropriate in the level of directness,

politeness, and formality. Expressions are more direct or indirect than the situation requires.

b. Post-test: *Excuse me, can I have an extension of the deadline for the paper?*
Evaluation: (3) fair. Somewhat appropriate in the level of directness, politeness, and formality. Expressions are more direct or indirect than the situation requires.

As may be observed in example (4), Lisa improved her appropriateness in requesting a pen from a friend (that is, a low-imposition situation) by using the conventional request strategy "Do you have.... I can borrow?" which was more appropriate than the expression *I was wondering* and the mitigator *maybe*, which are more appropriately used in high-imposition situations. In contrast, example (5) shows that she did not improve her appropriateness in requesting an extension of a deadline from a professor (that is, a high-imposition situation). Although she provided different answers in the pre- and post-tests, both answers were rated as *fair*, as she could have used a more polite and indirect strategy.

The present findings in relation to research question 1 have pointed out that the SA context is beneficial for the production of speech acts, particularly in low-imposition situations that involve conversations with friends. This suggests that during the first semester of immersion, students were probably mostly exposed to informal situations and interactions with other students rather than to formal conversations with professors. These results are in line with previous studies that have revealed that the first months of immersion in the SA context enhance production of low-imposition speech acts to a greater extent than that of high-imposition speech acts such as requests, refusals, and opinions (Taguchi 2006; 2011; 2013).

5.2 RQ2: To what extent, if any, does students' acculturation development influence gains in pragmatic competence?

The second research question of the study asked to what extent, if any, students' acculturation development was related to the gains in pragmatic competence reported above (see §5.1). Acculturation was quantitatively operationalized in terms of sociocultural adaptation, while a qualitative analysis accounted for both sociocultural and psychological adaptation.

To determine whether the participants experienced gains in their sociocultural adaptation, a Wilcoxon Signed-Ranks test compared pre-test adaptation scores ($M = 3.80$; $SD = 0.45$; Min = 3.24; Max = 4.66) with post-test ones ($M = 4.04$; SD

= 0.42; Min = 3.28; Max = 4.55). Results indicated a significant improvement (Z = 1.778; p = 0.075), and therefore confirmed that a semester of SA enhanced the students' sociocultural adaptation.

To examine the relationship between the reported sociocultural adaptation gains and the pragmatic gains, a Spearman rho correlation was conducted, with the significance level established at $p < 0.10$, and the analysis revealed a positive correlation (r = 0.604, p = 0.038). Therefore, we may hypothesize that adaptation to the SA context may have played a key role in learners' improvement of their ability to produce speech acts.

Next, post-hoc Spearman rho correlation tests between adaptation gains and gains in speech act production in high-imposition and in low-imposition situations were calculated. The results revealed that sociocultural adaptation was significantly related to speech act production in high-imposition situations (r = 0.527; p = 0.079), but it was unrelated to speech act production in low-imposition situations (r = 0.424; p = 0.169). This finding suggests that students who improved their sociocultural adaptation during the semester were also likely to improve their pragmatic ability in high-imposition formal situations that involve interacting with a professor. It could also imply that students who improved their pragmatic ability in such situations were also likely to improve their adaptation to the new context. Nevertheless, gains in pragmatic ability in low imposition situations such as interacting with friends were unrelated to sociocultural adaptation.

Next, the association between acculturation and pragmatic development was explored qualitatively. The participants' answers in the interviews at the beginning and at the end of the semester were analyzed, and individual profiles in terms of sociocultural and psychological adaptation were established. Table 5 illustrates the 12 individual profiles by showing descriptive data about their pragmatic gains (in high- and low-imposition situations) – expressed in percentages – their sociocultural adaptation gains – expressed in gain scores from the analysis of SCAS answers – and overall increase or decrease in sociocultural and psychological adaptation. The ordering of participants in the table is hierarchical, running from the student with the greatest positive gains in overall pragmatic competence to the one with greatest negative gains.

Table 5 shows that there were diverse individual trajectories of pragmatic learning and acculturation. Taking all the profiles into account, 3 patterns can be observed, which will guide the presentation of the qualitative findings in the following sections. Pattern 1 includes informants whose gains in pragmatic competence – either positive or negative – correspond with their gains in both overall sociocultural and psychological adaptation. Pattern 2 refers to partici-

Table 5: Descriptive information of the development of pragmatic competence and acculturation by 12 informants

| | Pragmatic competence | | | Acculturation | |
Participant	High imp	Low imp	Overall	Sociocultural	Psychological
David	2	1.75	1.9	0.97	Increase	Increase
Emma	1	1.75	1.4	0.89	Increase	Increase
Mike	1.75	0.5	1.2	−0.04	Decrease	Increase
Sean	0.5	1.25	0.8	0.48	Increase	Decrease
Lisa	0.5	0.5	0.5	0.6	Increase	Increase
Jeff	−0.25	1.25	0.5	0.41	Increase	Increase
William	0	0.75	0.4	−0.18	Decrease	Increase
Steven	0.75	0	0.4	−0.01	Decrease	Increase
Jason	0	−0.25	−0.1	−0.08	Decrease	Decrease
Ethan	−0.25	−0.25	−0.2	0.07	Increase	Decrease
Michelle	−0.5	0	−0.3	0.03	Increase	Decrease
Mark	−0.25	−0.5	−0.4	−0.27	Decrease	Decrease
average	0.44	0.56	0.5	0.24		

pants whose pragmatic gains only correspond with their psychological adaptation gains. Finally, pattern 3 includes one informant whose gains in speech act production only correspond with his gains in sociocultural adaptation.

5.2.1 Pattern 1: Interplay of sociocultural and psychological adaptation and pragmatic gains

The first category includes informants who have shown either positive or negative gains in pragmatic production and in both sociocultural and psychological outcomes of acculturation. David, Emma, Lisa and Jeff are gainers in this respect, while Jason, Mark and Michelle are non-gainers.

On the one hand, David, Jeff, Emma and Lisa all showed positive gains in pragmatic competence, sociocultural adaptation, and psychological adaptation. Their sociocultural adaptation was mainly determined by the successful integration strategy adopted: that of assimilation of US sociocultural values. They were the only participants that consciously tried to interact beyond their home-country cohesive group (in this case, Brazilians and Spaniards) and to assimilate host values. David and Lisa's integration can be largely attributed to making close US friends and, in the case of David, finding a NS girlfriend. Jeff and Emma's successful integration and therefore pragmatic development were mainly due to their enrollment in clubs – a theatre club for Jeff, and a music band and volunteering program for Emma. At the same time, the four improved their psychological adaptation thanks to social support from their home-country peers. In this sense, both David and Jeff expressed that living with their "Brazilian family" was what made the experience great. Similarly, Lisa expressed that although she tried to spend most of her time with her US roommates in order to integrate into the community, she also felt she had a Spanish family, and indeed all of the Spanish students developed a close relationship. In the case of Emma her improvement in psychological adaptation was primarily attributed to a reduction of language shock, which was a consequence of her integration into the L2 community.

On the other hand, Jason, Mark and Michelle decreased their scores of pragmatic ability, as well as in sociocultural and psychological adaptation. In the three cases, the students were not able to integrate into the L2 society, and instead preserved their own sociocultural values during the stay. This unsuccessful integration may be due to several reasons: an increase in language shock and a consequent change in personality in the case of Jason, academic pressure in the case of Mark, and ego permeability (also a problem related to personality) in the case of Michelle. Jason developed a wide network of Brazilian friends and did not gain confidence to interact with Americans. In the post-test interview, he expressed that his anxiety to speak in English had increased and that he was disappointed because he had expected to improve his speaking ability by coming to the US. Moreover, it seems that his language shock made him shy when using English, as he claimed to be extroverted and social with his Brazilian friends but could not interact with US students. Similarly, Michelle was aware that she was a shy person, and according to her, her introverted personality prevented her from interacting with NSs and from learning about their culture. As for Mark, his strong motivation to integrate into the society and to practice his English was evident: he enrolled in university clubs and also reached out to NSs. Nevertheless, he regretted feeling a lot of pressure to pass a TOEFL test at the end of the semester that would enable him to continue in the SA program. As a consequence, both Michelle and Mark also increased their language shock and at the end of the semester and reported being scared or ashamed of using their English at times.

5.2.2 Pattern 2: Interplay of psychological adaptation and pragmatic gains

The second case involves participants whose pragmatic gains corresponded with their psychological adaptation gains, but not with their sociocultural ones. William, Mike, and Steven experienced positive gains in speech act production and in psychological adaptation, while Ethan showed negative pragmatic development and a decrease in his psychological adaptation.

William and Mike experienced similar sociocultural and psychological adaptation paths. They reported having a phenomenal semester thanks to the Brazilian friends they made. Therefore, social support from their home-country peers seemed to have enhanced their well-being and their psychological adaptation. Nevertheless, limiting their contact to Brazilians made their sociocultural adaptation decrease. This situation was more striking in William's case, who openly admitted not making contacts outside his Brazilian peer group. William, however, claimed that he learned a great deal of English since sometimes the Brazilians spoke in English among themselves, so he attributes his language improvement to the meta-talk resulting from home-country peers correcting each other. Mike did integrate to some extent into the L2 community, and apart from Brazilian colleagues, he made friends with mainly other international students. In the case of Steven, his psychological adaptation increased during the semester from making friends of different nationalities, and his attitude towards the US improved as a result of this positive experience. Nevertheless, he did not experience immersion in US culture or make any NS friends. Steven's increased well-being could explain his moderate but positive pragmatic gains. Additionally, the fact that he was mainly concerned with improving his academic English (a reflection of his instrumental motivation) could account for his speech act production development in high-imposition situations.

Unlike William, Mike and Steven, Ethan did show gains in his sociocultural adaptation, mainly due to a progression towards a more positive attitude regarding US culture. Nevertheless, he experienced negative gains in his pragmatic competence as well as in his psychological adaptation. His decrease in psychological adaptation was mainly due to his lack of ego permeability. Ethan described himself as an introverted person whose preferred plan for a Saturday evening during the stay abroad was playing video games with a Spanish peer, who became his best friend. He also admitted not trying very hard to integrate with Americans since his main motivation in the program was to improve academically, not socially or personally.

5.2.3 Pattern 3: Interplay of sociocultural adaptation and pragmatic gains

The third category includes one student whose pragmatic gains corresponded to his sociocultural adaptation development, but not with his psychological one. This is the case of Sean, whose psychological adaptation decreased over the semester because his culture shock increased. His inability to cope with some cultural differences – particularly with the US custom of keeping dogs indoors and not removing shoes inside the house – led him to have arguments with his

American roommates and change his living arrangements. Sean finally felt well-adapted to the setting when, by the end of the semester, he changed from having two US roommates to living with two international students, one from Saudi Arabia and one from Thailand. He particularly felt his English improved more when sharing accommodation with international students since they interacted frequently. Sean's sociocultural adaptation improved during the semester abroad, which was mainly due to the fact that he felt more integrated into the L2 community once he had made real friends. Even if his friends were of other nationalities, going out with them gave him confidence to interact more with NSs.

In summary, a qualitative exploration of individual trajectories seems to indicate that gains in appropriateness of speech act production were somewhat related to overall acculturation gains. More particularly, the analysis highlighted the key role of the social variables of integration and of academic pressure, as well as the importance of the affective variables of social support from home-country peers and language shock in shaping the process of acculturation. It may also be hypothesized that psychological adaptation might lead to pragmatic gains to a higher extent than sociocultural adaptation, as only in one case (Sean) did sociocultural gains correspond with pragmatic gains, as opposed to the four cases in which only psychological adaptation was associated with pragmatic development (William, Mike, Steven and Ethan).

6 Discussion

The current study investigated whether acculturation was related to the development of pragmatic competence in the SA context. More particularly, it sought to discern (1) whether students developed their appropriateness of pragmatic production during a semester of study in the US, and (2) whether and how their sociocultural and psychological adaptation were related to the reported pragmatic gains. The objectives of the study drew on Schumann's (1978) proposal that the degree to which an individual acculturates socially and affectively to the L2 setting would determine the extent to which he/she learns the L2.

Firstly, the results corroborate previous longitudinal ILP studies that have reported that, despite the advantage of the SA context for pragmatic development, the process of learning pragmatic competence is variable and non-linear, as it is determined by different factors (e.g. Barron 2003; Félix-Brasdefer 2004; Taguchi & Roever 2017). Overall, the findings revealed that during the first 4 months of immersion in the US, participants improved their ability to formulate requests and refusals, as measured on a DCT. Nevertheless, this improvement was influenced by the type of situation, since learners showed higher gains in appropriateness of speech act production in low-imposition situations involving friends than in high-imposition ones entailing conversations with professors. This finding is, indeed, in line with a series of longitudinal investigations by Taguchi (2011; 2013) reporting that the development of high-imposition English speech acts (requests, refusals, and opinions) takes place at later stages of L2 immersion. It is hypothesized that low-imposition scenarios presented in this study (see Table 2) were encountered on campus more frequently than the high-imposition ones. This finding thus highlights the particularity of SA as an optimal setting for L2 learning given the opportunities it provides for interaction outside of class in different situations and for exposure to contextualized and authentic input (Taguchi 2015a).

Moreover, the study has revealed that pragmatic development was related in various ways to students' acculturation experiences. Therefore, it provides support for Schumann's (1978; 1986) Acculturation model of L2 acquisition and corroborates findings from previous studies that have provided empirical evidence for the relationship between acculturation and pragmatic acquisition (Schmidt 1983; Dörnyei et al. 2004). A quantitative analysis showed that sociocultural adaptation and pragmatic gains were significantly associated. Moreover, a qualitative exploration of individual trajectories of pragmatic learning and of acculturation showed that different factors sociocultural and psychological factors contributed to adaptation to the L2 setting and to subsequent learning of how to use the L2 appropriately as a function of interlocutor and situation. On the one hand, acculturation was determined by social variables that mainly included integration and academic pressure. On the other hand, it was influenced by affective factors, primarily social support from home-country peers and language shock. The most successful students in pragmatic learning were those who were able to integrate into the L2 community and those whose psychological adaptation increased thanks to the support from their home-country peers. In contrast, unsuccessful students were not able to integrate into US society mainly because of strong language shock and high academic pressure.

Although academic pressure and social support from home-country peers were not a primary focus of this investigation, they were found to be related to acculturation in the US. This finding has two main implications. Firstly, it supports Schumann's (1978) assertion that acculturation, rather than being a direct cause of L2 acquisition, is one of the main factors enhancing L2 learning. Secondly, it highlights the need to revise Schumann's (1978) framework so as to account for language learning in the current era of globalization, which has resulted in a dramatic increase of student mobility worldwide (see Mitchell et al. 2015; 2017). For instance, nowadays it is common to have large groups of students from the same nationality, and even from the same home university, at the same SA site, which makes social support from home-country peers an inevitable element to take into account when investigating the SA setting.

All in all, the findings from this study provide new insights into the investigation of SA program outcomes by reporting the relationship between pragmatic development and socialcultural and psychological adaptation. Therefore, the study has addressed the recent call for the need to investigate cultural and linguistic aspects of SA so as to have a more comprehensive understanding of the SA experience (Taguchi 2015b). To that end, future studies could draw from Schumann's (1978) framework of Acculturation.

7 Conclusion

This investigation focused on the interplay of acculturation and the acquisition of pragmatic competence in the SA context. More particularly, it discussed ways in which students' sociocultural and psychological adaptation during the first 4 months of immersion could be related to their ability to formulate requests and refusals appropriate to the given situation.

The main limitations of the study concern the relatively small sample size, and the merely qualitative assessment of psychological adaptation. A qualitative analysis of 12 case studies was, however, the most suitable methodology for the purpose of the study, since, as different scholars have noted (e.g. Dörnyei et al. 2004; Taguchi 2011), it allows for an in-depth exploration of the interplay between contextual factors and learners' individual differences. Nevertheless, future research should include a higher number of participants, as well as administer quantitative measures of psychological adaptation or overall acculturation.

Ultimately, the study makes a notable contribution to the field of ILP by highlighting the relevance of acculturation. Moreover, the findings have important implications for the design of mobility programs, as they highlight the need to maximize students' immersion experiences during SA programs, both at the social and at the affective level, to enhance their ability to use the L2 appropriately in the new sociocultural setting.

Acknowledgments

As a member of the LAELA (Lingüística Aplicada a l'Ensenyament de la Llengua Anglesa) research group at Universitat Jaume I (Castellón, Spain), I would like to acknowledge that this study is part of a research project funded by (a) the Spanish

Ministerio de Economia y Competitividad (FFI2016-78584-P), (b) the Universitat Jaume I (P1·1B2015-20), and (c) Projectes d'Innovació Educativa de la Unitat de Suport Educatiu 3457/17.

References

Alcón-Soler, Eva (ed.). 2008. *Learning how to request in an instructed language learning context.* Berlin: Peter Lang.

Alcón-Soler, Eva. 2014. Pragmatic learning and study abroad: Effects of instruction and length of stay. *System* 48. 62–74.

Arends-Tóth, Judith & Fons J. R. Van de Vijver. 2006. Issues in conceptualization and assessment of acculturation. In Marc H. Bornstein & Linda R. Cote (eds.), *Acculturation and parent-child relationships: Measurement and development,* 33–62. Mahwah, NJ: Lawrence Erlbaum.

Bardovi-Harlig, Kathleen & Maria-Thereza Bastos. 2011. Proficiency, length of stay, and intensity of interaction and the acquisition of conventional expressions in L2 pragmatics. *Intercultural Pragmatics* 8(3). 347–384.

Bardovi-Harlig, Kathleen, Marda Rose & Edelmira Nickels. 2008. The influence of first language and level of development in the use of conventional expressions of thanking, apologizing, and refusing. In Melissa Bowles, Rebecca Foote, Silvia Perpiñán & Rakesh Bhatt (eds.), *Selected proceedings of the 2007 second language research forum,* 113–130. Somerville, MA: Cascadilla Proceedings Project.

Barron, Anne. 2003. *Acquisition in interlanguage pragmatics: Learning how to do things with words in a study abroad context.* Amsterdam: Benjamins.

Beebe, Leslie M. & Howard Giles. 1984. Speech-accommodation theories: A discussion in terms of second language acquisition. *International Journal of the Sociology of Language* 46. 5–32.

Bella, Spyridoula. 2011. Mitigation and politeness in Greek invitation refusals: Effects of length of residence in the target community and intensity of interaction on non-native speakers' performance. *Journal of Pragmatics* 43. 1718–1740.

Berry, John W. 2003. Conceptual approaches to acculturation. In Kevin M. Chun, Pamela Balls Organista & Gerardo Marín (eds.), *Acculturation: Advances in theory, measurement and applied research,* 17–37. Washington, DC: American Psychological Association.

Brown, Penelope & Stephen C. Levinson. 1987. *Politeness: Some universals in language use.* Cambridge: Cambridge University Press.

Celenk, Ozgur & Fons J. R. Van de Vijver. 2011. Assessment of acculturation: Issues and overview of measures. *Online Readings in Psychology and Culture* 8(1). 3–22.

Dörnyei, Zoltán, Valerie Durow & Khawla Zahran. 2004. Individual differences and their effects on formulaic secquence acquisition. In Norbert Schmitt (ed.), *Formulaic sequences: Acquisition, processing and use*, 87–106. Amsterdam: Benjamins.

Ellis, Rod. 1994. *The study of second language acquisition*. Oxford: Oxford University Press.

Eslami, Zohreh Rasekh & Soo-Jin Ahn. 2014. Motivation, amount of interaction, length of residence, and ESL learners' pragmatic competence. *Applied Research on English Language* 3(1). 9–28.

Félix-Brasdefer, J. César. 2004. Interlanguage refusals: Linguistic politeness and length of residence in the target community. *Language Learning* 54(4). 587–653.

Félix-Brasdefer, J. César & Maria Hasler-Baker. 2017. Elicited data. In Anne Barron, Peter Grundy, Gerard Steen & Yueguo Gu (eds.), *The Routledge handbook of pragmatics*, 27–38. London: Routledge.

García, Carmen. 1989. Disagreeing and requesting by Americans and Venezuelans. *Linguistics and Education* 1. 299–322.

Gardner, Richard C., Richard N. Lalonde & Robert Pierson. 1983. The socio-educational model of second language acquisition: An investigation using LISREL causal modeling. *Journal of Language and Social Psychology* 2. 1–15.

Hansen, Doris. 1995. A study of the effect of the acculturation model on second language acquisition. In Fred R. Eckman, Diane Highland, Peter Lee, Jean Mileham & Rita R. Weber (eds.), *Second language acquisition theory and pedagogy*, 305–316. Hillsdale, NJ: Lawrence Erlbaum.

Hassall, Timothy. 2006. Learning to take leave in social conversations: A diary study. In Margaret A. DuFon & Eton Churchill (eds.), *Language learners in study abroad contexts*, 31–58. Clevedon, UK: Multilingual Matters.

Hudson, Thom, Emily Detmer & James D. Brown. 1995. *Developing prototypic measures of cross-cultural pragmatics* (Technical Report 7). Honolulu, HI: University of Hawaii at Manoa, Second Language Teaching & Curriculum Center.

Jiang, Mei, Raymond J. Green, Tracy B. Henley & William G. Masten. 2009. Acculturation in relation to the acquisition of a second language. *Journal of Multilingual and Multicultural Development* 30(6). 481–492.

Kasper, Gabriele & Kenneth R. Rose. 2002. *Pragmatic development in a second language*. Oxford, UK: Blackwell.

Krashen, Stephen. 1985. *The input hypothesis: Issues and implications.* Beverly Hills, CA: Laredo Publishing Company.

Lybeck, Karen. 2002. Cultural identification and second language pronunciation of Americans in Norway. *The Modern Language Journal* 86. 174–91.

Martínez-Flor, Alicia & Esther Usó-Juan. 2011. Research methodologies in pragmatics: Eliciting refusals to requests. *Estudios de Lingüística Inglesa Aplicada* 1. 47–87.

Mitchell, Rosamond, Nicole Tracy-Ventura & Kevin McManus (eds.). 2015. *Social interaction, identity and language learning during residence abroad* (Eurosla Monographs Series 4). Amsterdam: The European Second Language Association.

Mitchell, Rosamond, Nicole Tracy-Ventura & Kevin McManus. 2017. *Anglophone students abroad: identity, social relationships and language learning during residence abroad.* London: Routledge.

Mondy, S. 2007. *The acculturation model: A look into socio/psycho perspectives of SLA.*

Redfield, Robert, Ralph Linton & Melville Herskovits. 1936. Memorandum on the study of acculturation. *American Anthropologist* 38. 149–152.

Schmidt, Richard W. 1983. Interaction acculturation, and the acquisition of communicative competence: A case study of an adult. In Nessa Wolfson & Elliot Judd (eds.), *Sociolinguistics and language acquisition*, 137–174. Rowley, MA: Newbury House.

Schmitt, Norbert, Zoltán Dörnyei, Svenja Adolphs & Valerie Durow. 2004. Knowledge and acquisition of formulaic sequences. In Norbert Schmitt (ed.), *Formulaic sequences: Acquisition, processing and use*, 55–86. Amsterdam: Benjamins.

Schumann, John H. 1978. *The pidginization process: A model for second language acquisition.* Rowley, MA: Newbury House.

Schumann, John H. 1986. Research on the acculturation model for second language acquisition. *Journal of Multilingual and Multicultural Development* 7(5). 379–392.

Siegal, Mary. 1995. Individual differences and study abroad: Women learning Japanese in Japan. In Barbara Freed (ed.), *Second language acquisition in a study abroad context*, 225–244. Amsterdam: Benjamins.

Sykes, Julie. 2017. Technologies for teaching and learning intercultural competence and interlanguage pragmatics. In Shannon Sauro & Carol Chapelle (eds.), *The handbook of technology and second language teaching and learning*, 118–133. Hoboken, NJ: John Wiley.

Taguchi, Naoko. 2006. Analysis of appropriateness in a speech act of request in L2 English. *Pragmatics* 16. 513–535.

Taguchi, Naoko. 2011. Pragmatic development as a dynamic, complex process: General patterns and case histories. *The Modern Language Journal* 95(4). 605–627.

Taguchi, Naoko. 2013. Individual differences and development of speech act production. *Applied Research on English Language* 2(2). 1–16.

Taguchi, Naoko. 2015a. 'Contextually' speaking: A survey of pragmatic learning abroad, in class, and online. *System* 48. 3–20.

Taguchi, Naoko. 2015b. Cross-cultural adaptability and development of speech act production in study abroad. *International Journal of Applied Linguistics* 25(3). 343–365.

Taguchi, Naoko. 2017. Interlanguage pragmatics: A historical sketch and future directions. In Anne Barron, Peter Grundy, Gerard Steen & Yueguo Gu (eds.), *The Routledge handbook of pragmatics*, 153–167. London: Routledge.

Taguchi, Naoko & Carsten Roever. 2017. *Second language pragmatics*. Oxford: Oxford University Press.

Taguchi, Naoko, Feng Xiao & Shuai Li. 2016. Effects of intercultural competence and social contact on speech act production in a Chinese study abroad context. *The Modern Language Journal* 100(4). 1–22.

Ward, Colleen & Antony Kennedy. 1999. The measurement of sociocultural adaptation. *International Journal of Intercultural Relations* 23. 659–677.

Xiao, Feng. 2015. Proficiency effect on L2 pragmatic competence. *Studies in Second Language Learning and Teaching* 5(4). 557–581.

Zaker, Alireza. 2016. The acculturation model of second language acquisition: Inspecting weaknesses and strengths. *Indonesian EFL Journal* 2(2). 80–87.

Name index

Name index

Language index

Subject index

www.ingramcontent.com/pod-product-compliance
Lightning Source LLC
Chambersburg PA
CBHW080916100426
42812CB00007B/2300